Thomas Say

NEW WORLD NATURALIST

Drawn by T.R Peale.   40   Engraved by C.Tiebout.

Thomas Say

NEW WORLD NATURALIST

Patricia Tyson Stroud

UNIVERSITY OF PENNSYLVANIA PRESS

Philadelphia

FRONTISPIECE. The Tiger Swallowtail (*Papilo glaucus*) on a stem of *Aquilegia canadensis*, drawn by Titian Ramsay Peale and engraved by Cornelius Tiebout, from Thomas Say's *American Entomology*, 1824–1828, plate 40, volume 3.

Library of Congress Cataloging-in-Publication Data
Stroud, Patricia Tyson.
  Thomas Say : new world naturalist / Patricia Tyson Stroud.
    p.   cm.
  Includes bibliographical references and index.
  ISBN 0-8122-3103-1
    1. Say, Thomas, 1787–1834.   2. Naturalists—United States—
Biography.   3. New Harmony (Ind.)—History.   I. Title.
QH31.S316S76   1992
508'.092—dc20
  [B]   92-4528
                                                         CIP

See p. 322 for acknowledgments of manuscript sources quoted in the text.

For Morris

Contents

Illustrations

Jacket. *Thomas Say*, by Charles Willson Peale

Acknowledgments

T
HE INTEREST AND ENCOURAGEMENT of Robert L. McNeil. Jr., have been crucial to the realization of this project. My sincerest thanks for the support of the Barra Foundation.

Others to whom I am deeply grateful for assistance with this book are those anonymous benefactors of history who, at different times and places, had the foresight to save and collect letters from their correspondents, or those of their family or friends—famous or unknown—and donate them to libraries and other institutions, to be used by persons they would probably never meet and for purposes one could only hope they would have approved.

For one's contemporaries, thankfully, it is possible to be more specific. My warm gratitude goes to the library staff at the Academy of Natural Sciences of Philadelphia, who were tireless and always good-humored concerning my countless requests for manuscripts and books. They include Carol Spawn, librarian; Sylva Baker, former librarian; Janet Evans, former research librarian; and Bill Gagliardi, stack manager. Academy scientists George M. Davis, Robert Robertson, and Daniel Otte gave freely of their invaluable time and advice.

At the American Philosophical Society, my special thanks to Edward C. Carter II, librarian, for many important and helpful suggestions, and to Beth Carroll-Horrocks, manuscripts librarian. The staff at the Library Company and the Historical Society of Pennsylvania were most courteous and kind. Other institutions in Philadelphia where information was attained are the University of Pennsylvania, the College of Physicians, the Athenaeum, the Philadelphia Maritime Museum, and the Wagner Free Institute of Science. The staff at Historic Wyck, the ancestral home of Reuben Haines in Germantown, were most gracious in allowing me access to the collection of family papers (now housed at the American Philosophical Society). Another source of important manuscripts has been the Quaker Collection at Haverford College. Many books were borrowed from both Haverford and Bryn Mawr colleges. Institutions near Philadelphia with interesting Say connections, in addition to Wyck, include Bartram's Garden and Westtown School.

In Boston, Eva Jonas, librarian of the Museum of Comparative Zoology, granted me permission to quote from manuscripts in the library's collection, as did Rodney G. Dennis, curator of manuscripts at Harvard's Houghton Library. In Washington, the staffs at the National Archives and the Library of Congress were knowledgeable and helpful. James J. Holmberg at the Filson Club in Louisville, Kentucky, kindly granted permission to quote from letters in the club's possession. In London, my requests were graciously received at the Linnaean Society, the Royal Society Library, and the British Museum (Natural History).

On two highly successful trips to New Harmony, Indiana, I spent many hours in delightful conversation about "our loved ones" with Josephine Elliott, archivist emerita, Indiana State University, and author and "sage" of New Harmony, who provided me with quotes and sources on many occasions. Aline Cook, former librarian of the Workingmen's Institute Library, was most helpful, as was Ralph Schwartz, former director of Historic New Harmony.

Special thanks to William J. Orr, curator of manuscripts at the Center for Western Studies, Joslyn Art Museum, Omaha, Nebraska, for supplying me with a manuscript copy of his book on Prince Maximilian's diaries; to Joseph Ewan at the Missouri Botanic Garden for certain insights into nineteenth-century natural history; to Ian MacPhail, librarian of the Morton Arboretum in Lisle, Illinois, for information about Say; to Simon Baatz at the University of Pennsylvania for calling my attention to particular manuscripts and other source material; to Karl Koopman at the American Museum of Natural History for taxonomic information; and to Charles E. Mason at the College of Agricultural Sciences, University of Delaware, for compiling a long list of insects first described for science by Thomas Say. George Vaux, Robert Price, and Martha and Edmund Bray have given me valuable leads and ideas.

For illustrations I am grateful to the following institutions: in Philadelphia, the Academy of Natural Sciences, American Philosophical Society, Independence National Historic Park, Historical Society of Pennsylvania, Library Company, and Historic Wyck; and outside Philadelphia, Westtown School, National Portrait Gallery, Hunter Museum of Art in Chattanooga, Tennessee, Thomas E. Gilcrease Museum in Tulsa, Oklahoma, Joslyn Art Museum in Omaha, Nebraska, American Jewish Historical Society in Waltham, Massachusetts, New York Historical Society, and the Musée du Château de Versailles in France.

Individuals whose special assistance I have sincerely appreciated are

Edward F. Rivinus, former senior science editor at the Smithsonian Institution Press, for his editing and encouragement, and Gae Holladay for invaluable in-depth editorial aid in a final rewrite of the manuscript. Robert McCracken Peck, Fellow of the Academy of Natural Sciences of Philadelphia, has, in numerous conversations over the years, given me guidance, suggestions, and criticism which have been a constant source of inspiration. And last, special thanks to my three children for their unfailing faith in the project: Lisa Tyson Ennis, John Tyson II, who taught me to use a computer, and Peter Hutchinson Tyson, who has seen me through many revisions with encouragement, skillful editing, and uplifting humor.

If our utmost exertions can perform only a part of a projected task, they may, at the same time, claim the praise due to the adventurous pioneer, of removing the difficulties in favour of our successors.

THOMAS SAY, *American Entomology*

While in no sense denigrating the achievements of the great masters of science, we have to recognize the truth spoken by the first of the atom breakers, Lord Rutherford. "It is not in the nature of things," said Rutherford, "for any one man to make a sudden violent discovery; science goes step by step and every man depends upon the work of his predecessors. When you hear of a sudden unexpected discovery—a bolt from the blue, as it were—you can always be sure that it has grown up by the influence of one man on another, and it is the mutual influence which makes the enormous possibility of scientific advance."

LOREN EISELEY, *The Night Country*

Introduction

Eastward I go only by force, but westward I go free.

Henry David Thoreau

OR TOO LONG THOMAS SAY has been a nearly unknown
American historical figure. It has been sixty years since Say's only
biography appeared.[1] In the meantime, numerous letters in several
important collections have become available for research, making it possible as never before to engage in that "subliminal battle of imagination
between subject and biographer, upon which all life-writing ultimately
rests."[2]

In the course of this "battle of imagination," and based on Say's own
words—in his letters, but also in glimpses one happens upon here and there
in his scientific writings and expedition accounts—there emerged a very
different Thomas Say from the image that has prevailed for over 150 years.

Say was described in an 1834 memoir by George Ord, an early zoologist and contemporary of Say's at the Academy of Natural Sciences of
Philadelphia, as "bland" and "conciliating," with a character of such "modesty" and "retirement" that he was unfit for the "intercourse of society."
This nonsense, read at a meeting of the American Philosophical Society
several months after Say's death, was immediately rejected and suppressed
by Say's friends at the Academy. But Ord's words reappeared, unaltered,
when Say's collected entomological writings were published by John L. Le
Conte in 1859, thereby establishing a view of Thomas Say's character and
personality that has endured until now.[3]

In the following pages the reader will find a strong, self-determined,
highly motivated, even driving character, critical of his colleagues but
tireless in helping them and fiercely loyal. Although Say was totally uncon-
cerned—often foolishly—for his own personal comforts, and was modest
in terms of his selflessness and lack of conceit, he was fully determined that
his right of priority in naming certain species of insects and shells be
recognized. In this respect, he was very much a man of his own time and
place. His intensely nationalistic goal of establishing the authority of Amer-

ican scientists to name and describe the flora and fauna of their own country placed him squarely in the mainstream of postrevolutionary thinking.

In colonial times, what science there was had been international by necessity. Patronage, expertise, and extensive specimen collections were all abroad. John Bartram, the first American botanist of importance, for years sent American plants to his patron, Peter Collinson, in London, and enjoyed a lively and educational correspondence with Collinson that included a free exchange of ideas and information.

America's independence, however, was a tremendous impetus to an increasing number of North American naturalists, proud of their country's growing political and military strength, to establish a sense of national identity and forge a native style in their approach to science. Deference to Old World authority for identification, verification, and publication of natural history discoveries was at best tiresome and uncomfortable, at worst, humiliating. Thomas Jefferson had long lamented that, in the field of natural history, Americans had "done too little for [themselves] and depend[ed] too long on the ancient and inaccurate observations of other nations."[4] Alexander Wilson, a Scottish immigrant and Thomas Say's friend and fellow naturalist, was even more outspoken when he railed against "that transatlantic reproach of being obliged to apply to Europe for an account and description of the productions of our own country."[5] It had even been necessary to ship to England the plants collected by Lewis and Clark on their expedition of 1804–6 so the specimens could be named and their descriptions published.

The historian Robert V. Bruce has written that "scientific emphasis, style, and institutions bear the stamp of a nation's culture and circumstances."[7] The American natural science to which Say dedicated his life put its first emphasis on taxonomy. The vast wealth of species unknown to science demanded this. Plants and animals had to be found, then organized and described. Observations on behavior and speculation as to origins and relationships would necessarily come later.

Alexander Wilson stated this initial approach in the introduction to his classic work *American Ornithology* (1811):

> Well authenticated facts deduced from careful observation, precise descriptions, and faithfully portrayed representations drawn from nature, are the only true and substantial materials with which we can ever hope to erect and complete the great superstructure of Science;—Without these all the learned speculation of mere closet theory are but "the baseless fabricks of a vision."

By the time Henry David Thoreau wrote, some twenty years later, "Man cannot afford to be a naturalist to look at nature directly . . . He must look through and beyond her,"[8] it was clear that a change had taken place in scientific thinking. In the intervening years the "superstructure of [American] Science" had been erected by scientific explorers and classifiers, among whom Thomas Say was a prominent member. The way was prepared for the so-called cabinet naturalists not only to refine the classification of the enormous quantity of discoveries, but to "look through and beyond them" to theories of origin and change.

Peculiarly American were institutions such as the Academy of Natural Sciences, with memberships embracing a mix of nationalities, principally, besides American, English, French, and Dutch. A national style was also evident in the first books published on American natural science, such as Thomas Say's *American Entomology* (1824–28) and its prototype, Wilson's *American Ornithology* (1808–13). These seminal works were produced as elegantly as possible in order to stress the importance and sophistication of the New World. This aspect of American publication was often criticized for rendering books beyond the means of most Americans, however.[9]

Thomas Say was in many ways a transitional figure in the history of natural science. During the course of his life he bridged two approaches to science: the diffusion, nonspecialization, and self-sufficiency of the early method—a direct result of the New World's extensive land[10]—that initially characterized Say's career, and the larger scale, specialized, and interdependent effort of a later era that, as became increasingly and heartbreakingly evident, was necessary to his studies.

Say was also controversial. Some colleagues thought his descriptions too sparse; others, such as George Ord, thought them verbose. Say's lifestyle, that is, his decision to leave Philadelphia and live in New Harmony, was criticized by those who had no understanding of his motives or constraints, but his productivity was prodigious in spite of obstacles. In addition to competition over priority in naming new species, inadequate funds for research and publication were a constant problem, as were the lack of scientific institutions supported by informed laypeople and access to the great European libraries and collections.

The care and thoroughness with which Thomas Say conducted his research, despite the drawbacks of both time and (later) place, and the fairness with which he treated colleagues earned him the respect and admiration of his peers—including Ord, who said that Say's name was "synonymous with honor." More important, Say's approach to natural science helped to set a standard of excellence for scientific study in the New World that equaled or exceeded any in Europe.

Say's life story is remarkable and full. Adventure, romance, frustration, achievement, and tragedy are all there. It is my fervent hope that the man who lived this fascinating, obstacle-ridden life springs from the following pages with all the vigor and courage that were his.

I

METAMORPHOSIS
The Chrysalis Opens
1787–1818

Go, wond'rous creature! Mount where Science guides.

ALEXANDER POPE

CHAPTER 1
A Heritage of Science

I have sent thee a box of insects, numbered, and a paper with my remarks to each number.

John Bartram to Sir Hans Sloane,
Philadelphia, 14 November 1743

THOMAS SAY WAS BORN in Philadelphia on 27 June 1787.[1] Nearby in the State House an event was taking place of the utmost national importance: members of the Constitutional Convention were forging a document to weld thirteen separate and feuding entities into the United States of America. Say thus began his life not only in a burgeoning new country but in the city that was the center of culture and intellectual endeavor in the New World. The nation's spectacular economic rise in the nineteenth century, with its corollary social, political, and scientific upheavals, would sweep aside many traditional values, beliefs, and behaviors. In Philadelphia, where four generations of prominent Quaker ancestors preceded him, Thomas Say would always find his intellectual home.

Under Quaker influence since its founding, Philadelphia was cosmopolitan, egalitarian, and democratic. Although Quakers were considered anti-intellectual because they admired facts, distrusted theories, and scorned higher education, which they considered more theory than fact, Philadelphia Quakers traced their philosophical heritage to William Penn. Penn was learned enough to have been elected a Fellow of the Royal Society of London before founding Pennsylvania in 1682. According to historian E. Digby Baltzell, "the Quaker appeal to direct experience rather than to religious authority or tradition . . . was closely akin to the spirit of empirical science."[2] Therefore it is not surprising that among eighteenth-century Philadelphia Quakers there were many doctors, two of whom were Thomas Say's grandfather and father.

On Thomas Say's paternal side was a history of spirited dissenters who down the years became successful Quaker merchants, apothecaries, and physicians. Say's family, before his birth, had lived in Philadelphia for well over a hundred years. In the summer of 1682, before William Penn arrived in Philadelphia aboard the *Welcome* in October, Say's great-great-grandfather Thomas Paschall had set sail from the Quaker enclave of Bristol, England, to start a new life in America. Descended from French Huguenots who had fled to England in the seventeenth century to avoid religious persecution, Paschall's family, on becoming Quakers, had been subjected to indignities in Bristol that had eventually made their exodus to America a necessity.

The harassment of Quakers in England was economic as well as religious, motivated by the desire to eliminate ambitious Quaker merchants from competition. Quakers fined for nonattendance at church and unable to pay found their shops ransacked, looms broken, and implements and livestock seized. It was very different in the New World where they were welcomed and appreciated. Quakers became "an aristocracy not merely of wealth, certainly not of birth, but of virtue and talents."[3] Numerous and varied trades and crafts represented by the first Quaker colonists in Philadelphia contributed significantly to the city's rapid growth.

Business success was regarded as a sign of God's blessing. The Quaker belief in "the inner light"—the idea that God is within everyone—meant that God's will could be carried out in the marketplace as well as anywhere else. Armed with this philosophy and strong connections with their English counterparts, the Quakers were virtually guaranteed prosperity—especially given their high regard for industry, prudence, honesty, frugality, and orderliness. All these virtues would be deeply ingrained in Thomas Say's personality, except the Quakers' business sense.

Say's ancestor, Thomas Paschall, was listed as "pewterer" aboard the *Society of Bristol* in which he crossed the Atlantic with his wife and three children. Although a craftsman, Paschall wrote as an educated man in a detailed and articulate letter to a friend in England several months after his arrival.[4] His descriptions of a variety of trees and animals in his surroundings already anticipate the family interest in nature.

In addition to his resourcefulness as a pioneer and his familiarity with natural forms, Paschall apparently extended his talents into other fields. An essay on Pennsylvania's medical history, written two hundred years after Paschall's arrival, alludes to one of the men who settled Pennsylvania with William Penn as being "of French extraction, who, proud to have descended from the family of the recluse of Port Royal [Blaise Pascal, the seventeenth-century French mathematician and philosopher; see figure 1],

Fig. 1. *Blaise Pascal,* seventeenth-century French school. Courtesy of the Musée National du Château de Versailles.

and to bear his honoured name, had devoted his time and fortune to the study of the abstruse sciences, among others alchemy and astrology."[5]

Thomas Paschall's sons kept an apothecary store and dispensed "the produce of their father's laboratory."[6] Paschall's grandson, the elder Thomas Say (1709–1796), was a respected apothecary and physician, renowned for his mysticism and ability to cure by the laying on of hands. This Thomas Say's son Benjamin (1755–1813), father of the naturalist, was a trained medical doctor. The younger Thomas Say's heritage was thus one of alchemist, apothecary, and physician; centuries of scientific history were telescoped into four generations.

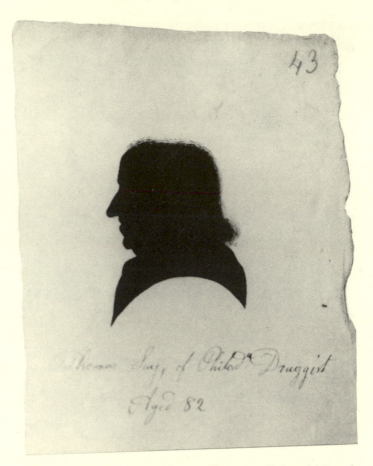

Fig. 2. *Thomas Say senior,* the naturalist's grandfather, by Joseph Sansom. Silhouette. Silhouettes were acceptable to Quakers, who regarded oil portraits as ostentatious. Courtesy of the Historical Society of Pennsylvania.

The elder Thomas Say (figure 2), for whom the naturalist was named, lived through most of the eighteenth century and contributed significantly to his native city of Philadelphia. He started his professional life as a saddle-maker's apprentice and in time set up his own business. Having a "natural talent" for medicine, according to a biography written by his son, he later sold his saddlery and opened an apothecary shop. In 1756 the botanist John Bartram's son Isaac joined him as partner. Apothecaries in colonial times were somewhat equivalent to today's general practitioners, but they prepared medicines for other doctors as well as for their own patients. With his benevolence and ability to cure "by the power of sympathy," the first Thomas Say exemplified the Quaker qualities of tolerance and compassion that would grace his grandson's character as well.

Say had a practical and civic-minded side that balanced his mystical leanings. He was among the original thirty members of the Fellowship Fire Company of Philadelphia, founded in 1738 just two years after Benjamin Franklin's Union Fire Company became the first organization for fighting fires in the country. He was also a manager of the Philadelphia Almshouse, a refuge for the poor founded in 1731.

During the French and Indian War the British government expelled thousands of French neutrals from Nova Scotia; many of these destitute people made their way to Philadelphia. Say, along with the Quaker educator Anthony Benezet, was tireless in helping them. His Huguenot ancestry may have given a special poignance to his sympathy for the plight of these French outcasts.

Unjust dealings with the Indians in Pennsylvania—which ran counter to William Penn's original precepts—were also the elder Thomas Say's concern. In 1760, he and other trustees of the "Friendly Association for Regaining and Preserving Peace with the Indians by Pacific Measures" addressed a document to Penn's grandsons stating that the Indians' "murderous behavior" was a direct result of the colonists' unfair treatment of them. To stop hostilities, conferences were held with several Mohawk leaders in Philadelphia and peace messages were sent to all tribal groups along the Susquehanna River. The society raised three thousand dollars in the hope that "the possession of Lands obtained by an equitable Purchase will . . . secure the Peace of the Settlers now as it did formerly, more effectually than the maintaining of superior Force can do; and thus the Frontiers may soon again be Peopled, the State of Tranquility formerly enjoyed in Pennsylvania restored."[7] In later years Say's sentiments would be reinforced by his grandson. The naturalist, who shared his grandfather's indignation at the imperious treatment of the native Americans, personally delivered messages of peace to Indians far west of Pennsylvania.

In his capacity as justice of the peace, the senior Thomas Say was empowered by the British crown to sign colonial paper money. In America, unlike England, the office was open to him as a Quaker because it required no oath of allegiance. Quakers refused to take oaths of any kind because they believed they owed allegiance only to God. Say's signature appeared on twenty shilling notes as early as 1757.[8]

The guardian of a number of orphans, Say adamantly supported the rights of blacks and served on Quaker committees for the education of both black and white children. Upon marrying his second wife, Rebekah Budd, he at once freed Rebekah's slave, Lot.[9] His action was consistent with the Quaker position on slavery, made clear when the Philadelphia Yearly Meeting voted in 1776 to disown all Friends who owned slaves.[10]

Say's first wife, Catherine Sprogell, who was descended from the earliest settlers of Germantown, had died in 1749. None of the eight children from this marriage outlived his or her father. Of two offspring from Say's second union, only his son Benjamin survived him. The legacy this venerable eighteenth-century gentleman bequeathed his grandson Thomas Say was one of generosity, humanitarianism, and drive. These traits, which the older man focused on religion and philanthropy, were no less evident in his descendant's pursuit of natural science.

Dr. Benjamin Say, son of the elder Thomas Say and father of the naturalist, was both prosperous and socially prominent. He owned extensive city real estate, including the handsome four-storied house where Thomas Say grew up. The mansion, with a coach house and stable behind it, was situated on fashionable Chestnut Street between Front and Second. The doctor's warehouse and wharf (figure 3) were several blocks away on the Delaware River's bustling waterfront. West of Philadelphia, high on a bank of the Schuylkill River near the floating bridge at Gray's Ferry—hastily erected by the British during the Revolution—stood Dr. Say's country seat, the Cliffs (figure 4), with its wide veranda and widow's walk. The artist and poet Alexander Wilson, a neighbor during Thomas Say's youth, celebrated this large brick house and the picturesque spot it commanded overlooking the Schuylkill:

> There upward where it gently bends,
> And Say's red fortress tow'rs in view;
> The floating bridge its length extends;
> A living scene forever new.[11]

Benjamin Say was also civic-minded. He was president of the Humane Society and a member of the Select Committee for the Abolition of Slavery in Pennsylvania. He served two years in the Pennsylvania Senate, and in 1808 he was called to the United States Congress to fill an unexpired term after which he was reelected. The Says were thus both respected and influential, and they had friends in high places. When Thomas Jefferson

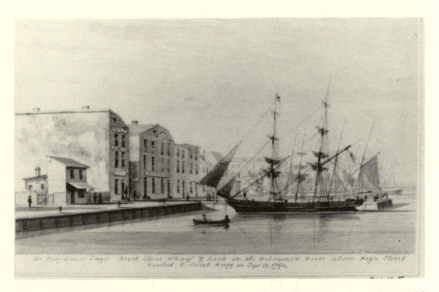

Fig. 3. *Dr. Benjamin Say's brick stores, wharf, and dock on the Delaware River,* by David Kennedy. Watercolor. Courtesy of the Historical Society of Pennsylvania.

Fig. 4. *Country residence of Dr. Benjamin Say at Gray's Ferry, Philadelphia,* by David Kennedy. Watercolor. Courtesy of the Historical Society of Pennsylvania.

was secretary of state, posted in Philadelphia, then the nation's capital, he rented a house for the summer of 1793 directly across the Schuylkill River from the Cliffs. Fifteen years later Jefferson had not forgotten his Phila- delphia neighbor. He wrote from the White House to William Bartram with regard to Benjamin Say, who was at that time new to the post of United States representative and wished to see the president, "An esteem for his [Dr. Say's] character, of very early date, as well as a respect for Mr. Bartram's friendships, will insure to Dr. Say the manifestation of every respect he [Jefferson] can show."[12]

Although he was a Quaker, Dr. Say supported the Revolution. Be- cause Quakers were pacifists these sympathies eventually caused his expul- sion from Meeting. Devout nonetheless, he and seven others organized their own Meeting known as the Society of Free Quakers or Fighting Quakers. Approximately one hundred sympathizers joined them and raised necessary funds by subscription to purchase a lot on the southwest corner of Fifth and Arch streets. There, in 1783, these "radicals" erected a meeting house that still stands.

Dr. Say was a man of many interests. In addition to his medical practice, political career, and religious pursuits, he was a member of the Company for the Improvement of the Vine, an organization that sought, unsuccessfully, to produce an indigenous American wine. An ardent sup- porter of John Fitch, inventor of the steamboat, Say served as treasurer of the company formed to promote Fitch, from 1787 until 1791 when Fitch's entire venture collapsed. Three generations of Says played a part in steam transportation's early history: Dr. Say and his father were shareholders in Fitch's company, and the doctor's son Thomas would be aboard the first steamboat to ascend the Missouri River as far as Council Bluffs, across the river from present-day Omaha, Nebraska.

The most important part of Benjamin Say's life was his career as a doctor. As one of the fellows of the prestigious College of Physicians and Surgeons, he associated with the best in the city's medical establishment.[13] Dr. Benjamin Rush, dean of the Medical School of the University of Pennsylvania and signer of the Declaration of Independence, was also a fellow and Say's close colleague.

When the deadly yellow fever epidemic of 1793 struck Philadelphia, many doctors fled the city. But Benjamin Say remained and tirelessly followed Rush's highly controversial practices. These involved massive purges, induced by large doses of mercury and jalap, combined with cold drinks, cold air, cold baths, and extensive bloodletting. (Rush thought the body contained twelve quarts of blood; it actually contains about six.) A number of Rush's colleagues regarded his methods as lethal, but Benjamin Say was not among them. When Say fell ill with fever he summoned his friend at once: "My dear brother, I feel myself considerably indisposed & wish to have the pleasure of seeing Dr. R—— this Evening."[14]

Benjamin Say recovered from yellow fever, but his wife Ann died in October, two days after the death of the couple's fifteen-year-old daughter Polly. Yellow fever, it was later discovered, is carried by a mosquito (*Aedes egypti*). One cannot help but note that, though he cannot have known of this connection, Thomas Say would devote his adult life to the study of insects. It was his mother's uncle, William Bartram, who first awakened his interest.

Dr. Say's wife, Ann Bonsall, was the granddaughter of botanist John Bartram (1699–1777) and thus a niece of the naturalist and artist, William Bartram (1739–1823), who lived nearby at his father's famous botanic garden in Kingsessing.

The eminent Swedish scientist Linnaeus called John Bartram, Thomas Say's great-grandfather, "the greatest natural botanist in the world." Named botanist to the king of England during colonial days, Bartram made countless forays into wilderness areas of eastern North America collecting hundreds of plants new to science. These he grew in his garden on the Schuylkill River and shipped in the form of seeds, roots, and plants to his many patrons abroad, principally to Peter Collinson in London. James Logan, William Penn's erudite secretary, encouraged Bartram to study Latin, the international language of science, and gave him John Parkinson's *Paradisi in sole paradisus terrestris, or A Garden of all Sorts of Pleasant Flowers* (1629), one of the earliest treatises on horticulture printed in English. Because little botanical knowledge of the New World could be found even in such an authoritative source, Bartram felt encouraged to pursue the subject on his own. Traveling on horseback and mostly alone through unmapped country, he filled his leather saddlebags with botanical specimens.

Thomas Say's participation in several western expeditions, beginning in 1819, would have pleased John Bartram, for it was he who first suggested a western survey to Benjamin Franklin. Franklin conveyed the idea to Jefferson, whose later instructions to Lewis and Clark were based on Bartram's original proposals.[15] These proposals would subsequently serve as Say's guidelines on his two expeditions with Major Stephen H. Long— journeys that Bartram's son William must have traveled vicariously, for President Jefferson had invited William fifteen years earlier, in 1802, to

Fig. 5. *William Bartram* (1739–1823), botanist, by
Charles Willson Peale, 1808. Oil portrait. Courtesy of
Independence National Historical Park.

accompany Lewis and Clark as naturalist. William had declined because of
his age.

William Bartram (figure 5) was fourteen when he first began traveling with his father. Later, after several unsuccessful business ventures, he
turned to natural science for his life's work (a pattern to be repeated by his
great-nephew Thomas Say). But art and literature rather than horticulture
were William's special delights. For many years John Bartram sent his son's
drawings of flowers, birds, fish, snakes, turtles, and alligators to his London
patron Peter Collinson. Later, William sent his exquisite drawings to his
own patron, Dr. John Fothergill, in London. Fothergill and his friends
considered them the best wildlife illustrations from America. William Bartram's *Travels through North and South Carolina, Georgia, East and West
Florida, the Cherokee Country, the Extensive Territories of the Muscogulpes or
Creek Confederacy, and the Country of the Choctaws* (1791) had a tremendous

influence on the English romantic poets, including Wordsworth and Coleridge. Still in print, it is recognized as a classic of American literature.

Many precedents for Thomas Say's own writings in natural science had been set by his maternal ancestors. John Bartram, in the mid-eighteenth century, wrote papers on insects and mollusks for the *Philosophical Transactions* of the Royal Society of London. In 1751 he made the first attempt at an American *materia medica* by adding an appendix of American plants and their medicinal values to Franklin's publication of Dr. Thomas Short's *Medicina Britannica*.[16] Bartram's cousin, Humphry Marshall, published in 1785 the first systematic botanical book to appear in the United States, the *Arbustrum Americanum,* an alphabetical catalogue of American forest trees. Bartram's son Moses published "Observations on Native Silk Worms of North America" in the *Transactions of the American Philosophical Society* in 1771; it was said to be the most original essay on the subject during the colonial period.[17] Moses Bartram's brother Isaac was appointed by the same organization to study the electric eel. Thomas Say's *American Entomology* would be the first book on a wide range of American insects, and his *American Conchology* the first on his country's mollusks.

Also in the tradition of Thomas Say's ancestors was his participation in the founding and forwarding of a learned society, the Academy of Natural Sciences of Philadelphia. John Bartram had first proposed what ultimately became the American Philosophical Society, which he and Benjamin Franklin founded. Isaac and Moses Bartram, as well as two other relatives of Say's, Isaac and Joseph Paschall, had been members of the American Society held at Philadelphia for Promoting and Propagating Useful Knowledge, the 1766 reorganization of Franklin's 1727 Junto. In 1769 the American Society, with Franklin as president, merged with a rival institution to become the American Philosophical Society. Since the term philosophy meant "pursuit of knowledge," the society embraced members engaged in a variety of intellectual disciplines. Membership was reserved for the most influential men of the age. Jefferson served as president of the American Philosophical Society for sixteen years, half of that time serving simultaneously as president of the United States. The Society was the American equivalent of the Royal Society of London. William Bartram became a member in 1786, and thirty-five years later, in 1821, Thomas Say would be named a curator of the society and would write many articles for its *Transactions.*

Although inspired to study nature by William Bartram, Thomas Say was essentially self taught after his early years. As a child he attended a local

Quaker school, and at age twelve, in 1799, he was enrolled at Westtown, a newly established Quaker boarding school some twenty miles outside Philadelphia. His father had remarried by this time and there were several more siblings, young and demanding. Say's profound dislike of the school may have been generated by feelings of rejection; he had been sent away not only from his home but from his Uncle Bartram, an important familial connection with his lost mother. Say remained at the school for three years, enduring the rigors of a strict curriculum and regimented life. He left at age fifteen, the limit imposed by the school, because, according to a twentieth-century Westtown alumna, "the system of whipping then in vogue failed to bring the older boys into subjection, and consequently to keep order, the said boys had to be kept away."[18]

Reuben Haines, Say's classmate at Westtown, described the students' crowded daily schedule in a letter to his father: "We have received new regulation vis. to rise at five go to School at six and stay till half past seven when we get our breakfast and go to School at nine o'clock and at two again to School when we stay until five and at seven get our suppers then at eight go to bed."[19]

The dormitory was a dimly lit attic; the dining room, narrow and bare, was furnished with long backless benches and boards set with pewter plates and porringers. It was said that the headmaster had "a genius for economy," for if a child left his food unfinished it was put in a cupboard and saved for him meal after meal. Because windows and doors were unscreened, insects presented a problem in summer. Haines wrote to his mother, "Please send all the old silk, and thread, stockings of Fathers & mine, that thee can spare, to put on us, the musquetos and gnats, bites us so." His aunt Catherine Hartshorne, the headmaster's wife, added to the bottom of Haines's letter that "they walk in the woods & bring them [fleas?] home at night. Sister would have smiled to see E. Porter and me with two pails, one night in the boys' room—one with salt and water the other sour buttermilk. Some capered, others cryed, some laugh'd, said they were pickled. When this was done, we had half pint bowl of cream tarter & Brimstone, gave them a dose and sent them to bed—& a fine night they had."[20]

Patterned after the Ackworth School in England, also Quaker, Westtown exceeded the traditional curriculum of reading, writing, arithmetic, and grammar. Notes from a lecture of 1801 introducing chemistry reveal quite an imposing content: "Uses of chemistry—its' application to Physiology, Pathology, Pharmacy, Materia Medica, Practice of Physic and the Arts, comprehending Tanning, Bleaching, Dying, Metallurgy, Mineralogy, etc., with its use in Agriculture."[21] A catalogue of the school's books from those years lists Fox's *Book of Martyrs,* Penn's *Works,* Livy's *Roman History* (in Latin), Milton's *Paradise Lost* (in German), Euclid's *Elements,* Cowper's poems, fifteen copies of *Pilgrim's Progress,* and thirty copies of the New Testament. This library, daunting for a child under fifteen, nevertheless provided a sound basis for Thomas Say's interest in literature and a fundamental resource for the quotations he would often use in his writings.

Say had an affinity for the arts, particularly literature, that would underlie and enrich his scientific mind for the rest of his life. According to a colleague, Thomas Say read extensively and compiled a "large volume of poetical abstracts, arranged alphabetically."[22] Say would use these abstracts frequently in his correspondence, embellishing his letters with quotations from the Bible, Pindar, Shakespeare, John Bunyan, and Alexander Pope. But poetry as a vocation did not suit him, and he soon replaced it with the study of facts as revealed in nature.

Religious services were mandatory at Westtown School, and students were admonished to keep in mind the Quaker maxim, "They who, in Meeting, have a wandering mind, are certainly to sin inclined."[23] Given his attitude toward organized religion, expressed often in his life, the mind of young Thomas Say as he sat in Meeting was more likely reviewing the structure of a newfound beetle than contemplating the state of his soul.

From the outset Thomas Say appears to have rejected all religious strictures. Although a birthright member of the Society of Friends, and the son and grandson of devout Quakers, Say had an ironic attitude toward the dictates and mysticism of formal religion. His own view of life being thoroughly pragmatic, he once jotted down, some years later after an Anglican sermon, that "if our priests would relinquish their grandiloquence about dogmas & notions which they cannot prove, & initiate such preaching as this, by inculcating precepts of practice rather than faith, they would have a much more moral audience; but this we cannot expect whilst the fleece & not the flock, is the object of the shepherd's care."[24]

Although John Bartram called priests "mystery mongers" and equated them with Indian "witch doctors," he nevertheless passed down to his great-grandson, through the intervening generations, a deeply personal belief in God. After Bartram had been disowned by Darby Meeting for refuting the divinity of Christ, he had carved in stone over his front door: "It is God alone, Almighty Lord, The Holy One, By me Adord." To his devoted English correspondent, Peter Collinson, Bartram wrote, "My head runs all upon the works of God, in nature. It is through that telescope I see

God in his glory."[25] Thomas Say's faith was equally pantheistic. Behind the intricate designs and infinite varieties of shells and insects he studied so closely, he was aware of an inexplicable creative force that compelled him to faith. Perhaps Say agreed with Pascal, who rationalized his belief in God's existence by his famous statement: "The heart has its reasons of which reason knows nothing."

Significant though the effect of Westtown must have been on Say's youth, a stronger and more positive influence was Charles Willson Peale's Philadelphia Museum. Founded by Peale in 1786 when his interests turned from portrait painting to natural history, this enormously popular museum contained hundreds of preserved birds, fish, mammals, insects, plants, and fossil remains. When, in 1794 Peale moved both the museum and his family from his own house into Philosophical Hall, Say may have been one of the neighborhood boys Peale enlisted for the move by arranging a parade. At the head of the brigade men carried aloft the larger preserved animals, such as the bison, while boys, decreasing in size, followed shouldering the smaller animals.

In the State House, where he moved his entire museum in 1802, Peale arranged his collection of some four thousand insects in an alcove where smaller specimens could be examined under microscopes. This was undoubtedly a fascinating place for Thomas Say. He grew up so interested in all living creatures it was said that as a child when he appeared at dinner his pockets would often be filled with specimens. Occasionally "a little snake, which had been sleeping in his warm pocket, would be aroused by the clatter of knives and forks, and raising its head and poking its neck forward, would send the family in terror from the board."[26]

Say and his brother Benjamin often went with the Peale children on collecting excursions into the meadows and woods outside the city. In addition to William Bartram, it may have been the first Titian Peale whose enthusiasm for insects first fired Thomas Say's lifelong interest in these invertebrates. Titian, one of Peale's older sons, died of yellow fever in 1799; his name was given to a later son. The second Titian Peale, although twelve years Say's junior, would be Say's companion on two major expeditions as well as the principal illustrator of his pioneering book on American insects.

After leaving Westtown in 1801, Say assisted his father in the apothecary shop Dr. Say ran in addition to his medical practice. In 1808, when he was twenty-one, Say was listed with his father in the Philadelphia City Directory as "Benjamin Say & Son, druggists & apothecaries, 163 High"

(Market Street). By 1812 Say had gone into business with John Speakman and was listed in the 1813 directory in his own right as "Thomas Say, apothecary & druggist, NW Corner High & 2nd."

During these years Say also took courses at the University of Pennsylvania's Medical School because his father wished him "to acquire a knowledge of medicine for the literature and learning incidental to medical studies."[27] Say more than likely studied anatomy, chemistry, materia medica, and the practice of medicine with such noted Philadelphia doctors as Caspar Wistar, James Woodhouse, and Benjamin Rush. The title "Doctor" given in later years to Thomas Say most likely resulted from these years of study.

Dr. Benjamin Say died in the spring of 1813. He left his three children—Thomas, Benjamin, and Rebecca—and his second wife, Miriam Moore (figure 6), whom he had married in 1795 two years after the death of Say's mother. There were also three children by Miriam—Caroline, William Penn, and little Miriam. Dr. Say was considered one of the richest men in the city because of his numerous real estate holdings and lucrative medical practice. None of his children inherited much at the time of his death, however, because he left the bulk of his estate to his wife (who outlived Thomas and Benjamin) and divided the remainder among his six children.

Unfortunately, neither Thomas nor Benjamin had a head for business. Thomas's venture as an apothecary failed several years after it began, largely as a result of a loan to Benjamin, whose partner in a brewery had embezzled a substantial sum of money. Dr. Say had anticipated this lack of business sense in his two eldest sons. Just two months before his death he made arrangements in a codicil to his will that would spare his wife and other children the burden of his sons' debts: "My appointment of my said sons Thomas and Benjamin as Executors, shall not operate as a release of any debt or debts which they or either of them now do or may owe me, but such debts shall be accounted for and paid to my Estate in like manner as if they were not named as Executors."[28]

It was fortuitous that, several months after Dr. Say's death, the wealthy and learned Scotsman William Maclure entered Thomas's life—at a meeting of the Academy of Natural Sciences—to fill a role left suddenly vacant. Maclure recognized the young man's uncommon abilities and encouraged his obvious devotion to science by offering moral and financial support. In many ways Thomas Say was more akin to William Maclure than to his own father because of Maclure's profound interest in improving

Fig. 6. *Mrs. Benjamin Say* (née Miriam Moore) (?–1836), by Rapha-elle Peale. Miniature portrait ca. 1810. Watercolor on ivory. Private collection.

societal conditions, his quest for adventure far afield, and his frugal life-style. Say's unconscious transference of filial duty from his father to Mac-lure resulted later on in a loyalty to Maclure so steadfast that it would restrict his own freedom.

Like Maclure, Say had a pronounced democratic bent, and he may have looked down on his father's deliberate cultivation of influential friends. Say professed to evaluate others on personal merit alone and to look for "the movements of the soul within"—a phrase he would later use in reference to a Cheyenne leader. Even so, his attitude in this regard was not entirely consistent. His enthusiastic friendship with Prince Charles Lucien Bonaparte, a nephew of Napoleon who was sixteen years Say's junior, may have stemmed from an unconscious sense of how much his father would have approved such a connection.

Say's "disdain of riches" would be explained by his wife years after his death as the result of his "prospective inheritance" stifling any economic worries as a youth.[29] After he lost the majority of his patrimony in the forced sale of inherited real estate to make up for funds embezzled by his brother's business partner, Say's disdain turned into a permanent dislike of money. Although growing up under the protective canopy of his father's affluence made it easier to indulge in a philosophical disregard of wealth, Say preferred to pattern his life on that of his mother's frugal relatives, John and William Bartram, who had led their lives devoted primarily to horticulture and botany.

In spite of the business debacle that ruined him financially, Say would remain close with his brother Benjamin throughout his life. Inspired by their mutual love of nature, they often went on short trips together; Thomas collected insects and shells while Benjamin gathered minerals and other geological specimens. When separated they corresponded regularly and often sought each other's assistance, both spiritual and financial. Benjamin eventually made a modest living as a brewer, but Thomas, in devoting himself to natural science, and particularly to zoology, chose a career that in effect did not exist.

Other than botany, which for centuries had been an important adjunct to medicine, courses in natural science were not offered at institutions of higher learning. Such studies were considered strictly an avocation for affluent gentlemen who set up "cabinets" and went on collecting forays. A school of pure science was not established at the University of Pennsylvania until 1816; it was then abandoned in 1828 because of "a lack of interest" as was stated in the trustees' minutes.[30] In fact it was discontinued because Thomas Say had moved to New Harmony and deserted the post of professor of natural science to which he had been appointed in 1822.

For a time Thomas's and Benjamin's lives ran parallel. Not only had they entered business only a few years apart, but they were members of the same scientific institution and both served in the War of 1812. In early September 1814, Thomas Say joined the First Troop Philadelphia City Cavalry, an organization formed in 1774 as the first group of colonial volunteers to maintain American rights against the British. In subsequent years this elite group of Revolutionary distinction, known as the Light

Horse of the City, featured prominently in every ceremonial occasion in Philadelphia. Still in active service today as a unit of the Pennsylvania National Guard, the First Troop is the oldest military unit in the United States in terms of continuous service since its formation.

The imminence of war had begun unnerving Philadelphians in 1811—a year before the declaration of war—when the British had blockaded the Delaware River, cutting off most of the city's trade. At the same time, warships had been clearly visible in Delaware Bay, though they had retreated down the Chesapeake, temporarily relieving the threat of bombardment. When the British sailed up the Potomac River in August, 1814, however, setting fire to Washington and burning the Capitol, president's house, and National Library, the war became a terrifying reality to the nation. A contemporary chronicler wrote that "already had the fears of some anticipated ere that moment the sacking of Baltimore, and not a few were to be found, who predicted the identical day when the enemy would dictate to Philadelphia the terms of her capitulation."[31]

Say, his brother Benjamin, and his cousins and friends were united in their determination to defend their country. Say might have seen Captain Charles Ross and thirty dragoons of the First Troop Philadelphia City Cavalry on 27 August 1814 as they paraded, completely equipped for the field, up Chestnut Street and down Broad; and he would have heard the signal for the march to begin: "six guns fired in quick succession at Fort Mifflin and at the Arsenal, and by the drums of the city beating to arms."[32] Less than a week later, Say joined Captain Ross's cavalry as a private. Benjamin was already a sergeant in the Second Troop City Cavalry, and a cousin, George Bartram, once a fellow student at Westtown, enlisted in still another unit. In the Delaware County Fencibles there were ten Bonsall cousins and a Paschall, and in the Washington Guards was Academy co-founder Nicholas Parmentier. Dr. Benjamin Say, as an organizer of the Fighting Quakers, would have been proud of his sons.

Say's detachment, composed of sixty-six dragoons, a trumpeter, and three servants, rode out to Mount Bull, strategically located at the head of the Chesapeake Bay. Here, commanding an extensive view, the men established permanent headquarters enabling them to monitor the enemy's movements. Mounted sentries were placed at intervals on a line reaching to Philadelphia. In this way Ross's detachment communicated daily with Camp Bloomfield at Kennett Square, the main rendezvous for the entire Advance Light Brigade, and with Camp Dupont, positioned to protect the gunpowder mills.

Say's daily tour of duty began at 4:00 A.M. when the entire troop was required to turn out, saddle, and remain ready to mount while the patrols made their rounds. Since Mount Bull was an outpost, no reveille was sounded, and the men were admonished to keep quiet. At daybreak when the patrols returned, horses were unsaddled, watered, and fed, and the regiment breakfasted. From 9:30 to 10:00 there was foot drill and sword exercise, from 10:00 to 11:30 mounted drill, and from 11:30 to 12:00, "sword drill for the awkward." The routine continued much the same until evening parade at 6:30, followed by supper, with fires and lights extinguished by 8:00, after which silence was mandatory.[33]

On the night of 12 September, Baltimore was attacked by the British. Because of the great outpouring of citizens, the enemy were soundly defeated and their commanding officer killed in battle. In November, Major-General Edmund P. Gaines, the district's American commander, ordered General Thomas Cadwalader and six hundred men to a position below New Castle. Fearing that the British, who throughout the fall had maintained their position at the mouth of the Delaware, would attempt to land on its western shore, General Gaines sent an officer daily to New Castle to collect intelligence of the enemy's activity from "travellers, sea faring people and water-men." Say's detachment relayed this information through the line of vedettes to Camp Dupont.[34]

Winter's onset deterred the British from proceeding up Chesapeake Bay, and the war was in effect over. The Advance Light Brigade arrived in Philadelphia on 2 December, three thousand strong, and marched through the city streets with all their equipment. Not since the Revolution had such a splendid sight been seen by the cheering populace. Because the mission of the First City Troop was considered too important to allow it to accompany the brigade, it remained on duty a short time longer, arriving in Philadelphia on 12 December with the same pomp and ceremony.

The next evening Say was present at the weekly meeting of the Academy of Natural Sciences. He lost no time in returning to science. The experience gained from his military career as a dragoon vedette would prove invaluable during future expeditions, when he would again endure physical hardships and sustain discipline and courage over long periods of time.

CHAPTER 2
Birth of the Academy

The unparalleled public spirit of the good people of this Province will shortly make Philadelphia the Athens of America, and render the sons of Pennsylvania reputable among the most celebrated Europeans in all the liberal arts and sciences.

Dr. Thomas Bond
Pennsylvania Hospital, 3 December 1766

AN IMPORTANT EFFECT OF THE WAR of 1812 was stimulation of the evolving sense of American nationality. Say and most of his peers in the natural sciences in Philadelphia felt this incitement acutely and would demand that dependence on European savants give way to American expertise in establishing American science. Fostering the growth of both museums and scientific institutions was an essential part of the plan, as they would be the seedbeds and sponsors of scientific investigation. According to one historian, it was necessary to have "recognized organizations for integrating studies and giving them common direction, an established community for judging, and media for disseminating the results of these studies."[1]

Philadelphia in 1812, when Thomas Say was twenty-five and beginning his career in natural science, had indeed become the "Athens of America" predicted nearly half a century earlier by one of Benjamin Say's mentors. The American Philosophical Society, the New World's counterpart of the Royal Society of London, listed the country's most prominent intellectuals among its members. Benjamin Franklin's Library Company was the first subscription library in the United States. The Pennsylvania Hospital, founded by Franklin and Dr. Thomas Bond, was the first of its kind in America, and the College of Philadelphia (in 1812, the University of Pennsylvania) had, in 1768, conferred the first American medical degrees.

A busy seaport, Philadelphia had lines of communication running to South America, Europe, and the Far East. The city's waterfront was alive with the loading and unloading of ships; the brig *South Carolina* awaited a charter to "any port in the south of Europe," while the *Concord* lay ready to sail for "the Brazils." Ever since the historic voyage of the *Empress of China* in 1784 from New York, the American China trade had been well established and had continued to fill Philadelphia markets with tea, blue and yellow nankeen, and porcelain.

Painting and sculpture were well represented in the city by, among others, Charles Willson Peale, his talented son Rembrandt, Thomas Sully, and the sculptor William Rush. Many works by these artists were displayed at the Pennsylvania Academy of the Fine Arts, founded in 1805. Philadelphia theaters, in the winter of 1812, featured the classics along with the newest hits: Shakespeare's *King Lear and his Three Daughters* and a stunning new work (1810), *The Lady of the Lake* by the young Walter Scott. And there were grand displays of horsemanship at the Circus.

Charles Willson Peale's Philadelphia Museum, with all its wonders, was now brightly illuminated with gas lamps two evenings a week. Basically a one-family operation, it combined exhibitions of the natural and physical sciences with public entertainments. Exhibits of preserved animals in their habitats, prefiguring modern dioramas, contained evocative painted backgrounds rendered by Peale and his artistic sons. At different times there were monkeys dressed in human clothes, a five-legged, two-tailed cow, and wax figures. One such figure showed Meriwether Lewis wearing a splendid ermine-skin mantle given to him by an Indian leader on his expedition to explore the West.

For years, Thomas Say had been fascinated by Peale's exhibits—not only the insect collection but also the animal specimens Lewis and Clark had brought back six years earlier, in 1806. Other specimens had been deposited in the museum soon after by Zebulon Pike.[2] Early one May morning in 1812, as Say strode toward the apothecary shop he ran with John Speakman, his attention may have been arrested by a sign advertising the "meat of a remarkably fine Missouri or Grisly Bear . . . procured by Major Pike."[3] Say knew well the story of Pike's return from the Rockies in 1807 with a pair of grizzly cubs he had presented to President Jefferson. Jefferson had given them to Peale for his museum. These animals from beyond the Mississippi attracted much interest, but they had grown so large and dangerous that Peale had recently shot them. The sign perhaps conjured up for Say a vision of the vast wilderness in which the grizzly lived—land containing countless secrets of American wildlife so fascinating to the young naturalist.

Thomas Say shared his passion for scientific knowledge with his friends, including doctors, chemists, distillers, and apothecaries like himself. These men had often met to discuss their common avocation of natural science and to examine the various specimens they avidly collected. As naturalists they were all amateurs since, at the time, professionalism in their field did not exist. Say had not been present in John Speakman's house on the evening of 25 January 1812 when, "at a meeting of gentlemen, friends of science and of rational disposal of leisure moments," as it was phrased in the original minutes, they had decided to formalize their get-togethers. The founders stated the object of their organization:

> The gentlemen present agree to form, constitute and become a Society for the purpose of occupying their leisure occasionally, in each other's company, on subjects of natural science, interesting and useful to the country and the world, and in modes conducive to the general and individual satisfaction of the members, as well as to the primary object, the advancement and diffusion of useful, liberal, human knowledge.[4]

Say, as an integral part of the group, was listed among the founders.

On 17 March 1812, Thomas Say did attend a meeting at 94 North Second Street in a rented room over a milliner's shop. There it was decided to call the fledgling institution "the Academy of Natural Sciences of Philadelphia." The new society was to be "perpetually exclusive of political, religious and national partialities, antipathies, preventions and prejudices" as being adverse "to the interests of Science."[5] It is tempting to take the banning of religious arguments as indicative of creationist views beginning to rub against ideas of evolution, as expressed, principally, by Lamarck and Erasmus Darwin (Charles Darwin's grandfather). Darwin, a physician, was unique in the history of evolutionism in that he was the only one to propose some of his ideas in the form of poetry.[6] Because of Say's reputed interest in poetry it is possible that he had read such works as Darwin's *Botanic Garden* of 1791 or the *Temple of Nature* of 1803, both of which were popular at the time.

In 1817, five years after the Academy's founding, there is mention in the *Minutes* of an "extinct" species of oyster from New Jersey being added to the collections. It would have been unusual then for scientists to describe species as extinct, since the idea that any species ever ceased to exist was so controversial. The acceptance, in academy discussions of this period, of the premise that species could disappear is therefore interesting, since Charles Darwin's earthshaking *Origin of Species* was still forty-two years in the future.

The exclusion of religious discussions as being "adverse to science" implies, in the context of the times, that theology was still explicit in the overall plan of things. It was just that academy members felt arguments over doctrine would be counterproductive. Scientists of the period saw themselves as demonstrating, through their various methods, the indisputable truth of the existence of God. Historian George H. Daniels observes that "it is impossible to overstress the importance of the pervasive belief that science was to be the handmaiden of theology, for it affected, in one way or another, most of the debates within the scientific community in early nineteenth-century America."[7]

The Academy of Natural Sciences of Philadelphia was formed exclusively for the exchange of ideas concerning natural science. It was distinct from the American Philosophical Society, which encouraged the arts as well as all the various disciplines of science, and from Peale's Philadelphia Museum, aimed primarily at mass education in scientific matters as well as at entertainment. Besides Thomas Say, the other six Academy founders represented a variety of professions and nationalities—a typical cross section of Philadelphia's cosmopolitan society: Jacob Gilliams, a prominent dentist who had treated Washington during his residence in Philadelphia as America's first president; John Shinn, a "manufacturing chemist"; the Frenchman Nicholas Parmentier, a distiller; the Dutchman Gerard Troost (figure 7), a former pharmacist from Le Havre who had been a pupil of the great French mineralogist L'Abbé René-Just Haüy and now earned his living making alum (a white mineral salt used in medicine and dyeing); Dr. Camillus Mann, described as an "Irish patriot and refugee"; and Say's business partner, John Speakman.

The friends determined to hold meetings in each other's houses and, until the society had sufficient funds to lease and furnish a suitable establishment, to rent several rooms as conversation hall, reading room, and a place to deposit their collections. The first Academy meetings cannot be reconstructed accurately. According to Troost, some thirty-five years later, the *Minutes* had been "carried off" and never returned by the secretary, Camillus Mann, when he moved to Baltimore after being expelled from the Academy for nonpayment of dues. "I doubt whether you have known that hot headed excentric Irishman," Troost wrote a colleague. "The original minutes of the Academy had more the appearance of an essay on Philanthropy and the benefits of Science on society than of a narrative of the proceedings of a meeting." Troost continued,

I found these minutes rather singular, they were not as similar minutes that I had heard in Holland—but it was the first meeting of the kind in which I was present in the United States—I thought every country has its peculiar customs. I met with Dr. Mann shortly after he left Phila—in disgust that he had been wronged etc etc—and speaking of the academy he told me then that he had the papers of that institution and that he did not expect to return them—whether they since have been returned I cannot say—I doubt because I found that Dr. Mann was some what crack brained and I avoided his company.[8]

Troost mentioned that a Dr. John Barnes was the first member elected to the Academy. He added with amusement that fifteen years later—and by then the Academy was a prestigious organization with members around the world—he had met Barnes on a Mississippi steamboat, and "the singular mode of his election" had formed their principal conversation. The Academy officers had closeted Barnes in the private room of a milliner's shop while they discussed his eligibility.

New members, either resident or corresponding, had been proposed at every subsequent meeting. The announcement by mail of one's election in the latter category employed a flattering rhetoric and opened the door wide to correspondence:

> The Academy of Natural Sciences of Philadelphia desirous of paying a merited compliment to a gentleman who has so highly distinguished himself in the Annals of Useful Science have elected you a corresponding member of their Institution. . . . Any inquiries you may be desirous to make relative to the Mineral, Vegetable or Animal productions of this country, its meteorologic peculiarities, the State and improvements making in Chemistry, Agriculture and the Arts shall be promptly replied to by the Academy and we shall feel particularly obliged by the favor of your occasional communications.[9]

Responses were usually prompt and were often accompanied by signed copies of the correspondents' works. Thus commenced in the United States a long list of Academy members—some of considerable distinction—and a library that, in its field, would become second to none.

Many of the first nominees would have a significant influence on Thomas Say's life. These included Dr. Daniel Henry Drake of Cincinnati, who would found a science museum in that city and employ John James Audubon to prepare animal specimens for display; the Frenchman François André Michaux, "the Naturalist of the forests" as he was described in the minutes; the educator Joseph Neef, who had an experimental school for children near the Schuylkill River; and Neef's associate Guillaume Sylvan

Fig. 7. *Gerard Troost* (1776–1850), geologist and mineralogist, by Charles Willson Peale, 1823–1824. Oil portrait. Courtesy of The Academy of Natural Sciences of Philadelphia.

Casimir Phiquepal d'Arusmont, or William Phiquepal as he called himself in America. But the most significant election for Thomas Say occurred in early June when Phiquepal paid his first visit to an Academy meeting and proposed William Maclure, described in the *Minutes* as an "amateur mineralogist."[10] Maclure at the time was in France.

Maclure was, in fact, no amateur in the sense in which we think of the term today. He had already, singlehandedly, made a geological survey of the entire eastern United States; this resulted in a pioneering paper, which he read before the American Philosophical Society in 1809 and later published in its *Transactions,* entitled "Observations on the Geology of the United States, Explanatory of a Geological Map." Phiquepal had met Maclure in Paris where the older man had subsidized his establishment of a boys' school. One of Maclure's most pressing enthusiasms was the implementation of the ideas of Swiss educator Johann Heinrich Pestalozzi (1746–1827).

Born in Ayr, Scotland, in 1763, Maclure had amassed a fortune in textile manufacture by middle age and then turned his considerable abilities to the study of geology, both in Europe and in America. Tall and imposing, with a temperament indicated—at least in his youth—by flaming red hair, he would be a great benefactor of the Academy of Natural Sciences as well as Say's patron.

Maclure's greatest contribution to Thomas Say's work, subsequent to this time, consisted of the numerous scientific publications he ordered in Europe and had sent to Philadelphia. Maclure continued this practice when Say moved to New Harmony in 1825, directing the shipments to that remote spot on the frontier. In the several years after Maclure's election to the Academy presidency in 1817—a post he retained until his death in 1840—this complicated, dogmatic Scotsman gave the new institution a large number of valuable books. Included were nearly fifteen hundred volumes on subjects covering natural history, antiquities, fine arts, travels, and voyages of exploration. Few institutions in America could boast of such an extensive library.[11] Among the treasures of natural history literature essential to Say in assisting his taxonomic pursuits in entomology were Guillaume Antoine Olivier's *Entomologie, ou histoire naturelle des insectes* (1789–1808), René-Antoine Ferchault de Réaumur's *Memoires pour servir à l'histoire des insectes* (1734–42), and Edward Donovan's *Natural History of British Insects* (1792–1813). Say would use the format of Donovan's book for his own pioneering work on American insects.

Long before he had access to Maclure's literary largesse, Say had immersed himself in the study of these invertebrates. In the summer of 1813 he read to his Academy colleagues an original essay introducing the science of entomology. Only a few others in America had preceded him in this area with occasional papers and insect collections. John Bartram and his sons had made some short studies, Benjamin Henry Latrobe had published "On Two Species of Wasp" in the American Philosophical Society's *Transactions* in 1809, and Frederick Valentine Melsheimer had published in the United States a booklet on beetles. But Thomas Say was the first to study a wide range of indigenous insects and to describe them in true scientific form.

Fig. 8. *Thomas Say,* by Joseph Wood, 1812. Oil on wood panel.
Courtesy of the National Portrait Gallery, Smithsonian Institution,
Washington, D.C.

(John Bartram had not known Latin well enough to describe his discoveries, although he was able to puzzle out the descriptions of others.)

Say continued his talks at subsequent Academy meetings that summer, delineating the structure of caterpillars and describing the various metamorphoses to which certain insects are subject. By December he was still featured at meetings with the same topic. Not everyone took him seriously. The *Minutes* record: "Thomas Say in pursuance of his appointment, delivered an Introductory Lecture on Entomology in which he endeavoured to defend it against the aspersions cast upon it by some writers and against the

Fig. 9. *Benjamin Say, Jr.* (1790–1836), by Joseph Wood, 1812. Oil on
wood panel. Private collection.

ridicule of the inconsiderate."[12] (The secretary was Say's brother Benjamin,
elected the previous June: see Figure 9.)

Unswayed by his detractors, Say continued these lectures during the
winter of 1813–14. Often he invited his colleagues to see specimens for
themselves under the microscope while he pointed out the "curious mecha-
nism of various parts of insects," including such minutiae as their sense organs and antennae. In essence, Thomas Say was creating the science of entomology in America. The scope of Say's work was, however, far broader,
for he also endeavored to convince American scientists to describe their
own fauna rather than send them abroad.

In the previous century, Dr. Thomas Bond had insisted that American medical students study in their own country rather than seek training in Europe. "No country . . . can be so proper for the instruction of youth in the knowledge of physic as that in which it is to be practiced," Bond had asserted in an introductory lecture at the Pennsylvania Hospital.[13] Stating the case for the value of indigenous knowledge, Bond noted that the Indians, without any medical training whatever, were more skillful in curing diseases "incident to their climate" than the most learned physicians, and that some of the "most valuable medicines" then in use were derived from Indian "discoveries."[14] An example could have been the treatment of goiter used by the Indians long before the arrival of European settlers in North America. The native peoples of a large region in what is now Ohio made regular visits to the Atlantic Coast to procure seaweed, which they dried in order to obtain salt. It is now known that a deficiency of iodine, contained in sea salt, is the cause of goiter. Benjamin Rush must have agreed with Bond, for he had been accused of refusing to prescribe anything but American drugs for his patients.[15]

It would indeed be an uphill struggle for Thomas Say to establish American scientific authority. He would have known the disparaging view of the New World that had been promulgated years earlier by the eminent French naturalist Buffon. Georges-Louis Leclerc, Comte de Buffon, superintendent of the Jardin du Roi (after the French Revolution renamed the Jardin des Plantes), had caused an enormous and ongoing controversy in America by his observations expounded in his forty-four-volume work, *Histoire naturelle, générale et particulière* (1749–1804). Although a brilliant and learned man, Buffon knew little about American wildlife, and he made many startling and ignorant statements based on his premise that New World fauna were inferior to that of the Old World. Animals degenerated because of the cold, humid climate, he said, which explained why in all of North and South America there were no mammals to equal the elephant or the rhinoceros. Buffon also maintained that domestic animals deteriorated when taken to the Americas. This last point, for different reasons, may not have been entirely erroneous, since it did take many years for the breeding of livestock to equal that of Europe.[16]

Thomas Say would have read Jefferson's *Notes on the State of Virginia* of 1785, in which Jefferson heatedly refuted Buffon, giving him a list of precise weights of American animals such as bear, beaver, otter, and marten that were heavier than their European counterparts. Jefferson had even sent Buffon the skin and skeleton of a large moose to vividly illustrate his point.

But most convincing of all was Jefferson's description, based on fossil remains, of the mammoth, an enormous brute six or seven times larger than an elephant. Jefferson was characteristic of his time in not accepting the idea that the mammoth was extinct, expecting that at any time the creature would be found roaming the western plains. Indeed, he steadfastly maintained that extinction was contrary to God's plan and therefore impossible.

Perhaps, because of his Quaker background of tolerance and equity, Say would have taken the most exception to Buffon's theory that the North American Indian was a degenerate creature because Indian men had no facial hair and were allegedly defective in ardor. Again Jefferson had leapt to the defense of his continent in the *Notes,* replying to Buffon that the Indian was brave, shrewd, and intelligent. Indian shortcomings were attributed by Jefferson to a way of life that included frequent hunger, everpresent danger, and constant hard work.[17]

Buffon inadvertently set a fire under the spirit of American nationalism that was spreading rapidly across the country by the year 1812. The Revolution had severed political ties with England, while the following years eroded economic dependence. The autonomy of American commerce would be a direct outcome of the War of 1812, but cultural ties would continue considerably longer. Natural science would be dependent on the expertise of European scientists as long as American flora and fauna were sent abroad to be described. Thomas Say and several of his colleagues shouldered the mission to stop this leaching of American knowledge once and for all.

By March 1815 the members of the Academy of Natural Sciences decided that larger quarters were badly needed. Say, Jacob Gilliams, the architect William Strickland, and Reuben Haines were appointed to find a new location. The next month these four resubmitted a plan proposed by Gilliams the previous year: to build a hall in the vacant lot behind Gilliams's father's house and rent it for two hundred dollars annually. The suggestion was accepted, the building built, and the Academy moved the following summer (figure 10).

Thomas Say also served on a committee to consider what European publications to buy for the library and how to go about the purchases. In spite of growing nationalism, Americans still had no choice but to turn to Europe for books on scientific subjects because so few had been published in America. The strength of Say's influence is evident in the list presented to the members in late September, 1815, as the great majority of books suggested dealt with entomology.

In addition to the numerous scientific papers Say read at meetings, he was busy with his duties as Academy curator. Not only were prodigious quantities of native shells, insects, birds, reptiles, amphibians, and mammals constantly donated by members, but a letter sent out to a number of sea captains concerning the procurement and preparation of articles for the museum was producing a rich harvest of specimens. The *Minutes* list a dried skin of a bird of paradise from the East Indies, a box of insects from China, "a small flying-fish" from a Captain Kitty, and "several fishes preserved in spirits." A collection of shells from the West Indies was given by a Captain Craycroft. From Madras, India, came the "petrified wood of a tamarind tree"; from Jamaica, several tarantula nests; and from Manila, a specimen of marble presented by Captain Hewitt of the *China Packet*. Correspondence with other scientific institutions around the world drew the Academy increasingly into the sphere of international science and added considerably

Fig. 10. *The Academy of Natural Sciences in 1817*, by David Kennedy. Watercolor. Courtesy of the Historical Society of Pennsylvania.

to its collections. A Mr. O'Kelly in Ireland sent one hundred specimens of shells; minerals arrived from Sweden, a group of birds from Italy, and eighty species of seeds from the botanic garden in Calcutta.

Just as the various scientific institutions around the world were connected by membership, exchange, and correspondence, so too were the naturalists themselves linked in interesting ways. The Abbé José Correa da Serra, a learned and distinguished Portuguese historian, statesman, and botanist who served for many years as his country's ambassador to the United States, presented the Academy with a slice from the trunk of a *Maclura aurantiaca*, the Osage orange. The botanist Thomas Nuttall, Say's friend and companion on visits to his uncle Bartram's garden, first saw the tree in 1810 in a St. Louis garden, where the *aurantiaca* had been raised from seeds collected by Meriwether Lewis in Osage Indian territory.[18] Nuttall described it for science and named it in honor of William Maclure, a patron of his western journey.

Thomas Say was soon spending all his time at the Academy of Natural Sciences organizing collections and books and using every free minute to study both. Even so, he was always available to discuss natural science with visitors. A friend, Dr. Benjamin Coates, wrote that Say's constant presence, warm personality, and enthusiasm were a strong encouragement to any who wished to study at the institution. In commenting that Say was a selfless and thoughtful man, Coates said—in what appears to be an observation of our own era—that "the contrast of these [qualities] with the manners of the times was occasionally so remarkable as almost to amount to eccentricity and satire." Concerning Say's willingness to share his time, knowledge, and collections with colleagues, Coates noted, "this generosity in bestowing upon others the results of his own industry, so highly characteristic of true genius and real love for Science, might be referred in part to a sense of his own strength.[19] Unafraid to assert his opinion, Thomas Say spoke out time and again on matters he considered unjust, especially when that injustice involved others. Over questions of scientific ethics he was consistently adamant—a mark of his increasing professionalism.

Say was so devoted to the Academy of Natural Sciences—the founding of which had fixed his destiny—that the institution virtually became his home. He spent day and night in the Academy's rooms, often sleeping in a tent made by throwing a sheet over a horse skeleton. Living on a frugal twelve cents a day for meals, Say was quoted as saying he wished for a hole in his side in which to deposit food and thus spare the time required to eat it. Say's friends said "his dinner frequently consisted of what he could carry with him in his pockets."[20] In this respect, Say's dedication resembled that of his ancestor. "So earnest was John Bartram, in the pursuit of learning," observed a nineteenth-century writer, "that he could scarcely spare time to eat, and might often have been seen with food in one hand, and his book in the other."[21]

Thomas Say's irregular diet and habitual disregard of his body's need for rest, which began in earnest after the Academy's establishment and his subsequent immersion in affairs of science, undoubtedly contributed to his eventual general physical decline. Throughout his entire adult life, and especially after his return from the first western expedition, Say suffered repeated bouts of illness, described in his letters as "bilious attacks." More than likely these seizures were caused by gallstones blocking the flow of bile from his liver and bringing about recurring jaundice.

The first mention of this problem in Say's extant letters is in a note to Jacob Gilliams in the spring of 1819 when Say was thirty-two and starting out on the Long Expedition to the far west: "I left my Dyspepsia in Philad[elphi]a & having had not the slightest symptom of it since my departure, now nearly 4 weeks, I think myself pretty well weaned from it."[22]

There may also have been a psychological explanation for Say's physical disorders, since from his childhood he appears to have suffered from underlying feelings of insecurity. The simultaneous loss at age six of his mother and older sister must have been a terrifying revelation of the fragility of existence, intensified by the inability of his doctor-father to save them. Yet painful though this crisis undoubtedly was, it no doubt deepened Say's appreciation of life in all its forms.

Although Say spent countless hours with Thomas Nuttall and other colleagues at the Academy of Natural Sciences, and particularly with Reuben Haines, Jacob Gilliams, and Gerard Troost, his association with the French naturalist Charles Alexandre Lesueur, both in Philadelphia and later in New Harmony, would be the closest and most intense, although it was also difficult at times. In 1816, when William Maclure arrived back in Philadelphia from a long sojourn in France, he brought Lesueur with him.

Born in 1778 at Havre-de-Grace, the son of a naval officer, Lesueur at age twenty-three had joined a three-and-a-half-year scientific expedition sent by Napoleon to explore the coasts of Australia. With his friend François Peron, who had studied medicine in Paris and joined the expedition as "medical naturalist," Lesueur collected numerous animal species new to science. Peron wrote accurate descriptions, and Lesueur made hundreds of drawings of these finds. A committee at the French Academy of Sciences composed of the eminent naturalists Pierre Simon Laplace, Louis Antoine de Bougainville, Bernard Lacépède, and Georges Cuvier, upon examining the collection, were amazed to find that it consisted of more than one hundred thousand animal specimens, including over twenty-five hundred new species. "If we call to mind," observed the committee in their report, "that the second voyage of Cook, fruitful as were its discoveries, made known not more than two hundred and fifty new species, and that all the united voyages of Carteret, Wallis, Turneaux, Mears, and even Vancouver, did not produce as great a number, it results that Peron and Lesueur alone have discovered more new animals than all the traveling naturalists of modern days."[23]

With such impressive commendation, Lesueur and Peron set out to publish their discoveries. But tragedy intervened in 1810 with Peron's death from tuberculosis. Grief-stricken over the loss of his friend, Lesueur was unable to continue their joint enterprise, and in an attempt to overcome his sorrow he turned his mind toward the New World. Fortuitously, at this time he met William Maclure, then living in Paris. Maclure was planning a trip to the West Indies and enlisted Lesueur's services as artist and naturalist. The two men reached the United States in the spring of 1816 after their tour of the Caribbean and then traveled through a number of eastern states before settling in Philadelphia the following fall.[24] Lesueur was welcomed at once by the scientific community, elected a member of the Academy of Natural Sciences in December, and soon became Thomas Say's intimate friend and companion. In Say he apparently found those qualities of keenness and industry he must have admired in Peron.

Some of Lesueur's friends and correspondents in Paris included the naturalists Anselme Gaetan Desmarest, Pierre-André Latreille, and Henri de Blainville. At the end of the following year all three were elected corresponding members of the Academy. Each was foremost in his field, regularly published his discoveries, and was willing to exchange knowledge and specimens with Thomas Say and his American colleagues. It was a large step in opening up important European channels for all the Academy's scientists.

Perhaps part of Say's enthusiastic response to Lesueur and other French naturalists, including Charles Lucien Bonaparte a few years later, stemmed unconsciously from his French Huguenot ancestry and specifically from his reputed descent from Pascal. In any event, Say's eagerness to communicate with these Parisian savants would soon find an additional vehicle, for the expanding Academy of Natural Sciences of Philadelphia was shortly to publish a journal of which Thomas Say would be the propelling force.

CHAPTER 3
The *Journal*'s Outreach

... with our efforts directed to the honour & support of *American* science.

Thomas Say to Thaddeus W. Harris
Philadelphia, 10 November 1823

IN A FEBRUARY 1817 MEETING, Academy members proposed that a committee be appointed to publish a periodical journal for the society. Say, the obvious choice to spearhead this endeavor, was eager to undertake it. The publication he and the others envisioned would be a forum for introducing new species of plants and animals to science and for exchanging ideas among institutions and individual naturalists. It was to be composed of original papers read at Academy meetings, as well as those submitted by corresponding members.

In the first issue of the *Journal of the Academy of Natural Sciences of Philadelphia,* published that May, the committee set forth their intent:

> The Members of the Academy of Natural Sciences of Philadelphia, desirous of acquiring knowledge themselves, and extending it among their fellow citizens, have for some years been accustomed to meet at leisure hours for the purpose of communicating to each other such facts and observations, as are calculated to promote the views of the society. By degrees, a collection of subjects in natural history was made, and has increased until a museum has been formed, which is already very valuable, and which is daily increasing. . . . In further pursuance of the objects of their institution, the Society have now determined to communicate to the public, such facts and observations as, having appeared interesting to them, are likely to be interesting to other friends of natural science.[1]

"Facts and observations" were part of the pragmatism—an obvious component of a democratic society—that characterized American science at the time and for many years afterward. Jefferson had laid the foundation with his inventions, new farming techniques, experiments in horticulture, systematic meteorological studies, and many other practical innovations. In the year of Thomas Say's birth, Jefferson had stated his attitude toward facts, as opposed to theories, in a letter to Charles Thomson: "I wish that persons who go thither [exploring the West for fossil remains] would make very exact descriptions of what they see of that kind without forming any theories. The moment a person forms a theory, his imagination sees, in every object, only the traits which favor that theory." Jefferson added: "We must wait with patience till more facts are collected."[2] Much in the mainstream of scientific thinking of the time, the *Journal* proposed to "exclude entirely all papers of mere theory" and "to confine their communications as much as possible to facts," as was stated in the first issue.

Throughout 1817 the *Journal* was printed for the society by a D. Heart. But this arrangement was apparently not successful. Part 2 (the second volume), which appeared in May 1818, stated on its title page that it was published and sold at 104 South Front Street. This was William Maclure's address, and it was there that the publication committee itself printed the *Journal* on a hand press purchased by Maclure. Say's unique importance in this venture is apparent in the *Journal's* disjointed chronology. Publication was discontinued after December 1818 and not resumed until 1821, approximately the two-year period he was away on an expedition.

The *Journal* was intended to be international in scope, based on the premise that mammals, reptiles, birds, fish, plants, shells, insects, and minerals, whether from Philadelphia or the Philippines, were all part of a worldwide study and of interest to naturalists around the globe. Therefore it was not inconsistent to have the first article of this American publication written by a Frenchman, Charles Alexandre Lesueur, an Academy member for only six months. Lesueur's essay described new species of fish that he and Peron had observed in the Mediterranean in 1809. The second article, by the Academy's prickly vice-president George Ord, discussed Rocky Mountain sheep, first sighted by Lewis and Clark and sometimes called the "white buffalo," an animal of as much interest to Europeans as to Americans because so few had seen it. The third piece, written by Thomas Say and entitled "Descriptions of Seven Species of American Fresh Water and Land Shells, not noticed in the Systems," dealt with an area of science virtually unexplored in the New World.

Say was conversant with the subject because a year earlier, in 1816, he had written an essay on conchology (called malacology today) for the American edition of William Nicholson's *British Encyclopedia, or Dictionary of Arts and Sciences*. The American rights to this publication had been acquired by the Philadelphia firm of Mitchell, Ames and White after Nicholson's death in 1815. Say's friend Samuel Augustus Mitchell had asked him to write on conchology, and the fifteen-page essay Say produced, identifying and describing many species of shells previously unknown to science, was the foundation of conchology in America.[3]

Classification, after detailed identification, was Say's dedicated task. He was not concerned with speculation on the evolution of species, since he accepted the still-current belief in the great chain of being—the idea that God had created life in one long unbreakable chain stretching from the lowest to the highest forms. When Say introduced the new genus *Alasmodonta* in his article on conchology, he was solely interested in its placement in the scheme of things. "This genus . . . will complete the chain of connection between the two genera *Unio* and *Anodonta*," he wrote.[4]

General doubts with the "chain" theory would emerge not long afterward in the scientific community, however. James DeKay, in an address to the New-York Lyceum of Natural History in 1826, stated that the theory was being "ridiculed" as a "philosophical reverie," and that "modern observation" more and more affirmed this opinion. He said that every day brought the discovery of "some extinct animal" whose structure varied in different ways with those of living creatures, and that it was to "comparative anatomy, and its companion physiology, that we must look for the most improvements and discoveries in zoological science." DeKay concluded that "the great chain of being" lay in a "confused heap," and that the links that appeared "to our partial and imperfect view" to be intimately connected were, very possibly, far apart.[5]

In his taxonomic work, Say at first adhered to the Linnaean system based on comparing obvious physical characteristics such as, in botany, the sexual parts of flowers. But later Say would be one of the first of his colleagues to use the natural system advocated by Lamarck and the entomologist Latreille. This system required a much broader knowledge of the field because a great number of related species had to be compared in order to arrive at an "overall affinity." In 1817, Say wrote in the preface of the first issue of *American Entomology* that the "corrections and improvements" of the Linnaean system of classification used by Latreille and "other illustrious observers" would be adopted. The natural method was unquestionably an advance over the Linnaean, which by Say's time was proving unsatisfactory for coping with the countless new discoveries, and he was quick to realize it. The development of natural science as a profession owed much to this improvement in classification. Science historian George H. Daniels has written that these innovations created "esoteric bodies of knowledge," whereas formerly, the artificial categories established by Linnaeus had been accessible to everyone.[6] In other words, the new method greatly expanded and deepened natural science, and put it in the hands of professional scientists.

Classifying shells was tricky, because it was difficult to decide whether to arrange them according to the animals who lived inside them or the shells themselves. "No one can deny," Say wrote, "that, if we proceed on principles strictly scientific, we must regard them as a department of zoology, and should, on that account, dispose them according to the nature and structure of the animals. . . . The best characters upon which to found all systems of natural history, must be those most obvious and accessible. All ranks of animals, as nearly as can be . . . should be arranged by apparent and external characters."[7] Say pointed out the difficulty of observing the animal inhabitants, which were usually dead or missing from retrieved shells. But he maintained that in studying shells "the animals that inhabit them should guide us in our researches; they alone are the fabricators of the shell, and the shell is only their habitation, to which they give the form, the bulk, hardness, colours, and all the peculiarities of elegance we admire."[8] Say's recognition of the importance of describing the soft parts as well as the animals' shells was an innovation in their study, since only in France had this aspect been considered.

Say criticized Linnaeus for the brevity of his descriptions. He theorized that, because of Linnaeus's methods, many discoveries had been lost to science—possibly from extinction, but more likely from insufficient description. In 1822 Say wrote:

> In common with the greater number of naturalists of the present day, I have very often felt the inconvenience of this imaginary improvement and real detriment in zoology, and heartily wish that brevity may be sacrificed to accuracy, as I am convinced that however desirable every describer may, and, indeed, ought to be, to represent the object before him in as few words as possible, he should, nevertheless, not hesitate to avail himself of as many expletives [descriptive words] as will in all probability obviously distinguish his object from others, regardless of the number of words that may be required for this purpose.[9]

By then Say had for some time felt constricted by the Linnaean system and was definitely advocating the broader natural approach.

Say observed that many distinguished zoologists thought it sufficient to give only cursory delineation, then refer the reader to a particular "cabinet"—a collection—for examination. Recognizing that to observe the specimen at first hand was essential, Say submitted that often the collection was inaccessible to the reader or (as would be the case with his own specimens) was damaged or destroyed. Say's descriptions were considered by some to be so accurate that future scientists would find no doubt as to their identifications.[10] In the days before "type" specimens (the specific individual from which the description was taken) were placed in scientific academies, accurate, detailed, hand-colored engravings in books were expected to serve the same purpose.

Say's 1816 article for Nicholson's *Encyclopedia*, containing four black-and-white plates, was printed separately later the same year under the title "Descriptions of Land and Fresh-Water Shells of the United States" and was received enthusiastically by other naturalists. Constantine Samuel Rafinesque (1773–1840), a colorful figure born in Turkey of a French father and German mother, who was involved in many areas of natural history, wrote to Reuben Haines from New York thanking him for sending Say's essay. Rafinesque said that he had read it "with great pleasure" and considered it to be "the base of American Conchology, a study totally new and which I have attempted to illustrate as well as Dr. Mitchell [Samuel Latham Mitchill] and Mr. Say." Rafinesque found it difficult to leave himself entirely out of any field of scientific inquiry. In his letter, however, he anticipated one of Say's most important works by mentioning that he hoped Say would delay no longer in undertaking "the vast and fruitful subject of American Entomology, which he is so able to enlighten. Let him give us as soon as he can a Synopsis of American insects."[11]

Say was, in fact, then working on *American Entomology*, the first book published in the United States that would, as it was planned, encompass all the known American insects. The slim volume of only twenty-eight pages, that appeared at the end of 1817, proved to be only Say's first attempt to publish his major work. The book was temporarily abandoned because the printer thought it was too costly, but Say resumed his study seven years later. Say wrote in the preface to volume one of the "real" *American Entomology*, which finally came out in 1824, that six of the plates had been printed in 1817, but because they had not been "properly published" it was "thought advisable to include them in the present work."[12] The second Titian Peale had been the artist for the first attempt. In later volumes,

Charles Alexandre Lesueur, William Wood, and Hugh Bridport would join Peale in illustrating Say's insect descriptions.

Say submitted papers dealing with the effects of insects on agriculture for subsequent issues of the Academy's *Journal*. In the third number he discussed a serious agricultural pest—*Mayetiola destructor*—peculiar to America: "This well known destroyer of the wheat has received the name of 'Hessian Fly', in consequence of an erroneous supposition, that it was imported in some straw with the Hessian troops during the revolutionary war. But the truth is, it is absolutely unknown in Europe, and is a species entirely new to the systems—being now for the first time described." After stating the way in which this insect devours wheat, Say demonstrated the balance of nature by describing another insect, *Ceraphron destructor*, which destroys the larvae of the Hessian fly. "It seems probable," he wrote, "that this insect prevents the total loss of our wheat crops, by restraining the increase of the [*Mayetiola*] within certain bounds."[13]

Say's task of educating the public concerning the vital link between agriculture and entomology, and thus the economic importance of insect crop depredation, continued to run into opposition. It was all of six years later when he could write encouragingly to his Boston colleague Thaddeus Harris—introduced to him by Nuttall through correspondence—that "entomology, which had so long been condemned in this country as a frivolous pursuit, seems now to be about to command that attention which its importance demands, & the formidable depredations of the insect race upon the vitals of the agricultural interest, compel the farmer to devote much attention to their manners & habits which he would not otherwise have deigned to bestow. This may be said to be the triumph of Entomology over the prejudices of the selfish."[14]

There were major difficulties in the study of this new science. Say noted to Harris that regardless of how much American entomologists wished to know about their subject, the distance from the rich libraries and collections of Europe, and from European scientists, worked against them. "We must therefore be content to labour onward as we may, with our efforts directed to the honour & support of *American* science, with *pro nobis* [for us] for our motto, not so much however in a *personal* as a *national* sense."[15]

Thomas Say was also much interested in the role of insects in human diseases. In a *Journal* article he discussed a South American insect that can

Color plate III. *William Maclure* (1763–1840), geologist, by Charles Willson Peale. Oil portrait. Courtesy of The Academy of Natural Sciences of Philadelphia.

Color plate IV. *Charles Alexandre Lesueur* (1778–1849), icthyologist, by Charles Willson Peale, 1818. An eel specimen in the portrait is symbolic of Lesueur's primary interest in fish. Oil portrait. Courtesy of The Academy of Natural Sciences of Philadelphia.

Color plate V. Titian Ramsay Peale II (1799–1885), by Charles Willson Peale, 1819. Oil portrait. Private collection.

Fig. 11. *George Ord* (1781–1866), by John Neagle.
Oil portrait. Courtesy of the Academy of Natural
Sciences of Philadelphia.

George Ord (figure 11), writing from Paris to request copies of the publication for the Jardin des Plantes, emphasized its significance: "Our little Academy, although undervalued by some at home, yet bears a good reputation abroad, particularly in Paris; and all this has been owing to its Journal. You may meet, and specify, and confabulate, and elect members, and enlarge your collections, and beautify your domicile, but if you publish not, down goes your character to the tomb of the Capulets."[21] From the beginning the *Journal* established the Academy's importance internationally and encouraged an exchange not only of ideas but also of publications and various plant and animal specimens. For Thomas Say—its driving force and most prolific contributor—the *Journal* was a principal means, along with correspondence, of entering the mainstream of world science.

The outpouring from foreign naturalists of all disciplines was exciting.

Sir William Jackson Hooker of Glasgow, Scotland, sent the Academy copies of his *Flora Scotia;* Dr. Leach at the British Museum promised to send a collection of crustacea; and William Jones in Calcutta wrote that he intended to ship specimens of all the snakes in India! The Baron Hyde de Neuville, in Paris, sent the prospectus of a book by Baron J. D'Audebert de Ferussac, a prominent conchologist, mentioning—in regard to Say—that de Ferussac wished to exchange French "molluscous animals" for those from America. Say immediately sent de Ferussac a large box of shells, together with all he had published on the subject.

In conjunction with a long list of descriptions included in an accompanying letter to de Ferussac, Say remonstrated against the endless changing of scientific names, asserting that such alterations served only to "embarrass the student, whose memory is already surcharged almost to plethora with generic synonyms." He added,

> certainly posterity will rise up in judgement against all those pirated names & indignantly strike them from the list. That new genera must constantly be made to keep pace with discoveries cannot be denied, but I think it impolitic to overwhelm the science with unnecessary names, unjust to wrest from an author his property in the name of a genus, in order to apply to it a name of our own inventing, which, in its turn, is equally liable to be rejected by a succeeding naturalist who has an adequate share of vanity.[22]

Say felt so strongly about priority—the right of the person who published first to be credited with the description—that he would not alter even an inaccurate name. In discussing the "apple tree borer" with Thaddeus Harris, he submitted that the designation *"Saperda 2-fasciata"* was "a very bad one inasmuch as the insect is not banded but is ornamented with two white longitudinal broad lines; notwithstanding this, as the name has been given, & to my knowledge, I cannot stoop to the knavery of changing it."[23]

Several years prior to writing to de Ferussac, Say had encountered an unfortunate instance of the "knavery" to which he so adamantly objected. Rafinesque, eccentric and brilliant, but with a predilection for rushing into print descriptions of new finds in many branches of natural science in order that he could be the first to publish them, had submitted to the *Journal* a paper on a certain species of fish; he had already published a description of this fish elsewhere, however, using a different species name. Say, as editor, unknowingly accepted and printed the essay. Either Rafinesque in his haste to publish had been unaware of his error, or else he had hoped to be credited with two discoveries.

Several months later the *Journal* included a retraction of Rafinesque's article; it was most likely written by Say in view of sentiments he would express in correspondence: "In concluding the present volume, the publishing committee consider it a duty which they owe to the readers of the Journal and to themselves, to state, that when the paper of Mr. Rafinesque was admitted into the preceding pages, they were not informed that a portion of it had already appeared in a contemporary journal." Rejecting Rafinesque's article was "indispensible for the interest of science," since "no direct reference" had been given by which the identity of the species might have been "detected." This notice finished with the disclaimer that responsibility for the contents of the publication's papers rested solely with their authors.[24]

In mid-January 1819, Rafinesque read before Academy members a paper discussing a new genus of fossil medusa, or jellyfish. Afterward, when he submitted this paper to the *Journal*, it was promptly rejected—the first time in fact that any article had been refused. Rafinesque's duplicity with the publication committee had not been forgotten. Also in 1819, Yale University's Benjamin Silliman returned to Rafinesque several papers that he refused to publish in his *Journal of Science and Arts*.

Rafinesque's enthusiasm for being first with as many discoveries as possible inevitably made his name anathema to men like Say, whose ethics were solid as marble, and who insisted on an exacting scientific approach to the naming of plants and animals. Say wrote to de Ferussac a few years later that

> with respect to Mr. Rafinesque I am sorry to say that I cannot place any reliance upon his writings & I therefore do not consult them at all; if you wish for my reasons I am ready to give them, though I am unwilling to injure him in the estimation of European naturalists who seem willing to publish his writings which cannot now be admitted in any scientific work in this country. I would not have made these observations if you had not requested me to give a synonyma between his species & mine.[25]

When Rafinesque died in 1840, the botanist Asa Gray wrote an essentially satiric obituary mentioning that Rafinesque had once submitted to a learned scientific journal (probably Silliman's) a paper "describing and characterizing in natural history style, twelve new species of thunder and lightning!"[26] It was unfortunate that Rafinesque so alienated himself from the scientific community of his day, because Gray himself, however unwittingly, found evidence of an original mind. In the obituary, Gray, speaking of botany, touched upon one of Rafinesque's ideas that we can now see was an anticipation of Darwin's theory of the evolution of species: "According to his [Rafinesque's] principles, this business of establishing new genera and species will be endless; for he insists, in his later works particularly, that both new species and new genera are continually produced by the deviation of existing forms, which at length give rise to new species, if the foliage only is changed, and new genera when the floral organs are affected."[27]

Although Thomas Say was basically mild-mannered, his heated reactions to what he considered questionable scientific standards showed him on occasion to be energetically assertive. His handwriting, found on notes approving or rejecting articles for the *Journal*, indicates this. Large, bold, and forward-slanting, it is that of a man forceful and confident in his convictions. Yet, at the same time, the sweeping oval line with which he invariably underscored his signature reveals the poetic nature that could describe a butterfly as "resplendent with all the brilliance of polished silver."[28] And hard though he was on Rafinesque, whose eccentric and impulsive behavior was the antithesis of his own, Say was a loyal and helpful friend to those he esteemed. When Charles Alexandre Lesueur first became an Academy member he spoke little English. The *Minutes* record that Say not only read Lesueur's essays for him at meetings, but also prepared his friend's papers for the *Journal*. In return Lesueur helped Say improve his French, enabling him to correspond with and read the works of the prominent French naturalists of his time. He also drew exquisitely detailed illustrations for Say's *Journal* articles.

Say often rewrote papers for the dentist Jacob Gilliams, a close friend at whose house he boarded for several years. Some time later, the fastidious George Ord wrote to Reuben Haines from Paris concerning the new edition of Cuvier's *Règne animal*: "What shall we think of Jacob Gilliam's name appearing in the formidable list of *Savants*? The author of two trifling articles, which were not written by him—which he was not capable of writing. . . . This will make T. Say chuckle, for no one better than himself knows who wrote the papers in question."[29]

The Dutchman Gerard Troost, who had moved to the South to find work, also received considerable aid from Say in preparing his papers for publication. "I not have forgotten our Academy nor its members particularly my friend Tom Say, [whose] assistance I put in requisition, being not abel of writing the English language," he wrote to Say. Troost spoke of assistance in preparing an article, and of sending the first part with the request that Say would put it into good English for him. He hoped to have his paper included in the next issue of the *Journal*.[30] Say, as editor, could not at the time include Troost's paper because the *Journal* was suspended at the end of 1818. This was owing in part to the difficulties of printing it by hand at Maclure's house, but mostly in consequence of Say's absence from the city on the Long Expedition of 1819–20. When publication resumed in 1821, however, an article by Troost appeared in the first number; Say had not forgotten his old friend.

A third "pupil" who received more help than all the others combined was Charles Lucien Bonaparte, Prince of Canino and Musignano and the nephew of Napoleon Bonaparte. Raised in Europe, Bonaparte's English was halting, but he was only twenty-two when his first book was published in that language. It had first appeared in parts in the Academy's *Journal* and was a continuation of Alexander Wilson's *American Ornithology*. In it Bonaparte described birds Wilson had not mentioned. In reference to his project, Bonaparte wrote in 1824 that he was glad to learn Say had completed correcting all the descriptions he had sent, though he was afraid that Say was not finished, "since you have besides Sylvia Celato and Fringilla Grammaca two others to copie or correct and the preface!"[31]

Both these birds, the orange-crowned warbler and the lark finch (sparrow), had been discovered by Say on his western journey and were later described by him in the expedition's report. Not surprisingly, their descriptions in Bonaparte's book are remarkably similar to those of Say's in the 1823 *Account of an Expedition to the Rocky Mountains* . . . . Say's aid to Bonaparte had a precedent in his own family, since William Bartram had assisted the much younger Wilson, also a foreigner, with his identifications and descriptions of birds.

"Notwithstanding *not to keep you idle*," Bonaparte continued in his letter, "I send you some more things to correct; you will observe they have nothing to do with my work, but I must proceed with my observations; those . . . Muscicapa [flycatchers] have given me a devilish trouble and I am very anxious to get rid of them; as soon as you will have sent them back to me I shall come in town the next Tuesday to read them at the Academy." He ended his letter, "I am very glad to see you occupie yourself with the Turtles [Say's researches extended to reptilia] and live always in the hope of seeing you at Point Breeze before the day of judgement."[32]

Point Breeze, an estate on the Delaware River near Bordentown, New Jersey (figure 12), had been purchased in 1816 by Charles Bonaparte's uncle and father-in-law Joseph Bonaparte, formerly king of Naples and of

Spain.[33] When he arrived in the United States a year earlier under an assumed name, Joseph Bonaparte was advised by his brother Napoleon to reside somewhere between New York and Philadelphia where news from Europe could easily reach him. At Point Breeze he built a large house and in time added numerous acres to his original holding.[34] Highly esteemed and popular in Philadelphia, he welcomed friends to his elegant gardens and stately mansion, where his art collection of European masters was regarded as the finest in America. Say occasionally visited Bonaparte at Point Breeze, as did other mutual friends. Reuben Haines, writing to his cousin, gave a vivid account of one of those visits, describing the sumptuous gardens ornamented with exotic birds and marble statues, the breathtaking paintings by Titian, Rubens, and Van Dyke, and "a library of the most splendid books I ever beheld."[35]

Impressive though this library was, in the domain of natural history it could not compare with the library at the Academy of Natural Sciences, which had been steadily enriched by gifts from abroad and by the munificence of Maclure. Ord wrote Haines from France that in his "cases" Haines would find "fresh proof" of Maclure's generosity: "On informing him that

Fig. 12. *Manor House* [Point Breeze] *of Joseph Bonaparte near Bordentown* (New Jersey), by Karl Bodmer, 1832. Watercolor. Courtesy of the Joslyn Art Museum, Omaha, Nebraska.

I discovered the great and valuable work of Labrun on sale in Paris, a work which, I believe, no one in Philadelphia possesses but Peale, he without hesitation requested me to buy it for the Society, at the price marked on the Invoice. Say's heart will throb with delight at the sight of it."[36] These books were essential for Say's work, and their aesthetic layout would prove to be a source of inspiration. When it came to publishing Say's *American Entomology*, the format of these volumes of natural history, as well as those of Alexander Wilson, would determine its appearance.

At the end of 1821, the *Journal* paid special tribute to Maclure, stating that his gifts included "many very rare, costly and splendid works on Natural History, which . . . constitute one of the most valuable and extensive Libraries of Natural History in the United States."[37] With the aid of this library and the Academy's ever-increasing specimen collections, in addition to those both preserved and alive at Peale's museum, Say was able to pursue his studies of many animal forms, including not only insects and shells but reptiles and fossils. He was gradually and thoroughly educating himself to become a zoologist, specializing in the largely unexamined fields of entomology and conchology—studies not then seriously undertaken in America.

Occasionally Say discussed mammals as well in his essays. When placing in a new genus a gigantic South American rat recently given to Peale's museum, he was able, by means of the Academy's library, to compare his scientific description with those of other naturalists: "This specimen does not at all agree with either of the [giant rats] mentioned by Buffon, Gmelin, D'Azzara or Cuvier," he wrote in the *Journal*, "but it agrees tolerably well with the description of the Patagonian Cavy, by Pennant." It is a tribute to his sense of the ridiculous that Say could not resist the kind of humorous footnote about the creature's behavior these older writers would never have included: "This animal had the singular habit of resenting the obtrusive caresses of strangers, by rearing upon its hind legs, and discharging a sudden and copious jet of urine upon them; females and children were more generally the objects of this disagreeable salutation."[38]

It was an engaging time for a naturalist. Undescribed animals, birds, and fish not only were sent from abroad—a welcome switch from earlier times—but were appearing close to home. In an article on snakes, Say wrote about an "individual" found by Haines on the second floor of his Germantown house; another was caught by a friend near Philadelphia.[39] A giant shark, discovered in Delaware Bay, elicited an excited letter to Say's brother Ben, then living in New Jersey: "I have just now returned from examining the 'Leviathan or huge Sea Serpent,' now exhibiting in Market St. It is a species of Shark closely allied to the Basking Shark, & my present impression derived from this first examination, is that it is a new species. . . . Its throat is very capacious & certainly capable of admitting Jonah, [while] that of a whale, tho' a much larger animal, certainly is not. Mr. Lesueur is engaged in making a drawing of this great fish, & when that is finished we shall, perhaps, be able to determine its affinities with some exactness."[40] This demythicizing of nature through scientific explanation would be one of Thomas Say's major contributions to the science of his time.

At the next Academy meeting he discussed the enormous shark, calling it "Squalus maximus." But since ichthyology was really Lesueur's department Say referred to him the scientific description of it. Lesueur observed (perhaps with a smile) that the creature had been exhibited in the city under the deceptive title of "Wonderful Sea Serpent," and that "in order the more effectually to attract the attention of the multitude, the long appendices which generally distinguish the male, and which accompany the ventral fins, were declared to be feet."[41]

Interesting though these local finds might be, scientific expeditions to the country's frontiers had been, and would continue to be, for Thomas Say the most fruitful and fascinating source of natural history specimens. Since he collected and described the fauna himself, misinformation and faulty identifications could be kept to a minimum.

CHAPTER 4
Spanish Florida

Mr. Maclure . . . invited me to accompany him on a journey to Florida, this invitation you
may be sure I thankfully accepted.

Thomas Say to John F. Melsheimer
Washington, D.C. (en route), 12 December 1817

A T THE END OF 1817, William Maclure invited Thomas Say,
George Ord, and Titian Peale to accompany him on a sailing excursion to the islands off the Georgia coast and to Florida, still owned
by Spain.[1] Peale, although only eighteen, was probably suggested by Say,
since for well over a year he had been working on illustrations for Say's
American Entomology, just issued.[2] Say must also have regarded the enthusiastic and well-trained young man as an able assistant in preserving specimens, a role he would fill again on a later expedition.

Maclure had contacts in Spain, having visited the country on several
occasions. He even planned to purchase land there to establish an agricultural school. Even so, his feat of obtaining a letter of safe-conduct from the
Spanish king, Ferdinand VII, had been quite an accomplishment under the
prevailing circumstances. In 1783 the British had returned Florida to Spain,
its previous owner, but relations between Spain and the United States had
never been easy. When the War of 1812 seemed imminent, the American
government asked Spanish permission to occupy east Florida to prevent the
British from establishing a base of operations there, but because Great
Britain was Spain's European ally, the request was refused. In spite of this
refusal, in the spring of 1812 United States forces seized the Spanish town of
Fernandina on Amelia Island, just off the Florida coast, and pressed southward to St. Augustine on the mainland. In the face of Spanish outrage, the
American government officially denied its action, but American frontiers-
men from border towns in Georgia continued fighting Spanish-incited
Indians caught in a crossfire between two nations. These southern border
areas were a hotbed of trouble, and late 1817 was not the most propitious

time to launch an expedition. But Maclure had often before been present in places of political turmoil—Paris during the French Revolution, for example—and his motives for the excursion were probably as political as they were scientific. Maclure's friend and lifelong correspondent, the American diplomat George William Erving, who had been sent to Spain to resolve the Florida question three years before Maclure's expedition, may have secured Maclure's assistance in assessing the situation firsthand. A year later, in 1819, unable to maintain its hegemony, Spain would sell Florida to the United States.

Say and Maclure left Philadelphia by carriage in December, traveling "by easy journies" to Charleston with a short stopover in Washington. Here Say dashed off a letter to his fellow entomologist John Melsheimer, advising him that he was thus far on his journey to "that promised land, not flowing with milk & honey it is true, but abounding in insects &c which are unknown, & if they remain unknown I am determined it shall not be my fault."[3] Say's focus was entirely on natural science, not politics, and he probably took little interest in Maclure's ulterior motives for the expedition, if he even knew them.

Say's friendship with the Melsheimer family, who shared his passion for entomology, was of some years' duration and greatly benefited his studies. John's father, Frederick Valentine Melsheimer, had in 1806 published privately a *Catalogue of Insects of Pennsylvania*, a slim volume of sixty pages that dealt solely with beetles and was an invaluable reference guide for Say. It remained, except for a few articles, the only American publication on insects until Thomas Say's *American Entomology* of 1817. The elder Melsheimer had come to America in 1776 as chaplain to a company of Hessian dragoons; later, as a Lutheran minister, he taught German, Latin, and Greek at Franklin College (later Franklin and Marshall College). His son John, also a minister, corresponded and exchanged specimens with Say until the former's death.

Say told John Melsheimer that he, Say, had received and sent on to him a collection of insects from "Mr. Oemler of Savannah." Augustus Gottlieb Oemler, whose zeal in entomology and botany had gained him Academy membership in early 1815, may have been sponsored a few years earlier by Alexander Wilson (who had died in 1813). Wilson had met Oemler in 1808 on his southern journey to collect new bird specimens and to sell subscriptions for his book. It was probably through Wilson's acquaintance with Oemler that Say met the Charleston naturalists Stephen Elliott and John

Eatton Le Conte, both of whom Say nominated for Academy membership. Until his death in 1830, Elliott, whom Oemler deemed "the first botanist of the South," regularly sent Say new shell specimens. Le Conte, however, would do little to promote American natural science per se and, much to Say's fury, would persistently mail his North American specimens overseas for identification.

On reaching Charleston, Say and Maclure sent the carriage ahead and took a steamboat to Savannah, where they met Ord and Peale, newly arrived from Philadelphia by packet. The four naturalists agreed to get under way immediately. Their main reason for haste was to escape an unexpected avalanche of southern hospitality. Word had spread that famous scientists from Philadelphia had come to study the native wildlife, and a number of merchants and planters not only wanted to meet them but insisted on sending letters to every island along the Georgia coast soliciting friends to extend all possible assistance. Although well intentioned, these civilities would prove a nuisance, since invitations at each stop had to be answered. Maclure repeatedly sent word that the party was equipped only for scientific pursuits and was unprepared to visit.

In just two days, after Maclure had sold the carriage and horses and chartered a thirty-ton sloop, the party cast off, accompanied by Maclure's servant, three sailors, and Ord's hunting dogs. The plan was to sail along the Georgia coast, stopping at the Sea Islands, then to travel by water into Florida's interior. Say wrote to Jacob Gilliams that they expected "to ascend as far as convenient the river St. Johns, pursuing pretty much the track of Bartram my excellent & ingenious relative; but whether or not we shall go further than he did will entirely depend on circumstances."[4] "Circumstances" referred to the Indian problem, something William Bartram had not had to contend with during his travels in Florida from 1773 to 1777.[5]

At the first landfall on Wassaw Island, the naturalists unwittingly caused a stir by shooting birds for their collections. On hearing shots, the local inhabitants assumed that runaway slaves were slaughtering their cattle; yelling and cursing, they rushed for their own guns. Although Say and the others were able to reassure the irate farmers as to their strictly scientific intentions, they decided to cut the stopover short. Upon reaching the next destination, Ossabaw Island, Ord and Peale collected specimens of the jackdaw (boat-tailed grackle), later the subject of Ord's *Journal* article scientifically describing the bird. In it he noted that Bartram had claimed to have seen the jackdaw in New Jersey. But, observed the acerbic Ord, the sighting must have been a rare occasion indeed, because he had never seen one there.

The men found the inlets "filled with multitudes of beautiful Medusae and other Molluscous animals, their phosphoric light giving brilliancy to the water."[6] At night they examined and discussed the day's collections. Since conchology was Say's second major area of scientific investigation, he may have viewed these crustacean-rich inlets as the "promised land" he had hoped to find. Further south the sloop stopped at Cumberland Island, described by Bartram as "large, beautiful and fertile, yet thinly inhabited, and consequently excellent haunts for deer, bear and other game."[7] Taking Bartram's hints the men took time out for deer hunting.

With everyone back aboard, the sloop continued on to circumvent the island, but shortly afterward it ran aground on a sand bar. Help was fortunately not long in coming, and with it an invitation to visit the plantation of a Mr. James Shaw. Say wrote Gilliams that they "were conducted by a negro along a winding road closely lined on each side by evergreen live oaks, waving from their branches the long pendant Tillandria [Spanish moss], by the Adam's Needle (Yucca Gloriosa), & various plants clothed with luxuriant foliage, all novel to the northern eye, this road terminated by a very extensive orange grove, loaded with fruit . . . which led immediately to the mansion."[8] The plantation house had been built by Mrs. Shaw's father, the distinguished Revolutionary War general Nathaniel Greene; his portrait, Peale noticed, had been painted by his father. Constructed entirely of oyster shells, the house featured an unplastered interior with thousands of shells protruding from the walls, giving an incongruous appearance to the vast hall, elegant with imported furniture, where the visitors sat down to a formal dinner.

The Shaws' extensive gardens of orange groves, lemon-tree hedges, roses, and other flowers in full bloom afforded Say excellent collecting opportunities. Among the many specimens he collected there, he discovered a distinct species of spider and a strange snail later described for the *Journal*. In the warm evening as he stood atop the flat roof of the house he could see far across the inlet to "the ocean which washed the shores at about ¼ of a mile distant, of the celebrated Amelia Island, of orangeries—vessels of war, privateers &c."[9] These last must have heightened Say's excitement as well as his concern over a journey into such contested land.

When the sloop was at last freed from the sand bar, the party sailed on to St. Marys Island, off the southern coast of Georgia, where they anchored for several days. Say wrote Gilliams,

We are now refitting with as much rapidity as possible for our voyage up the river St. Johns—Mr. Ord is purchasing stores at this moment, Mr. Maclure is looking for a pilot, Mr. Peale is sitting by our cabin fire (though it is not so cold as to need one) reading Bartram's Travels, and I am writing on a table near him to my friend. Our Captain is mending his sails, taking in water, &c. We shall be off in about 3 or 4 days for the promised land, a portion of which is indeed now in sight. . . . We entertain no fears from the hostility of the Indians; we could even repell the attack of a few of them as there are 8 souls of us—armed with guns & pistols.[10]

Although Bartram had claimed these waters abounded with fish, Say told Gilliams that he had found only a very few for Lesueur, even after repeated attempts with casting nets and hook and line. The fish he did find, however, constituted several new species, one of which Lesueur would ascribe to a new genus. At the letter's end, Say could not resist commenting on his bête noire, Constantine Rafinesque: "In the number for this month of the N.Y. Monthly Magazine, Mr. Rafinesque describes many fishes in a rough manner and in the same manner criticizes Purshe's [Pursh, a botanist] work and ranks himself (as he has often done before) with Jussieu, Decandolle & Brown."[11] Rafinesque's self-aggrandizement never ceased to annoy Say, who was himself so often characterized as modest to a fault.

Say's dislike of Rafinesque had been particularly exacerbated by his review of *American Entomology* in the previous month's issue of this same magazine. Say may have just had time to read it before leaving Philadelphia. Although Rafinesque had begun with a compliment—"The United States can at last boast of having a learned and enlightened Entomologist in Mr. Say . . . [who] shows himself acquainted with the details and improvements of the science"—he castigated Say severely for patterning his work after Edward Donovan's book on British insects, rather than that of the Danish entomologist Johann Christian Fabricius, imitating the former's "uncouth arrangements, desultory style, pompous publications, and costly performances." He acknowledged that the reading public was offered an "elegant specimen of typography" but lamented that the price was "two dollars." Estimating that at that rate it would require $2,000 to see illustrated the eight thousand species of North American insects, Rafinesque had concluded dryly, "It would be well if this style was left for the use of the princes and lords of Europe."[12]

On 3 February the travelers sailed for Fernandina on Amelia Island. They found the town partly deserted and the few remaining inhabitants near starvation as a result of fighting between indigenous Indians and

Americans defending territory not legally theirs. When Say and the others sighted a graveyard on the outskirts of town, they were surprised at the many Indian burials and conjectured that these deaths had resulted from "patriot knives."

When the sloop entered the St. Johns River the scientists saw great numbers of porpoises, pelicans, herons, and egrets, and extensive forests of live oak, palm, and *Magnolia grandiflora*. They sailed past many burned and deserted plantations before finally landing at one covered with orange trees heavy with fruit. This may have been the "orange groves of Mr. Fatio" that Say would mention in the *Journal*, where he found several new land shells. On another excursion ashore Say discovered a large tortoise, later described for science and called by him *Testudo polyphemus*. On spying a tortoise burrow along the river bank, he and Peale dug down some ten feet before reaching the end and "securing the inhabitant."[13] Limited to the southern states, and particularly Georgia and Florida, the tortoise was known in Bartram's day as the "Gopher"; today it is an endangered species with a severely limited range.

When the following day the party reached Fort Picolata, Say was intrigued to see the ruins of the Spanish fortress that John and William Bartram had found "dismantled and deserted" nearly fifty-two years earlier. William Bartram had described it in his *Travels* as having a thirty-foot square tower and high wall "without bastions."[14] Peale made a drawing of the site while Say unearthed crustaceans from beneath the old structure and on "oystershell hammocks" near the sea. Say would later watch one of these creatures with infinite patience, contradicting the opinions of later critics who stated that his studies were limited to taxonomy and that he had no interest in behavior: "I have often had the opportunity of observing the feet of this species [Say called it *Lupa hastata*] regenerating. One of the joints, I think the third, appeared first, the remainder of the foot was as it were doubled, and was gradually elongated until the tip of the foot was disengaged."[15]

After leaving the fort the men continued collecting and hunting for the rest of the day. Toward dusk they were surprised on being approached by two Americans who had heard their shots and had come to investigate. From them Say and the others learned the distance to St. Augustine, the capital, where they planned to present the Spanish governor with Maclure's royal "passport." With one of the men engaged as guide, Say, Ord, and Peale set out overland the next morning. Maclure, then 55 and suffering from chronic rheumatism, considered the 23-mile trek too arduous and remained aboard the sloop; the prospect of substandard accommodations may also have influenced his decision.

After passing through pine barrens and swamps, often waist-deep in water, the men reached the gates of St. Augustine toward sunset. Wet and miserable, they presented themselves at the governor's house and were shown into the guardroom. Upstairs the governor was entertaining two British officers, and on being informed that several bedraggled visitors wished to see him, bade them wait below while he finished his dinner. Shivering with cold and increasingly hungry, Say and his companions grew impatient in their damp quarters while listening to the laughter and the clinking of glasses above.

When at long last summoned to the dining hall, the mud-caked travelers were scrutinized with annoyance by the governor and with an equal amount of boredom by the British officers. But when presented with a passport bearing the royal seal and signature, the governor leaped to his feet as if shot. "From the King!" he exclaimed in consternation, and bowing low, expressed his deepest apologies. He urged his visitors to join him for dinner, but they refused, by then having lost all appetite and wanting only to find lodgings, bathe, and retire. While servants were dispatched in every direction, Say, Ord, and Peale enjoyed several glasses of wine and stretched out in leather armchairs before a roaring fire.

The following morning, in the course of a lavish breakfast, they asked the governor's advice about proceeding with their expedition. He warned that because of Indian hostility it would be foolish to venture any further up the St. Johns River and suggested that instead they explore the Mosquito River and the coast more to the south. This recommendation was agreed upon when the three men were reunited with Maclure, and the sloop was turned around.

The next day Say persuaded the others to accompany him ashore to investigate Indian mounds, possibly the very ones William Bartram had found in this same location. Bartram had conjectured that "the aborigines" must have had a "great town in this place" because of the large "tumuli" and "conical mounds of earth and shells" he had found.[16] Say paced off one of them as ninety feet in circumference and ten feet high. In it he found three flint spear heads, a stone hatchet, lumps of red paint, and a large conch shell he assumed was extinct since it belonged to a species never found on the North American coast. Again this unresolved question of extinction presented itself.

These few artifacts were all Say would see of Indians on this journey, even though he had been continually on the lookout for them. "As we redescended the river," he wrote Melsheimer, "we heard of parties of Indians who had been committing depredations, & one person informed us that a few days previous, his plantation was totally destroyed by them & his son killed. He narrowly escaped with the remainder of his family. . . . The Indians then took the road to Picolata; so that we departed from that place in good time, as it seems probable they went in quest of us."[17]

The naturalists coasted along the St. Johns as they headed back to the ocean, stopping repeatedly to collect and observe wildlife. For food they harpooned fish at night by torchlight and often dined as well on now-extinct Carolina parakeets. On reaching the Atlantic, Say transferred with Maclure—who refused further ocean travel—to a boat bound for Amelia Island. Ord and Peale continued on in the sloop but, caught in a sudden storm, were driven much farther out to sea than they intended.

When the party at last reconvened at St. Marys, Georgia, at the end of January, 1818, Ord announced that because of business matters he would have to return to Philadelphia; Say, Maclure, and Peale agreed to continue exploring. Several weeks later, on reaching Savannah, Say wrote Ord: "We arrived here this morning all well, after jaunting among the Sea Islands, halting at every inlet & examining the adjacent beach; I need not say to you, who know so well all our arrangements, that the time has passed very agreeably." He added that, "notwithstanding all our sanguine anticipations of discoveries amongst the Islands now that the season is rapidly advancing; we have not met with a single new vertebral animal & but very few new ones in the Invertebral departments, one additional new Genus we hope to add to the Crustacea."[18]

Nevertheless, Say and the others had already amassed such a large collection of finds that they would be describing them in *Journal* articles for the next few years. This Florida journey was the first in a long line of distinguished expeditions sponsored by the Academy of Natural Sciences, including sending Admiral Peary to establish Greenland as an island and Brooke Dolan to study Asian wildlife and bring back to America the first specimen of a giant panda.

A note of loneliness is sounded in Say's letter to Ord: "We have for a considerable time been anxious to arrive at this place [Savannah], only to receive the letters which we most confidently expected from our relatives & our friends. I alone have been disappointed & this disappointment rendered your very friendly note the more acceptable."[19] Say was thirty-one, unmarried, and perhaps beginning to feel isolated by the demands of his career from the warmth of intimate relationships. Little information on his private life is to be found at this period, which may account for a colleague's observation that Say's "correspondence with distinguished foreign natural-ists occupied a large portion of his time . . . and thus superseded much of his domestic letter-writing."[20] Matters of science had for too long taken precedence over affairs of the heart.

Say mentioned to Ord that he wished Lesueur had been along. "It is very much to be feared that all those fine Medusae &c. will have to remain yet longer unknown to the scientific world, but nothing shall be wanting on our parts towards succeeding in bringing them to his eye, yet I very much doubt the possibility of preserving those very delicate objects so perfectly as to be delineated even by his magic pencil; We shall however try other antisepticks besides whiskey for their preservation."[21]

Although Say had made many new discoveries and collected numer-ous species of crustacea, shells, sponges, and gorgonia, as well as a few fish for Lesueur, he was disappointed that the expedition had been foreshort-ened and that he had not been in Florida during a season auspicious for insects. "Thus, in consequence of this most cruel & inhuman war that our government is unrighteously & unconstitutionally waging against these poor wretches whom we call savages," he complained to Melsheimer on his return to Philadelphia in May 1818, echoing his grandfather's indignation at the treatment of Pennsylvania Indians over a half century earlier, "our voyage of discovery was rendered abortive, as we were not in Florida at the season we wished, the Spring. We therefore obtained but very few Insects & these few of but little consequence—My discoveries were principally in the Crustacea."[22] Say read a paper on American crustaceous animals to Academy members soon after his return, and the following week he deliv-ered another on several new shell species.

He had written Melsheimer shortly before embarking for Florida: "I have made considerable advances in a distinct work which may be entitled *Descriptions of the Insects of North America*, this is to be without plates, it is a work I have fixed particular attention upon, but it will occupy a consider-able time & will be the product of much, & unremitted, labor." (This book was to be in addition to *American Entomology*, but it was never published. The information it contained was used in Say's numerous contributions to periodicals.) "You will see in the 'Journal' that I have been describing the Crustacea of our waters; but my dear sir," he added, "I assure you that Shells & Crustacea are but secondary things with me, INSECTS are the great objects of my attention. I hope to be able to renounce everything else & attend to them only."[23]

Say did not then realize that the flame of enthusiasm for far-flung expeditions that had been kindled inside him by this journey to Florida would divert him from an exclusive study of insects for the next several years. Ten months after his return from Florida he would be setting out on a hazardous adventure as the first zoologist to explore the American West. "The continent was covered by penumbras," as Daniel J. Boorstin has written, "between the known and the unknown, between fact and myth, between present and future, between native and alien, between good and evil."[24] To Say the challenge was irresistible.

II
FLIGHT
Expeditions and Publications
1819–1825

Hills peep o'er hills, and Alps on Alps arise!

ALEXANDER POPE

CHAPTER 5

Destination: Council Bluffs

I have been so continuously occupied in preparing for our Western Expedition that I have
hardly time even to write to my friend at parting.

Thomas Say to John F. Melsheimer
Philadelphia, 13 March 1819

THE PITTSBURGH WATERFRONT on the morning of 4 May
1819 was a scene of great activity and excitement as onlookers jostled
each other for a better look at the steamboat *Western Engineer*
(figure 13). With its figurehead—a huge serpent—spewing steam from
enormous nostrils and its stern wheels lashing the waves, the boat had been
designed to awe the Indians as it carried to the West the United States
government's first expedition of exploration to be accompanied by trained
scientists. Thomas Say, William Baldwin, Augustus Jessup, and Titian
Ramsay Peale composed the scientific arm of this coterie led by Major
Stephen Harriman Long of the U.S. Topographical Engineers.

Resplendent in handsome new uniforms, also designed to impress the
Indians, the "gentlemen of science," as they were referred to by other
members of the expedition, stood ready to embark on an eighteen-month
journey to discover species of North American plants and animals unknown to science, examine fossil remains, and study the numerous Indian
groups they expected to encounter. Not since the travels of Lewis and
Clark, thirteen years earlier, had such an enterprise been attempted. And
then no scientists had been along, although the two leaders were charged
by President Jefferson to collect animal and vegetable specimens and to
study the Indians. Because of the fame Thomas Say had achieved at the
prestigious Academy of Natural Sciences in Philadelphia in his mission to
name American faunal species, he was considered "perhaps the most brilliant zoologist in the country."[1]

At thirty-two, Say—his face framed with unruly black hair and full
sideburns—was handsome and confident. His uniform of gold-buttoned

Fig. 13. *Western Engineer,* by Titian Ramsay Peale, 1819. Pencil sketch. Courtesy of the American Philosophical Society.

green jacket with high collar and black military trousers encased his lean, muscular figure to advantage. Six feet tall, Say was said to have had "pro-digious" physical strength before the chronic illness that plagued him seriously undermined his health.[2] Titian Peale's flushed color and lively eyes denoted not only the vigor of his twenty years, but the eagerness he felt for adventure. Peale was in love, and the fact that his father disapproved of the young woman may have added to his slight air of defiance. The robust aspect of both men contrasted markedly with that of William Baldwin, who at forty was hollow-eyed and pale from years of struggle with tuberculosis. Baldwin's misguided decision to join the expedition was based on his belief that the journey would be therapeutic.

In regard to the selection of these men, Major Long had written to Secretary of War John C. Calhoun that numerous applications have been made by gentlemen of science to accompany the expedition out of which I have made three selections: vis.—one in favour of Dr. Baldwin of the Navy, who agreeably to the best information I can obtain stands unrivalled in this country as to his acquirements in Botany; one in favour of Dr. Say of Philadelphia, who ranks equally as high in Zoology; and the other in favour of Dr. John Torrey of New York, who was strongly recommended to me by the Lyceum of Natural History of that City, as well versed in the sciences of Mineralogy and Geology.[3]

Torrey, a 22-year-old New York physician, declined Long's offer because he much preferred to have the position of botanist already offered to Baldwin. He also took a dim view of the fact that the scientists were to serve without pay (this decision was subsequently changed and they received two dollars a day). After Baldwin's death Torrey—who would make quite a name for himself in botany—arranged for publication Baldwin's botanical writings from the journey. In Torrey's place Long appointed a fellow Academy member, Augustus E. Jessup. Jessup at twenty-nine was a wealthy Philadelphia merchant with a keen interest in geology and mineralogy. It was thought he would be a congenial member of the expedition because he was a friend of Thomas Say's. Jessup had provided Say with the examples of fossil shells Say had used to write his pioneering article on paleontology for the first issue of Silliman's *American Journal of Science* in 1818.[4]

The botanist William Baldwin (figure 14), a Quaker, was born in Chester County, Pennsylvania. While living in Downingtown he became a close friend of Dr. Moses Marshall, nephew and heir of Humphry Marshall, founder of the well-known botanic garden at Marshalton and cousin of John Bartram. This friendship with Moses Marshall introduced Baldwin to the study of botany, although his formal training was that of a medical doctor. In 1817 he was sent by the U.S. government as ship's surgeon aboard the frigate *Congress* to Buenos Aires and other South American ports, and from these regions he added a quantity of new material to his botanical collections. The herbarium Baldwin amassed served to enrich the works of Frederic Pursh and Thomas Nuttall, and his copious correspondence with the botanist Henry Muhlenberg added much information to the latter's important catalogue of North American plants.

Major Long told Secretary Calhoun that he had met Thomas Say "after having received the most flattering accounts of his talents as a gentleman of science, from the most respectable authority." Say's name was not unknown to Calhoun. In early September 1818, Thomas Jefferson himself

Fig. 14. *William Baldwin* (1779–1819), botanist, by Charles Willson Peale, 1819. Oil portrait. Collection of Mrs. Richard Cassin Thatcher, courtesy of the Hunter Museum of Art, Chattanooga, Tennessee. Photograph by William Parsons.

had referred to Calhoun the names of Say and Nuttall—the latter by now a botanist of authority with the publication in 1818 of his seminal work on the taxonomy of American flora, *Genera of North American Plants . . .* —to serve as scientists aboard the ship *Macedonian*. Dr. Thomas Cooper, representing a special committee at the American Philosophical Society, had written to Jefferson asking for his influence with President Monroe "to send out in some capacity or other our Mr. Thomas Say and Mr. Thos. Nuttall . . . as Zoologist and as Botanist in the Macedonian. *They have done more than any two other men of late to extend our scientific reputation abroad.*"[5]

Monroe handed the matter to Calhoun, who replied to Cooper that he had consulted with the Navy Department and had found that the *Macedonian* was "under sailing orders" and would probably depart in a few days, "so that the wishes of the young gentlemen cannot be complied with for the present." It was just as well. The *Macedonian* would cruise the waters of the Pacific off the coast of South America for two years, protecting American whaling and trading ships; it would have little need of naturalists. Calhoun added that "it would have been a source of pleasure to me, to contribute in any degree to afford so good an opportunity to persons so eminently qualified as Mr. Say and Mr. Nuttall appear to be, to add to the stock of science and their own and their country's reputation. It is not improbable that a similar opportunity may shortly again present itself."[6] This prophecy was soon realized when Say was asked to join the Long Expedition, although Nuttall, possibly because of his English nationality, failed to get a similiar government appointment. Consequently, Nuttall, sponsored by Maclure and several members of the American Philosophical Society, set off alone in the fall of 1818 to explore the Arkansas Territory.[7]

The leader of the present expedition, Major Stephen H. Long (figure 15), short in stature but imposing, had all the attributes of a good soldier: motivation, courage, and an air of authority. A graduate of Dartmouth College, he had been an instructor at West Point before giving up a teaching career to enter the military. At thirty-five, he was recently married, and though reluctant to leave his bride he knew that this was only the first of many necessary separations in his projected army career. Long had already explored the headwaters of the Mississippi and the wilds of the Arkansas Territory, where he had established Fort Smith in 1817.

During the winter before the explorers left Philadelphia, Charles Willson Peale painted their portraits, commenting dryly that "if they did honour to themselves in that hazardly expedition that they might have the honour of being placed in the Museum and if they lost their skalps, their friends would be glad to have their portraits."[8]

Before leaving home, William Baldwin described in a letter the experience of having his portrait painted by Charles Willson Peale: "My portrait is completely finished, and ought to be, as I have sat little short of 12 hours. The old gentleman considered it one of his most finished performances, and spoke of sending it (on this account and not, I presume, on account of my beauty) to the Academy of Fine Arts, as a specimen of his finished workmanship." Baldwin said that he, Say, Titian Peale, and Long had requested that their portraits be "nameless," and be placed in a private room where

Fig. 15. *Major Stephen H. Long* (1784–1864), by Charles Willson Peale, 1819. Oil portrait. Courtesy of Independence National Historical Park, Philadelphia.

friends could see them. According to Baldwin, only Major Long's portrait was finished when he left the city. "The Major's, I think, is defective," he noted, "particularly about the eyes. The old gentleman complained of his [Long's] never sitting well, and the last time he sat, he was drowsy from loss of sleep (in consequence of his wife's indisposition.) This drowsiness is manifest in the picture."[9]

The portrait Peale painted of Thomas Say shows him at the peak of his physical and mental health, attested to by his high color and erect bearing. The introspective hazel eyes, with somewhat hooded lids, convey a hint of sadness, though it is counterbalanced by the slightly upturned corners of the mouth, indicative of Say's turn of phrase and the wit and irony that repeatedly sparked his writings. His head, held straight and high, is that of a man of strong moral conviction, although one so resolute as perhaps to narrow his opportunities.

Essentially mild-mannered and genial, Say had a slight lisp that "gave to his naturally gentle voice a musical softness."[10] He was known for his excessive modesty, a trait he willingly showed to others when it suited his purposes. For example, his reputed modesty allowed him to be less than candid when pleading incompetence, though this was usually a ploy to avoid tasks that did not interest him. On this journey he would decline to keep the expedition's journal, claiming a lack of literary expertise despite having amply demonstrated his skill in articulate articles for the *Journal of The Academy of Natural Sciences*. More than likely Say was reluctant to give up time from naming and describing zoological specimens. Such purposeful, if minor, deception in a man of such integrity may account for the intensity with which he reacted to the least hint of dissembling in others.

The value of the explorers' enterprise would be expressed to Major Long by Secretary of War Calhoun in a letter some months into the journey: "The Country takes a deep interest in the success of the expedition and I feel the strongest confidence that you and the gentlemen associated with you will use every exertion to meet the high expectation which is entertained. The cause of Science as well as the interest and reputation of the Country is involved in the success of the expedition."[11] By "the interest and reputation of the Country" Calhoun alluded to the government's utilitarian motives—its interest in opening the West for settlement. This objective was considered "in the public good" and justified—in pragmatic America—the spending of public funds. Knowledge for its own sake had to appear as a secondary consideration.[12]

It had been the same with Jefferson and the Lewis and Clark expedition—that is, stated objectives had camouflaged deeper motives. Military and economic goals had served as a convenient front for Jefferson's intense interest in the natural history of the West and his eagerness to answer many questions, such as the existence of the great mammoth in which he firmly believed.

The "Yellowstone Expedition," as originally conceived by Calhoun and of which the Long Expedition was only a part, had military, diplomatic, and commercial as well as scientific aspects. A thousand troops were to be transported by the recently invented steamship to the headwaters of the Yellowstone River where it joins the Missouri in what is today northern Montana. Here the men were to establish a military post in order to secure respect from hostile Indians on the upper Missouri. The military presence was also planned to discourage Canada-based British traders who were in virtual control of the northwest fur trade.[13]

Difficulties with the British, who clung tenaciously to this lucrative source of trade, had continued since the War of 1812. A newspaper article of October 1818 stated that the establishment of this post would be an "era in the history of the west" and that it would "go to the source and root of that fatal British influence which has for so many years armed the Indian nations against our western frontiers. It carries the arms and power of the United States to the ground which has heretofore been exclusively occupied by the British North West and Hudson's Bay Companies, and which has been the true seat of the British power over the Indian mind."[14] Calhoun wrote General Andrew Jackson in December that Jackson was no doubt "aware of the great importance I attach to the expedition to the mouth of the Yellow Stone."[15]

Several months later, Calhoun addressed the Academy of Natural Sciences on the scientific aspects of the enterprise. He said that the "immediate object" of the expedition was to "acquire a more accurate geographical knowledge of an interesting portion of our country." It was also the government's wish, however, to render the journey "useful to the Sciences." Because the Academy took such a deep interest in the advancement of science, "particularly in our own country," he asked for any suggestions that might be useful in carrying out the expedition's scientific objectives.[16]

The subject was brought up at subsequent Academy meetings, but by the time an answer to Calhoun's requests was drafted it was too late—the expedition was already under way.

In his role as zoologist on the journey, Thomas Say was charged with classifying all collected land and water animals—including birds and insects—and describing fossil remains, as well as studying and reporting on Indian habits and manners. The study of zoology was so all-inclusive in the early nineteenth century that John Davidson Godman, in his *American Natural History* of 1828, eight years after the return of Long Expedition, included a study of Indians along with his discussions of mammals.

Titian Peale, designated "assistant naturalist," was to collect, preserve, and sketch specimens. Long described him to Calhoun as "a young gentleman of much promise," who would be a valuable addition to the party for "he paints with a good degree of execution" and "is well skilled in preparing birds and other animals."[17] Titian's older half-brother Rembrandt recommended that he practice sketching from nature immediately: "Get into the habit of making notes of everything as it occurs, no matter how short. Memoranda written at the moment have always an interest of accuracy that distant recollections never have."[18] Since Titian was an excellent shot and had acquired his knowledge of taxidermy and drawing from his father, he was certainly well qualified for the job.

Samuel Seymour, the expedition's landscape painter, was an associate of Thomas Sully and other Philadelphia artists, and had worked for William Russell Birch as an engraver for Birch's magnificent collection of Philadelphia views, published in 1800. Born in England, Seymour had lived for many years in Philadelphia.

Long also included two army officers and a West Point cadet in his cadre. Major Thomas Biddle, Jr., aside from his military duties, was to serve as official journalist. Unfortunately, Biddle would have several bitter quarrels with Long—one nearly ended in a duel—and refuse to keep the journal; he then resigned in mid-1819. Lt. James D. Graham, a twenty-year-old West Point graduate, was to help run the steamboat, while William H. Swift, a cadet who would graduate with his West Point class while traveling westward, was to be Long's topographical assistant.[19]

In his letter to Calhoun of 24 December 1818, Long set out his proposed route, a difficult course given the modes of transportation then available and the problems inherent in such a journey. He said that, in order "to survey the waters of the Mississippi," he planned first to ascend the Missouri to the Platte, explore this river, and "return with all possible dispatch." Then he would travel up the Missouri and arrive at its junction with the Yellowstone "at or *before* the arrival of the troops." Subsequently, he and his men would explore the Yellowstone, after which he would follow the Missouri as far as the falls and "up as many of its tributaries below that point as the season would allow."[20]

This colossal plan, with its punishing schedule, was in place on 13 March when Say wrote Melsheimer, "if I recollect rightly I informed you of our destination to examine all the immense Western waters—the Mississippi, its tributaries, some of the Lakes & perhaps some of the rivers still further south. . . . Our Steamboat at Pittsburgh is nearly ready & it is ordered that we depart from Philad^a in all next week—It is further determined that we shall return to Pittsbg to winter next season—All this is *inter nos*."[21] Secrecy was essential so as not to alarm British traders.

The trip from Philadelphia to Pittsburgh had taken a week in a jolting carriage over bad roads, and a raging snowstorm greeted the travelers on their arrival in early April. In spite of the weather, Pittsburgh was an exciting city to be in. Thomas Nuttall had seen it a year earlier and described it as the "Thermopylae of the west, into which so many thousands were flocking from every christian country in the world." He had written that the banks of the Monongahela River were lined with nearly one hundred steamboats, barges, keels, and "arks."[22]

The expedition's steamboat was, unfortunately, far from ready when the scientists arrived, forcing them to wait an entire month. But they were well occupied. Baldwin recounted that "Mr. Say has been very successful in finding new fishes, lizards, etc.; Jessup has collected many stones; Mr. Seymour sketched a number of romantic views, & Mr. Peale has painted most of Say's fishes and amphibia."[23]

On 17 April, when most of the boat's initial problems had apparently been solved, Say wrote Jacob Gilliams that they were "busily occupied" with preparations for their departure and were "highly pleased" with the vessel:

> Though we have not yet had a trial of her speed, our cabin is neat & commodious, & everything is so contrived as to be condensed into the smallest space; our clothing, etc., is placed beneath our seats, which form an uninterrupted bench around the cabin; our books are placed in lockers conveniently constructed which form a continuous series around the sides of the cabin over our heads when seated on the benches; the table will be composed of separate parts, each of which can be removed to the most advantageous position & used as a writing desk.[24]

Titian Peale noted in his journal that "on the quarter deck there is a bullet proof house for the steersman, on the right hand wheel is [painted] James Monroe in capitals, and on the left J. C. Calhoun, they being the two propelling powers of the Expedition."[25]

The books mentioned by Say constituted a considerable library of natural history to be used for reference while collecting western flora and fauna: five volumes of Fabricius's entomological works, four volumes each of Turton's *Linnae* and Cuvier's *Règne animal*, twelve volumes of Nicholson's *British Encyclopedia*, European articles on crustaceology and entomology, and nine parcels containing the *Journal of the Academy of Natural*

Sciences. Say worried rightly that the *Journal* would be discontinued during his absence. In this regard he had written Melsheimer that "if I can make the necessary arrangements for its continuance, I will certainly direct copies to be transmitted to you. In order to facilitate its publication I shall leave papers for it."[26]

Say was also concerned about the approaching hiatus in his correspondence with European scientists. The English naturalist William Elford Leach had written in January: "Your remarks on Ocythoe [a crustacean] interested me so much that I instantly forwarded that part of your letter to Sir Joseph Banks to be read before the Royal Society, in whose transactions it will doubtless be published."[27] Joseph Banks was an eminent British scientist and explorer who as a young man had accompanied Captain Cook on his circumnavigation of the globe. Say had suppressed his excitement in mentioning this letter to Gilliams: "I have much to regret that time will not permit of a reply to the kind letter [of] Dr. Leach which Ben copied for me, this must of necessity be deferred until next winter, when if no casualty prevents, I hope to visit Philadelphia."[28] Say would not know for many months that his remarks to Leach were indeed published in the prestigious *Philosophical Transactions of the Royal Society.*

For the present Thomas Say's concerns centered primarily on difficulties surrounding the steamboat. After he and the others had stowed their belongings aboard, the weight of baggage, guns, and provisions caused the boat to ride much lower in the water than anticipated. This fact, coupled with a poor quality of wood fuel, made the necessary quantity of steam hard to maintain. On its maiden voyage the *Western Engineer* grounded on a sand bar in mid-river. During exertions to free the craft a leak was discovered in one of the boilers.

Despite these setbacks, Say and his companions did their best to maintain an optimistic outlook. The philosophic Baldwin reasoned to a friend that when "we take into consideration the complicated structure of a steam boat, and that everything must at first be stiff in its operation, I do not see that anything has happened which might not reasonably have been expected, and that we have no just cause to doubt of future success."[29]

Success in defense seemed almost assured by the quantity of weapons taken aboard. "The Armament is such as in time of need will probably stand us in good stead," Say wrote. "We have four fine brass Howitzers, two of which are mounted on travelling wheels for land operation and were used by General [Anthony] Wayne in his Indian wars; a shifting brass four pounder in the bow; four wall pieces; and a sufficient number of rifles, muskets and sabres with which to defend our boat if the natives venture an attack upon it; there are 10 of us, 10 soldiers, and 10 crew; 30 in all. A few rockets will be taken along."[30]

Certainly the boat's most interesting feature was its steam ejection pipe, ingeniously crafted in the form of an enormous snake emerging from beneath the bow and extending up and beyond it. The snake hissed out vast billows of steam and gave the entire construction a menacing aspect. The impact of this artifice, designed to impress the Indians with the expedition's power and importance, would unfortunately be negative. When the *Western Engineer* reached Franklin, Missouri, several months later, a local resident described the boat and the native peoples' reaction to its design: "In the place of a bowsprit, she has carved a great serpent, and as the steam escapes out of its mouth, it runs out a long tongue to the perfect horror of all Indians that see her. They say, 'White man bad man, keep a great spirit chained and build fire under it to make it work a boat.'"[31] Popularly referred to as "Long's Dragon," the *Western Engineer* must indeed have resembled a huge creature with a boat on its back as it puffed its way up the Missouri River, its myth occasionally enhanced by the discharge of a howitzer.

Say himself may have suggested this ingenious design to Major Long. In 1817 Say had written to William Elford Leach at the British Museum of well-publicized incidents concerning strange sightings at sea and their subsequent notoriety. Such fantasies as sea-serpents had been spotted in the Atlantic for years, but when a certain Captain Rich was summoned to his ship's bridge to see a frightful creature whose curved body appeared out of the water in waves, he sent a boatload of men to harpoon it. What they caught was one of a school of albacore, which swim in rows and could be taken for an enormous animal.

Leach had forwarded Say's comments to the prestigious Société Philomatique of Paris, which printed them in its Bulletin of 1818 under the heading, "Scientific News: The American Sea Serpent." In his letter Say had expressed regret that many learned European journals had taken the absurd tales from the American East Coast seriously—tales attributed to "erroneous observation" that had created "extraordinary fear"—when "the monster," reputedly a hundred feet long, was in fact a school of harmless fish, each only nine or ten feet in length. He concluded that natural history was indebted to Captain Rich for "purging its pages" of a ridiculous myth.[32]

Here again was a subject on which Say and Rafinesque had been at odds. In October 1817, a year before the publication of Say's remarks, a magazine article by Rafinesque had appeared describing a sea serpent "about 100 feet long" with a round, dark brown body nearly two feet in diameter and covered with "long scales in transverse rows." He had even proposed a name for the creature—*Megophias monstruosus*![33]

When the strange steamboat at last left its mooring in Pittsburgh and began its voyage down the Ohio, myriad aspects of river life unfolded before the explorers' eyes. They passed crude barges transporting pioneer families along with their household possessions, cattle, horses, and agricultural implements. Nuttall had observed in his own trip down the river some months earlier, "A stranger who descends the Ohio at this season of emigration, cannot but be struck with the jarring vortex of heterogeneous population amidst which he is embarked, all searching for some better country, which ever lies to the west, as Eden did to the east."[34]

Carried along by the strong current, the steamboat narrowly missed the sunken trees that proved treacherous to all forms of navigation, but snags on the river were taken as a matter of course. Since it was early May, the trees had leafed out, birds sang, and all nature in its rebirth seemed to be encouraging the explorers in their venture. They saw pelicans, sandpipers, and turkey vultures, and in the evenings heard the cry of whippoorwills. In observing the enormous American plane tree along the banks of the Ohio, they noted that its fruit was the favorite food of the Carolina parakeet and that "large flocks of these gaily-plumed birds constantly enliven the gloomy forest of the Ohio."[35]

Because Baldwin was ill and in need of treatment and the boat needed minor repairs, the expedition docked at Cincinnati for nine days. In his journal Peale described the town as having "risen like a mushroom from the wilderness," adding with special interest that the inhabitants had founded a college and museum for which they had collected mostly fossils and animal remains. Dr. Daniel Henry Drake, a corresponding member of the Academy of Natural Sciences, had been instrumental in establishing this institution.[36] His presence there was fortunate for Baldwin, whose disease had taken a turn for the worse.

Also at the Western Museum was the French-descended naturalist John James Audubon, employed to preserve and mount animal specimens and to paint backgrounds for exhibits. Audubon, at thirty-four, had a series of business disasters behind him but was on the threshold of his sensational career as an artist. Virtually unknown at the time, he must have been impressed by the Long Expedition's members—especially Thomas Say, the notable zoologist from the Academy in Philadelphia. Years later Audubon recalled meeting the explorers and the effect his bird paintings had made on them. "The expedition of Major Long passed through the city . . . and well do I recollect how he, Messrs. T. Peale, Thomas Say, and others stared at my drawings of birds at that time."[37] When Audubon recorded these words he may have seen Titian Peale as a rival, since the latter had published his drawings of birds collected on this expedition in Charles Bonaparte's continuation of Alexander Wilson's *American Ornithology*.

Baldwin rejoined the party when fit enough to travel, and the boat resumed its journey to St. Louis. En route the explorers steamed past a flotilla containing Yellowstone Expedition troops, also bound for St. Louis before proceeding to Council Bluffs on the Missouri River. They, too, were encountering endless difficulties with travel by the newly invented steamboat. On the *Western Engineer* leaks occurred regularly in the steampipe; mud in the boiler also reduced the quantity of steam. Sawyers, or trees embedded in the river with their branches projecting to the surface, frequently brought the hapless vessel to a standstill, forcing the men to drop down into waist-high water and push.

When the boat finally entered the Mississippi and attempted to head upstream, the current, favorable in the Ohio, was now in opposition, and the pilot hugged the bank, making progress slow and tedious. Nuttall had portrayed the Mississippi as "a labyrinth of danger, so horribly filled with black and gigantic trunks of trees, along which the current foamed with terrific velocity—Scylla on one hand, and more than one Charybdis on the other."[38] Because of the slow pace caused by these difficulties and the constant stopping to chop down cottonwood trees for fuel, Say was able to go ashore and search for specimens. Several new insect species he found would appear a few years later in his *American Entomology*, painstakingly sketched by Titian Peale.

On 9 June the expedition arrived at St. Louis, saluted by a large cannon on the bank and several guns aboard the Yellowstone Expedition steamships moored in the harbor. The fanfare impressed young Peale, who noted in his diary that "the day after our arrival the Citizens gave us a dinner at which all the officers of the 5th and 6th regiments, the rifle regiment and all the Captains of the Steamboats in port were invited, making a Concourse that I never expected to see here. We were entertained by the band of the 6th regiment while dining."[39]

While in St. Louis, Say and Peale investigated Indian mounds in the vicinity. They exhumed several of them, and, with a tape measure and pocket compass, carefully measured twenty-seven mounds and prepared a map. On finding rattlesnake bones in one grave, Say wondered whether the native peoples of America, like the Egyptians, had worshiped snakes and buried them with their dead. A current myth alleged that a pygmy race had lived there; Say and Peale discredited this story by asserting that the bones they found were those of children. For Say, this discovery was further refutation of Buffon's theory that man and beast in the New World were somehow smaller and inferior to those in the Old World.

"It is probable," Say wrote in 1819, "these piles of earth were raised as cemeteries, or they may have supported altars for religious ceremonies. We cannot conceive any useful purpose to which they can have been applicable in war, unless as elevated stations from which to observe the motions of an approaching enemy; but for this purpose a single mound would have been sufficient, and the place chosen would probably have been different." Forty-two years later, Peale published an article with the map he and Say had prepared. In it he wrote that the opinions he had quoted of his "much-respected friend" concerning these earthworks had "since been corroborated by other observers."[40] Today, these extensive Cahokia Mounds, located east of St. Louis in Illinois, and numbering one hundred or more, are believed to have been a ceremonial center.[41]

After a few days ashore the voyage was resumed. Baldwin confided to a friend that he doubted the *Western Engineer* would measure up to the "sanguine expectations formed of her. . . . This boat, hastily constructed and built entirely of unseasoned timber, is almost daily in want of repairs, and is so leaky and wet that we have not a dry locker for our clothes. A great part of my stationery has been wet and a portion of it entirely lost. It will be with the utmost difficulty that I shall save the specimens I may collect. . . . Mr. Say makes the same complaint." Baldwin, depressed by the obvious severity of his illness, stated emphatically that "a steamboat is not calculated for exploring." He complained that no stopping had been permitted except for repairs and to take on wood and water, and the naturalists had not been allowed a moment to explore, thus bypassing many "productive situations."[42]

At St. Charles the expedition was joined by Major Benjamin O'Fallon, agent for Indian affairs in the Missouri Territory and nephew of General William Clark, and O'Fallon's interpreter, John Dougherty. O'Fallon had only recently been appointed to the post by Secretary Calhoun, who correctly believed that the military operations he planned against the British would be greatly facilitated by Indian cooperation. O'Fallon was to accompany Long's advance party, ahead of the troops, in order to prepare the way for their reception by the Indians. This he hoped to accomplish by guaranteeing the military's peaceful intentions and by distributing a generous number of presents. He had been cautioned by Calhoun not to excite the suspicions of British traders until the military posts were established, at which time he was to give notice that all trade was prohibited except that authorized by the United States government.

At this stage in the journey, Say, Peale, Jessup, and Seymour decided they had had enough of the steamboat and would travel by land. They saddled a horse, packed it with blankets and provisions, and set off on foot to explore the countryside. But the excursion was doomed when the pack horse ran away on the first evening. Though they managed to recapture it, it again made off two days later. Food and water supplies soon proved inadequate, and prairie flies and intense heat plagued the men unmercifully. Exhausted and ill they rejoined the boat several days later at Loutre Island in the Missouri.

Although the adventure had been fraught with problems, Say was able to look back with amusement when recalling it to Jacob Gilliams:

> Your commiseration would hardly have restrained a smile at the uncouth appearance we exhibited on our march, our rough dress suited for the forests, our blankets, provisions, shooting apparatus, &c. slung upon our backs, our procession in Indian file, peeping cunningly through the occasional skirts of forest that intersected our rout & our silence now & then interrupted by a remark called forth by a change of scenery, or by the presentation of some natural object new to us; & my companions trudging along with sore feet would have reminded you of Pindar's facetious story of the Pilgrims & the Peas.[43]

On 13 July, when they arrived at Franklin, Missouri Territory (Missouri would not become a state until 1821), Baldwin decided he should remain behind since his disease had progressed alarmingly. Ever thorough, he made his withdrawal official in a letter to Long: "In consequence of being afflicted with a pulmonic disease the symptoms of which I now find becoming aggravated by confinement on board of the boat under your command, so as to endanger my life, I feel myself under the painful necessity of requesting that you will permit me to land at this place, and remain until so far recovered as to be enabled to rejoin my colleagues, or otherwise return home."[44] Baldwin hoped to increase his botanical collections by exploring the area, but he grew steadily worse and died six weeks later, his brilliant career cut off before he could publish any of his innumerable discoveries.

A week after arriving at Franklin and outfitting themselves for the frontier by purchasing moccasins and skins to make leggings, a detachment consisting of Say, Jessup, Seymour, Dougherty, and Biddle departed on horseback for Fort Osage. The fort, an outpost established in 1808 by Meriwether Lewis, was located, at the time of the Long Expedition, at the extreme frontier of the settlements. Later, Peale, Swift, and five soldiers joined Say's detachment while the *Western Engineer* chugged slowly up the Missouri.

Say would write in *American Entomology* that "after encountering many obstacles and privations which it is unnecessary to enumerate, the party arrived at the village of the Konza [Kansa] Indians, hungry, fatigued, and out of health." In his usual dignified prose Say described the party's reception: "Commiserating our situation, these sons of nature, although suffering under the injustice of white people, received us with their characteristic hospitality, and ameliorated our condition by the luxuries of repletion and repose."[45] The explorers, lodged in the house of the Kansa leader and seated on bison robes around large wooden bowls, were served maize soup enriched with slices of bison meat, grease, and beans.

"Whilst sitting in the large earth-covered dwelling of the principal chief," Say wrote, "in the presence of several hundred of his people assembled to view the arms, equipment, and appearance of the party, I enjoyed the additional gratification to see an individual of this fine species of *Blaps* [a beetle] running towards us from the feet of the crowd. The act of impaling this unlucky fugitive at once conferred upon me the respectful and mystic title of 'medicine man,' from the superstitious faith of that simple people."[46]

The following day the party left the Kansa village, accompanied by three tribal members. After traveling some seven miles they encamped beside a small creek in a narrow but beautiful prairie bottom, while the interpreter, Dougherty, with one of the Indians, went in search of game. The rest of the men had just passed around pipes and tobacco when suddenly a large cloud of dust rising from the plain called their attention to a galloping band of at least one hundred Indians. Immediately the three

Kansas leaped up and disappeared, leaving the explorers alone to face what appeared to be a hostile party armed with tomahawks, clubs, knives, and guns, and fully decorated for battle. To the astonishment of Say and his companions, the Indians began shaking hands with them, hugging them, and raising their palms toward them in signs of peace. But these expressions of friendship soon vanished when other warriors seized the expedition's horses and plundered a tent erected for Say, who was unwell, taking Say's pistols among other articles.

Say and his companions quickly heaped their baggage together and formed a circle around it. The Indians demanded whiskey and tobacco, smiling all the while. During the next half hour the tension mounted appreciably, especially when one warrior cocked his gun while another attempted to seize a soldier's knapsack. The owner clamped his foot on it and aimed his gun, but the Indian jumped back with a laugh and "drew his arrow to the head." Another warrior "put a war whistle to his mouth" and held it there for an unnerving length of time, though he refrained from blowing it.[47]

Dougherty appeared at last and shouted something at the war party, but by then the Indians had begun to move away. They did so slowly, so as to give the impression the maneuver had nothing whatever to do with Dougherty's commands. After the Indians departed, Jessup set out for the Kansa village to get help while the rest concealed their baggage in the bushes and awaited his return. At dawn a group of thirty friendly Kansas rode up to escort the explorers back to their village. The other Indians, they said, were Pawnees, who were at war with the Kansas.

Raiding was a way of life for the nomadic Pawnees, who depended principally on hunting and pillage for their sustenance, particularly in the fall and winter. Like most other plains Indian tribal groups they saw only occasional white men, who always traveled, it seemed to them, in small bands without women and children. Because of this they could not conceive that these people could compare in strength to the Pawnee nation, and they were not afraid to attack them.[48]

Such a life of violence and plunder was somewhat recent in origin. Until the Spaniards introduced the horse into North America at the end of the sixteenth century—the indigenous equine having been extinct since the great glacial melt—the inhabitants of the plains had subsisted principally by means of agriculture. After Indians acquired the horse, which enabled them to hunt bison more effectively, an entirely different culture evolved. Indians from all over the west converged on the plains, "the lands of the agriculturists were usurped, and the plains became a maelstrom of varied and often conflicting cultures."[49]

Finally secure in the same spacious lodge they had previously occupied, the explorers had just fallen asleep when a large group of Indians, armed with bows, arrows, and lances and shouting jubilantly, burst in upon them. Say and his companions grabbed their guns in fright and prepared to defend themselves. On realizing the invaders were Kansas and seeing the serene demeanor of several accompanying women, however, they understood that no harm was intended. The Indians ringed the fire in the center of the lodge, chanting, beating drums, and shaking rattles made of stringed deer hooves. Taking no notice of their startled audience, they continued dancing for some time, eventually leaving as promptly as they had arrived, "raising the same wolfish howl, with which they had entered; but their music and yelling continued to be heard about the village during the night." Say learned later that this ceremony was the Kansas' Dog Dance, which had been performed in their guests' honor.[50]

When Say and the others finally arrived at Isle au Vache in the Missouri, where they planned to rendezvous with the steamboat, the troops that were temporarily anchored at the island informed them that Long had not received Say's message establishing this meeting place and had moved on. Say and Jessup, who were by then both ill, elected to remain with the troops while the others set off at a gallop to intersect Long at the confluence of the Wolf and Missouri rivers. They were in time to hail the steamboat as it passed by. Thomas Biddle left the expedition at this point. He claimed that his "defeat" at the hands of the Pawnees would damage his military career.[51] Undoubtedly Biddle's animosity toward Long was much involved with his decision.

On 19 September 1819, nearly five months after departing Pittsburgh, the *Western Engineer* arrived at the location on the west bank of the Missouri, some thirteen hundred miles from Philadelphia, where the explorers planned to establish winter quarters. It was less than a mile above the fur trading fort of the legendary Manuel Lisa, credited as the first white trader to ascend the Missouri after Lewis and Clark, and five miles below Council Bluffs where the army troops were to be stationed. Council Bluffs, named by Lewis and Clark in commemoration of a council held there on 3 August 1804 with the Oto and Missouri Indians, possessed a superb command of the surrounding area from its position high on a bank above the river. Since there was almost no wood or stone within a convenient distance, however, Long's party selected a camping place lower down, where a narrow beach covered with trees stood between the river and the gradually ascending bluffs behind, and abundant building supplies were within easy reach.

A week later Say and Jessup, nearly recovered and in high spirits, arrived from Isle au Vache with several members of the military. In a short time they joined the others in cutting timber and quarrying stone for the winter base camp all agreed to call Engineer Cantonment.

CHAPTER 6
Winter Encampment

We have here very comfortable winter quarters, snug log houses, amply large, with
capacious fire places & plenty of fuel around us.

Thomas Say to Benjamin Say
Engineer Cantonment, 10 October 1819

AT THE NEARLY COMPLETED Engineer Cantonment (figure 16),
much excitement surrounded the arrival on 3 October of one hundred Otos and a contingent of Iowas (a name supposed to be from
the Dakota word *Ayuhwa* meaning "Sleepy People") to attend a council
called by Major O'Fallon. When at last the tribes had arrived and the principal leaders had seated themselves, Shonga-tonga (Big Horse), a portly man
with a commanding presence, arose and addressed Major O'Fallon: "My
father, your children have come to dance before your tent, agreeably to our
custom of honouring brave or distinguished persons."[1] With a wave of his
hand the dancing began, accompanied by the measured beats of a gong, a
group of vocalists, and the bodily swaying of the entire Indian assembly.
Several sets of dances followed, during intervals of which a different warrior each time stepped forward, struck a flagstaff with a stick, and recounted
his martial exploits. These included stealing horses from the Kansas, Ietans
(Comanches), and Pawnees, and beating the bodies of slain warriors belonging to these and other tribes, including Osages, Omahas, and Sioux.
This latter practice was considered an act of the utmost bravery because the
enemy was usually watching and would most certainly retaliate.[2]

As Thomas Say looked around at the Indians, he noticed three youthful leaders completely painted black, a sign, he had been told, of their positions of authority and duties as peacekeepers. One, called Hashea or Cut
Nose, whose profile made Say think of an engraving he had once seen of
Voltaire, seemed much amused by the proceedings and frequently aroused
the laughter of those around him by his remarks and gestures. He was
handsomely dressed in a robe of white wolf skin.

The council itself took place the following morning. Benches, arranged in a semicircle with Indians on one side and expedition members on the other, faced a large American flag snapping in the wind. Sentries patrolled the periphery. Several howitzer rounds opened the meeting, and after the last reverberations died away Major O'Fallon stood up and made his address. At the ceremony's close he presented gifts of blankets, kettles, shrouding, tobacco, guns, and powder. Cut Nose in turn gave the major a magnificently decorated bison robe.

Five days later, three tribes of Pawnees—the Grand Pawnees, Pawnee Republicans, and Pawnee Loups—also summoned to council, arrived ceremoniously on fine mules and camped some distance from the cantonment. The Pawnee Republicans were hesitant and wary because of their past attack on Say's exploring party, and Major O'Fallon attempted to reassure them: "Pawnees, encamp here and smoke your pipes in security; you have conducted yourselves badly, but the whites will not harm the red-skins when they have them thus in their power; we fight in the plains, and scorn to injure men seated peaceably by their fires. Think well of what you will

Fig. 16. *Engineer Cantonment,* by Titian Ramsay Peale, 1819. Watercolor. Courtesy of the American Philosophical Society.

have to say to me in council to-morrow."[3] At that very moment, three boatloads of troops from Council Bluffs on an errand to obtain provisions fired guns in greeting accompanied by "a brassy blare of trumpets" as they approached the dock. The Pawnees, convinced of an ambush, dashed in a body for cover. It took some time for the leaders, who from having been in St. Louis were somewhat accustomed to hearing cannons fired, to reassure their tribesmen.[4]

The guns and trumpets must have been unnerving to the Pawnee leaders as well, for they were faced with a serious situation. After the raid on Say's party, Major Long had sent word that all traders were to be stopped from dealing with the Pawnee Republicans. Since the tribe was preparing to set out on hunting and war expeditions and urgently needed supplies, such prohibition was a serious impediment.[5] At the council, forced by their position to make concessions, the Pawnee Republicans returned most of the articles stolen from Say's detachment. Included were "one buffaloe robe, one horse, one pair double-barrelled pistols, one bird-bag, one toma-hawk, one axe, one powder-flask [and] one shot-bag."[6] But O'Fallon's order to surrender the warriors responsible for the raid was refused out-right, since the tribe had never relinquished anyone at the demand of another tribe. In lieu of this, the leaders promised that those responsible would be whipped. Major O'Fallon acquiesced, though aware that the likelihood of this promise being carried out was remote.[7]

A week later, when the cabins at Engineer Cantonment had been completed and supplies taken in for the winter, Major Long decided to return East to confer with Secretary Calhoun about the expedition's further progress in the face of the 1819 economic crisis. Accompanied by Augustus Jessup—who had resigned, possibly because he was disenchanted with exploring—Long left in a canoe on 11 October for St. Louis on the first leg of his journey to Washington and Philadelphia. Say sent with him a letter to his brother Ben expressing concern over their family and his own ongoing financial problems. He ended the letter by sending his "most sincere love to mother [his stepmother], Caroline [his half-sister], & the children [perhaps his other half-siblings William Penn and Miriam]—I should delight to hear from them & from Rebecca, but this latter I cannot hope for."[8] Whether his sister Rebecca was at odds with him or was simply not a good correspon-dent is unknown.

Before leaving the encampment, Major Long wrote down his expecta-tions for the men during his absence. The field for observation and inquiry

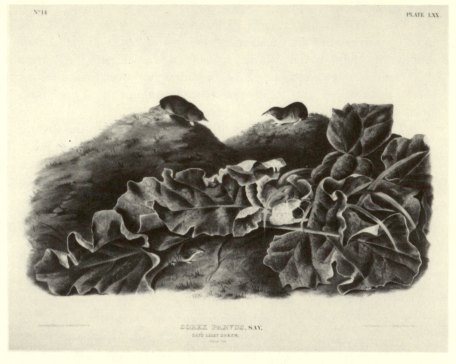

Fig. 17. *Say's Least Shrew, Sorex parvus,* by John James Audubon, from *The Viviparous Quadrupeds of North America* (plates issued in 30 parts of five folios each in 1845 and 1846). The text of the volumes appeared in 1846–54.

is here so extensive," he noted, "that all the gentlemen of the expedition will find ample range for the exercise of their talents." He hoped to return to "a rich harvest of useful intelligence."[9]

Thomas Say's ethnological studies would be much advanced during this period because of the opportunity afforded him of living near the Missouri Indians for many months. And a rich harvest would be reaped from his animal observations, though some years would elapse before all of them were published. He and Peale planned a large-scale work combining Say's descriptions with Peale's drawings of western animals, but the book never materialized, perhaps because other interests took precedence.[10] Not until thirty-five years later, in 1854, did Audubon and the Reverend John Bachman accomplish this goal with the publication of their *Viviparous Quadrupeds of North America.* Audubon featured in his book a group of

Fig. 18. *Prairie Wolf, Canis latrans, Say,* by John James Audubon, from *The Vivipa-rous Quadrupeds of North America* (1845–46).

animals collected by Peale on the Long Expedition and described by Say, including Say's least shrew (*Sorex parvus*; see figure 17), a molelike creature caught in a pitfall that Peale had dug to trap a wolf.

Thomas Say was the first to describe the coyote for science. He called the animal *Canis latrans—latrans* meaning "barking," because the animal sounded to him on its first two or three notes like a small terrier, even though these barks were "succeeded by a lengthened scream." Say observed that coyotes—or "prairie wolves" as he referred to them (figure 18)— hunted at night, roaming over the plains in considerable numbers and frequently uniting in packs to overtake and kill deer. They often came near the explorers' camp and were seen eating wild plums and other fruits. Although nearly indigestible, these fruits served to distend their stomachs and thus relieve their hunger.

Say thought coyotes were very intelligent because they managed to evade the variety of traps Peale devised for them. Say's type specimen (the one from which his description was drawn) was finally caught in a trap baited with a wildcat. He wrote of the coyote that it "does not seem to be known to naturalists . . . [and] is most probably the original of the domestic dog, so common in the villages of the Indians of this region, some of the varieties of which still retain much of the habit and manners of this species."[10] Audubon also included in his book a painting of the coyote (which he, too, called the prairie wolf).

Later Say would bring back his specimen of the black-tailed deer (*Cervus macrotis*; see figure 19) and deposit it in Peale's museum along with the rest of the collections. Unfortunately, by that time the skin was so badly damaged by insects that only the head could be used for exhibition. It was cleverly placed under a coyote's foot. Say noted that *Cervus macrotis* was "probably the species mentioned by Lewis and Clark . . . under the name of

Fig. 19. *Black-tailed Deer, Cervus macrotis, Say,* by John James Audubon, from *The Viviparous Quadrupeds of North America* (1845–46).

black-tailed deer, and more frequently in other parts of the work, by that of mule deer." He added that it was undoubtedly a new species, "not having been hitherto introduced into the systems." Say's name, *Cervus macrotis,* is currently considered a synonym of *Odocoileus hemionus* (Rafinesque, 1817), the mule (or black-tailed) deer, and he is not credited with its discovery.[12]

In Audubon's *Viviparous Quadrupeds* the mule deer is shown, uncharacteristically, with a bullet hole in its side, and in the distance there is a small depiction of the artist himself carrying a gun. The painting Audubon made of a western squirrel that Thomas Say had described shows a small cabin in the background, perhaps representing the hut Say used during his stay at Engineer Cantonment. The squirrel was later named *Sciurus sayi* after him.

Guidelines for Thomas Say's Indian studies, in addition to Jefferson's instructions to Meriwether Lewis, had been developed by a special committee at the American Philosophical Society. This group included Peter S. Du Ponceau, Dr. Samuel Brown, Dr. Robert M. Patterson, Robert Walsh, and Dr. Thomas Cooper, who had tried to get Say a berth on the *Macedonian.* Walsh wrote Calhoun that the society had "full confidence in the knowledge and sagacity of the men of science attached to the party" and recommended two books as essential to the explorers' investigations: Captain Jonathan Carver's *Travels through the Interior Parts of North America in the Years 1766, 1767 and 1768* (1778) and Professor Benjamin Smith Barton's *New Views of the Origin of the Tribes and Nations of America* (1797).[13] The first contained accurate descriptions of Indian customs and manners and a vocabulary of the Sioux language, while the second incorporated a comparative vocabulary of many Indian languages.

Included with Walsh's letter were copious notes from other committee members concerning inquiries about American native peoples. Since three of the five men on the committee were doctors, the majority of questions understandably dealt with the human condition. In reference to disease, the doctors wanted to know if Indians suffered from "the sea or land scurvy," Saint Vitus's dance, cancer, hernia, rheumatism, hepatitis, and hysteria. They were curious as to the general state of the Indian stomach when fed entirely with animal food during long hunts, noting that during the War of 1812 spies claimed they could easily distinguish which were Indian evacuations because of their diet. Medicines used by the native peoples were also of much interest because cures for so many afflictions suffered by the white population had yet to be found.

Many questions had to do with menstruation and childbirth: How was the placenta removed and the cord tied? Were Indian pulses "slower than the whites as Dr. Rush affirms," and did they acquire "notions of anatomy" by dissection of the human body? Perhaps the most surprising questions were those dealing with racial color. "Is the color of the Indian white at his birth, and if so, when does the child take the copper hue? Is it innate or produced by exposure to the sun and ointments?"[14] Say made every effort to find specific answers to these questions and would later use them to structure his portion of the expedition's published account.

Aside from his first-hand encounters with Indians, Say also derived much information from John Dougherty, who had a thorough knowledge of their customs. As the bitter cold and lengthened evenings of winter set in, Say spent long hours talking with Dougherty about the Missouri tribes, especially the Omahas. In the expedition's account, Say wrote that "this gentleman with great patience . . . answered all the questions which I proposed to him, relating to such points in [the Indians'] manners, habits, opinions, & history."[15] To a friend, Say excused his negligence in letter writing by "the numerous demands upon my time as Zoologist & Journalist." He added, "I could tire your patience with stories of our red brethren."[16]

Dougherty told Say of the Omahas' life in their principal village about a hundred miles north of Engineer Cantonment, which they occupied for some five months of the year. He said that during the month of May the inhabitants planted maize, beans, pumpkins, and watermelons and dressed bison skins procured during the winter hunt. Young men continued to search for beaver, otter, deer, muskrat, and elk within a large radius of the village. In June, when planting and fur trading ended, a feast was held to which all the distinguished men of the nation were invited. The proud hosts, having spread bison skins as seats, would pass the peace pipe, serve the delicacy of a boiled fat dog, and discuss plans for the summer hunt.

The women enjoyed the prospect of this hunt and prepared for departure by mending moccasins, readying packsaddles and dogsleds, and burying all unneeded possessions. Tepees were folded and packed on horses, already heavily burdened with domestic articles. The whole load might also be surmounted with an infant.

Along the way the men searched for game—keeping always on the alert for enemies—and when a herd of bison was sighted the tribe would pitch camp. The next morning all able-bodied men would ride out in pursuit, halting briefly for a pipe-smoking ceremony officiated by the

Color plate VI. Thomas Say (1787–1834), entomologist and conchologist, in the uniform of the first Long Expedition, 1819, by Charles Willson Peale. Oil portrait. Courtesy of The Academy of Natural Sciences of Philadelphia.

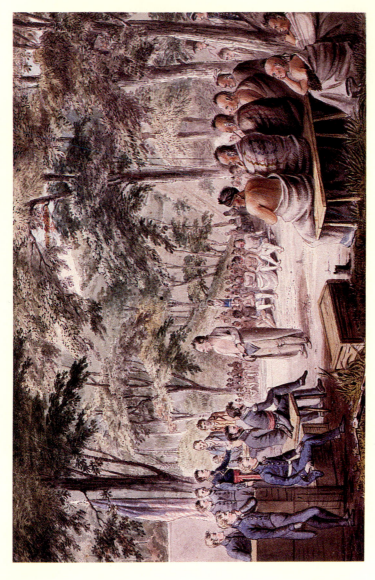

Color plate VII. Oto Council, by Samuel Seymour, 1819. Thomas Say, with his strong profile accented by heavy dark sideburns, sits erect to the left of Major Long, while Major O'Fallon, standing behind them, gestures to an Indian leader in the center of the picture, possibly Cut Nose. Watercolor. Courtesy of The Academy of Natural Sciences of Philadelphia.

Color plate VIII. View of New Harmony, by Karl Bodmer, 1832. Lucy Say described the painting in an 1843 letter to Alexander Maclure: "The view of the town appears to have been taken from some distance down the river . . . the Hall, Church, Granary and No. 5—are seen . . . the Island and River and opposite shore are very distinctly given—forming a very beautiful picture and giving a very correct idea of the locality." Watercolor. Courtesy of the Joslyn Art Museum, Omaha, Nebraska.

Color plate IX. Sayornis saya, Say's phoebe, by John James Audubon. Original watercolor for *The Birds of America.* Courtesy of the New York Historical Society.

medicine man. To ensure success, smoke would be puffed toward the bison, the heavens, the earth, and the four cardinal points: the sunrise, the sunset, the cold country (north) and the warm country (south). Then, at a sign from the leader, the hunters would split into two bands and ride at full gallop with bows and arrows positioned to kill.

Say noted in the expedition's account that "the force of an arrow, when discharged by a dexterous and athletic Indian, is very great, and . . . it has been known to pass entirely through the body of a bison, and actually to fly some distance." Since each individual knew his own arrows, "the man whose weapon penetrated the most vital part" was credited with slaying the animal.[17] The skin was used to cover lodges, and every eatable part of the bison was preserved. The Omahas dried, or "jerked," the meat in the sun, then concealed it in the earth for safekeeping while the tribe pursued other herds.

In addition to preserving bison, the women scratched ground-peas from beneath the soil surface. If they found them hoarded in the winter homes of field mice, they always replaced the peas with other food to keep the animals from starving. Say noted that when Indian women engaged in these field labors, "young warriors are very officious in offering their services to the squaws as protectors . . . and from the opportunities they enjoy of making love to their charge in the privacy of high weeds, it is extremely common for them to form permanent attachments to the wives of their neighbors, and an elopement to another nation is the consequence."[18]

Say recorded the reflections of an old Oto leader who had told Dougherty, "I was once fool enough to be jealous, but the passion did not long torment me." He realized that women were often alone while their husbands were hunting, and even if the husband was at home the wife needed to go some distance to draw water or collect wood. "I am not so silly as to believe that a woman would reject a timely offer," he said. "Even this squaw of mine, who sits by my side, would, I have no doubt, kindly accede to the opportune solicitations of a young, handsome and brave suitor."[19] The man's wife laughed heartily but did not refute her husband's statement. Say observed in his notes that this often liberal attitude toward conjugal relations could extend to Indian hospitality as well, since "the offer of one of their wives for company during the night, though it might call on our politeness for a return of thanks, was no cause of surprise to us, during our stay at their villages."[20] His careful wording gives no indication of the explorers' response to this form of generosity.

The activities of medicine men were of particular interest to Say, the healing arts having been so much a part of his background. He noted that when a healer was asked to attend the sick, he washed, painted himself with red clay, and took along a medicine bag and a dried gourd filled with pebbles. Upon reaching the patient, the medicine man smoked his pipe and spoke to Wahconda—"believed to be the greatest and best of beings, the creator and preserver of all things"—after which he mixed herbs in warm water and administered them. Finally, as Say recorded, "he rattles his gourd with violence, singing to it with great vehemence, and throwing himself into grotesque attitudes." All this might be repeated daily until the patient either recovered or died. Fees for the medicine man's services were proportional to the seriousness of the illness and the patient's wealth, and might include horses, kettles, blankets, and other prized possessions.

Although Say remonstrated against "the impostures which these priests practise on the credulity of the people," he reasoned: "How can we wonder at this facility, with which a simple people are blinded, through the medium of their superstitious faith, when we know that infinitely more monstrous absurdities . . . excite the fears of thousands of civilized men, in the most enlightened cities of Europe and America, and that the horseshoe, even at this day, is frequently seen, attached to the threshold of a door, as a security against the entrance of a witch?"[21]

Say described the Missouri Indians as tall and lean, with glossy black hair, Roman noses, and prominent cheekbones, although "not angular like those of the Mongul." He mused that "the [Indians'] active occupations of war and hunting, together perhaps with the occasional privations, to which they are subjected, prevents that unsightly obesity, so often a concomitant of civilization, indolence, and serenity of mental temperament."[22]

Say undoubtedly witnessed such complacence in the prosperous, comfortable lives of his fellow Philadelphians, but the severity of his censure was a direct result of his own personal code of harsh abstinence—by this time a lifelong conviction that was slowly undermining his health. Perhaps his Quaker background of thrift and sparing use of material resources—the very traits that made the Quakers such successful merchants—accounted in part for his strict moral idiosyncrasies. The object of his self-denial was primarily self-mastery.

Say wrote in his journal of the Indians' cleverness—how they often imitated the cry of an owl or the howl of a wolf when approaching enemies, to give the impression that the animals present were undisturbed. He also noted the treatment of prisoners. Women were used as servants, young men were assigned to the care of horses, and children were looked after as the tribe's own offspring and were initiated as full tribal members when they reached the proper age.

According to Say, the Indians considered themselves superior to white people in industriousness and "in natural intelligence, and . . . have a greater capacity for undergoing with fortitude, the many evils to which they are subjected . . . , such as exposure to great heat and cold, hunger, thirst, and pain. They appear to esteem themselves more brave, more generous and hospitable to strangers." For instance, if a stranger entered an Indian lodge, a pot would invariably be put on the fire, and meat—even the last of the stores—served the visitor.[23]

Say was intrigued that "the free and independent spirit of the Indian is carried even into their language," for they refused to employ English or French words to describe certain manufactured articles received from traders. They invariably rejected the names they were told and invented their own.[24]

In relating Indian myths that dealt with the personification of animals, Say revealed his own attitude toward religion—not surprisingly, the pragmatism of a scientist: "That the inferior animals did, in ancient times, march to battle with simultaneous regularity, that they conversed intelligibly, and performed all the different actions of men, many of them appear to admit, with as much faith as many equally absurd doctrines are believed in Christendom."[25]

Say also collected accounts of Missouri Indian dances and rituals, performed for such purposes as to enhance crop fertility or to honor a guest. "On some particular occasion," he was told, in a Minnetaree village "a large inclosure was constructed . . . [and] covered with jerked meat, instead of skins. The distinguished warriors who were concerned in the ceremony . . . summon[ed] a certain number of the handsomest young married squaws, who immediately repaired to the meat-covered lodge with the consent of their husbands'." The women were then undressed before these warriors. After the conclusion of certain rituals (not mentioned), a young warrior entered the lodge leading a fine horse. Upon selecting a woman whose beauty struck him, he placed the horse's halter in her hand. "She accepted the present, and immediately admitted him to her favour. Other warriors appeared in succession, leading horses, all of [whom] were very readily disposed of in the same manner." Say noted that this ceremony "occurred during the day, and in the presence of the whole assembly."[26]

Say was occasionally able to discern the reaction of the Indians to himself. Several Omaha trappers, on an errand of trade with Manuel Lisa, stayed overnight at Engineer Cantonment. Say invited one of them to share his room. But, he recounted, the man "became alarmed at my repute as a medicine man, fearing that I would cast some spell upon him, or otherwise injure him by the operation of some potent mystic medicine: [so] he removed his quarters to the adjoining room where he seemed to think he was safe from my incantations."[27]

Thomas Say's Indian data added to the ethnological studies that preceded him, although, strangely, Edwin James received the credit. Even such an authority on the American Indian as the historian George E. Hyde states in his book on the Pawnees that James "wintered on the Missouri in eastern Nebraska in 1819–20, and during his stay in this district collected from traders and Indians a fairly complete history of the Indians in Nebraska from about 1770 to 1819."[28] In fact, James did not arrive at Engineer Cantonment until late May of 1820. The collecting of Indian data during the winter encampment and on the rest of the expedition as well was, as assigned, entirely carried out by Thomas Say.

Winter had definitely set in by the end of December when the temperature dropped regularly to zero. At night Say could hear starving wolves howling close to his hut. He and his companions depended largely on venison and other game, including an occasional skunk, which they found "remarkably rich and delicate." On one hunting excursion, Dougherty and Peale shot twelve bison, enough to occasion a feast with the fur trader Manuel Lisa and his family.

Say would have known for many years about the famed Manuel Lisa, probably from Thomas Nuttall who had traveled with him to the Mandan Indian villages on the upper Missouri in 1811. Lisa had opened this region for fur trading with many Indian tribal groups by establishing a number of forts from which he sent out explorers. These men had trapped beaver on both sides of the continental divide and by so doing had made known to the British and Spanish that America was intent on making the most of its Louisiana Purchase.[29] Lisa's knowledge of the area and its inhabitants had been invaluable to the United States government during the War of 1812. Lisa can, in fact, be credited with saving the fur-trading empire for the United States by thwarting the efforts of a British trader, Robert Dickson, to turn the northern Indians—the Sioux, Omahas, and Poncas—against the Americans.[30]

In preparing their hunting banquet for the Lisa family, Say and his fellow chefs cooked the rump of a bison using the Indian method: they placed it in a hole in the ground previously heated by a strong fire, then covered it with at least a foot of earth and cinders. Another fire, built on top, was kept burning for twenty-four hours.

Say, who was habitually plagued with digestive disorders, noted that all members of the party except himself were in good health. But the troops at Camp Missouri, the military post at Council Bluffs, were suffering from scurvy. The cause of the disease was unknown, although Say observed that the hunters who had been absent from camp for long periods escaped it.

Early in April, 1820, Say, Seymour, Lieutenant Graham, and a Lieutenant Talcott from Camp Missouri rode out on a week-long excursion to locate the source of the Boyer River, which flows eastward into the Missouri. One morning Say awoke to the loud cries of sandhill cranes circling the camp in search of pea-vine tubers growing nearby on the riverbank. His account of this flock demonstrates not only his ability for precise observation, but the poetic quality of his finest writing: "They were now in great numbers, soaring aloft in the air, flying with an irregular kind of gyratory motion, each individual describing a large circle in the air independently of his associates, and uttering loud, dissonant, and repeated cries. They sometimes continue thus to wing their flight upwards, gradually receding from the earth, until they become mere specks upon the sight, and finally altogether disappear, leaving only the discordant music of their concert to fall faintly upon the ear."[31]

Several weeks later, Say again departed the encampment, this time to accompany Major O'Fallon, Lieutenant Graham, Dougherty, several officers from Camp Missouri, and a guard of twenty-seven soldiers on visits to Pawnee villages along the Platte River (called *Nebraska,* or "Flat Water," by the Otos).

After the men had circled the Grand Pawnees' village, they trotted into its center accompanied by bugle, drum, and fife. In the expedition's account Say tells of the villagers' delight, especially the children's, as they ran alongside the strange musicians. "Of these instruments the bugle was most decidedly the favorite," he wrote. "We passed by and saluted the mansions of the chiefs, at each of which an American flag was hoisted." He noted that one lodge was mistakenly flying a Spanish flag, which "was struck as soon as the cause of the procedure was understood."[32]

After a brief stay the men departed and galloped over a wide, beautiful plain extending along the Loup River fork of the Platte. There were antelope in the distance and sandhill cranes overhead. Two miles from the Pawnee Loup encampment they were stopped by a messenger who re-

Fig. 20. *Sandhill Cranes, Grus canadensis,* by Titian Ramsay Peale, 1820. Watercolor.
Courtesy of the American Philosophical Society

quested that the party await a proper reception from his leaders. Say recounted that soon a large number of Indians emerged as if from the plain itself, for a ravine had hidden them from view. "It is impossible . . . to do justice to the scene of savage magnificence that was now displayed," he recalled. "Between three and four hundred mounted Indians, dressed in their richest habiliments of war, were rushing around us in every direction, with streaming feathers, war weapons and with loud shouts and yells. The few whom we had observed in advance of the main body, and whom . . . we recognized to be the chief men, presented a perfect contrast to the others in their slow movements, and simplicity of dress."[33]

His attention was drawn to a tall, muscular, strikingly handsome young man, apparently the leader, whose "head dress of war eagles' feathers, descended in a double series upon his back like wings, to his saddle croup; his shield was highly decorated, and his long lance was ornamented

PETALESHAROO

A PAWNEE BRAVE

Fig. 21. *Petalesharoo,* by Charles Bird King, from
McKenney and Hall's *History of the Indian Tribes of
North America,* 1836. Courtesy of the Library Company
of Philadelphia.

by a plaited casing of red and blue cloth." Say later learned that the man,
considered his nation's most fearless warrior, was Petalesharoo (Generous
Chief), son of Latelesha (Knife Chief).[34]

The name of Petalesharoo was familiar to Thomas Say from information he had gleaned from traders concerning Petalesharoo's determination
to abolish a custom "at which humanity shudders." In a rite peculiar to the
Pawnee Loups among all other North American tribal groups, human
sacrifice was offered as propitiation to Venus, the "Great Star."[35] Performed
annually, the ritual was judged essential to crop success. Presumably igno-

rant of his or her ultimate destiny, a prisoner was selected, richly clothed, and fed the choicest food. On the appointed day, bound to a cross and encircled by a solemn dance, the sacrifice was then slain by tomahawk.

Sometime previously, Latelesha had returned from a visit to General William Clark in St. Louis with an altered perception of his ancient customs, particularly human sacrifice. Disregarding their leader's admonitions, however, one group of tribesmen had bound a Comanche woman to a cross in preparation for her sacrifice. Coming on the scene by chance, Petalesharoo had instantly leaped off his horse before the captive woman and declared to those assembled that, because his father demanded the ceremony be abolished he, Petalesharoo, would willingly lay down his life to enforce the decree. While the tribesmen watched in astonishment, the young brave cut the cords, carried the woman to his horse, and rode away. Had Petalesharoo not already distinguished himself as a warrior, he would not have survived such a feat.

When Say's party had set up camp along the Platte, a huge feast was held and a council planned for the following day. The afternoon after this council, Say and the others were surprised to see a large part of the Pawnee Loup population—"painted, armed, and decorated as if for war"—advancing toward their camp. Petalesharoo rode out ahead and announced that his tribesmen had come to honor their "American father" (President Monroe). Forty performers then began to dance, accompanied by the rhythmic beating of a deep-toned gong and other instruments as well as the occasional firing of a gun with its muzzle to the ground. At the conclusion of the performance the young chief asked his visitors to play their own music to accompany the next dance. When Say's companions started up with bugle and drums, however, the Indian dancers were thrown into confusion. Several vain attempts by his men to adjust to the strange sounds caused Petalesharoo, barely able to suppress his amusement, to end the performance.

The next morning, after trading merchandise for fresh horses, Say and his companions departed on their return journey to Council Bluffs. On the way they stopped at the village of the Pawnee Republicans, whose warriors had pillaged Say's tent the previous fall. Say expected to recognize the culprits, having committed to memory the features of several. As the tribesmen filed past, shaking hands, he scrutinized the face and figure of each but could identify only one individual with certainty. "I knew him immediately," Say wrote, "and judging from the Indian character, he knew me equally well; yet his physiognomy, on presenting me his hand, was not varied in the slightest degree from the expression with which he regarded my companions, many of whom he had not before seen." When the men were invited into the lodge of Fool Robe, the principal leader, Major O'Fallon spoke "at considerable length . . . of the great power of the United States; he detailed the glaring offences of the Pawnee Republicans," to which, in reply, Fool Robe "spoke well, but with evident embarrassment."[36]

After a quick stop at the Grand Pawnees' village to barter for sixty horses for themselves and the troops at Camp Missouri, the contingent returned to Engineer Cantonment. Within two months Thomas Say would be leaving his winter quarters on the Missouri and striking out across the great plains toward the Rocky Mountains. He fully expected this territory to be rugged and hostile.

CHAPTER 7

To the Shining Mountains

The route here specified would embrace a region of which we at present have no certain knowledge.

Major Long to Secretary of War Calhoun
Washington City, 3 January 1820

O N 6 J U N E 1820 the expedition set out westward by land for the Rocky Mountains. Congress had canceled funds for the military operations at the headwaters of the Yellowstone River, partly because of the severe economic depression caused by the Panic of 1819 and partly because of the excessive corruption and bungling of the quartermaster in charge of the Yellowstone Expedition's supplies at Camp Missouri. But Major Long had convinced Secretary Calhoun to redirect Long's scientific party to follow the Platte River to its source, explore southward along the base of the Rocky Mountains, and then divide into two groups for the return to the Mississippi. One group would go by way of the Arkansas River and the other by the Red River, after locating its source.

When Long was in Washington, Calhoun had cautioned him to carry out his expedition on as tight a budget as possible because Congress was closely scrutinizing the War Department's funds after the embarrassing fiasco with the military segment of the expedition. To justify the expenditure, the men were to gather as much interesting and useful material as possible in the time allotted. But distance and speed were to be given priority over thoroughness of scientific investigation.[1]

To the "gentlemen of science"—Say and Peale—and the landscape painter—Seymour—was now added the twenty-eight-year-old Edwin James. Major Long, who had arrived back at Engineer Cantonment a week before departure, brought James with him as botanist to replace the deceased William Baldwin. James, a Vermont native, had graduated from Middlebury College and then studied medicine for three years. He had

Fig. 22. Detail of map of the Long Expedition to the Rocky Mountains in 1819–20, showing the "Great Desert," from *Account of an Expedition from Pittsburgh to The Rocky Mountains Performed in the Years 1819, 1820. By Order of the Hon. J. C. Calhoun, Secretary of War, Under the Command of Maj. S. H. Long, of the U. S. Top. Engineers. Compiled From the Notes of Major Long, Mr. T. Say, and other gentlemen of the party,* by Edwin James. London, 1823.

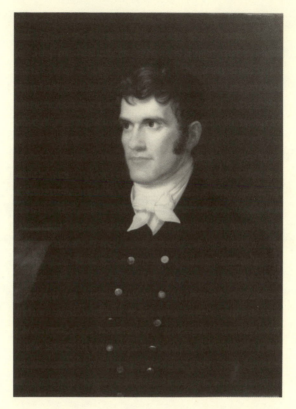

Fig. 23. *John C. Calhoun* (1782–1850), Secretary of War, by Charles Bird King, 1819. Oil portrait. Courtesy of the National Portrait Gallery, Smithsonian Institution, Washington, D.C.

been recommended by John Torrey because of the botanical knowledge James had acquired in conjunction with his medical studies. Although enthusiastic about the expedition, James was less so regarding his commanding officer. "I am not entirely satisfied with Long," he had written to his brother from New York City the previous March, "but I hope I may find him better than I fear he is. I have great apprehensions that his pretensions to the character of a man of science are like those of certain great bugs in this humbugging society."[2]

Major Long headed the military contingent consisting of William Swift, assistant topographer; Captain John R. Bell of the Light Artillery, an instructor in tactics at West Point who would assume Biddle's duties, including keeping the expedition's journal; and one corporal and six privates. Also signed up were John Dougherty's brother, Henry, as hunter; Stephen Julien, as French and Indian interpreter; a Spanish interpreter; a "baggage master"; and two "engagees" (expedition factotums). Lieutenant Graham was left in charge of the *Western Engineer* and instructed to bring the steamboat to Camp Girardeau on the Mississippi to meet the explorers on their return.

Several Indians witnessing the explorers' preparations scoffed at their prospects of surviving such a journey. Parts of the country through which the men proposed traveling, the Indians claimed, were entirely without water or grass to feed the horses. Say wrote in a letter that the same advisors also assured them that "the country was covered with hostile indians, who would not fail to massacre every individual of our small party."[3] But despite the negative admonitions and what were probably inadequate supplies, Say and his companions embarked in good spirits.

It was not long after entering the Platte river valley, however, that their enthusiasm began to wane as a vast expanse of level prairie, with scarcely a tree in sight, opened out before them. The Indian warnings assumed an uncomfortable credibility as the way west appeared to be on increasingly less fertile soil. Such wildflowers as phlox and delphinium, which had grown in profusion between St. Louis and Council Bluffs, gave way to milk vetch and a few other insignificant species. As for wildlife, they saw a few wary antelope in addition to curlews, marbled godwits, and "Bartram's sandpiper."

The expedition halted at the Grand Pawnees' village only long enough to hear the leader's warning that they must have "long hearts . . . that would reach from the earth to the heavens" to undertake such a journey.[4] Still, Say and his colleagues were inclined to shrug off the chief's words in the belief that he wanted to keep them from passing through his hunting grounds.

At sunrise the men rode out from the Indian village. The foremost rider carried a white silk flag bearing a peace emblem. Its design featured a saber crossed with a tomahawk. At the next Pawnee village Major Long engaged two Frenchmen who had made a permanent home with the tribe: Abraham Ledoux to serve as hunter and blacksmith and Joseph Bijeau as guide and interpreter. Both had been to the Platte and Arkansas headwaters to hunt and trap beaver. Thomas Say especially welcomed the addition of Bijeau, who not only knew several Indian dialects (especially Crow, "extensively understood by the western tribes") but was also proficient in sign language. Since this form of communication was universally understood amidst the plethora of languages and tribal dialects, it was indeed a valuable skill.

Just outside the last Pawnee village, the explorers, in fording the Platte, experienced greater difficulty with the powerful current and treacherous sand bottom than anticipated. At the head of the column, Say and Long, having just reached the far shore, were thrown into the river when their horses' hooves plunged into quicksand. When the two men at last struggled ashore and stood erect, a volley of shouts went up from the watching Pawnees lining the opposite bank. Edwin James would note facetiously in the expedition's account that "Mr. Say, having lost the greater part of his furniture at the river of Souls, by the ill-timed activity of his horse, was now, in a great measure, unencumbered with baggage."[5]

As he rode along, Say was constantly on the lookout for wildlife. Fascinated with the countless prairie dog villages he saw along the Platte, he wrote of this "interesting and sprightly little animal" that it had been given "the absurd and inappropriate name of Prairie dog, from a fancied resemblance of its warning cry to the hurried barking of a small dog."[6]

Also of much interest to Say was the unusual burrowing owl, which lives in abandoned prairie dog dwellings. Titian Peale's sketch of the bird, with a prairie dog in the background standing in its village, would later be published with a full description of both animals in Charles Bonaparte's book of ornithology. In his chapter on the owl, Bonaparte paid special tribute to Thomas Say: "The votaries of natural science must always feel indebted to the learned and indefatigable Say for the rich collection of facts he has made whenever opportunities have been presented, but more especially in the instance of this very singular bird, whose places of resort in this country are far too distant to allow many the pleasure of examining for themselves."[7]

Where the Platte River divides in two, the men ascended the north fork for a few miles, then waded across the shallow river—following the route of a pair of elk—and headed for the south branch.[8] Upon gaining the summit of a gentle rise, they saw an immense herd of grazing bison—as many as ten thousand—spread out on the plain beyond. Since it was getting dark, the men set up camp with high hopes for a morning hunt. But by dawn, incredibly, the entire herd had disappeared, so they packed up and continued on to the south fork.

Although the Platte was broad and its current rapid, it was so shallow the men were able to cross it without dismounting or unpacking the mules. Once again they saw vast herds of bison, followed by "famine-pinched wolves and flights of obscene and ravenous birds."[9] In addition, the countryside teemed with deer, badgers, hares, coyotes, eagles, ravens, and owls. These animals and birds, together with the vegetation that was new to the scientists, made the otherwise hot and dreary plains a fascinating place. There was certain pain in dismounting to examine anything, however, because the sharp thorns of the ubiquitous prickly pear (*Cactus ferox*) easily pierced moccasins.

It all seemed worthwhile to Say when he first beheld the Rocky Mountains early on the morning of 30 June 1820. Initially, Say was uncertain whether what he saw were indeed mountains or only large banks of cumulus clouds. As the "bright parts" continued to retain their shape and position, he was convinced that the great snow-covered range—known to the Indians as the "Shining Mountains"—lay before him.[10]

Every attempt was made to reach the Rockies by the fourth of July,

Fig. 24. *View of the Chasm Through Which the Platte Issues from the Rocky Mountains,* by Samuel Seymour, 1820. Watercolor. Gift of Paul Mellon. Courtesy of The Academy of Natural Sciences of Philadelphia.

since it was thought fitting for the expedition to celebrate the "great national festival" at their journey's destination, but on that day the exhausted explorers were still some distance away. It was not until the morning of the sixth that they arrived at "the boundary of that vast plain" across which they had traveled for nearly a thousand miles.[11] They pitched camp in front of a large chasm not far from present-day Denver, through which the Platte plunges from the mountains. Seymour painted the dramatic setting on an elevation a bit to the south. His watercolors would be the first views of the Rocky Mountains ever published.

Say and his companions made short climbing forays into the foothills, always keeping in view the white peace flag flying far below at the camp. After several days, the expedition moved on, but only when all had recovered from the violent headaches and vomiting most experienced from eating "currants." Since their diet had consisted of only meat, the men concluded that their stomachs were unable to digest vegetable matter. Say, with his ever-present internal problems, suffered severely. Altitude sickness may also have been to blame, since the Rockies rise from five thousand feet at the valley bottom to over fourteen thousand feet, and it is likely that none of the explorers had ever been much above four thousand feet.

On 10 July Peale shot a beautiful pigeon that Say described for science as *Columba fasciata,* the band-tailed pigeon. Audubon would paint this bird, depicting it perched on a bough of the western dogwood (*Cornus nuttalli*) which Thomas Nuttall had brought back from the "Arkansa Territory." Thus three great naturalists—contemporaries and sometime friends—are brought together in one magnificent plate of Audubon's *Birds of America.*

Another painting shows a male and female of Say's phoebe (later named *Sayornis saya* by scientists at the British Museum) eyeing an insect while several butterflies flit below them. The inclusion of insects is possibly a reference by Audubon to Say's primary importance as an entomologist. Peale had shot the bird near the Rocky Mountains, and Bonaparte later described it for science. To his description Bonaparte added, in typical nineteenth-century rhetoric, "I dedicate [the phoebe] to my friend, Thomas Say, a naturalist of whom America may justly be proud, and whose talents and knowledge are only equaled by his modesty."[12]

As the expedition traveled along the base of the Rockies, the mountain came into view that Zebulon Pike twelve years earlier had designated the highest peak in the range. It was decided that a small detachment should attempt to climb it. Edwin James and four soldiers were selected.

The contingent reached the summit after several arduous days, including a night spent just below the snowline without food or blankets. On returning to their base camp, abandoned several nights earlier, the men found that the cooking fire they had neglected to extinguish completely had ignited not only their provisions but also several acres of forest. Apprehensive that the smoke would attract Indians who might take advantage of so small a party, they returned to the main camp with haste.

Because Long believed Edwin James was the first person, either white or Indian, to reach the summit—Indians and hunters knew of no one who had ascended it, and though Pike had been the first to record seeing the mountain, he did not climb it—he named it James's Peak. Many years later, however, when the explorer John C. Fremont came to the same place, he found that the mountain was called Pike's Peak. Thus this aspect of James's effort has not been recognized by history.[13] But James would not go unrecognized entirely, for the botanical specimens he brought back from his ascent were among his most important finds. They constituted the first collection of American alpine plants and added significantly to botanical knowledge of the area. John Torrey would base his introduction of the natural system of classification to American botany on the over five hundred plant specimens—many of which proved to be type specimens of new species—collected on this expedition by Edwin James, and earlier by William Baldwin.[14]

On 19 July the explorers left the mountains and moved eastward down the Arkansas River. Say regretted abandoning the area, with its great variety of natural history specimens that he had not had time to examine. But Long hurried the expedition along at every point both because of Calhoun's instructions to make the journey as economical as possible and because of the paucity of supplies. Since the little food remaining was reserved for hospital stores, the expedition was now entirely dependent on the hunters—one of whom, out alone after deer, was nearly lost to a grizzly bear.

The grizzly had been known to exist for some time. In 1815, using Lewis and Clark's and Pike's accounts of the animal, George Ord had named it *Ursus horribilis*, but at the time of the Long expedition the animal had not yet been described as a distinct species.[15] Say had carefully observed the behavior of a half-grown male grizzly in the yard of Manuel

Lisa's Missouri Fur Company. Fed only vegetables because it became "furious" when given meat, the captive bear had spent his days pacing back and forth to the extent of his chain.[16]

When the point was reached where the expedition was to split, the division of personnel and the two routes were decided on as follows. Thomas Say would join Captain John Bell; Samuel Seymour; Lieutenant Swift; the interpreters Bijeau, Ledoux, and Julien; five riflemen; two dogs; and the majority of pack horses to proceed down the Arkansas to Fort Smith. Major Long, Edwin James, Titian Peale, and seven soldiers would head south to search for the Red River's source and then follow that river to the rendezvous at the fort.

The following morning at five—the usual hour for setting out— Major Long's party crossed the Arkansas and gave three cheers from the opposite bank. Say and his companions returned their farewells and the two detachments got under way. Say noted that all were encouraged in thinking that their journey's major objective (reaching the Rockies) was accomplished, that the men had been compatible, and that no accidents had occurred. But he shared the general anxiety at the thought of a thousand-mile trek across a "trackless desert" traversed by "lawless war parties of various nations of Indians."[17]

That afternoon a violent thunderstorm broke, causing the terrified horses to turn in circles. Julien was slightly shocked by lightning, and the entire party were soaked to the skin. But two uneventful days then followed, and on the morning of the third day the men spotted a number of tepees along the far bank of the Arkansas. After fording the river, the explorers were soon surrounded by a welcoming group of Indians who offered to share their lodges, but the expedition's interpreters explained that the strangers carried their own accommodations. Women brought presents of jerked bison meat, and a council was arranged for the following day.

In the early morning, four leaders representing the Kiowa, Kaskaia, Cheyenne, and Arapaho tribes presented themselves at the explorers' camp. Preparations for the leaders' reception had been made by spreading bison skins, hoisting the peace flag, and selecting a few gifts of knives, combs, and vermilion. Say wrote that the Indians "arranged themselves with due solemnity and the pipe being passed around, many of them seemed to enjoy it as the greatest rarity." One eager individual filled his lungs and mouth "top full of smoke," inflated his cheeks "as in an ecstacy," and held the smoke until he nearly exploded. Say added that he and his companions restrained themselves "with some effort from committing the indecorum of a broad laugh."[18]

One of the leaders spoke Pawnee, and by means of translating English into French, French into Pawnee, and Pawnee into Kiowa and the other languages, it was possible to communicate. Captain Bell told the dignified chief that his party belonged "to the numerous and powerful nation of Americans," whose great father had sent them to examine part of his territories. Bell explained that "we had been traveling for many moons . . . and had passed through many red nations, of whose hospitality we largely partook." One leader replied that he was glad to see them and expressed the hope that traders would be sent to his nation now that a path had been opened. Bell assured him this would happen if his own party could report on their return that they had been treated hospitably while traversing his territory.

After an exchange of gifts the council concluded, and the village's entire population pushed in close to the explorers: "the women brought jerked meat, and the men skin and hair ropes for halters, to trade with us for trinkets." Even after trading was officially finished, much to the annoyance of Say and his companions, the curious Indians persisted in crowding about. The explorers were nevertheless amused "at the appearance of the naked children mounted on horses, sometimes to the number of three or four on each, fearlessly standing erect, or kneeling upon their backs to catch a glance over the heads of the intervening multitude, at the singular deportment, costume, and appearance of the white strangers."[19]

At last the Cheyenne leader stood up and, with a wave of his hand, ordered his people to disperse. Say described him as a man "endowed with a spirit of unconquerable ferocity" who had certainly been born to command. He was "tall and graceful," Say noted, "with a highly ridged aquiline nose, corrugated forehead, mouth with the corners drawn downward, and a rather small, but remarkably piercing eye, which, when fixed upon your countenance, appeared strained in the intenseness of its gaze, and to seek rather for the movements of the soul within, than to ascertain the mere lineaments it contemplated."[20]

At dusk, accompanied by an interpreter, Say visited several Indian lodges to gather information. Notwithstanding hooting children and snarling dogs, he was "kindly received," and the villagers were generally cooperative.

Later that night women were brought to the camp, but the explorers refused their services, though not without difficulty, as the brother of the Arapaho leader Bear Tooth continued to pester the men on behalf of a particular woman. The brother was at last "directed to begone, and the sentinel was ordered to prevent his further intrusion."

At dawn Say was awakened by a cry of "Tabbyboo" (a name applied to white people) shouted by two handsome mounted Arapahos. They had been sent by Bear Tooth to inform the explorers that their people would be moving on. Say marveled at "the remarkable facility with which the lodges disappeared, and with all their cumbrous and various contents, were secured to the backs of the numerous horses and mules."[21] These nomadic tribes had no permanent town, but followed bison herds inhabiting the headwaters of the Platte, Arkansas, and Red rivers. Before leaving, the Kiowa leader complied with Say's request for samples of the Kiowa vocabulary. He smiled benignly as Say attempted to imitate the sounds while rapidly writing them down.

Several full days of riding—interrupted with camping at midday to avoid the oppressive heat—followed the explorers' departure. Then one clear morning, the men, almost in unison, spied a spear-carrying horseman silhouetted like a statue atop a distant bluff. They sent Julien ahead to reconnoiter and were aghast to see the sudden appearance of a band of warriors who quickly surrounded him. As Say and the others spurred their horses, they saw the Indians abandon Julien, wheel around, and gallop at full speed down the steep slope toward them, singing what they all realized with horror was a scalp song.

When the Indians reached Say and his companions, they reined in their horses abruptly and began shaking hands with "a kind of earnest familiarity" Say felt was rather disagreeable. On being questioned as to which tribe they belonged, the warriors answered yes to every nation mentioned. Such evasion, combined with their warlike dress, a fresh scalp hanging from their leader's spear, and their superior numbers, kept the explorers on their guard.[22]

Bijeau addressed the Indians through a Crow prisoner and learned that they were a Cheyenne war-party returning from an expedition against the Pawnee Loups. During the exchange, Say, unwilling to miss a single opportunity to make notes of his experiences regardless of the circumstances, recorded words of the Cheyenne dialect, assisted by a warrior positioned behind him. The Cheyennes' persistent demands for tobacco, which the explorers denied possessing, caused the latter to slowly withdraw, mount their horses, and ride away. When out of the Indians' sight, Say and his companions congratulated themselves that their deportment had appeared to be more that of caution than of consternation.

On 7 August Bijeau and Ledoux bade the expedition farewell and headed north on a three-hundred-mile journey to their homes in the Pawnee villages on the Platte. They had served well as hunters, butchers, and cooks, as they had in their principal roles as guides and interpreters. Say was particularly sorry to lose them, since their assistance to him in gathering Indian information had been invaluable.

On each succeeding day the landscape stretched out hotter and more monotonous than the day before. Both men and horses suffered from a plague of green-headed flies and were on constant alert for rattlesnakes, especially when passing through prairie dog villages. At night, barking coyotes, howling wolves, and the lowing of thousands of bison kept up a steady din, often making sleep impossible. Daytime temperatures averaged in the mid-nineties, and a brilliant glare reflected from the white sandy soil irritated everyone's eyes. Only a few withered sunflowers hung despondently here and there, and an occasional eagle soared overhead.

Food stores were running out and game was scarce—even at times nonexistent. Three meals were reduced to one, which consisted of a meager soup made from moldy bread crumbs, a small amount of grease, and a boiled skunk. At one point everyone's hopes were raised upon hearing what sounded like a prairie dog. But the dwellings of these marmots had long ago been passed, and it was soon realized that the sound came from a small bird—not enough for a single meal. Lack of tobacco caused additional hardship for some of the soldiers. Say overheard one, who was suspected of having a cache, rebuff a pleading companion: "Every man chaws his own tobacco, and them that hasn't any chaws leaves."[23]

The lack of food and tobacco was as nothing, however, compared to the great misfortune that occurred on 31 August when Say awoke to find the saddlebags containing his manuscripts stolen. Also gone were other bags packed with clothing and Indian gifts, and three of the expedition's best horses. "This greatest of all privations that could have occurred within the range of possibility, suspended for a time every exertion, and seemed to fill the measure of our trials, difficulties, and dangers," Say wrote later.[24] Gone was the work of months. Five of his notebooks were missing, including one on Indian manners, customs, and history, another on animal habits with descriptions of various species, a journal, and two books containing Indian vocabularies—all Say's writings since he left Engineer Cantonment. It would tax his memory to the utmost, back in Philadelphia, to reconstruct their contents for his own considerable portion of the expedition's report. Three missing soldiers—Nolan, Myers, and Bernard—were obviously the culprits. They had been chosen by officers at Camp Missouri, but all three had proved indolent, pugnacious, and generally worthless. Nolan, it was discovered later, had deserted on two other journeys.

To this day scientists lament the theft. The specific identity of a two-legged lizard that Say mentions in the expedition's account as having been found on 27 June in the present state of Colorado remains a mystery, because this genus of lizard (*Chirotes*, called *Bipes*) is now restricted to the Mexican border and southwards.[25] Say's specimen and its detailed scientific description were both in his stolen saddlebags. As for Say's notes about the Indians, the historian Walter Prescott Webb has written, "Those lost records would be of inestimable value to the student of life on the Plains."[26]

Through the following days' extreme heat the explorers proceeded in silence, scanning the horizon in the hope of seeing their destination, Fort Smith. There was little to cheer them at night when the hunters returned with only a few grapes and some unripe persimmons.

In the late afternoon of 1 September, having at that point traveled for several weeks without encountering another human, the men were "very agreeably surprised by hearing an Indian whoop, in our rear . . . a mounted Indian was observed upon a rising piece of ground, contemplating our movements." Quickly hoisting the white peace flag, they encouraged the single young warrior to approach. Through Julien, they learned that he was a member of the Osage tribe whose village was nearby. On hearing of the travelers' lack of provisions, he produced a number of ripe plums, a pipe, and tobacco, and promised to bring them meat. At sundown the youth returned with six companions, bringing a fat buck hanging in pieces from his saddle and the welcome news that Fort Smith was within four days' ride. That night, after all had retired, it was strange yet beautiful to hear the young warriors chant "in a wild and melancholy tone a kind of hymn to the Master of Life."[27]

The next morning the explorers were greeted warmly by Clermont, the principal leader, at the Osage village. Say had hoped to surprise the thieves because, according to the young warriors, they had been several days in their village, but the culprits had quickly departed before the expedition arrived. A reward of two hundred dollars was subsequently offered at Fort

Fig. 25. *Fort Smith, Arkansas,* by Samuel Seymour, 1820. Watercolor. Gift of Paul Mellon. Courtesy of The Academy of Natural Sciences of Philadelphia.

Smith for the recovery of Say's manuscripts, but to his lifelong dismay they were never found.

On 9 September, after laboriously hacking through two miles of canebrake, the men came out on the riverbank and saw Fort Smith (figure 25) like a mirage before them. After much shouting they were ferried across the Arkansas River, welcomed by post-commander Ballard, and comfortably housed after ninety-three days of continual exposure to the elements.

Four days later, a pistol shot on the river's far side signaled the arrival of Major Long, James, Peale, and the other soldiers. The reunited explorers had many tales to share concerning their past month's adventures. Long's detachment had suffered unduly from hunger, excessive heat, "blowing flies," and wood ticks. For much of the time they had been unable to find water to bathe so their filthy clothes had been a source of great discomfort. Edwin James would write in the expedition's account that the country they had traversed had a soil rich enough "to support a dense population," but that "the want of springs and streams of water must long pose a serious obstacle to its occupation by permanent residents."[28] These discouraging words helped to defer the region's settlement for many years.

The disparaging view that Say and his colleagues took of the western territory through which they had traveled would not be news to Secretary Calhoun upon their return. The idea of this region being a desert stretched back to Coronado's letter to the Spanish king in the mid-sixteenth century: "It was the Lord's pleasure that, after having journeyed across these deserts seventy-seven days, I arrived at the province they call Quivira."[29] Major Long, James, and Say would all agree with the assertion of a more recent explorer—Zebulon Pike, who had traversed the region nine years earlier—that the great plains were barren and desolate and would serve as a barrier to western expansion. Expansion, they all feared, would overly disperse the country's population and weaken the young nation.

Say would write to John Melsheimer that the Platte and Arkansas rivers were not navigable for large boats and that "the country within about 500 miles of the Mountains is destitute of timber and miserably poor, thus furnishing us with an excellent frontier in that direction, which is totally unfit for the tillage of civilized man, & which may for ages afford an asylum to the cruelly persecuted indian and its immense herds of Bisons."[30]

From the expedition's report, and in particular from the map prepared by Lieutenant Swift (figure 22), Major Long's assistant topographer, would emerge a solid concept of the "great American desert." Swift had used the designation "Great Desert" for the region from the South Platte to the Canadian River and from the Rocky Mountains east to the ninety-ninth meridian of longitude.[31] Mapmakers for many years afterward borrowed Swift's phrase for that portion of the West.

The acceptance of the desert's existence over the years since the Long Expedition account was published was conditioned by two factors: human and environmental. The desire to contain Americans in order to prevent population diffusion, and extended periods of drought (the 1850s, 1890s, and the Dust Bowl years of the 1930s), supported the idea of there being a desert.[32]

For a few years in the middle 1860s, a prolonged wet period on the plains helped to change this concept, and railroad companies promoted development along their tracks. The vast Ogallala aquifer underlying the plains would be discovered and, over the years, tens of thousands of wells dug to tap it.[33] (The irony of the late twentieth century is that the aquifer's water is being so severely overdrawn that, in combination with global warming, the plains could again become a desert.)

It was of course not known at the time of the expedition that irrigation and hardy strains of wheat would turn these plains into the nation's bread basket. The desert myth would first be questioned by Randolph Marcy in 1854. Marcy, who located the source of Red River, which Long had failed to do, would describe the buffalo grass country of the Texas Panhandle as an "interminable meadow."[34]

For Major Long, the severest disappointment on this last part of the expedition had been the realization that the river he had been following for nearly a thousand miles was the Canadian, not the Red—which had been his assignment—and that time would not allow his mistake to be rectified because the detachment's stores were nearly exhausted. James claimed that as they "had no time nor no wish to make the examination necessary to furnish [them] with a knowledge of the country and its streams," they had simply called it "the head of Red River."[35]

After a week's rest at Fort Smith, Say, Long, Peale, and Seymour, with the Spanish interpreter, baggage master, and two engagees—Julien and the soldiers having stayed at Fort Smith—set off on the three-week journey to Cape Girardeau, three hundred miles away on the Mississippi. There they met James and Lieutenant Swift, who had left earlier to take a different route, and Lieutenant Graham, who had just arrived from St. Louis with the *Western Engineer*. Major Long rode off almost at once for St. Louis.

James wrote to his brother from Cape Girardeau with disgust, echoing many of the same grievances as his predecessor, William Baldwin:

> I am full of complaining and bitterness against Maj. Long on account of the manner in which he has conducted the Expedition and if I cannot rail against him, I can say nothing. We have travelled near 2000 miles through an unexplored and highly interesting country and have returned almost as much strangers to it as before. I have been allowed neither time to examine and collect, nor means to transport plants or minerals. We have been hurried through the country as if our sole object had been, as it was expressed in the orders which we received at starting "to bring the expedition to as speedy a termination as possible." After stating this you can judge how sickened I am with the thoughts of the little I have done and the nothing which I have to say for myself.

He added, however, that he had "seen many strange things," had been to the Rocky Mountains and "shivered among these eternal snows in the middle of July." But, he concluded sourly, he had gone hungry for a long time, had "eaten tainted horseflesh, owls, hawks, prairie dogs, and many other uncleanly things, the like to do, and to record for the amusement of the publick seems to be the sole ambition of our scientific commander."[36]

Ironically, when at last they were warm, dry, and comfortable at Cape Girardeau, with plenty to eat, Say, Graham, and Seymour were almost simultaneously struck with "intermittent fever" (malaria). Each morning Say awoke feeling listless and depressed, with fits of shivering followed by a gradually rising fever. His symptoms would regress by evening, only to resume the next day. Long was also affected by the disease, which was evident when he returned from St. Louis. Though still unwell, he departed several weeks later for Washington with Captain Bell.

By 1 November, Say, Seymour, and Graham were sufficiently re-covered to proceed. Accompanied by Peale, they took a small boat to the mouth of the Ohio and boarded the riverboat *Yankee* for New Orleans where they embarked by packet for Philadelphia. Swift and James, the latter being too ill to travel, later took the *Western Engineer* to the falls of the Ohio to be moored for the winter.

Say arrived back in his native city at the end of December 1820 and at once immersed himself in the all-absorbing assessment of his discoveries from "the unknown portions of our territories," as he described the region to a European colleague.[37] It was a major undertaking to arrange and describe his specimens and to prepare a catalogue for the War Department "embracing the zoology of the country," in Major Long's words to Secre-tary Calhoun. By previous arrangement the collections were to be depos-ited in Charles Willson Peale's Philadelphia Museum. Peale had repeatedly petitioned the federal government to take over and run his enterprise as a national institution, but he had been consistently turned down. Even so, his museum was the obvious repository for the fauna and flora brought back from this first government-sponsored scientific expedition to the West. The precedent had already been set by Jefferson's order that the Lewis and Clark specimens be housed with Peale.

Say's life during the following fall and winter after his return was devoted largely to writing a considerable part of the expedition's narrative. Secretary Calhoun, eager for the account to be published in order to encourage settlement of the vast, newly acquired portion of the country it would describe (although possibly apprehensive about the description of a great desert he knew it would contain), had authorized Major Long to rent a room in Philadelphia, order sufficient wood fuel for the winter of 1822, and engage Thomas Say and Edwin James to compile the document at the same pay they had received on the expedition, two dollars a day.

It was fortunate Say had such a good memory—probably trained by the numerous literary quotations he had once committed to it—for he was able to reconstruct most of the information stolen with his saddlebags. Luckily, he still had the notes he had taken up to and including his stay at Engineer Cantonment. Major Long supplied the topographical data, while James added his botanical observations to William Baldwin's. Since Captain Bell's journal had been deposited with the army in the form of a report, it was unavailable and was therefore not included. In fact, it was probably suppressed. James had written to his brother from Smithland, Kentucky the previous March where he was still with the *Western Engineer*: "In your letter of Dec. 21 you complain of the meagre and erroneous communication of Capt. Bell's relating to our expedition. I have never seen that communication but from what I know of the author's mean and illiberal prejudices against almost every member of the party, I have no doubt you have judged it correctly. You are already acquainted with my opinion respecting the manner in which the Expedition was conducted, but I was in hopes there was not such an ass in the party as would, to gratify a contemptible figure [presumably Bell himself], come forward and exhibit to the public, our mean performances in a[n] unfavorable light."[38]

Although Say, as senior scientist, most likely should have assumed the task of compiling his writings with those of Long, Baldwin, and James, James took over instead. Probably Say was too involved with writing *American Entomology* and editing and writing for the *Journal of the Academy of Natural Sciences*. Nevertheless he was much occupied with editing the expedition's account. Say wrote to his brother Ben in October 1822 that although he earnestly wanted to visit him, it was "at present altogether out of my power consistently with my duties" because he had "proof sheets" to examine and correct every morning.[39]

James had apparently very much wanted the job of writing the expedition's account, most likely because he was virtually penniless at the time. But he told his brother that he felt "wholly incompetent to it." "It has been as you know a matter of my own seeking and if I shall hereafter be thought to have failed in it, on my own head be the mischief." He added that, even so, he would probably be "able to shift a part of the responsibility from myself by the proper construction of the title."[40] Which he did: the title page states that the account is "compiled from the notes of Major Long, Mr. T. Say, and other gentlemen of the party."

The account's introduction explains that the original observers' words were used at all times, even though that required the sacrifice of stylistic uniformity. It was assumed that entire passages would be recognized as written by either Say or Long, though the authors were seldom identified. Certainly Say's style can be singled out because it is distinctively witty, detailed, and at times, eloquent. Long's style, on the other hand, is terse and humorless. At the beginning of chapter 9 the account states that "the transactions at and near Council Bluff . . . we copy from the journal of Mr. Say." This amounts to the next four chapters.

Say wrote to his friend John Melsheimer, "in addition to contributing my aid in the ordinary diatribe of the work, it falls to my lot to describe the new Quadrupeds, birds & reptiles which we met with, as well as to give an account, both moral and physical, of the natives of the country through which we passed."[41] Say added that recording meteorological observations had also been his assignment. He had compiled morning, noon, and evening temperatures; wind direction and approximate velocity; precipitation figures and storm activity; cloud forms and movements; and barometric readings. Say's extensive weather data, in conjunction with information collected at the time by the Surgeon General's office, provided "the first basis in historical sources for comparative studies of weather and climate" in western America.[42]

According to the *Account*, the expedition brought back "several thousand insects, 60 skins of new or rare animals, and a number of land and freshwater shells." Say preserved his own insect specimens, while Charles Willson Peale's son Rubens worked on other items. Rubens wrote to his brother Titian the following summer that he had been "amusing" himself in his leisure "preparing a number of them—yesterday I mounted seven of the fish. . . . The shells form a very handsome case, Mr. Say is delighted with it and is progressing with the Insects."[43]

Say told Melsheimer that he was having "much difficulty" preserving his insects, and confided that, though many of them were interesting, "they are not numerous." He said he was describing new species of which "the greater portion . . . are inhabitants of Pennsylvania, as well as of the Missouri and Arkinsaw countries."[44] He assured his friend that he would preserve the names already used by Melsheimer's father in his catalogue and would, of course, acknowledge those names Melsheimer himself had given to him.

As usual, Say neglected his health; he slept too little and was careless about regular meals. Characteristically, he was overzealous in describing for science his zoological and ethnological discoveries. Meticulous in his descriptions of fauna unknown to science, Say was also tireless in ferreting out all previous references to particular species, in order not to name as new those that had been previously described in published articles.

Aware that he was in the vanguard of establishing America's own natural science, Say was devoted to proving its credibility. Clearly it was time for American naturalists to name and describe their endemic creatures. The preface of the expedition's account, undoubtedly written by Say, states:

> We cannot but hope, that the enlightened spirit which has already evinced itself in directing a part of the energies of the nation, towards the development of the physical resources of our country, will be allowed still farther to operate; that the time will arrive, when we shall no longer be indebted to the men of foreign countries, for a knowledge of any of the products of our own soil, or for our opinions in science.[45]

Say planned to do for American insects what Alexander Wilson had done for American birds in his *American Ornithology*, written and illustrated between 1808 and 1813. Wilson's zeal in creating his pioneering book stemmed from an almost mystical belief that the heritage of America's wildlife was a unifying element that linked its citizens, of diverse nationalities and cultures, into a common destiny.[46] Say embraced this philosophy wholeheartedly. Since his own field was entomology, he could make his fellow citizens aware of their common heritage of North American insects. Except for Frederick Melsheimer's catalogue (written in Latin) and John Abbot's study of the insects of Georgia (published in England) no one had written on the insects of the United States. After this expedition Say felt qualified to take on such a task.

In fact, Say planned to delve into many disciplines of natural history. Four years after his return from the Rockies, when his second volume of *American Entomology* was in press, Say wrote to a friend that he had "commenced a work in the same style on the Reptiles and amphibia of N[orth] Amer[ica]"—unfortunately it was never completed—"& propose to undertake another on our shells."[47] These two fields were nearly virgin territories of study. Americans had, after all, spent the previous two hundred years creating a place for themselves out of wilderness and freeing themselves from foreign domination. Most areas of natural science had, of

necessity, been left unexplored. With his keen observation and his meticulous care with taxonomy, Thomas Say appeared at the right time to name
and describe the insects, reptiles, and shells of North America.

Although the Long Expedition did not succeed in finding the sources
of the Platte and Arkansas rivers, and mistook the Canadian River for the
Red, the first sentence of Secretary Calhoun's orders to Major Long of
8 March 1819, "to explore the country between the Mississippi and the
Rocky Mountains," was well carried out, at least in scientific terms, in spite
of James's observations to his brother. Thomas Say made American scientific history by technically describing for the first time such predators as the
coyote, the swift fox, and the plains gray wolf, as well as species of birds,
reptiles, rats, squirrels, shrews, bats, insects, and land shells unknown to
naturalists. The historian Bernard Jaffe has said that Say "helped not only to
illuminate many of the hidden biological corners of the continent, but also
to pile up information which helped in the creation of a new and fundamental biological synthesis."[48]

The *Account of an Expedition from Pittsburgh to the Rocky Mountains,
Performed In the Years 1819, 1820*, published in Philadelphia (1822) and London (1823), was a success. Long told Secretary Calhoun that there were
"numerous demands for the work." The *Port Folio*, a popular magazine
published in Philadelphia, stated: "It affords us great pleasure to learn that
[the *Account*] . . . is received with that liberality of patronage which it so
well deserves."[49] *Niles' Weekly Register* said that the book "abounds with
interesting information of the manners and habits of the Indians, and the
geography, geology, botany of the regions traversed, with ample notices of
its animals, and natural curiosities, &c. It will no doubt be extensively
read."[50]

The work even entered into American historical fiction, when several
years later James Fenimore Cooper used aspects of the Long Expedition in
the last of his Leatherstocking tales, *The Prairie* (1827). Cooper's comical
character Dr. Obed Battius—possibly a composite of Nuttall and Rafinesque, both of whom were known to be eccentric—is the personification of
the early nineteenth-century idea of a naturalist. Dr. Battius gives a Latin
name to every bird, animal, and flower he encounters. At one point in the
story, at dusk, he is terrified by the sound of what he thinks is an undescribed beast, and immediately names the creature *Vespertilio horribilis*,
only to find, to his chagrin, that this great unknown is none other than his
own mule—*Asinus domesticus*.

The character and description of that "Apollo-like person," the Pawnee warrior Hard-Heart, were patterned on Petalesharoo. Perhaps Say saw Petalesharoo in Philadelphia in 1821, as did Cooper, when the Pawnee warrior visited that city as part of an Indian delegation. Petalesharoo, in his elegant headdress of eagle feathers and ermine tails, was painted by John Neagle in Philadelphia and Charles Bird King in Washington. The historian John C. Ewers believes that these pictures were the first of what has become the stereotype representation of the American Indian.[51]

Another Indian Say had met, the Omaha leader Ongpatonga, or Big Elk, was also part of the 1821 delegation. Say's colleague at the Academy of Natural Sciences, Samuel George Morton, now known as the father of physical anthropology in America, would use a lithograph of the portrait John Neagle painted of Big Elk as the frontispiece of his *Crania Americana* in 1839.[52]

The year following his return from the West, Thomas Say was elected a member of the American Philosophical Society and also named a curator of that institution. He simultaneously held the post of curator at the Academy of Natural Sciences, a position to which he had been annually elected for ten years. The Academy's collections, built by its foreign and domestic members, continually increased in size, as did the voluminous correspondence dealing with its specimens. By 1821 the institution included over a hundred scientists, close to thirty of whom met on a weekly basis to present monographs on their individual spheres of inquiry.

In the spring of 1821, still another job was scheduled for Say's already crowded agenda when he was asked to serve as "professor of zoology" at Peale's museum. A series of lectures in various branches of natural history had been planned by the board of trustees, and Say was an obvious choice for the post of zoology, since he had been working at the museum all winter describing the expedition's fauna specimens. Dr. John Davidson Godman, who had married Rembrandt Peale's daughter Angelica, and whose *American Natural History* (published in 1828) would be based almost entirely on the Peale collections, was given the chair of physiology. Dr. Richard Harlan was to lecture on comparative anatomy and Gerard Troost on mineralogy.

Unfortunately, the courses given by Godman and Troost were poorly attended, and probably for this reason Say and Harlan did not lecture at all. Say may also have overcommitted himself. He often lacked discretion about his own time constraints and agreed to undertake more than he could handle. This inevitably led to procrastination on projects which he did not consider of the first importance. Two years later, Charles Willson Peale wrote to his son Rubens in reference to Thomas Say with obvious impatience: "I have insisted on Mr. Say to commence his duty as a Professor of Zoology in the Museum. I tell him that when I deliver my lecture on Natural history connected with the Museum, I will give notice that he will deliver a lecture at a given time."[53]

Whether or not Say complied is unknown, but when he later placed "Philadelphia Museum" on the title page of his 1824 *American Entomology*, it may have been a token of apology and an emblem of the regard he felt for the venerable old man whose collections he had used since childhood. This acknowledgment made it appear that the book was printed under Peale's auspices.

Say had no choice but to use the museum's collections when writing his book, because his own insects had been destroyed. He wrote to the distinguished German entomologist Jacob Sturm, in Nuremberg, that "upon my return to this place [Philadelphia] I found that my collection of insects which I had been many years in assembling together were so much injured by the depredations of the Anthrenus, Dermestes [microscopic insect predators] etc, as to be worthless for exchanging." Say said that he wished to procure European insects to compare with American, and he accepted Sturm's offer to supply him specimens at the rate of $1.07 a hundred. He asked Sturm to send him one thousand as soon as possible, including as many of the modern genera as possible, and mentioned that he "did not crave rare insects," but that if the specimens should be examples of "the most modern divisions" (that is, sorted into the most recently established genera), then his "purpose" would be answered.[54] Say was in the forefront of his time in seeking specimens from abroad for comparison, since natural history would become increasingly international as the century progressed.

That all his shell specimens were placed with Charles Willson Peale "by order of the Secretary of War" was also disappointing to Say. "I do not possess a single specimen of them," he wrote to his colleague Daniel Barnes the following summer. This situation was especially inconvenient because, as he confided to Barnes, he was contemplating a book on the subject: "I have several times since my return from the West, consulted a bookseller of this city, about publishing an account of our shells, with colored plates; whether or not he will undertake to do it, I cannot at present say, but he appears very well disposed towards it."[55] Seven years would elapse before this project was realized, but in the meantime Say was building a considerable reputation for expertise on the subject. Although conchology had been promoted by Linnaeus, Buffon, and Lamarck in Europe, Thomas Say was the first American to pursue it as an independent study.

In March 1822 Say was named "Professor of Natural History including Geology" at the University of Pennsylvania. The position was purely honorary; he drew no salary, and his lectures were to be delivered on his own initiative. Remuneration of professors, at the time, usually came only from student fees, and if attendance at the few lectures given by Godman and Troost at Peale's museum was any indication Say most likely received little or no monetary compensation from his appointment. The trustee minutes of the university record that the chair of natural history was discontinued in 1828.[56] By then Say had been away from Philadelphia for nearly three years, and since no letter from him exists in the university's archives, he had probably neglected to resign.

Exploring, not teaching, was certainly Say's preference, and another opportunity to delve into the mysteries of western zoology slowly materialized. Before the expedition to the Rockies, Secretary Calhoun had written to Major Long that, because the extreme northern bend of the Missouri was thought to be a strategic spot, Long should survey it. (Lewis and Clark had proposed this many years earlier, as had Long himself.) Secretary Calhoun also wanted to establish the forty-ninth parallel marking the northern boundary of the United States, in order to put a stop to the hostilities between American and British traders. Because these goals had not been accomplished on the 1819–20 expedition, the subject was reopened by Major Long in 1823.

In February of that year, Long wrote an influential friend in Washington proposing a topographical survey of the entire country to establish the proper measurements of latitude and longitude from which accurate maps could be made. As an officer in the Topographical Engineers, a branch of the army established during the War of 1812 to plot military positions, Long was uniquely placed to conduct western surveys. The Corps of Topographical Engineers was, in the words of historian William H. Goetzmann, "a central institution of Manifest Destiny."[57]

By April, Major Long had his official orders from Secretary Calhoun to undertake an expedition from Philadelphia to Lake Superior. He was to survey the intervening territory, describe the plant and animal life, and study Indian customs. Long immediately contacted Say to accompany him again as zoologist and antiquary (paleontologist).

CHAPTER 8
Expedition to St. Peter's River

My time has recently been fully occupied with preparations for another
western Expedn under the orders of the Secretary of War.

Thomas Say to John F. Melsheimer
Philadelphia, 26 April 1823

T HOMAS SAY AND SAMUEL SEYMOUR were the only members of the new expedition who had been to the Rockies with
Major Long. It was hoped that Edwin James would also join them
as botanist, geologist, and physician, but he could not be reached. As a
backup Long signed on William J. Keating to serve as mineralogist and
geologist. Keating was twenty-four, had studied at the School of Mines in
Paris, and held a master's degree from the University of Pennsylvania. Two
years earlier he had published a book on mining that was said to be the
first scientific work on the subject written by an American. This talented
young man, who for the past year had been teaching mineralogy and
chemistry at the university, was so eager to study the geology of the West
that he agreed to serve without pay should James join the expedition
after all.

Long requested that the Lieutenant Talcott he had known at Camp
Missouri in 1820 serve as his assistant, but Talcott was given another
assignment; his place was filled by James Edward Colhoun, brother-in-law
and cousin of Secretary Calhoun (despite the different spelling). The affable
Colhoun was a twenty-seven-year-old midshipman whose travel experience
included South America and China. His appointment to the expedition had
occurred purely by chance. At breakfast one morning with the secretary, the
subject came up of Talcott's inability to join Long. Colhoun asked his
brother-in-law if he might fill the position, and his request was granted
at once.[1]

Thomas Say and Edwin James were to have acted jointly as the expedition's journalists. Keating would replace James in this role, and Say agreed

to collect botanical specimens, reluctantly, because he did not feel qualified to undertake the task. He was more confident about assuming James's duty as physician. Such doubling up of jobs was one result of the government's penurious allocation of funds for the journey. Long's purchases for himself and "the gentlemen of science" before leaving Philadelphia included one small surveyor's compass, one "mercurial case," a pocket sextant, a protractor, a patent lever watch, thermometers, lenses, a pocket compass, blank books, lead pencils, and camel hair brushes. For food his voucher listed only "portable soup" for the men's sustenance. Six horses and an assortment of arms, including "one pair [of] bayonet pistols," a "double gun," and a rifle, completed the bare necessities.[2]

Long was also armed with a letter from Stratford Canning, the British minister in Washington, directed to all the post commanders in British territory. This bit of diplomacy was necessary since the expedition would be crossing over the forty-ninth parallel—the boundary agreed upon at the Convention of 1818 dividing Canada from the United States west from the Lake of the Woods to the Rockies—and traveling through British territory to Lake Superior. The letter stated that the objects of Long's expedition were "purely scientific," and that he, Canning, had been requested by the U.S. government "to recommend that officer [Long] and his party to the civilities of His Majesty's officers and subjects in the Northwest territory."[3]

Canning was, in fact, deeply concerned about the American government's hidden motives for the expedition. He wrote to his cousin George Canning, Britain's foreign minister, that he had apprised Lord Dalhousie, governor-in-chief of Canada, of the expedition, and that he had "submit[ted] to His Lordship's judgement how far it may be worth while to give directions for observing its movements."[4]

Word would spread quickly to the post commanders to monitor the expedition's route carefully as the explorers traveled east from the Red River settlement of Pembina (today northernmost North Dakota) through country under the dominion of Great Britain. Speculations about American plans for establishing a military post to watch the British and for acquiring knowledge about the country "in case of war" would be put forward by various British representatives.[5]

Secretary Calhoun officially set down in his letter to Long of 25 April 1823 that the expedition's objective was to make "a general Survey of the Country," along with a "Topographical description of the same"; to examine and describe the flora, fauna, and minerals of the region; and to "enquire into the character, customs, etc. of the Indian Tribes." The unwrit-

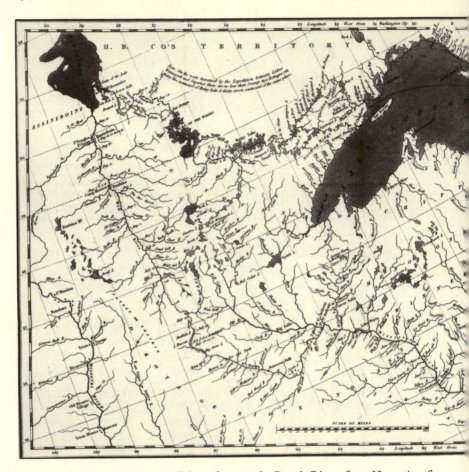

Fig. 26. Map of the Long Expedition of 1823 to St. Peter's River, from *Narrative of an Expedition to the Source of St. Peter's River, Lake Winnepeek, Lake of the Woods, etc. Performed in the Year 1823, by order of the Hon. J. C. Calhoun, Secretary of War, Under the Command of Stephen H. Long, U. S. T. E. Compiled from the Notes of Major Long, Messrs. Say, Keating, & Colhoun,* by William Keating. London, 1825.

ten objective, however, was apparently to officially locate and mark the location of the forty-ninth parallel—that is, the U.S.-Canadian border.

The expedition, consisting initially of Say, Long, Keating, and Seymour, set out from Philadelphia on 30 April 1823. As the season was late, frost lingered in the mountains even though the dogwood was in full

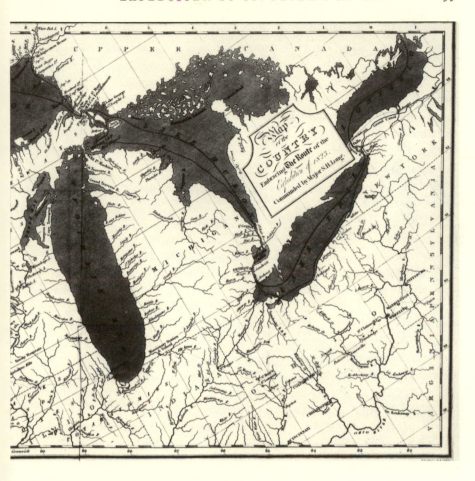

bloom. Unusually heavy rains during the preceding month had made the roads muddy and difficult, and the men were glad to sell their carriages at Wheeling and proceed on horseback. The route mapped out would take them to Chicago via Fort Wayne, to Fort Armstrong on the Mississippi, along the river to Fort St. Anthony (the site of present-day Minneapolis/St. Paul), and on to the source of the St. Peter's (Minnesota) River. The explorers would then head up the Red River of the North to establish the forty-ninth parallel at Pembina, proceed along the northern boundary of the United States to Lake Superior, and return home by the lakes.

After Colhoun joined the expedition at Columbus, Say persuaded Long to halt for a day at Piqua on the Miami River in order to examine ancient Indian fortifications. In pursuing his assignment as antiquary, Say unearthed a quantity of arrowheads among which he found interesting distinctions. An arrowhead used in battle, intended to break off and remain buried in the enemy's body, was engineered so as to make it difficult and painful to remove from a wound. The hunting arrowhead, firmly attached to the shaft, could be easily extracted and reused.

After four days of wet and uncomfortable riding, often through immense swarms of mosquitoes and horseflies, the party reached Fort Wayne. To Say, the town's population of Canadians, French, and Indians made it seem like a different country. In regard to the clash of cultures, he noted that "the awkward and constrained appearance" of Frenchmen who had exchanged their usual attire for the "breech-cloth and blanket" was as comical as that of an Indian who donned the "tight body coat of the white man."[6] Say observed a French-Canadian fur trader having difficulty with a loosening loincloth and a gaudy Indian blanket that slid off his shoulders as he packed and weighed animal pelts. Several Indian women with small boys in tow stood nearby watching and giggling.

Say concurred with the others that the town's position at the confluence of three rivers—the St. Mary's, St. Joseph, and Maumee, with its access to Lake Erie—would prove a prosperous spot for long-term settlement. He and Long were aware of the value of such observations to future settlers, since their previous expedition had generated interest in new territory. They wished to pay special attention to the subject on this journey, because their assessment of the great plains as arid and unfit for cultivation had been so discouraging.

While at Fort Wayne, Say was shown the grave of the legendary Miami leader Little Turtle, who had attempted to unite fellow Indian tribal groups around the country to preserve their ancestral lands and resist the encroaching white population. When Little Turtle realized that the time for such a plan had passed, he had urged his tribespeople to make peace with the intruders and adopt their ways in order to survive. Say considered exhuming Little Turtle's skull and examining it for indications of superior intellect. Both he and Keating had studied the new science of phrenology, which held that mental capacity could be determined from skull configurations.

Say thought it would be in the interest of future generations to preserve the head of one of America's foremost aborigines, but agents in the Department of Indian Affairs convinced him that Little Turtle's people would regard any disturbance of their leader's grave as a sacrilege—undoubtedly one with dire consequences.

Because Say was also assigned to gather Indian data, while at Fort Wayne he arranged an interview with a Potawatomi warrior, Metea, whom he described as having a "haughty and tyrannical mien," adding that "if ever an expression of pity or of the kinder affections belonged to his countenance, it has been driven away by the scenes of bloodshed and cruelty through which he has passed."[7] Say made notes that polygamy was common among Potawatomis, with the number of a man's wives dependent on his ability as a hunter; that boys were initiated as warriors at the age of twelve; and that mercy killings of the terminally ill were frequent. From sources other than Metea, principally traders, he heard that cannibalism was allegedly practiced by the Chippewa, Miami, and Potawatomi Indians, who believed that by consuming a brave enemy's organs they would acquire his characteristics.

On 29 May, with the addition of a guide, Private Jesse L. Bemis, and a free black youth named Allison to act as "waiter," the explorers set out on the two-hundred-mile journey to Chicago, often riding through nearly impenetrable swamps dense with mosquitoes. For days their horses had insufficient grazing, and on occasion when the horses had wandered off during the night searching for food the men lost valuable time rounding them up. The forests were so thick in places that Say and the others had to dismount and, knee-deep in mud, lead the horses. When the animals leaped over fallen logs, baggage was invariably thrown off and more time was lost tying it back on. On one particularly trying day, Keating noted that to "the younger explorers it was a source of much gratification to find that the fatigues of that morning had exceeded all that their experienced companions had ever met with."[8]

When they reached the Carey Mission Station, a school for Indian and mixed-blood children, time was allotted for the mission's blacksmith to shoe their horses before they struck out for Fort Dearborn. In a week, averaging about twenty-seven miles a day, they arrived at the fort in Chicago (a Potawatomi word meaning either skunk or wild onion), thought to be one of the oldest Indian settlements in the country. Numerous ancient trails coming together indicated that the site had once been an extensive

Indian village, but Say saw only a few rude huts belonging to people of mixed blood. He and Keating noted that though the present village might one day become a well-populated settlement because of its position in a direct line between the Great Lakes and the Mississippi River, "the dangers attending the navigation of the lake, and the scarcity of harbors along the shore, must ever prove a serious obstacle to the increase of the commercial importance of Chicago."[9]

Say and his party left Fort Dearborn in mid-June guided by an old Frenchman, Joseph St. Peter Le Sellier, who would also act as interpreter. Rather than take the usual route by the Mississippi and Fort Armstrong, the men headed across the prairie toward Fort Crawford at Prairie du Chien to save time. Their course took them due west across low, swampy prairie thickly covered with aquatic plants. Say noticed prairie hens, reedbirds, sandhill cranes, and curlews, and, in drier parts, land pockmarked with badger holes.

When Le Sellier became unsure of the route, a Sauk Indian guide, Wanabea, was hired at the next village. Say found him cooperative in answering questions about religion and recorded that he believed in a female deity residing in the moon whose duty it was to cross man in all his desires, and a male god living in the sun who was all goodness and "propitiation." On the subject of women, Say noted that the young warrior, "feeling a little encouraged, continued in a strain so obscene as even to put to the blush our old interpreter, Le Sellier; which with a Canadian trader, might be supposed not to be an easy thing."[10]

The expedition crossed a great rolling prairie where the soil was fertile enough, Long rightly observed, someday to be heavily populated by farmers. In a few days the party reached the Wisconsin River. Because it was too wide and deep to ford, the men built a small raft and sent Bemis across to obtain boats from Fort Crawford. That evening Lieutenant Martin Scott and another soldier pulled ashore from the fort, bringing with them a welcome bottle of wine. After crossing the river, a three-hour ride lay ahead to reach the fort, but the evening was cool and still and the moon was full. "Our way lay across a beautiful country," Say would recount in the expedition's narrative, "where steep and romantic crags contrasted pleasantly with widely extended prairies, which, seen by the uncertain light of the moon, appeared to spread around like a sheet of water. Our party was sufficiently numerous to form a long line, which assumed a more imposing character from the dark and lengthened shadows which each cast behind him."[11]

Five days were spent at Prairie du Chien—named after the Dog

Indians, whose site it had been—outfitting for the journey up the St. Peter's River. Ten men commanded by Lieutenant Scott were detailed to accompany the expedition, tired horses were exchanged for fresh ones, and an eight-oared mackinaw barge with a "tent-fly" for a sail was furnished to transport the baggage and part of the group up the Mississippi. The expedition embarked on 25 June in two divisions. Say, Keating, and Seymour, with Lieutenant Scott and his men and a mixed-blood interpreter, went by boat, while Major Long, Colhoun, Allison, two soldiers, and a Dakota Indian guide took the land route.

Say's detachment had not proceeded far up the Mississippi when trouble started. It seemed that before leaving, while he and Scott had been discussing the route with Long, several soldiers had helped themselves liberally to a keg of whiskey. They were now drunk and fast becoming unmanageable. Scott loaded his pistols and warned them that anyone attempting a mutiny did so at the risk of his life. Subdued by this action, they fumbled for the oars, but they were obviously too intoxicated to pull against the strong current so Scott ordered the boat to shore. By late afternoon they were sober enough to continue rowing until nightfall.

Fig. 27. *The Maiden's Rock on the Mississippi,* by Samuel Seymour, 1823, from *Narrative of an Expedition to the Source of St. Peter's River, Lake Winnepeek, Lake of the Woods, etc. Performed in the Year 1823, by order of the Hon. J. C. Calhoun, Secretary of War, Under the Command of Stephen H. Long, U. S. T. E. Compiled from the Notes of Major Long, Messrs. Say, Keating, & Colhoun,* by William H. Keating. London, 1825.

The next day was clear and warm and the scenery magnificent. Islands dotted the river, and the landscape with its features, as Say noted, "so bold, so wild, so majestic," altered with every bend of the Mississippi. In some places the river was three or four miles wide and bordered by bluffs and countless ravines. Say's enjoyment of the scene was spoiled, however, by a soldier apparently suffering from *delirium tremens*. When he became uncontrollable, Scott ordered him tied to the mast, where all day he alternated between abusive language and wild bursts of laughter. At camp ashore he broke loose and was found hours later hiding in a swamp. As the expedition's doctor, Say treated the man as best he could, but when it became obvious his refusal to row was a ruse, Say "prescribed the use of an oar as a sudorific, by which he soon recovered the use of his lost senses."12

That night the party camped on the prairie between the Raccoon and Bad-Axe rivers, but mosquitos forced them to reboard the barge and continue upriver, aided by a strong breeze. The wind increased rapidly and soon a heavy storm broke, making further progress impossible. The men tied up at the bank and huddled under blankets as torrents of rain threatened to swamp their boat. Thunderclaps reverberated off the rocky bluffs and flashes of lightning illuminated the wilderness. By morning the sky was clear and the journey resumed after several hours of drying clothes around a roaring fire. While encamped, Say, in examining the head of a rattlesnake he had caught, punctured his thumb on its fang. The pain was initially excruciating, but after he gouged the spot with his knife the painful swelling slowly subsided. At Fort Wayne, Metea had told him that Potawatomis treated rattlesnake bites by covering them with poultices made of the "Seneca snake-root" plant and drinking quantities of violet tea. Say probably ignored these remedies because he doubted the efficacy of plants as a snakebite cure. He had written in an article on herpetology for the Academy's *Journal* that when a snake's reservoir of venom is empty, which is often the case when one is bitten, the reptile is harmless, "and the most inert plant would then stand a good chance of gaining reputation with the credulous as a specific."13 Indians held rattlesnakes in high esteem because of their timely warning of an enemy's approach and for this reason seldom killed them unless their rattle was wanted as an ornament. In that case they usually left a piece of tobacco by the carcass in atonement.

It was sunset when the expedition made camp by Lake Pepin. The men had been warned that heavy swells from high winds could make the lake dangerous—"Le lac est petit, mais il est malin," cautioned their interpreter—but next morning the lake was like glass and they crossed without mishap. Say was excited by the catch of a large paddlefish, a specimen of which Lesueur had described for science in an early issue of the *Journal*. In observing a live specimen, Say could add many details unavailable to Lesueur working only with a dried one. Later the men landed on an island and shot for food dozens of passenger pigeons in only a few minutes. (In less than eighty years this bird would be extinct.)

On 1 July the expedition was reunited at the village of the Dakota leader Redwing. Invited to his lodge to smoke, Say and his companions seated themselves opposite a group of warriors. Redwing rose and delivered his welcoming speech, periodically punctuated by his companions' deep-toned responses of *ah-hah*, signifying approval. Long described the expedition's purpose and presented Redwing with tobacco, powder, and shot. Redwing seemed pleased with these gifts but explained, facetiously, that his warriors were painted black to signify their grief over the recent loss of relatives and friends in battle, and he had hoped for a present of "the Great Father's milk to gladden their hearts." Long responded sternly that whiskey only served to make Indians "crazy, quarrelsome and sick," and that his stock was strictly for medicinal use. Redwing reluctantly accepted Long's response, and after circulating the peace pipe, he presented him with the three-foot stem as a token of respect.

Late at night on 2 July, the barge entered the St. Peter's River—*Watapan Menesota*, meaning "river of turbid water" in Dakota—and proceeded to Fort St. Anthony (later renamed Fort Snelling and located in present-day St. Paul). The fort had been erected by Colonel Henry Leavenworth in the late summer of 1819 on a bluff rising high above the right bank of the Mississippi—a spot recommended in fact by Major Long on an 1817 expedition. The garrison now contained five companies of the Fifth Infantry under Colonel Josiah Snelling, who made sure that the explorers were comfortably housed and served excellent meals enhanced with vegetables from the soldiers' gardens. Colonel Snelling was as helpful as he was hospitable. After sending back the guard from Fort Crawford with the proviso that Lieutenant Scott conduct them, but return with all possible speed to rejoin the expedition, the colonel assigned twenty-one soldiers commanded by Lieutenant St. Clair Denny to accompany the scientists. Since the guide from Prairie du Chien had proved completely inept, he was replaced by another, also a man of mixed blood.

The expedition was again divided in order to explore the land as well as the river. This time Say took the land route, along with Colhoun, Denny, nine soldiers, and a boy to serve as guide and Chippewa interpreter. Long, Keating, Seymour, and the rest embarked in four canoes. Also joining the water party was a colorful Italian the explorers had met at the fort, J. C. Beltrami. Beltrami got on reasonably well with all except Long, for whom he developed an intense dislike. For Say he had nothing but praise, describing "the Professor at Philadelphia" as the only naturalist on the expedition "who deserved the designation," and admiring him as a scientist "distinguished at once by modesty and merit."[14]

Say's land detachment set off from Fort St. Anthony with twenty horses into *terra incognita*, as Colhoun described it. After a week of difficult riding, much of it through boggy ground, the men rejoined Long's contingent and the decision was made to abandon travel on the river, as it was becoming increasingly winding, shallow, and filled with snags and sandbars. The explorers hesitated to disregard government orders to ascend the St. Peter's to its source, but other expedients took precedence. The guide cautioned that if they proceeded by water they would lose precious time and arrive at Red River after the buffalo had gone. This advice was reinforced by an Indian family encountered along the way who warned of a food shortage. They said their nation was near starvation because of the delayed arrival of the herd. In addition, the guide warned that if too much time was lost it would be impossible to reach Lake Superior before winter.

The decision was thus made to continue by land, while half the military guard returned to Fort St. Anthony in the canoes. Nine horses were "allotted to the officers and gentlemen," with the rest carrying baggage and provisions; the remaining soldiers were "obliged to walk." Among the scanty wildlife, Say collected a few specimens of sandhill crane, yellow-headed blackbird, black-breasted tern, and blue-winged teal. To the herbarium he added several beautiful lilies, including *Lilium philadelphicum* and *Lilium superbum*. Besides birds, the only animals Say observed were several snakes and a few muskrats, although coyotes were often heard howling in the distance as the expedition proceeded north. Where the St. Peter's widened into Lac qui Parle, two wolf puppies were caught; Say hoped to bring them back, but they escaped during the night. Fresh buffalo tracks were spotted, and several Indians later told the party that a tremendous herd had halted near Lake Traverse.

The St. Peter's at last widened into Big Stone Lake. After reaching the head of this lake they portaged to Lake Traverse, the source of the Red River of the North. Say made note of the curious phenomenon of two rivers rising in the same valley and flowing in opposite directions—the St. Peter's, south, eventually emptying into the Gulf of Mexico, and the Red River, north into Lake Winnipeg.

On the shore of Lake Traverse the explorers visited a Yantonai (Dakota) village where the young leader, Wanotan, was renowned as a warrior. Say described him as over six feet tall, uncommonly handsome, with "an intelligence that beams through his eye," and noted that he was especially revered for having undergone the "Blood sun dance," a ritual including self-torture practiced by the Dakotas and many other Plains Indian tribes in fulfillment of a pledge to the sun for help in stealing horses or other adventures.

Invited to Wanotan's lodge for a feast, the naturalists and officers helped themselves liberally to the buffalo meat but were less enthusiastic about the three boiled dogs served by their host as a delicacy. Say forced it down, and the guide cautioned him to replace all the bones in his dish because the Dakotas treated them with deference, washing and burying them to show that no disrespect was meant to the dog species and to guarantee the animal's reincarnation. Say was sympathetic with this example of the Indians' integral relationship with other forms of life, their thoughtfulness and respect toward them, and their concern for their renewal. In the future, such concepts would be lost on the majority of encroaching settlers, whose brutal exploitation of all natural resources would consistently confound the native peoples.

The next day Wanotan paid the expedition a formal visit. Say was much taken with the dignified man's impressive regalia, describing him as "worthy of the pencil of Vandyke, and the graver of Berwick"[15] in his white buffalo-skin cloak decorated with small tufts of owl feathers; a jacket, leggings, and moccasins profusely ornamented with human hair; a huge necklace of grizzly bear claws hanging around his neck; and nine red sticks representing the number of gunshot wounds he had received plaited in his hair. His face was painted with vermilion, and he carried a large fan of turkey feathers. His eight-year-old son was equally magnificent in a mantle of ermine skins and an immense headdress of eagle feathers.

Wanotan assembled a group of warriors to entertain his visitors with the Dog Dance. Say could not help smiling at some of their ornaments, obviously obtained from traders: several wore two and three pairs of eyeglasses suspended around their necks, while others displayed open papers of straight pins hanging from their headdresses. The performers formed a ring and, beating time with bird wings, began singing in a "low tone," as Say wrote, "gradually rising it for a few minutes, then closing it suddenly with a shrill yell."[16] The performance lasted almost an hour.

On 26 July Say and his companions commenced their journey north along the Red River to Pembina and Fort Douglas, two posts of the Hudson's Bay Company. The town of Pembina—named for the high-bush cranberry growing in the area—was thought to be situated almost squarely on the forty-ninth parallel. Both the American and the British governments were aware that most of Lord Selkirk's Red River settlement at Pembina was located south of the border. It would be Long's job to resolve the issue.

Thomas Douglas, fifth earl of Selkirk, was a Scottish philanthropist who gained control of the Hudson's Bay Company in 1810. The company granted him a vast tract of land in the Red River valley near present-day Winnipeg, Canada, where he founded a settlement of Scottish peasants forced to emigrate during the Highland clearances, when agricultural land was reclaimed by the lairds to graze their enormous flocks of sheep.

Four Canadian fur traders with six carts of provisions accompanied the expedition northward. It was a relief to sight a sizable buffalo herd soon after starting; the hunters shot several to be cooked over a surprisingly odorless fire of dung. A few days later Lieutenant Scott caught up with them after traveling a total of eight hundred miles to Prairie du Chien and back. Say was particularly pleased to see him since he had a reputation as a crack shot and would be invaluable in collecting bird and animal specimens.

The next day, having spotted a small group of elk, Colhoun, Beltrami, and a guide galloped off to give chase. The rest continued on, moving slowly because of the carts and to accommodate the men on foot. Suddenly a gun went off near the river, announcing a band of Indians running toward them across the prairie. Wearing only loincloths, but well armed with guns and bows and arrows, the Indians appeared friendly at first, until their demands that Long's party move away from the buffalo and accompany them to their camp to speak with their leader took on a threatening tone. During the conversation Say noticed that they had cleverly intermixed themselves with the exploring party, so that "every one of our number was placed between two or more of theirs." As the situation intensified, Long mounted and ordered his men to move on. The Indians offered no opposition but immediately followed.

Minutes later another Indian group galloped up. Since those behind shouted that their leader was among them, the explorers reined up and waited. But when Long saw there was no leader he commanded the expedition to proceed. At that instant several warriors raced to the head of the line, fired across the explorers' path, and formed a crescent in front of them. There were now seventy or eighty warriors and only twenty-five men in Long's party. "It was probable that they did not care much to harm our persons," Say recounted later, "but they were anxious to pilfer our baggage, and especially to secure our horses; and as we were resolved not to part with them without a struggle, it was evident that the first gun fired would be the signal for an attack, which must end in the total destruction of our party."[17]

Long once more acted with resolve and waved the expedition on. Perhaps thinking a night attack would be more successful, the Indians made no move to follow them. Had it not been for the three missing hunters, the explorers would have ridden all night; as it was they halted at dusk. With the horses staked in a circle on short ropes, and guns checked and loaded, they waited around a signal fire. When the three at last appeared, it was decided that, because the Indians would probably attack just before dawn, the expedition would leave as the moon was rising, after the hunters' horses had rested. Preparations were made in relative silence and they departed without notice. After riding all night they halted even though gunfire in the woods indicated the Indians were still tracking them.

During the first few nights following this incident, it was decided that more night sentinels were needed. The "officers and gentlemen of the party" each agreed to a watch. When Say took his turn, the occasional harsh bark of a coyote cutting through the lowing of a bison herd was all he could hear. A full moon cast its eerie glow across the grasslands. As Say tried to make out strange shapes in the landscape created by the low light and his imagination, his attention was drawn to something moving on the prairie. The dark shape that approached stealthily appeared to be a wolf. Say thought he recognized the "stratagem of the wily Indian, who, to conceal his approach, had assumed a false garb." He was strongly tempted to shoot, but resisted, not wanting to alarm the camp. After a tense stillness, the creature "scampered off on his four legs, with a rapidity and agility that satisfied [Say] that this was its natural posture."[18]

The explorers were apprehensive enough about pursuit that for several days they continued to break camp very early, until one morning they saw behind them spreading billows of smoke rising into the sky. This could only mean the Indians had returned to their usual routine. In order to keep the land open for bison to graze, they periodically set the prairies on fire—a further example of their symbiotic relationship with the endemic wildlife.

Although the party encountered no further difficulties with the Indians, a new problem presented itself. Water was getting scarce. Stream beds were dry, and the men were forced to drink from stagnant pools, "the quality of which was not much improved by its having been resorted to by buffaloes." Temperature fluctuations from extreme heat in daytime to biting cold at night generated heavy dews, which soaked them and made guard duty especially onerous.

After more days of monotonous travel, Say and his fellow explorers arrived at the Hudson's Bay Company's post at the disputed location of Pembina. Since the party's main objective there was to decide whether the town was north or south of the forty-ninth parallel, the men halted for four days in order for Long and Colhoun to make topographical calculations. On 8 August 1823, a ceremony was held at "Camp Monroe"—with parading and flag raising—at which Long declared that, by the authority vested in him by the President, the country south of the pole erected by the soldiers was United States territory. The inhabitants of Pembina cheered, for the entire town, with the exception of one house, was on the United States side. There was little subsequent dispute by either group regarding Long's calculations.

At Pembina the explorers were advised that travel by horseback to Lake Superior would be impractical, since the entire length of the journey was covered with marshes and lagoons. Instead it was suggested they follow the principal streams by bark canoe, a light boat that could easily be carried from one body of water to another. After the horses were traded for canoes and supplies and several engagees hired, Long rode ahead to Fort Douglas to enlist more help. Say and the others followed by barge up the Red River with stops en route for Say to collect plant and animal species. He found a rare plant, a monandria, and later was so intent on collecting insects he nearly missed a rare antelope (*Antelocapra americana*, Ord) that came quite near him, perhaps attracted by the white beaver hat he invariably wore. In the soft mud along the river bank he saw elk, bear, and wolf tracks.

The expedition left Fort Douglas in mid-August with twenty-nine men in three thirty-foot canoes. Donald McKensie, the fort superintendent, had treated the Americans with every courtesy. McKensie had, in his day, been quite an adventurer. He has been described as one of the greatest of those men who explored beyond the Rocky Mountains.[19]

On entering the Winnepeek (Winnipeg) River, the men calculated that they had reached the furthest point in their expedition, which had

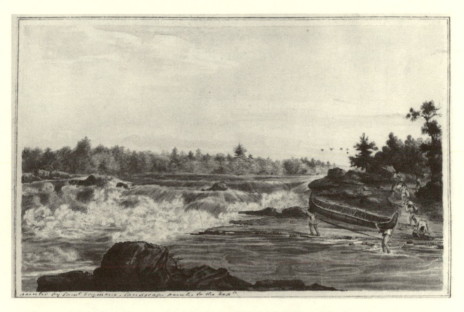

Fig. 28. *Major Long's party crossing the lower falls on Winnepeek river, August 20, 1823,* by Samuel Seymour. Watercolor. Courtesy of the American Jewish Historical Society.

covered eleven hundred miles in 112 days. Ahead of them lay a long water journey broken by seventy-two portages between Lake Winnipeg and Lake Superior. Say noted that sturgeon, salmon, and pike battled their way upstream, while eagles and hawks watched from above for fish hurled on the rocks by the raging current. The river became a series of lakes connected by rapids. That they were treacherous was made all too plain by clusters of wooden crosses seen periodically along the bank. But the boatmen's constant singing was cheerful, in spite of the loon which flew by screaming its fabled, but accurate, prediction of stormy weather.

After crossing Lake of the Woods and navigating the Rainy River, they stopped at another Hudson's Bay Company post, Rainy Lake Fort, to repair their canoes, damaged from shooting rapids. The chief factor, Simon McGillivray, welcomed them and asked Say to examine an injured white man, John Tanner. In conversation with Tanner—a challenge, because the man's native tongue was obviously an Indian language and his English was minimal—Say learned his most unusual story. As a child he had been kidnapped by a band of Ottawa Indians. Treated with great kindness, he grew up with the tribe, assuming its language, habits, and manners. Years later as a grown man he had met Lord Selkirk at his Red River settlement. The Scotsman took a special interest in him and after complicated investigations located Tanner's natural family. Tanner by then had two Indian wives and several children, some of whom he had already taken to the United States to live. Recently he had been shot by one of his wives during his attempt to kidnap his two teen-aged daughters, who had been living with their mother near Lake of the Woods.

The explorers took Tanner aboard when the canoes were patched and ready. After only a few miles, however, he was in such pain they put him ashore to return to the fort, aided by a man from the post they saw fishing on the bank. Say regretted losing the opportunity for further conversation with Tanner because of his remarkable first-hand experience with the life and manners of the Ottawa and Chippewa tribes. Several years later Tanner would tell the story of his years with the Indians and his difficult readjustment to Euro-American culture to Edwin James, who would publish the account in New York in 1830.[20] James met Tanner at Fort Crawford (now Prairie du Chien) while serving as an assistant surgeon at the fort.

As the expedition progressed, Say collected a ruby-throated hummingbird, a pileated woodpecker, and many Canada jays and golden plovers. He observed that the clouds of tiny ephemeral insects arising at night like "snow showers" never saw the sunrise but lived out their entire life within a few short hours after emerging from the pupal stage. In the lakes he found a number of leeches, including four new species.

At Fort William (present-day Thunder Bay, Ontario), one mile from Lake Superior, the canoes were exchanged for a flat-bottomed rowboat. Although old, ill-formed, and barely large enough, it was considered more seaworthy than the canoes. Disappointingly, the only food supplies available from the fort were maize and suet.

The explorers began their voyage along the north coast of Lake Superior on 15 September. Anxious to cross a section of the lake known to be dangerous when the wind was up, they took advantage of the calm weather at night and continued after supper. "The effect of that evening scene was beautiful beyond description," Say wrote in the expedition's narrative. "Tall cliffs filled with caverns, and curiously indented by numerous little coves, rose abruptly from the smooth and undisturbed surface of the lake, whose unbounded expanse lay then open to view."[21]

Lake Superior was not always so serene. The season was in fact "unusually boisterous and severe," with rain, hail, or snow inundating the explorers much of the time. Occasionally waves rose so high the men were forced to wait for several days until they subsided. Once a fierce storm erupted during the night, sending heavy swells rolling into the harbor where they had moored. The waves would have dashed their old boat to pieces had they not secured it on logs. The boat was essential, because it would have been impossible to travel along the shore with its countless swamps and dense undergrowth.

Weather alone was not always to blame for the discomfort. One night a soldier decamped with various articles and foodstuffs—a serious theft when provisions were dangerously low. As a last resort, Say and his companions ate a lichen the boatmen called "tripe de roche"; no amount of red or black pepper could render it palatable, and all agreed this "black matter floating in liquid" was "as unsightly in appearance as its taste was disagreeable." When they finally landed at a fishery on the Michipicoten River, Say's fierce hunger overcame his initial intent to take back to Lesueur the unusual trout he was served.

At the end of September he and the others reached their destination of Cantonment Brady at Sault Ste. Marie, where lakes Superior, Michigan, and Huron come together. During a few days' rest Say compared experiences with the explorer Henry Rowe Schoolcraft, an authority on Indian ethnography stationed there as Indian agent with his Ojibway wife. In 1820 he had explored some of the same territory as Say; he would later, in 1832, be credited with discovering the Mississippi's source. From a book Schoolcraft published in 1839, recounting legends of the great Iroquois statesman Hiawatha, Henry Wadsworth Longfellow would take the name for his famous poem.

After this respite, the expedition continued by boat to Mackinac Island, where Lieutenants Scott and Denny and the soldiers left for the arduous trip back to Fort St. Anthony. Say, Long, Keating, Colhoun, Seymour, and Allison embarked aboard the cutter *Dallas* for the three-day voyage down Lake Huron to Detroit, then took a steamboat across Lake Erie to Buffalo. After seeing Niagara Falls, they traveled by land to Rochester and down the Erie Canal to Albany. Healthy and exhilarated, Say and his fellow explorers reached Philadelphia on 26 October 1823 after six months and four thousand miles of travel.

The expedition had accomplished its political objective of providing the United States government with considerably more information than it already possessed about that triangular portion of the country's new region encompassed by the Missouri, the Mississippi, and the northern U.S.

boundary. And the explorers had passed through British territory without incident; surprisingly, every civility had been extended to them. This fact alone must have been something of a relief in Washington.

The collections of fauna and flora, however, were perhaps not as abundant as had been hoped for. Not being a botanist, Say had lacked the enthusiasm to gather a large number of plants and instead concentrated his energies almost entirely on insects. The information he had amassed on new insect species would allow him to represent enough of the country to commence writing his long-planned book. Now he could truly consider his subject *American* entomology.

The *North American Review* in Boston, in discussing the published narrative of the journey, which appeared the following year, praised the expedition's accomplishments while deriding the government for not providing sufficient funds. The *Review* mentioned Thomas Say's 150-page appendix on natural history, "the merits of which we do not pretend to speak, being fully convinced that no better pledge of its value can be desired by the public, than the name of the author."[22]

Viewed from abroad, the expedition's most important contribution was the Indian data that had been collected. A London literary magazine observed, "In the course of a few years, it will become more and more difficult to ascertain the original opinions and practices of Indian nations, and to discover what changes may have been introduced by a more frequent intermixture with white men, on which account the information in these volumes will become a valuable record, as it appears to have been selected with much diligence, and a scrupulous attention to truth."[23] This praise Say could have justly taken to heart, since, as noted in the narrative's preface, "much of the matter relating to the Indians" had been taken from "Mr. Say's notes."

CHAPTER 9
American Entomology

For beauty and elegance of execution, this work surpasses any other that has been printed in this country.

North American Review, July 1825

SEVERAL MONTHS AFTER the explorers' homecoming, Maclure, writing from Spain to his friend Madame Marie Duclos Fretageot in Philadelphia, expressed relief at her news of Thomas Say's safety: "I'm glad to learn that Mr. Say is returned as I had some fear of the indians and consider him as a usefull man in the cause of the propagation of knowledge."[1] Say was indeed making himself useful. In addition to his duties as curator at the American Philosophical Society and sometime lecturer at the University of Pennsylvania, he served at the Academy on the zoological, library, and publication committees and continued his duties as curator. For the *Journal* he wrote a long essay, which would appear in installments in 1823 and 1824, on beetles obtained from his expedition to the Rockies, as well as papers on sea and land shells.

The major thrust of his work in 1823 was preparation of *American Entomology or Descriptions of the Insects of North America* for the press. Volume one would be published in Philadelphia the following year, as would *Narrative of an Expedition to St. Peter's River.* Say's involvement with his *Entomology* likely precluded his compiling any more of the expedition narrative than the Indian vocabularies he had collected and the appendix notes in which he described shells, fossils, leeches, and insects new to science. The plants he had gathered were turned over to Thomas Nuttall to sort out, but Nuttall was called off to England after finishing only five descriptions, so the rest of the herbarium was given to Lewis David von Schweinitz, a Moravian minister who was also an avid botanist. Unfortunately, the expedition had moved too fast for Say to collect both flower and fruit of the same species, which of course occur at different seasons. This made many identifications and descriptions difficult.

"We passed over that immense country in six months," he wrote to John Melsheimer, "so that you will be well aware that we had not much leisure to make very abundant collections; nevertheless I obtained some insects that are of some interest."[2] Of the collections Say made during the expedition, that of insects was by far the most extensive, since not only was entomology his favorite pursuit, but many of the other types of specimens had been lost. The shells he had collected on the St. Peter's River were packed in a box and sent back with the soldiers who returned from Pembina to Fort St. Anthony, but the shells were never located; nor were the specimens he sent back from Chicago. On the last leg of the trip, Say had put all the shells he had collected into a canteen that he carried constantly, but it was left by mistake on Mackinac Island when the canoes were being reloaded. An even more important package containing skins of quadrupeds, birds, reptiles, and fishes was also missing. These losses were very disappointing to Say, but at least the insect collection was intact.

Say's interest in entomology eclipsed his curiosity in other spheres of scientific inquiry. Once, in a request to Melsheimer for insect specimens which was accompanied by a long list, he had written: "You can well conceive the pleasure that the reception of any of the insects corresponding with the above numbers or indeed any other natives of our country, would yield me, when I assure you that the fondness for these pursuits to which they lead, seems to increase with my age, or in other words, it has hitherto 'grown with my growth & strengthened with my strength.'"[3] Say underlined his enthusiasm by quoting Pope's *Essay on Man*, a poem he had found inspirational since his youth.

The first volume of *American Entomology*, which incorporated the text and six illustrations from the 1817 edition, was published at the end of 1824. Say planned his book to be issued in unpaged parts with paper covers, so that when the entire set was eventually bound in leather (a typical nineteenth-century procedure) insects of the same genera could be arranged together. The work was dedicated to William Maclure, "distinguished as a successful cultivator and munificent patron of the Natural Sciences," and Say signed himself Maclure's "much obliged, and most obedient servant"—a prophetic designation as it would turn out.

Say's feelings for Maclure likely went deeper than those of obligation to a patron. As mentioned before, the older man had entered Say's life at a critical time—Say was only twenty-six and attempting to establish himself—and he may have filled the role left vacant when Say's father died. In many ways it was Maclure's character, philosophy, and interests—rather

Fig. 29. Frontispiece of Thomas Say's *American Entomology,* by Charles Alexandre Lesueur. Black and white steel engraving.

than those of Say's father—that mirrored the young man's own personality and aspirations. In any event, Maclure's advent released Say from essential financial worries and made possible the publication of his *American Entomology* in the elegant style he had hoped to present it.

The detailed black-and-white frontispiece by Charles Alexandre Lesueur, taken from the book's 1817 issue, shows a large tree framing a distant view of Philadelphia across the Delaware River, with the graceful steeple of

Christ Church rising behind sailboats and steamboats plying the river. About the tree, beetles, ants, termites, bees, spiders, and butterflies pursue instinctive routines. The book's hand-colored engravings of American insects, prepared by Cornelius Tiebout, were after drawings by Titian Peale. Say stated in the preface that the drawings "represent the present state of the arts in this country." Species of different genera are not shown on the same plate, an innovation advanced over the work of Wilson, Say's mentor in matters of concept and style.

Say asked his readers' indulgence concerning errors by submitting that whatever might be the book's "merits or defects, we must observe, that it is the first attempt of its kind in this country." He compared his "enterprise" to "that of a pioneer or early settler in a strange land," whose objective is to become knowledgeable with the "various productions" (insects) he meets with, "in order to select such as may be beneficial, either as regards his physical gratification, or his moral improvement, and in order to counteract the effects of others that may have a tendency to limit his prosperity."[4]

The book was well received by the press. After extolling the beauty of its plates and the rich layout, Boston's *North American Review* affirmed the prominence of Thomas Say as a naturalist: "No person, who has paid any attention to the advancement of science in this country for the last ten years, can be ignorant of the doings and movements of Mr. Say, or of his particular devotedness to the subjects of which he has treated in this volume."[5]

No praise from other quarters, however, could equal the endorsement of Say's peers at the Academy of Natural Sciences. It must have been immensely gratifying when Charles Lucien Bonaparte rose at the meeting of 14 December 1824 to make a motion, enthusiastically approved by his colleagues, "that in order to show the interest which the Academy take in the Advancement of The Natural History of this country and particularly in the labours of one of their most industrious and most successful associates, the Librarian be instructed to subscribe in their name for a copy of the American Entomology by Thomas Say."[6]

It strengthened Say's reputation abroad to send the book to his correspondents. A copy accompanied insect specimens he shipped to the German entomologist Christian Rudolph Wilhelm Wiedemann in Kiel, Germany. Say mentioned to Wiedemann that he hoped now to carry on the project "with some spirit" and would send him subsequent volumes as they were published.[7] He wrote Baron de Ferussac in Paris that he had posted copies to Count Pierre François Marie Auguste Dejean (a leading European entomologist who had been one of Napoleon's generals) and Anselme Gaetan Desmarest, as well as to the baron himself.[8]

By this time Say had already commenced volume 2. Besides Titian Peale, who had entirely illustrated the first volume, other artists would contribute their work to the second volume: Hugh Bridport, a painter of miniatures, associated for a time with the architect William Strickland; William W. Wood, an artist, entomologist, and publisher; and Lesueur. The number of artists employed in the work are an indication of Say's difficulty in getting any one of them to undertake the task alone. He wrote to his entomologist-friend Nicholas Marcellus Hentz in Northampton, Massachusetts: "Many thanks for your kind offer to assist me with your excellent drawings, if you resided here I should gladly avail myself of it, for we have not one here who can aid me as I could wish in this respect."[9] Hentz was an excellent painter of miniatures who was one of the first to study and draw American spiders. Forced to flee from his native France in 1816 after the fall of Napoleon, Hentz had lived for a few years in Philadelphia where he became an intimate friend of Lesueur's.[10] Hentz's drawings would undoubtedly have still further enhanced Say's *American Entomology*.

Because the second volume contained more anecdotes of insect behavior, Say had probably taken to heart the admonition expressed by the *North American Review* concerning his descriptions: "We are not sure that [Say] has decided wisely in confining himself so exclusively to rigid science, and introducing so little that can be interesting to the unskilled."[11] Sometimes he enhanced his exact scientific descriptions with visual images as vivid as the watercolors of his illustrators. Speaking of wood-boring beetles (family Buprestidae), he wrote that "many of these insects are gaily ornamented with the most splendid colours, which often shine with metallic brilliance. Some have a general coppery tint, whilst others present the beautiful contrast of fine yellow spots and lines, on a polished green or blue surface, and others exhibit the appearance of burnished gold, inlaid on emerald or ebony."[12] His poetic account of the behavior of certain moths sketches on the mind an indelible picture: "They are never seen to shoot, like meteors through the air, from flower to flower, balancing the body at each, in order to extract sweets from the nectary, but, unlike the Sphinx and Humming-bird, their flight is heavy and reluctant, and they receive food only in the state of repose."[13] Say opened volume 2 of *American Entomology* (1825) with a long essay on an agricultural pest, the peach tree borer, which he called *Aeperia exitiosa*—the right to name it being his as its first describer. He offered several methods for dealing with this destroyer of garden crops, orchards, and forest trees, and quoted various works on the subject. Among other insects that might "limit man's prosperity," Say named three new species of grasshopper and described in graphic detail the devastation wrought in Africa by their relatives, the locusts. "During their migrations in search of food, they move in immense dense masses, which resemble huge thunder or hail clouds, and at the termination of their career, every leaf is soon devoured, and the atmosphere is finally loaded with putrid exhalations from their dead bodies, producing pestilence in the train of a general famine, which is the consequence of their voracity." It was fortunate this species was not found in the United States, he said, but several American species "have already proved a very serious evil."[14]

In his discussion of the wasplike ichneumon fly, Thomas Say was the first to point out the insect's fascinating behavior in rearing its young and the resulting benefits to man: "Having found a caterpillar of suitable magnitude . . . [the female] places her eggs either upon the skin, or by puncturing it, within the body, notwithstanding the convulsive efforts of prevention made by the victim." The larvae, having emerged from the eggs of the insect, then feed on the body "of their Promethean victim, which continues to walk and feed as usual." He added that "the depredators are by no means indiscriminate in their choice of food" but dine on the fatty parts of the caterpillar, saving the vital organs for last when the larvae are nearly full size. Caterpillars destroyed by the parasitic ichneumon sawfly are the larvae of such pests as the gypsy moth and the cabbage looper.[15]

In speaking of the colorful scarab beetle, called *Scarabaeus tityus* by Linnaeus, Say explained the name's mythical origin: "Tityus in the heathen mythology, was a gigantic son of Jupiter and Elara, whom Apollo killed for offering violence to his mother Latona." It was Linnaeus, he said, who "endeavoured to connect Entomology with Mythology and the civil history of antiquity." Say referred to specimens of this beetle belonging to Frederick Melsheimer (John's father), whom he called "the parent of Entomology in this country"—a title often given to Say himself.

In a practice begun by Linnaeus, Say honored his friends by naming new species after them. Near the base of the Rockies he had first found the rare beetle he named after Thomas Nuttall, *Lytta nuttallii*. Nuttall not only had been Say's intimate friend since their initial meeting at William Bartram's house and through their many hours spent together at the academy; he was also one of Say's primary collectors. Nuttall had brought him numerous insect specimens from his 1818 trip on the Arkansas River.

Say had other friends at the Academy who encouraged his endeavors, including his old schoolmate Reuben Haines, a farmer deeply interested in agricultural science, and of course Lesueur. The camaraderie of these friends is evident in a note Haines wrote his mother from Wyck, his ancestral farm in Germantown, outside Philadelphia: "T. Say and Lesueur walked up to breakfast with me on 7 day [Quaker Saturday]. We spent the morning in exploring the pond in the woods for insects etc. . . . After dinner, by previous appointment T. Nuttall had an excursion for plants on the banks of the Wissahickon."[16] Two of Say's more youthful colleagues were his former zoological assistant, Titian Peale, and Charles Bonaparte, in a sense Say's protegé. In early 1824 Say and Lesueur nominated the latter, newly arrived from France, for Academy membership. Bonaparte was described at that time by a visitor to the institution as "a little, set, blackeyed fellow, quite talkative."[17] He was supposed to have borne a remarkable resemblance to his uncle, Napoleon.

Beginning in 1825, Charles Lucien Bonaparte (figure 30) published his continuation of Alexander Wilson's work on American birds. This exhaustive supplemental study, which appeared shortly after the second volume of Say's *American Entomology*, contained many entries written by Say, as well as numerous others reformed by him into proper English. The same Academy visitor who described Bonaparte also indicated, after attending an Academy meeting, the popular attitude in the 1820s toward detailed scientific studies of fauna: "To a novice, it seems curious, that men of the first intellect should pay so much attention to web-footed gentry with wings."[18] Still far in the future was the exact science of ornithology.

The publication of books by both Say and Bonaparte was of much interest to another devotee of "web-footed gentry," the capricious but brilliant John James Audubon, who hoped to publish *The Birds of America* in the United States. Since Say's own study had recently been published and enthusiastically received, Audubon may have thought to enlist his influence with the Philadelphia publishing establishment, and perhaps to avail himself of Say's scientific expertise. Aware that his English was imperfect, he may have had Say and his translations for Bonaparte in mind when he suggested to Haines that "your Lyceum [the Academy] . . . might give *one* Member who would be willing to spend some of his time daily to Anglicize my observations."[19]

Audubon was unpopular at the Academy, however. Much of the animosity toward him could be traced to the vice president, George Ord, who, at considerable personal expense, had completed Wilson's last two

Fig. 30. *Charles Lucien Bonaparte* (1803–1857), ornithologist, by T. H. Maguire, 1829. Stipple engraving. Courtesy of the American Philosophical Society.

volumes after the ornithologist's untimely death in 1813. Ord jealously perceived Audubon as an upstart intent on replacing Wilson as the expert on American birds. In any case, Academy members rejected Audubon's nomination for membership in 1824 because they did not respect him as a scientist. "Although many of my drawings are called Historical Illustrations of Birds More than real Ornithological representations," Audubon wrote resentfully to Haines in May 1825, "observations of a few of our best Judges in America I hope would soon counterpoise the opinion of a Paire [Ord and Alexander Lawson, Wilson's engraver] of Initiated Minds towards the Public Sanction."[20]

By the following December, Audubon despaired of publishing his book in America. Say apparently had evinced no desire to help him with his project, which may account for Audubon's negative reaction when he received from Haines a copy of Bonaparte's *Continuation*. Although Audubon described it as "handsome and scientific," he also said that "*nature has not put her stamp* upon it. There are great errors in it and yet some valuable parts, but, if it is not Willson who speaks, it is *Monsieur Say qui n'est qu'un homme d'Esprit*—Bonaparte *I think* has been abused and misled." He added that he was "surprised at the scarcity both of Subjects and Matter contained in it," and if Bonaparte would listen to him instead of to Thomas Say, he "would acknowledge, that although I have read but Little, I have seen a Great deal—in the woods."[21]

Audubon must have regarded Say as a "closet naturalist" despite his extensive field experience—Audubon had, after all, met Say in Cincinnati in 1819 while the latter was on his way to the Rockies. But more to the point, Say's meticulous scientific descriptions were markedly different from the anecdotal text, *Ornithological Biography* (1831–39), with which Audubon accompanied his bird paintings.

Audubon should not have expressed his sentiments about Bonaparte's *Continuation* to Haines, who was given to gossip. According to Bonaparte, Haines had the "kindness, not to say, simplicity" to repeat Audubon's derogatory appraisal. "He [Audubon] does not even grant me the honor of my errors," Bonaparte complained indignantly to a friend. "I have been *misled, betrayed*, says he, and if I had confided in him instead of having my pretended work written by Mr. Say (who, after all, says he, is but a *man of wit*) he would have stamped his hand upon it, whilst now it is altogether in contradiction with it! I have one part of his remarks which I read yesterday to several members of the Academy."[22]

Although Say was aware of Audubon's artistic talent, having seen his impressive watercolors in Cincinnati, he would not have liked the Frenchman's opportunistic and volatile personality. Perhaps Say was reminded too much of Constantine Rafinesque.

In 1825 Say was deeply involved in writing volume 3 of *American Entomology*. With his initial description, that of the walkingstick (family Phasmatidae), an insect related to the grasshopper, cricket, and mantid, he was one of the first American naturalists to discuss an insect's form and color for the purpose of survival in its environment. "Walkingsticks," he wrote, "are probably indebted for safety from the attacks of their enemies the birds, to their deceptive appearance, and by their general similarity in point of colour to the object on which they rest."[23]

Say's discussion of this curious insect brought new objectivity to old superstitions and, through rational explanation, contrasted traditional attitudes toward nature with modern scientific thought. The following excerpt from Thomas Say's *American Entomology* focuses on the persistence of myth in his own era:

> We are told that there was a time, when a piece of wood was transformed into a serpent, and even in the present age of knowledge, a hair fallen from the tail or mane of a horse into a stream of water, is believed by many to become animated into a distinct being; dead leaves shed by the parent tree are said to change gradually into animals of singular shape, and to have changed their place of abode under the eye of the historian who related the wonderful tale; dead sticks also were said to sprout legs, to move from place to place, and perform all the functions of a living body. These, and a thousand other equally ridiculous tales, were at one period or another, generally admitted as indisputable truths. . . . And although at present the possibility of making a living serpent out of wood, and the story of animated leaves and sticks would be despised as absurd, yet many are to be found both in Europe and America, who firmly believe in the reanimation of a horsehair.[24]

Say believed, however, that the most glaring errors often rested on the merest shadow of truth. The person who wrote of the walking leaf may have been fooled by a certain mantis whose wings resemble leaves, and the account of ambulating sticks could indeed be attributed to the insect under discussion. Walkingsticks were indigenous to many parts of the country in Say's time. He had found one crawling up an orange tree in Cumberland Island, Georgia, during his trip to Florida with Maclure, another in Missouri, and a third near Niagara Falls at the end of the expedition to the St. Peter's River. And during an excursion in the summer of 1825 with Maclure, he would come across several specimens at Franklin, New Jersey.

In the family Pompilidae, Say christened three new species of spider wasp and gave a detailed account of their habits, once again belying the accusations of critics that he was not interested in insect behavior:

> These insects associate by pairs, and make their nest in the earth. The female digs a hole in a sunny bank or declivity; when this is accomplished, she goes in search of a spider or caterpillar, which she punctures with her sting, and places

at the bottom of her nest. Having deposited an egg, either in or upon the prey, she closes the hole with earth, and abandons it. The young, hatched from the egg, has an abundant and convenient supply of food, in the body of the interred insect. . . . Descending the Arkansaw river, with Major Long's party, I was one day surprised to see a species of this genus, dragging along the ground the body of the gigantic Bird-catching spider.[25]

Say's great-grandfather John Bartram had sent wasp nests filled with spiders to both Peter Collinson in London and Dr. J. F. Gronovius in Leiden in 1744. Bartram's account of the wasps' use of spiders appeared in the *Philosophical Transactions of the Royal Society* in 1745.

Say concluded his study—which would remain in manuscript for several years—with one of the most familiar and beautiful of North American insects, the monarch butterfly, *Danaus plexippus*. The monarch had been named in the eighteenth century by Linnaeus in his *Systema Naturae* (1745), but Say added a few observations of his own: "[The Monarch] feeds on different species of Asclepias [butterfly weed], and is very abundant in the neighborhood of Philadelphia."[26] The watercolor illustration of a monarch by Titian Peale published in Say's *Entomology* was the first representation published in America of this now well-known insect. Mark Catesby had drawn it nearly a hundred years earlier, but his book had been published in England, as was John Abbot's *Natural History of the Rarer Lepidopterous Insects of Georgia* (1797), which also included a plate showing the monarch butterfly, although it was not named as such.[27] The modern entomologist Arnold Mallis states that Say's reputation as a pioneer taxonomist is today "solidly based because of such publications as *American Entomology* and [later] *American Conchology*."[28]

During the late summer of 1825, Say, Lesueur, Haines, Troost, and Say's cousin James Carmalt accompanied Maclure on a seven-week tour through parts of Pennsylvania, New Jersey, and New York. The journey's object was to visit a number of mineral sites, including the large anthracite coal mine at Mauch Chunk (present-day Jim Thorpe), Pennsylvania (figure 31). Coal, particularly the recently discovered anthracite (hard coal), was becoming increasingly valuable as fuel to replace wood in heating American buildings. For Say, the excursion was an opportunity not only to spend nearly two pleasant months with his colleagues but to collect insects from still other areas of the country. He would include several discoveries from the trip in the third volume of his book.

As the party followed the Schuylkill River, they passed Valley Forge—

"the now deserted ramparts peopled in 1777 by our suffering band of heroes," Haines wrote to his wife, Jane—and headed for Reading. The travelers dined at local taverns, eating only two meals a day to save time, and put up at inns recommended by friends. Comfortably ensconced in a coach and a two-wheeled gig, they progressed by easy stages. "Our company as I expected is a very pleasant one," Haines observed. "We travel leisurely, Maclure is willing to stop just where we please—a part walk on in advance, Lesueur with his gun and Say with fly catchers. Lesueur sketches all the interesting views."[29]

They visited mills, forges, and iron works, as well as the anthracite coal mine at Mauch Chunk, where Say and the others watched large amounts of "black gold" being extracted from the mountain. At the Moravian settlement in Nazareth, Pennsylvania, they saw the school, church, and gardens of the establishment, but decided to forgo an evening church service on learning it would be conducted in German and consist of a reading of letters from Europe.

Fig. 31. Large open pit coal mine with men working, Mauch Chunk, Pennsylvania, by Charles Alexandre Lesueur. Pencil sketch. Geology expedition with Say, Maclure, Troost, Haines, and Say's cousin, James Carmalt, in the summer of 1825. Courtesy of the Musée d'Histoire Naturelle du Havre, Le Havre, France. Copy at the American Philosophical Society.

There may have been a deeper reason than tourism for visiting the Moravians, since conversation during much of the journey had centered on the Welsh philanthropist Robert Owen and his recent purchase of the entire town of Harmonie, Indiana. Owen had bought the land and buildings from George Rapp, leader of a German religious community whose lifestyle was similar to that of the Moravians. At New Harmony, as the town was renamed, using the Harmonists' houses, dormitories, churches, mills, factories, and granaries, Owen was attempting to establish a new experimental society—a self-sufficient utopia of industrious, democratic inhabitants who owned everything in common except the land.

Maclure had been interested for years in radical improvements to society, especially to the country's educational system, but while intrigued by Owen's venture he remained hesitant about Owen the man. Say had met Owen in Philadelphia the previous year, had found him charismatic, and was philosophically interested in his plan for a new world, as were several of his more forward-thinking friends.

Soon after Say's return to Philadelphia in mid-September 1825, Maclure suggested that he and Lesueur accompany him to Mexico—the possible "land of milk and honey" that Say had sought but not found in Florida—with a stopover along the way to look at Owen's "utopia."

III

ALIGHTING
New Harmony, Indiana
1826–1834

My soul, do not seek immortal life,
but exhaust the realm of the possible.

PINDAR

CHAPTER 10

"The Boatload of Knowledge"

I now write to inform you that I expect to set out in the course of 2 or 3 days on a journey for the winter in company with Mr. Maclure; we shall visit Mr. Owen's settlement on the Wabash & thence proceed down the Mississippi.

Thomas Say to Thaddeus W. Harris
Philadelphia, 21 November 1825

S AY HAD BEEN AWARE of Robert Owen's ideas for social reform for several years from reading Owen's articles reprinted in the Philadelphia newspaper *Aurora*.[1] Say was a liberal thinker, an attribute inherited from his Quaker family and fostered by idealists like John Speakman. Impatient with the smug, entrenched society he saw around him in Philadelphia, Say had found Owen's plans for communitarian living inherently appealing.

Organized communities were part of Owen's attempt to reorder society so that men and women might more easily adapt to an industrial environment. Owen envisioned a "new moral world" void of "individualizing" institutions such as personal wealth, religion, and marriage, and he proposed a system of cooperation, with value based on labor. Karl Marx would develop this theory more fully in later years. Owen's approach was essentially nonpolitical, however, and was not based on class struggle or violent overthrow of the state.

The American and French revolutions had altered forever the structure of society on both sides of the Atlantic by giving the common people a voice in their own destiny. In America, where many sought new organizations in which to exercise their liberty, Owen found sympathetic listeners. A modern historian has said that "the origin of many aspects of Owenism lies in those elements of Enlightenment thought which were also influential in the early days of the Republic, so that a common base for sympathy and understanding was provided. Agrarianism, Deism, and Jeffersonian ideals [of freedom and the dignity of human rights] struck an answering chord in many Owenite breasts."[2]

One of the first of Say's friends to become an avowed Owenite was John Speakman, his partner in the ill-fated apothecary business the two men had opened in 1812. In the intervening years Speakman had moved to Pittsburgh, where he became involved with an Owenite group led by Benjamin Bakewell, a prominent glassmaker. A year or so before Say met Owen or heard anything about New Harmony, Speakman had written to him:

> It is the intention of some of us as soon as we can acquire the necessary funds to purchase and improve some insulated spot, and then form a community something like the Harmonites & Shakers, who we see have arrived at the height of prosperity although governed by Phantoms [mystical beliefs], and would it be slandering common sense to suppose that a number of rational beings could not do as well, in a community so organized that the interest of each individual depended on the prosperity of the whole. But our object is not riches, rather a school for ourselves and children; as it is particularly intended that the knowledge of nature shall be the polar star or grand object to which all our exertions shall tend.[3]

He concluded that there were no "learned or scientific men" among his group, but that "our grand object will be to make our Community a heaven for men of that description."

Speakman did not know how prophetic his letter was. A short time later Owen would purchase Harmonie in order to test his ideas of cooperative living, and the skeptical Maclure would join Owen's enterprise to promote his dream of an educational system coupled with an advanced scientific community.

Robert Owen, who has been called "the father of British socialism," was born in Newtown, Wales, in 1771, the son of a blacksmith. Owen's father belonged to a station in life higher than his profession would indicate, but fell on hard times. His son was thus forced to seek work at the age of twelve, after a scant formal education. Intelligent and enterprising, Owen became manager of a large cotton mill in Manchester, England, by the time he was nineteen. He was the first industrialist in Great Britain to import American sea-island cotton—grown on the islands off South Carolina and Georgia. In 1800, he moved to New Lanark, Scotland, to take charge of the largest cotton-spinning mill in Great Britain, which he and several partners had bought from David Dale, a Scot whose daughter Owen subsequently married.

The next quarter century, encompassing the industrial revolution's beginning, was especially challenging for Owen. Factory conditions all over Britain were appalling, but at New Lanark Owen pioneered reforms to ease his workers' long hours and squalid living conditions. A benefactor of his country's economic growth, he nevertheless saw the means as too exacting to justify the results, and although initially he was a reformer only of factory conditions he gradually came to believe that society in general needed reorganization. Over the years Owen developed the ideas of communitarianism and cooperation that he would attempt to put into practice in the New World.

Owen planned to improve his workers' lives through mass education, founding infant schools and instituting continuing studies for adults. Although his reforms were widely discussed and New Lanark became an object of pilgrimage for other reformers as well as for statesmen and even royalty, he was discouraged with the actual practice of his theories. They were not accepted as he had hoped, primarily because he advocated, among other sweeping changes, that the deeply entrenched and revered institutions of religion and marriage be abolished—a proposition put forward earlier by the influential English reformer William Godwin. This was too much for the people Owen intended to help, and they turned against him, forcing him to realize the existing social order's overwhelming power. Clearly, he believed, if his educational plans were ever to succeed, the entire society as it then existed would have to be radically altered.[4]

When the American philanthropist Richard Flower offered for sale the German evangelist George Rapp's entire town of Harmonie, Indiana, Owen saw an opportunity for the practical application of his concepts. Flower was amazed that Owen was willing to exchange his comfortable life in Scotland for the hardships of the American frontier. But, observed Owen's son Robert Dale Owen, "he [Flower] did not know that my father's one ruling desire was for a vast theatre on which to try his plans for social reform."[5] Owen's dream would not develop the way he envisioned it, but it has been said that "of all the dozens of backwoods Utopias reflecting the spirit of the Enlightenment that struggled hopefully to take root on American soil in the nineteenth century, none would be more significant than New Harmony."[6]

Throughout the first quarter of the nineteenth century, the life of William Maclure, who was eight years older than Owen, had paralleled that of the younger man in ways important to their eventual joining of forces. In Great Britain Maclure had, like Owen, been a successful businessman early in life and had become wealthy by middle age. Imbued with ideas of social change fostered by the French Revolution, with which he sympathized, Maclure believed that only through education could life for the masses be improved. He was convinced that the old "monkish system" of classical education had been useless in his mercantile life, and he saw no reason to provide it for the common people; scientific knowledge would be more beneficial. Combining this theory with the advanced educational reforms of the Swiss educator Johann Heinrich Pestalozzi, who incorporated physical labor into his regimen, Maclure set out to put his concepts into practice. While Pestalozzi advocated retaining class distinctions, however, because he thought society would always have rich and poor, Maclure wanted to abolish all such divisions.

Maclure moved to Philadelphia in 1799 and became an American citizen. Several years later, with the idea of establishing a Pestalozzian school in his adopted country, he persuaded one of Pestalozzi's Swiss coworkers, Joseph Neef, to emigrate and found a school in Philadelphia that Maclure would subsidize. During the following years Maclure indulged in his other passion—geology—crossing the Allegheny Mountains at least fifty times, by his own calculation, in order to prepare the first geological map of the eastern United States. His map was published by the American Philosophical Society in 1809, and in an enlarged and corrected version in 1818. Because of his work in this field, Maclure has been called the father of American geology.

In 1819 Maclure returned to Europe, where he bought from the liberal Spanish government then in power ten thousand acres of confiscated church land on which to establish agricultural and mechanical schools.[7] At the same time Maclure became involved in Paris with two other Pestalozzian teachers, Marie Duclos Fretageot and William Phiquepal. Maclure had known Phiquepal in Philadelphia some years earlier when he had been Joseph Neef's associate in Neef's school at Schuylkill Falls. It was Phiquepal, proposed by Academy founder Nicholas Parmentier, also French, who had nominated Maclure for Academy membership.[8]

When Maclure's Spanish schools and land were taken over by the reactionaries of a succeeding government in 1824 and he was personally threatened with kidnapping, he returned to America to pursue his philanthropic goals. He wrote Benjamin Silliman at Yale that he was "fatigued and tired with the injustice, cruelty, oppression, and folly of despotism" that he had found in Spain.[9] Besides, he had always had America in mind as a place to try out his ideas of educational reform. Three years earlier he had provided the means for Mme. Fretageot to emigrate and start a school in

Philadelphia, and in 1824 he sent over Phiquepal for the same purpose. A year after that, when all the excitement over Owen came to a head, Maclure was understandably reluctant to move the two schools he had so recently established to the western frontier.

Although impressed with Owen's theories, Thomas Say initially shared with some of his acquaintances a less-than-serious attitude regarding John Speakman's proposal for a radical utopian community. Early in 1824, Mme. Fretageot wrote from Philadelphia to Maclure in Spain:

> Mr. Say read to me the letter you wrote dated 30th November in which you do not approve the community of wealth. I inquired about the project, and laughed much when asking how many they were to form such society. He answered that first they were a great number but now they remain but 2 or 3, that the others under different pretexts declined of joining the society. After some pleasant remarks I told they would never put such project in execution if they cannot have some ladies among them.[10]

But by November 1824 it was no longer a joking matter to Mme. Fretageot. She had heard of Owen's intention to buy Harmonie, and when the philanthropist visited her in Philadelphia on his way to make the historic purchase she wrote excitedly to Maclure: "You have no idea what pleasure I felt when I was talking by the side of a man whose actions and principles are so much in harmony with mine."[11]

Say, too, was interested in meeting Owen. Donald MacDonald, a young Scottish captain in the Royal Engineers who had accompanied Owen to America, noted in his diary that on returning to his hotel after visiting the Academy, where he had met "the librarian, Mr. Say," he had "found Mr. Owen & several gentlemen [Say and Lesueur] looking at his plans & discussing his views."[12]

In early January 1825, Robert Owen purchased the entire town of Harmonie, Indiana—which he renamed New Harmony—from the German religious group called Harmonists, led by the zealous George Rapp. Owen left his son William in charge while he returned east to promote his new community. Approximately eight hundred people flocked to New Harmony in the first months of its existence, spurred by Owen's immensely successful publicity campaign.

Owen returned to Philadelphia in early February and made strenuous efforts to reawaken interest in his project. In this he was extremely successful, especially with Mme. Fretageot, who hinted to Maclure the idea of combining efforts with Owen: "After all that I know concerning his plan, I have no doubt you will change something in your intention about [her Philadelphia school], I talked with [Owen] on the subject. He said that the more good means are reunited the more effects are powerful." Mme. Fretageot attempted to persuade Maclure by telling him of his friends' interest in the project: "There is already a great many persons of this town making their preparations. Several of them are your acquaintances Doctor Troost, Mr. Say, Mr. Speakman, [a] great many others, who expect you will join them."[13] Troost and Speakman had every intention of joining the community, but Say's later letters to Thaddeus Harris and Nicholas Hentz stating that he was going "to visit" Owen's "establishment on the Wabash" suggest that he did not anticipate moving to New Harmony.[14]

Owen spent the rest of February and March in Washington promoting his plan, even delivering two speeches on his ideas to a large crowd in the Capitol's Hall of Representatives. President James Monroe and the newly elected John Quincy Adams were in the audience for his second speech, as well as members of the Cabinet, Supreme Court, and Congress.

On returning to Philadelphia at the end of March, he wrote to Maclure, who was still overseas: "I am surrounded by your friends here & we have had much conversation respecting you & your charitable objects. The result of which is a great desire on the part of all of them to see you here & to have your direction in various important matters which they have before them."[15]

Maclure remained dubious about this American experiment, however, even though he had visited New Lanark in August 1824, only weeks before Owen was offered the option to buy Harmonie. Maclure had been duly impressed by Owen's improvements in the Scottish town, but even so, he cautioned Mme. Fretageot that the people attracted to a community like New Harmony would be "stubborn, crooked and too often bent in an opposite direction from their own most evident interests."[16] He recommended that she remain in Philadelphia rather than join in such an "arduous" undertaking.

When Maclure arrived in New York in July, he wrote to her that the only object of most of the people he had met since landing was to make money, and that they had no interest in Owen's ideas: "Wild speculations and golden dreams entirely occupies the upper stories of most of the Bipeds. If I was to take the nation from the sample I have seen, I should be apt to think Mr. O. had taken silence for consent, when it was only indifference bordering on contempt." But he added that "in spite of the mania I see here, am much gratifyed by the general improvement in Society, and think Mr. O. may advance more rapidly than I had expected, but still the experiment is to be tryed."[17]

Owen visited Philadelphia again on 4 July 1825, and his presence excited much enthusiasm. Since the previous winter the intelligentsia of the city had been hotly debating his ideas for a "new moral world." Reuben Haines, writing facetiously to his vacationing cousin Ann, reflected the general feeling that July: "As I know thee likes a little excitement I may perhaps as well let thee know how much thee has lost by not accepting my invitation to return home last 7th day. Our breakfast company this morning were Mr. Owen, Dr. Price, Mr. Phiquepal . . . T. Say." Had Ann been present, Haines said, she could have taken part with Owen in a discussion of almost three hours. "[Owen] has now 1000 people at New Harmony, when with 5 weeks instruction in the New System he leaves [them] to govern themselves whilst he goes to Europe to bring out his wife and family and endeavors to bring to a close all his concerns in the old world . . . T. Say and myself expect to accompany him in the steam boat to Point Breeze."[18]

MacDonald recorded this visit to Haines in his journal, mentioning that Owen had spent the subsequent night in Bordentown, New Jersey, at Joseph Bonaparte's, "who had been most anxious to make his acquaintance, & sent his carriage down to the landing place on the banks of the Delaware to receive him. Mr. Owen was accompanied by Mr. Say the naturalist. They sat inside the carriage & Lucien & Murat's [Napoleon's brother and brother-in-law respectively] sons on the box, one driving & the other opening the gates. The party were much interested and delighted with the New Plans, & promised a visit to Harmony next year."[19]

In October 1825 Say still regarded his forthcoming trip to New Harmony as a digression from his journey to Mexico. He wrote to Nicholas Hentz: "I suppose you have heard that our worthy president Mr. Maclure has returned to us [from Europe], I shall accompany him this winter on a western & southern journey. Mr. Speakman & Dr. Troost, our fellow members, have gone with their families to join Mr. Owen's establishment at New Harmony on the Wabash."[20]

On 6 November 1825, Robert Owen landed in New York from Scotland where he had returned the previous July. He met at once with some of the people ready to join his new community, including young Lucy Way Sistare and her two sisters, whose mother ran a fashionable boardinghouse on Broadway. The girls were pupils of Mme. Fretageot in Philadelphia. Owen's entourage included his son Robert Dale Owen, Donald Mac-

Donald, and an English architect, Stedman Whitwell, who had designed an elaborate complex of buildings for New Harmony. Whitwell's large model was displayed in New York and later in Philadelphia and Washington.[21] Before leaving for Philadelphia, the party called on many prominent New Yorkers, including the governor.

Owen and his companions left for Philadelphia on 12 November and that evening conferred with Say, Maclure, Haines, and other members of the Academy. Again there was a flurry of activity that included visits, meetings, and preparations. On the front page of the *Aurora General Advertiser*, amid notices for mackerel, ox hides, bees wax, and bombazines, an announcement called for "Artificers and Mechanics—Wanted Immediately at New Harmony." There followed a long list of job vacancies for skilled workers, including farmers, "vinedressers," weavers, dyers, distillers, bricklayers, and bookbinders.[22]

The weeks preceding Say's departure for the West were frantic. Since he had not put himself through such a maelstrom of activity before his other expeditions, he may have had a premonition that he would be away for a long time. Although he did not resign from any of the committees on which he served at the Academy and elsewhere—and he was duly reelected to them all for the following year—the Academy *Minutes* reflect Say's desperate efforts to deliver to the members all the papers he had been working on. For the 18 October meeting he read an essay describing marine shells recently discovered on the American East Coast; the following week he presented an addendum to his paper on shells and read another on "New Coleopterus Insects [beetles] of the United States." The first two weeks of November he continued his insect essay, in which he refuted three names recently published by John Le Conte that he himself had previously published—two in the *Journal* and one in *American Entomology*. (Le Conte would have his revenge for this questioning of his scientific integrity.) In a final letter to Thaddeus Harris in Boston, Say mentioned that "on this expedition" he hoped "to obtain some additional materials" for "Descriptions of the Insects of the U.S.," which he had been working on for several years.[23] He left behind a record number of five papers to be approved for publication in the *Journal*.

Say, Lesueur, Maclure, and Mme. Fretageot with her assistant, Lucy Sistare, and Lucy's teen-age sisters, Frances and Sarah, left Philadelphia on the stagecoach for Pittsburgh at 3 A.M. on 27 November 1825, a clear but cold

Sunday morning. Local inns where the party put up were pleasant and the roads were reasonably good. It was a relief to Say that Maclure paid all the bills because his own funds were almost gone. This perpetual indifference to the need for money can certainly be attributed as much to Say's personality as to his profession. Also, he may have regarded Maclure's subsidy as payment for continually giving in to the older man's plans.

At Pittsburgh a week was spent outfitting a keelboat—the water level being too low for a steamboat—for the journey down the Ohio. Named the *Philanthropist* by the party (see figure 32), it was later dubbed "the Boatload of Knowledge" by a New Harmony resident because of the eminent scientists it had brought to the colony. Eighty-five feet long by fourteen feet wide, the craft was divided into four compartments: one to accommodate the six boatmen hired to man the oars—"sweeps"—and three for the passengers, including a large cabin for dining and general activities, a kitchen, and the ladies cabin, called "Paradise."[24]

Besides Say, Lesueur, Maclure, Mme. Fretageot and the three Sistares, the party now included Owen, his son, a servant Schmidt; a Swiss artist who had accompanied Mme. Fretageot from Paris; Phiquepal, with ten students, including Mme. Fretageot's two nephews Peter and Victor Duclos; and Dr. and Mrs. William Price from Philadelphia with their three children. Dr. Price, whom Say had known since their childhood years at Westtown, had been intrigued with Owenism for some time and had even visited Owen's factory town at New Lanark. Also on board were several workmen recruited from the advertisement.

In the early afternoon of 8 December, the *Philanthropist* pulled away from its Pittsburgh mooring and moved down the Allegheny into the Ohio, with its passengers all in high spirits. But the mood changed the following day when the boat ran aground and remained fast despite concerted efforts to free it. Eventually six men came from Economie—the new town only seven miles away where George Rapp had relocated his followers—and dislodged it with long poles.

A few days later, ice on the river began to thicken, and with great effort the boat was rowed to shore. Say took the opportunity, with Robert Dale Owen and several others, to hunt in the woods bordering the river. On his return he learned of a further mishap: Phiquepal had struck his head severely in a fall and had been taken to a nearby farmhouse for care. The evening grew colder and it began to snow. Robert Dale wrote in his journal that "the ladies" were becoming "disgusted" and that one of them had been

Fig. 32. Interior of the *Philanthropist,* 8 December, 1825, by Charles Alexandre Lesueur. Pencil sketch. Courtesy of the Musée d'Histoire Naturelle du Havre, Le Havre, France. Copy at the American Philosophical Society.

Fig. 33. Pittsburgh waterfront showing the *Philanthropist,* 8 December 1825, by Charles Alexandre Lesueur. Pencil sketch. Courtesy of the Musée d'Histoire Naturelle du Havre, Le Havre, France. Copy at the American Philosophical Society.

in tears that morning at breakfast; "It is somewhat of a good education for her and for all of us," he stated philosophically. "As for myself, seldom have I had a better time."[25]

Say, having been designated captain, took the myriad inconveniences of the journey with his usual composure. "[He] goes about it competently and handles the crew in the most clever manner," Owen's son observed.[26] Not so Maclure. A week later, suffering from a bad head cold and having had quite enough of the *Philanthropist*, he set out overland with Mme. Fretageot for the town of Beaver, Pennsylvania.

One night Say was awakened by a thunderous roar that sent him and everyone else on deck. It proved to be the ice breaking up in the river. Fearing the boat might be crushed, he ordered passengers and baggage ashore. It all seemed more of a game than a catastrophe to the sleepy voyagers, who joked and laughed as they gathered up their possessions. When at last it appeared that most of the ice had gone by, Say summoned the passengers back on board. The following day Maclure and Mme. Fretageot rejoined the boat party with the unwelcome news that masses of ice still clogged the river upstream. Much discussion followed about whether to start off before it floated past.[27]

New Year's day dawned bleak and cold. The ice had not broken up, nor would it for another week. Say read, hunted, and chopped wood for the stove. The keelboat had become quite homey, with sounds of quiet conversation and the comforting smell of baking bread filling the compartments daily. An array of specimens destined for the future museum at New Harmony, including preserved birds, fish, and small mammals, were hung each day on the walls of the main cabin, despite some objections.

The occupants in general adjusted as well as could be expected to the primitive, confining life, except for Maclure, who was no longer used to such discomfort and grew impatient with the interminable delay. Once again he took to solid ground with Mme. Fretageot and headed by carriage for Steubenville, further down the Ohio. MacDonald and Whitwell caught up with the boat at that point, having taken Owen's New Harmony model first to Washington and then to Monticello for the aged Jefferson's approval.

For Thomas Say, the trip was in one way perhaps the most pleasant he had ever taken. Forced by the cramped quarters and long days to become intimate with everyone, Say, who had not since his childhood been in such close proximity to women for such an extended period, found himself seeking the company of Lucy Sistare, Mme. Fretageot's pretty young

Fig. 34. Say and Maclure reading aboard the *Philanthropist,* by Charles Alexandre Lesueur. Pencil sketch. Courtesy of the Musée d'Histoire Naturelle du Havre, Le Havre, France. Copy at the American Philosophical Society.

protégé and assistant. Never had he felt so attracted to a woman as he was to this vivacious young teacher, while she in turn seemed pleased by his attentions. At twenty-five, she was thirteen years his junior, yet in conversation they were completely at ease, laughing at the same things and sharing similar opinions about their fellow travelers. Say found Lucy's sharp wit especially entertaining. To Lucy, the tall naturalist who had been to the Rocky Mountains was soft-spoken and kind; at the same time she had seen him brusque and authoritative as the boat's commander. He certainly knew a great deal about nature, medicine, and Indian lore, as well as history, literature, and art. This last interested her particularly.

On 8 January Say and the other men decided to cut a path through the ice to allow the boat access to an open channel—an arduous procedure that

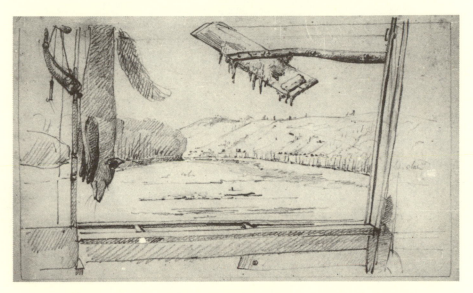

Fig. 35. View looking toward Five Mile Creek through a window of the *Philanthropist*, showing a fox skin hanging up to dry, and an ice-covered sweep, by Charles Alexandre Lesueur. Pencil sketch. Courtesy of the Musée d'Histoire Naturelle, Le Havre, France. Copy at the American Philosophical Society.

took an entire day (see figure 36). But after four weeks of deadlock, with Phiquepal back on board and with plenty of wood and provisions, the *Philanthropist* was ready to continue. At dawn it moved down the Ohio, making good time as both men and women took turns at the sweeps. That evening the boat reached Steubenville, where the ten-year-old son of Judge Benjamin Tappan, a prominent anti-slavery leader and future U.S. senator, came aboard, destined for Maclure's school at New Harmony.

At Wheeling the next day Maclure and Mme. Fretageot reboarded, Owen having gone ahead in the mail stage. To reach Cincinnati would require nine days vigorous rowing—exercise that both Say and Lucy Sistare enjoyed because it helped keep them warm in the biting cold of early January. At night lively conversation and reading filled the hours agreeably, and on occasion, when the evening was mild and the moon bright, others joined them on the top deck for music making (figure 37).

At Louisville, a pilot was taken on board to guide the boat over the two-mile-long rapids. With the river high from melting ice and "with all hands to the sweeps," this was accomplished swiftly and without incident.

During a brief stopover at Louisville, Say and Maclure talked with Joseph Neef, who had moved his family there after his school failed in Philadelphia, apparently because he had refused to teach religion. Both were pleased to hear that Neef intended selling his farm and moving to New Harmony.

After the pilot of the *Philanthropist* was put ashore at Shippingport, a steamboat was hailed and Schmidt, Owen's servant, boarded to go to New Harmony in advance of the party and there hire wagons so he could meet the *Philanthropist* at Mt. Vernon for the passengers' overland transportation.

Four days later Schmidt was at the Mt. Vernon landing, as planned, flanked by several wagons. It was high time to quit the *Philanthropist*—the river was freezing up once again and all were eager to escape another prolonged imprisonment. Half the passengers, including Say and Lucy, perhaps out of sheer bravado, elected to stay aboard and chance the journey

Fig. 36. Safe harbor, 8 January 1826, by Charles Alexandre Lesueur. Pencil sketch. Men cutting a path through the ice to the Ohio River to liberate the *Philanthropist* in foreground. Courtesy of the Musée d'Histoire Naturelle, Le Havre, France. Copy at the American Philosophical Society.

Fig. 37. Passengers on the roof of the *Philanthropist,* 10 January 1826, by Charles Alexandre Lesueur. Pencil sketch. Courtesy of the Musée d'Histoire Naturelle, Le Havre, France. Copy at the American Philosophical Society.

Fig. 38. Departure of the *Philanthropist* from Cincinnati, by Charles Alexandre Lesueur. Pencil sketch. Courtesy of the Musée d'Histoire Naturelle, Le Havre, France. Copy at the American Philosophical Society.

up the Wabash to New Harmony, while the rest loaded the wagons and set off posthaste. Two days later when the river began to freeze in earnest, Say and his companions had to abandon the boat and head overland after all.

On the night of 25 January 1826, almost two months after leaving Philadelphia, Thomas Say arrived at the local tavern in New Harmony, Indiana, and fell deeply asleep in Robert Owen's "utopia."

CHAPTER 11
Utopia Confronted

Having arrived here, we became interested in the singular spectacle which this place presented: we were involved in the vortex of experiment to realize the dreams of perfection in human association, which had been so confidently and imposingly promulgated.

Thomas Say to Thaddeus W. Harris
New Harmony, Indiana, 4 January 1829

S AY AWOKE TO THE EXCITEMENT and debate of a town in transition. Owen had arrived two weeks earlier, had discarded the "Preliminary Society" that he had inaugurated the previous May, and was now forming his "Community of Equality." Although Say was theoretically only a visitor, it was impossible not to become involved. He found himself listening to numerous arguments, for hardly anyone agreed on the community's ideal operation. Owen had succeeded too well in promoting his utopian dream. His initial mistake in throwing open the doors without discrimination had brought nearly a thousand people to New Harmony in only one year. Hangers on and ne'er-do-wells of all types were attracted by the prospect of partaking equally of the renowned British philanthropist's benevolence. Few were the skilled workers—farmers, manufacturers, and merchants—so urgently needed to make a cooperative community work. Those who stayed away understood only too well the fundamentals of competition underlying such an organization; they had no wish to share the fruits of their labor with the shiftless and lazy.

With George Rapp's once-thriving community to serve as model, Owen believed that, given freedom from religious and marital constraints and the "negative pressures" of accumulating individual wealth, his new society would go far beyond Rapp's. But he failed to take into account that religion and superstition were the unifiers that made the German community so cohesive and productive.

Rapp's followers, Lutheran dissenters from Wurttemberg, in present-day Germany, revered him and surrendered themselves completely to his protection. He had brought them to America in 1803 to settle in western

Pennsylvania but decided that a more southerly climate was needed to cultivate grapes. In 1815 he purchased twenty thousand acres in the far southwest corner of what became in 1816 the state of Indiana. This land lay near the Wabash River, with its commercially important connection to the Ohio and Mississippi. These industrious peasants, who called their settlement Harmonie, set about building houses, barns, mills, kilns, and granaries. They also constructed a school for free education, two churches, a bank, a general store, a tavern, and a post office. By 1819 they had fenced and planted nearly three thousand acres of grains, tobacco, cotton, flax, and sugarcane, as well as vineyards and peach, apple, and pear orchards. Each family had a well-built house, a neatly fenced yard, and a cow; single people lived in dormitories. Although life was rigorous and hours were long, it was said that a small orchestra played while the workers labored and that vases of flowers decorated the factories.[1]

Religious beliefs were based on millennialism, the idea that after two thousand years—time near at hand—Christ would reappear and life would cease. As it was pointless to bring children into a world shortly to end, celibacy was advocated. Rapp's beliefs were so well known abroad, from foreign travelers and social theorists, that Byron used them as part of a witty discourse on marriage in his poem *Don Juan* published in March 1824:

> When Rapp the Harmonist embargo'd marriage
>   In his harmonious settlement—(which flourishes
> Strangely enough without miscarriage,
>   Because it breeds no more mouths than it nourishes,
> Without those sad expenses which disparage
>   What Nature naturally most encourages)—
> Why call'd he "Harmony" a state sans wedlock?
> Now here I have got the preacher at a dead lock.[2]

Rapp's decision to sell Harmonie and move back to Pennsylvania was principally based on the animosity of neighboring settlers, who had to pay high prices for the Harmonists' excellent manufactured goods, and also the economic advantage the new site offered on the Ohio.[3] Outsiders theorized that Rapp had found the atmosphere unhealthy, "subject to heat and confined air."[4]

The incoming New Harmony community, of which Thomas Say soon found himself an unwitting part, would be substantially different. Instead of a peaceful, subjugated populace led by an absolute ruler who monitored each aspect of community life, there was a chaotic, diverse mob, few of whom felt even a moral commitment to the town's absentee owner. Robert Owen's twenty-three-year-old son William, who had been left for seven months to govern the Preliminary Society when Owen returned to England in June 1825, entertained serious reservations about his father's experiment: "The enjoyment of a reformer is much more in contemplation, than in reality. . . . I doubt whether those who have been comfortable and contented in their old mode of life, will find an increase of enjoyment when they come here."[5]

Marie Fretageot was initially impressed with the look of New Harmony but was somewhat apprehensive about the residents. She wrote to Reuben Haines's mother that some of the houses would be found "handsome" even in Philadelphia, but because of the large number constructed of logs, the town itself did not "appear in its proper light." She found the inhabitants a mixture of Americans and Europeans with "manners" so different that very few families could live together "in good harmony."[6]

Economic difficulties also were all too apparent, since the town's manufacturing apparatus had been allowed to slump. A cotton-spinning factory that generated three to four hundred pounds of yarn per week under the Harmonists now turned out a fraction of that amount, while the spacious brick dye house with its large copper kettles was closed and locked. The sawmill lay idle, as did the water mill, which had produced sixty barrels of flour in a twenty-four-hour period. New Harmony boasted no potters, saddlers, harness makers, leather dressers, coppersmiths, brush or comb makers, glaziers, or bookbinders, although soap, candles, glue, hats, and shoes were produced with varying degrees of sophistication.[7] The policy of exchanging work for staples, such as food and clothing, by using certificates to be "cashed" at the central store, did not work. It was virtually impossible to evaluate a person's work-time equitably; neither cerebral nor physical endeavor could be equated with goods.

Say was confronted on his arrival with a raw frontier town seething with variant ideas on how things should be run. As the days passed and Maclure made no mention of continuing their journey, it was impossible not to be drawn into the "vortex of experiment." Maclure's interest in New Harmony was solely to effect social change by establishing schools where the teaching of science would be paramount, thereby putting his educational theories into practice. But there would be more to it than that, and he would soon become entangled in the community's multitudinous affairs.

Maclure could see at once that the constitution adopted on the very day he and Say arrived did not come to grips with the basic economics of running the organization. Astonishingly, nothing was mentioned about the ownership of land, and within two weeks the document was scrapped. "The new voyage had begun, but the chartroom was empty," as the historian Arthur Bestor described it.[8] His statement neatly characterizes the next few months at New Harmony. Disillusionment set in as plan followed plan and schisms formed in the community. A group of backwoodsmen, refusing to accept Owen's ideas on religion, created their own faction, which they called Macluria in the mistaken belief that Maclure was more orthodox in his religious views than Owen. Three weeks later a group of English farmers formed a third community. Justifiably dissatisfied with the agricultural practices employed until then, they bought 1,400 acres from Owen for $7,000, to be paid in installments. "Feiba-Peveli," the curious name they gave their community, was derived from a scheme put forward by the architect Whitwell whereby the name of every town in the United States would be based on its geographical location, with letters representing the numbers of its latitude and longitude—an idea soon rejected.

Owen finally offered to turn over the buildings and land to the community for a sum of $126,520, to be paid over twelve years at 5 percent interest.[9] After protracted deliberation, a group of twenty-four agreed to take on this responsibility, but this plan, too, was doomed to fail: when labor was turned into remuneration, no way could be found to relate the work of the skilled craftsmen with that of the unskilled, and malingerers presented an ongoing problem. Maclure suggested still another reorganization, in which similar occupations would be grouped together in separate societies, while all still contributed to the whole. This arrangement was agreed upon and the School of Education, the Agricultural and Pastoral Society, and the Mechanic and Manufacturing Society were formed. The residents were still required to spend additional time in manual labor, including washing, cooking, making shoes, farming, or participating in other communal activities.

For a while after Maclure's plan was adopted, the majority entered into the spirit of communal living and developed a lively social life. Weekly cotillions were held in the large brick hall, Rapp's former church, in addition to frequent concerts interspersed with poetry readings. A dance called "the new social system" was introduced at balls, and a community costume was adopted in order to illustrate the idea of equality. Ironically, only the "literati," as they were called, wore the costume, thereby accomplishing exactly the opposite result from that for which it was designed.

Karl Bernhard, the Duke of Saxe-Weimar, who visited New Harmony in April 1826, described the women's outfit as a coat reaching to the knee and worn over pantaloons "such as little girls wear among us." The men's costume consisted of "wide pantaloons buttoned over a boy's jacket, made of a light material, without a collar." The duke noted in his journal his meeting with Thomas Say, who was dressed in this singular fashion. "I renewed acquaintance here with Mr. Say," he wrote in his journal, "a distinguished naturalist from Philadelphia, whom I had been introduced to at the Wistar Party there; unfortunately he had found himself embarrassed in his fortune, and was obliged to come here as a friend of Mr. M'Clure. This gentleman appeared quite comical in the costume of the society, before described, with his hands full of hard lumps and blisters, occasioned by the unusual labour he was obliged to undertake in the garden."[10]

Say's first six months in New Harmony were enough to make his head spin. He wrote philosophically to Charles Lucien Bonaparte that "so many events have occurred since we left Philadelphia, that years seem to have been condensed into the space of a few months & our span of life to have been correspondingly expanded; after all, it does not seem to be the length of time we exist, but the number of interesting or agreeable incidents that crowd it, that make the lease of life worth holding." He added that he had been "agreeably employed," but because he lacked his books and collections he had not been able "to labour in the fruitful vineyard with as much assiduity as could have been desired."[11]

Say wrote this letter from Columbus, Ohio, while on an excursion with Maclure through Ohio and Kentucky from early June until early October. Their purpose was to visit other experimental communities, such as those at Yellow Springs and Xenia, Ohio, to see how they were managed. By this time Say realized that on his return to New Harmony in the fall he would probably be living there permanently. He had written the Academy of Natural Sciences to this effect, for the minutes of 25 July 1826 record, "Mr. Say's resignation as a member of the Committee of Publications was offered and accepted." The trip to Mexico had been indefinitely postponed.

Say wrote Bonaparte of his position in Maclure's communities of education, agriculture, and mechanics, saying that he belonged "to the first of these, & must therefore be supposed to know more of it than of the others." Maclure planned to invest $49,000 in the education society, which, Say explained, would allow his community to pay Owen for "two thirds of the town & 900 acres of land for the experimental farming Schools; we have the large hall, the church, boarding school, Mansion House, large

Granaries, besides a number of brick & frame houses capable of accommodating from 1000 to 2000 pupils between the ages of two & 18 years; and hope to have every facility of imparting a good & rational education."[12] Maclure's purchase would encompass the nucleus of the town, including the most important buildings.

Say's remarks on the educational ideas he and Maclure evolved on their journey have a decided echo of Maclure but indicate an enthusiasm and sense of involvement on Say's part that ring of conviction. Regarding his future students, he told Bonaparte, "it is not intended that they shall have 7 years at latin, greek or lilliputian & that the remainder of their time shall be devoted to what cannot be understood or to what no one can gain an accurate knowledge of." The students would be taught natural history "in its most comprehensive sense," mathematics, and the arts, "so as to make them useful members of society." Say assured his friend that, although he was interested in education, he was still primarily devoted to science, adding that with the assistance of a good library and a printing press for colored plates, he intended to print his own books on natural history.[13]

Maclure would attend to both these requirements, and would, in addition provide a wealth of equipment. The preceding February a New Harmony resident had written to his son: "There are now at New Orleans on their way hither a vast collection of books, philosophical apparatus & musical instruments weighing upwards of 50 tons. In Harmony there will be the best Library & the best school in the United States."[14] These supplies had been shipped from Philadelphia to New Orleans, then up the Mississippi to Shawneetown on the Ohio, where they were picked up by the *Philanthropist* and finally delivered to New Harmony when the ice melted sufficiently to allow the boat to proceed up the Wabash. A printing press arrived later.

Maclure wrote to Mme. Fretageot from Cincinnati, where Say spent most of August 1826 at the natural history museum describing a large collection of newly acquired specimens, that he had "given an order . . . for books, copperplates etc. wanted for the publications of Lesueur & Say's works."[15] At the same time Say wrote to induce both the printer and engraver of *American Entomology* to join the New Harmony community. The printer, Samuel Augustus Mitchell, refused Say's invitation, but the engraver, Cornelius Tiebout, arrived in early October. He was an accomplished artisan, well known and respected in the Philadelphia art world, and Say considered his coming a stroke of good fortune.

Behind all Say's plans for intellectual endeavors lurked a personal reason for staying in New Harmony: he had fallen in love with Lucy Way Sistare. Spirited and intelligent, Lucy was described, along with another young woman, by the Duke of Saxe-Weimar as "the handsomest and most polished of the female world" at New Harmony.[16] One of ten children whose mother had been widowed early, Lucy was descended from a Spanish sea captain, Gabriel Sistare. In 1771 the captain had been blown off course in a hurricane while transporting a load of spices and sugar from Havanna to Cadiz, Spain. He eventually landed at New London, Connecticut, which so suited him that he remained there for the rest of his life. From such an enterprising forebear, Lucy inherited the zest for adventure that led her to New Harmony.

Now she needed additional courage to confront the idle talk springing up around her affair with Thomas Say. Perhaps the jealousy of other women, who also found him attractive, was involved in the gossip. Mme. Fretageot wrote to Maclure that Whitwell was trying "to set the females of the society against one another" by spreading the rumor "that Lucy was in a family way by Thomas Say." Insulted by Whitwell's implication that this talk had originated with her, Mme. Fretageot stated indignantly that "Lucy interests me to much that I would ever say any such thing."[17]

Radical ideas on marriage were current that summer. Owen had brought feelings to a boil on 4 July 1826 when he delivered his "Declaration of Mental Independence." In his speech he promoted "mental revolution," exactly fifty years after the adoption of the Declaration of Independence, by advocating the abolition of individual property, "irrational systems" of religion, and traditional marriage. When these ideas circulated outside New Harmony, the greatest stir was caused by his view of sexual relations—a virtual endorsement of free love. Of all Owen's pronouncements, this seems to have done the most to give New Harmony a bad name. "I did not conjecture that Mr. O. was quite so amourous as the stories make him," Maclure wrote facetiously to Mme. Fretageot from Cincinnati. "The wives of the greatest part of those that have left you lately have declared to their husbands that it was in consequence of the freedom that Mr. O. took with them that they could not think of remaining under such dreadful risk of their virtue."[18] Several damning articles appeared in national newspapers as a result of the indignation expressed by these women.

Lucy's mother, far away in New York, was greatly disturbed by the negative reports. In addition to what she may have read in the press, she could have heard Whitwell's gossip from her other two daughters, who were also at New Harmony. Maclure took it upon himself to reassure her in a letter that was eventually published in the Philadelphia *United States Gazette* and the Washington *National Intelligencer*. He wrote to Mme. Fretageot from Springfield, Ohio, that

> from the state of misery, fear and tribulation manifested by Mrs. Sistare in most of her letters [undoubtedly related by Lucy to Say] I was induced (in hopes of alleviating part of her troubles) to volunteer a long letter assuring her of the morality of the inhabitants of Harmony being more correct than in any part of the Earth I ever was in, touching on the pivot of all the lyes, the sexual intercourse. I expected that the married were more faithfull and the young more chaste than in any part of the Globe I had visited . . . I contrasted the simplicity, innocence and moral conduct of the members of our Society with the extravagance, debauchery and vice of New York.[19]

Another member of the community defended her companions, despite the fact that she herself was quite unhappy in New Harmony, in a letter to her aunt in Pittsburgh: "I hear that our society bears a very ill name in the neighborhood, and I believe very undeservedly. There are a few bad members among us, but it seems hard that the whole should suffer for the faults and follies of the few."[20]

Other problems plagued the struggling "utopia." Mme. Fretageot complained to Maclure that the inhabitants of Macluria and Feiba-Peveli were withdrawing their children from her school because they refused to pay tuition. Eighty children remained, and Mme. Fretageot had them under her care in the mansion formerly occupied by George Rapp and now designated Community House No. 5. To complicate matters, Phiquepal, who ran the other school, had proven mentally unstable, his condition possibly being a result of the head injury he had received on the journey west. Maclure, while on his summer travels with Say, directed Mme. Fretageot to put the educational materials in Lesueur's charge so that "the Schools might not be deprived of them by the whim or caprice of one [Phiquepal] so full of all extravagant fanceys."[21] He insisted that a substitute be found for Phiquepal since, "from his physical weakness and moral uncertainty it will not be prudent to suspend the school every time any derangement of his faculties takes place."[22]

But all other difficulties were minor beside the significant breach fast developing between Maclure and Owen. In addition to their disagreements on how the society should be organized and operated, they held opposing opinions on educational methods. Owen preferred learning by rote, with older children teaching the younger, while Maclure advocated learning by demonstration, with a faculty composed of the best scientific minds available. These conflicting ideas caused factionalism. Mme. Fretageot, surprisingly, appeared to embrace Owen's methods, still apparently seeing him as somewhat of a hero, while Joseph Neef doggedly followed those methods he and Maclure had worked out years before. "His system I have watched the practice of for upwards of 25 years," Maclure wrote of Neef, "and cannot be such a fool as to abandon it for the wild speculations of a Visionary who does not see the rocks and shoals on which he and his flimsy bark will be dashed to pieces."[23]

Maclure was convinced that only Owen's continual input of funds was keeping the community afloat. After visiting the Owenite experiment at Yellow Springs, he chided Mme. Fretageot: "You seem to think that no community will succeed but under his [Owen's] management. Quite the contrary is the fact. All have failed by following the blaze of his wild theories without possessing the wealth which alone has supported him." Maclure felt that all was not lost, however: "What I have at stake I can lose without being ruined, and I'm decided not to augment the risk by any farther advance but for the conducting of the Schools on rational principles."[24]

Say detached himself as best he could from these arguments and concentrated on his scientific work. When he and Maclure returned to New Harmony on 7 October 1826, affairs had briefly stabilized. Three schools, run by Mme. Fretageot, Neef, and Phiquepal, were in operation. Toward the end of November Maclure, who was much in need of a warmer climate to control his rheumatism, embarked for New Orleans, reasonably assured that his plans would progress essentially as he hoped.

On 4 January 1827, a month after Maclure's departure, Thomas Say and Lucy Sistare were secretly married by civil ceremony in the courthouse at Mt. Vernon, Indiana, attended only by Virginia Dupalais (a former student of Mme. Fretageot's in Paris) and Neef's daughter Louisa. All went smoothly until the return journey to New Harmony when the carriage—perhaps driven too fast in the exuberance of high spirits—turned over, slightly injuring Virginia and Louisa.

Say's new life with Lucy was the tranquil eye of the Maclure-Owen storm that was gathering force around them. Gerard Troost wrote Benjamin Tappan that "the conduct of our monied men, our Patrons or Masters has been shamefull, and coincided not very much with the expressions we have often been obliged to hear of philanthropy, community of property, disinterestedness etc." Much to Maclure's consternation, Owen chose to disregard the agreement he had made to sell Maclure the land and buildings for the education society. When Frederick, George Rapp's adopted son, came to New Harmony in late April to collect the installment due on the town's purchase money, Owen, being unable or unwilling to pay, asked Maclure, just returned from New Orleans, to do so. Maclure agreed, on condition that he first be given a deed to his property. But after paying the bill and not receiving the deed, Maclure sent Say to the county seat to file suit against Owen. When Owen did not produce it, according to Troost, "on the first of May, the day of the payment, Mr. Say had the sheriff here to get Mr. Owen in prison. Mr. O. kept his room and got in the same time a rit against Mr. Maclure, so that we every moment our two great men expected to see going to Mount Vernon to spend some days in prison."[25] Bills were posted all over town warning everyone not to trust Owen on Maclure's account. But at last, after four days of heated debate with the sheriff, Maclure got his deed and matters were settled.

By this time it was clear that the utopian experiment in communal living had failed. The *New Harmony Gazette* of 28 March 1827 officially announced its demise in an article written by Robert Dale Owen and his brother William: "One form of government was first adopted, and when that appeared unsuitable another was tried; until it appeared that the members were too various in their feelings and too dissimilar in their habits to govern themselves harmoniously as one community." From now on the inhabitants were on their own to govern themselves in any way they saw fit.

Although Owen's experiment had collapsed, Maclure's survived. Even so, Maclure's reputation in Philadelphia had suffered from his association with Owen. Benjamin Tappan, writing from Steubenville, Ohio, to Reuben Haines, defended Maclure as well as Say and the others:

> We owe to your friend Maclure the first planting of science in the western territory, & there is promise already of a vigorous growth & a rich abundance of fruit from his exertions—Le Sueur & Troost & Say are industrious, the former plies his graver & pencil with but little interruption & with exquisite skill while the others are arranging & describing new species of fishes, shells & minerals as well as insects—the world will be benefited as science will be enriched by their labours.[26]

Troost told Tappan that he did not know what would happen to Maclure's education society, but that "Phiquepal must leave the place—Neef will be treated in such manner that he will be obliged to look for another home—a certain woman, a former *Soubrette* or *fille de chambre* as

Stern has it, has the government of Mr. Maclure and the schools."[27] He added to this uncomplimentary description of Mme. Fretageot that anyone who disagreed with her was obliged to leave.

Marie Fretageot was not popular in New Harmony. One community member wrote that "some have found reasons for believing that this same female teacher was at the bottom of most of the overturning manoeuvres of this place, as being willing by ingratiating herself with Owen and M'Clure, to promote her own interest exclusive of others."[28] Say, given the difficult circumstances of his financial dependence on and moral obligation to Maclure, and Maclure's trust in Mme. Fretageot, tried diplomatically to get along with her. The others did not bother. "If Say was only occupied with the dissection of his Insects, I would consider him just as I do with Troost and Lesueur," she had written Maclure in early March. "They are shut up in their cabinet, the former with speculative Mineralogy, the latter with the collection of Fish, Shells, Birds, Drawings, perfectly useless to the happiness of mankind. Yet calculate the expense they carry with them and tell me what benefit will arise from their work to the present and even the future generations. That is the case with all Scientific people. Their knowledge is not only useless (because their is no application of it) but hurtful; it carries the mind astray, in fact it is false knowledge." Recalling that Maclure was a geologist, she assured him he was exempt from this criticism since his knowledge had been applied.[29]

In spite of Mme. Fretageot's demands, Say would have been totally occupied with entomology if only his collections and papers had arrived from Philadelphia. By June they still had not come. He wrote anxiously to Jacob Gilliams, who was supposed to have sent them: "Do please inform me of the fate of my cabinet etc., I entertain the greatest apprehensions of having lost them. Mr. Maclure left New Orleans the beginning of May [late April], having waited a considerable time to receive them, but he at length feared that they had been shipwrecked!"[30]

Say planned to continue adding volumes to *American Entomology*, with Tiebout engraving plates from Lesueur's drawings. He asked Mitchell to forward the copperplates for his third volume so he could have them corrected and then return them to Philadelphia for publication. The plates could be executed in New Harmony, he told Gilliams, but the letterpress would have to be done in Philadelphia, "as we cannot print it with sufficient elegance here. The Mss. for the 3rd Vol. is in my cabinet, which if it be lost with my books will render me incapable of prosecuting my labours in Natural history perhaps for years to come, & perhaps forever."[31]

By the end of August 1827, Say had still not received his manuscript, nor had he heard from Mitchell in respect to continuing the publication of *American Entomology*. But a letter to Benjamin Tappan shows he was busy with the printing office all the same: "Two Nos. of Mr. Lesueur's work on Fish with coloured plates have already been published & the third No. is nearly ready to be printed off. The first plate is now engraving for my work on Shells. So you see that we are at least making something of a spirited commencement as publishers."[32]

By mid-October the missing manuscript, the majority of his insect specimens, and most of Say's books at last arrived, but several books and instruments that he needed desperately had not been included. Say asked Dr. Isaac Hays at the Academy to ship his micrometer and a six-inch ivory scale, saying that without these two instruments he could not give dimensions for the insects he described daily. He found it immensely frustrating not to have the tools of his trade, especially the books he needed for reference. In describing new species it was of the utmost importance not to name something as new that had already been published by someone else. "What other things are missing if any, I do not know," he continued to Hays. "I discover the loss of a book etc. only when I wish to refer to it." Also, Say had received letters from his European correspondents mentioning boxes of insect specimens that had been sent to him, "not one of which has been forthcoming."[33]

By the fall of 1827, Say had begun to feel acutely isolated from the scientific community. "If you can convey to this remote backwoods region, any scientific news or particulars of any of our friends or even of our enemies, if we have any, I would be most obliged to you for them," he wrote Hays.[34] He had lived at New Harmony for over a year and a half, and several of his colleagues had left for various reasons. Troost had moved in midsummer to Tennessee to assume a position as professor of chemistry, geology, and mineralogy at the University of Nashville. One of the reasons for accepting the position was his wife's indignation at Owen's attitude toward religion. The previous May, with Tappan's assistance, Troost had tried to secure a job for Lesueur and himself "constructing a geological map," but nothing had come of it.[35] Although Say's closest friend and longtime associate, Lesueur, was still in residence, he was not content with his life. According to Neef, who had departed shortly after Troost, the Frenchman's stay in New Harmony was tenuous: "Lesueur, I know, from what he often told me, considers his situation as being extremely irksome, and I am sure he will only remain in it until he can change it."[36]

Say definitely felt the absence of Joseph Neef, since he was a good educator and a fine musician, and was proficient in several languages. Robert Dale Owen described Neef as "straight forward and cordial," but other aspects of his behavior may have caused his downfall with Mme. Fretageot. "To his earlier life, as an officer under Napoleon," wrote Robert Dale, "was due a blunt, off-hand manner and an abrupt style of speech, enforced, now and then, with an oath—an awkward habit for a teacher, which I think he tried ineffectually to get rid of."[37]

Much of the school staff's general dissatisfaction could be traced to continual change. Maclure, deeply dissatisfied with Owen's experiment, had been in residence since April 1827, allowing him ample time to reorganize his favorite philanthropy. Say explained Maclure's disenchantment and reasons for change to Tappan, who was concerned about the quality of his son's education:

> [Maclure] came here from his confidence in the judgement & integrity of Mr. Owen & hoping to find more toleration for introducing his [Maclure's] plan of education, under the community system, in all of which he has been grossly deceived, finding that the aversion to the system of education was 100fold augmented by the unpopularity of Owen's system; & finding himself too old to contend any longer against the ignorance & deeprooted prejudice of parents he gives up all attempts at giving a rational education to those who can afford to pay for the education of their children, & returns to his original plan of giving knowledge cheap to the poor & oppressed. It has always been his intention to diffuse knowledge amongst the great class of productive labourers; this was the only object that induced him to meddle with education, being thoroughly convinced, by all his experience that the inequality of knowledge is the source of all the evils that torment humanity, & giving knowledge to the rich is the certain way of increasing that inequality. . . . The cost of ten months experiment on two hundred unproductive people, the school community, was also a discouraging reason.[38]

However much Say may have concurred with Maclure's ideas for social reform—and there is every indication that he was in accord with them—the implementation of the school for poor children was now entirely up to Marie Fretageot. Say's teaching would be suspended for some time to come, since he planned to leave New Harmony for the winter on the long-anticipated scientific expedition to Mexico.

CHAPTER 12

Travels and Trials

I am here with Mr. Maclure on our way to Mexico for the winter, & we have to regret that
your multifarious labors prevent you from participating in our excursion.

Thomas Say to Charles Lucien Bonaparte
New Orleans, 6 January 1828

ALTHOUGH SAY had been married less than a year, the opportunity to accompany Maclure, in December 1827, to a part of the
world he had not seen was more than he could resist. Since Lucy
was fully occupied with drawing and coloring illustrations for *American
Conchology*, the idea that she would join him was not considered. She had
even been obliged to turn down Benjamin Tappan's invitation to spend the
winter with him and his wife in Steubenville, because her occupations
required that she remain in New Harmony.

Say regretted that Charles Lucien Bonaparte was unable to accompany
him to Mexico. He wrote to his friend that he and Maclure expected to find
"much novelty in that interesting region . . . something better and more
permanent than milk & honey, the anticipated produce of the land of
Canaan." Such uncharacteristic cynicism derived not only from his disenchantment with religion, but also from his recent experience. He told
Bonaparte that "with respect to communities at Harmony I have been
altogether disappointed . . . no such thing now exists in the town." Robert
Owen had sold his portion of the property to a Colonel Taylor, who
established a monopoly on the principal trades, such as the retail store and
the distillery. Maclure's deed had forbidden his entering into competition
in these spheres, but his primary interest—the free school—still func-
tioned. Say mentioned that Owen had returned from Europe and was
presently aboard a ship in the New Orleans harbor on his way to New
Harmony. "What he may do there I cannot even conjecture," Say said. He
added that Frances Wright had returned from Europe and had left New
Orleans two days earlier for her settlement at Nashoba.[1] Frances Wright

was a wealthy young English activist who initially had been drawn to New Harmony by Owen's plans for a cooperative society. Because of the prejudice against blacks inherent in Owen's scheme, however, she had left to found her Nashoba community in the Tennessee woods, where freed slaves were welcomed and treated equitably.

Since Say's departure from Philadelphia, affairs at the Academy of Natural Sciences had been as chaotic as those in New Harmony. In early April 1826 the naturalist William Cooper had written Bonaparte from New York concerning the institution: "We hear nothing from there but refutations, excuses, . . . jealousies & disquiets of every degree."[2] Trouble had started as soon as Say, Maclure, and the others had gone. Of the five papers Say had left to be published in the *Journal*, two had immediately been withdrawn from publication. This was the first time since its inception, eight years earlier, that anything written by Say for the *Journal* had been rejected. Politics were surely involved in what appeared to be questioning of Say's scientific expertise. His absence from the Academy, where he had been prominent for so long, allowed jealous colleagues an upper hand. His friends, Charles Bonaparte and Titian Peale, had been unable to attend the meeting at which Say's papers were turned down.

Say's short article criticizing John Eatton Le Conte's essay on beetles, which had appeared in the first volume of New York's *Annals of the Lyceum of Natural History*, was one of the withdrawn papers. Le Conte was a member of both the New-York Lyceum and the Academy, and because the world of scientific inquiry at the time was such a tightly knit circle, members of each organization favored certain cohorts in other institutions. Le Conte undoubtedly had his coterie at the Academy. To Bonaparte, Say defended his discarded remarks:

> Capt. Leconte has much scientific knowledge in Nat. Hist., he has observed much & well, & is capable of doing much in the field, where the harvest is great & the laborers are few, but he must not be discouraged by criticism, or suppose that it is intended to irritate. My observations on one of his papers were called forth from me by necessity & I said no more relative to it than the truth, & what I hope for from other naturalists relative to my own writings. If I have not put the truth only in my observations let him reply to it.[3]

Of the five Le Conte names that Say himself had previously given to each insect, one had even been depicted in plate 10 of *American Entomology*. Say asserted there could be no doubt as to his own priority.

This debate had seethed for three years. Fortunately for Say he had friends at the New-York Lyceum as well as at the Academy. James Ellsworth Dekay, a prominent member of the organization, had written Bonaparte in 1825 on the subject: "With regard to Le Conte's paper & observations respecting Mr. Say's description, I can only repeat what I said in my former letter, that Entomology must be far behind every other department of Nat. History if descriptions as minute & detailed as Mr. Say's are, cannot be at once recognized. No man has a higher respect for Mr. Say's acquirements than myself & this respect is only exceeded by my personal regard." Say may have written his paper on Le Conte's insect names in response to Dekay's remark to Bonaparte that the correction of Le Conte's mistake would come with "a better grace" and more authority from Say himself than if the Lyceum should have to publish a retraction, since Le Conte was one of their members.[4]

As might have been anticipated because Le Conte could reasonably have expected Say to write to him and ask him to correct his mistake, Le Conte was sorely offended by Say's criticism and lost no time in striking back. Say wrote Bonaparte: "I shall not inquire whether or not Capt. Leconte stated that Count Dejean would not notice me or my works, for the work of that distinguished Entomologist (the 2nd Vol.) would at once show the falsity of any such remark."[5]

Say was not alone in controversy. Bonaparte had his own battles to fight, since he had dared to continue Alexander Wilson's *American Ornithology*, thus treading on the toes of George Ord, keeper of Wilson's flame. Audubon had made this contention a triangle and would ultimately sweep up most of the glory.

Fierce competition raged between scientists in the struggle to be first in naming a new species. This battling over nomenclature was unavoidable in the early years of natural science studies in America, when so much was new and taxonomy took precedence over all other aspects of scientific debate. Taxonomy formed the foundation without which the study of theory and behavior could not proceed. "Whatever the fate of natural history theories," a modern historian has written, "natural history descriptions are not so likely to be superseded as they are to be elaborated and refined. The history of scientific progress, therefore, has a place for those who wrote the early descriptions."[6]

A schism within the Academy of Natural Sciences was the inevitable outcome of all this quarreling, and certain disgruntled Academy members founded what was called the Maclurian Lyceum. Say was asked to serve as president, in absentia, while Bonaparte and Gilliams were to be vice presidents. Say wrote to Bonaparte from New Harmony that he had told the members of the Lyceum that he "conceived it prejudicial to the interests of the institution to have a chief officer at so great a distance," and that it was his "opinion & wish" that Bonaparte occupy the position, but that "on a reiteration of the request" he could not but "accept of the honor," as long as it was understood that his resignation would be ready "at any moment that the interest of the society requires it."[7]

In its first issue of January 1827, the new alliance's publication, *Contributions of the Maclurian Lyceum to the Arts and Sciences*, stated the circumstances of its founding with appropriate tact: "In consequence of an increasing taste for scientific pursuits, it was thought advisable to form another institution in this city, which should afford additional facilities for the acquisition of knowledge."[8] This rival organization's founders could not have been unaware of the irony implicit in naming it after Maclure, since the elderly philanthropist was still president of the Academy and would remain so until his death in 1840. The Lyceum had even more of the Academy than its president's name: the previous spring the Academy had moved to new quarters in a former Swedenborgian church at Twelfth and Chestnut streets, and the curators' year-end report noted that the majority of the Academy's cases, as well as tables, benches, and the stove from the meeting room had been sold to the Maclurian Lyceum for one hundred dollars.

It was as though the Maclurian Lyceum had been set up as a forum in which rebuttals could be made to the work of Academy members who might have suppressed such rejoinders. Say must have known that the observations he made about Richard Harlan's paper on reptiles, which had been published in the *Journal* after Say's departure from Philadelphia, would cause a stir. "I have examined the specimen of Scinus described as new . . . and believe it to be no other than an aged individual of the *Quinquelincatus*," Say wrote in the first volume of *Contributions*. In the same paper Say managed to annoy George Ord as well by stating that the "agama" Ord described was no other than the "*tapayaxin* of Hernandez." Say claimed this reptile had been shown in Benjamin Smith Barton's 1806 *Medical and Physical Journal*, where "he applied the specific name Tapayaxin to the very individual represented in Mr. Ord's excellent plate." Say continued that, whatever the question of identity, "no one can hesitate to admit that the name selected by Dr. Barton has the priority, and consequently, bad as it is, the exclusive right."[9] The Academy's Dr. Isaac Hays confirmed

Say's statements by producing a friend's letter from Mexico, which said the animal in question was common in the neighborhood of Mexico City and was the one described by Hernandez. Ord would not forgive the shadow cast on his integrity by Say's candid remarks.

In answer to Bonaparte about a heated Academy meeting during which Ord had questioned a paper of the prince's, Say wrote his friend:

> I thank you much for the particulars relative to the Academy & the Lyceum & I regret exceedingly that I was not present during the transactions you narrate, in order to second the firm & upright stand you made. But I sincerely hope I have misunderstood one sentence of your letter . . . speaking of the Academy you say in brackets ("for nothing less did I consider the burning of my papers.") Have I not misunderstood your meaning! Were papers of yours on Nat. Hist. burned, intentionally burned? It cannot be, such vandalism could not occur in our country; however ignorant the society, 12 men could not be got together at random, who would be guilty of such a thing. I cannot therefore come at your meaning in that passage.[10]

Beneath his gentle exterior Thomas Say was a passionate man often blinded into naivete by what he considered injustice. Surely Bonaparte had meant that he was so frustrated with prevailing circumstances that he considered burning his own papers rather than turning them over to others.

Say said in the same letter to Bonaparte that he assumed all the papers he had left with the Academy were now in the Lyceum's possession. One of them at least—the paper on Le Conte's names rejected by the *Journal*—would be printed in the Lyceum's *Contributions*.

Although factionalism existed among Academy members, Say had friends who continued to look after his interests. To Jacob Gilliams he mailed two papers on insects for the *Contributions,* one naming new species of hymenoptera (wasps and bees) and the other on diptera (flies). The first appeared in volume one of the *Contributions* in 1828, while the *Journal* published the other the following year. As a member of both organizations, the diplomatic Gilliams wanted to keep peace with the Academy for Say as well as for himself. And Gilliams knew that Say still contemplated the collaboration with him that had been in back of Say's mind for several years. Say mentioned to Benjamin Tappan, when telling him of his various New Harmony printing projects, including Lesueur's book on fish and his own on shells: "I fear you will think we are leaping at stars in the brook, when I inform you, that . . . I am corresponding with a friend in [Philadelphia] who has proposed to me to publish a work on the Amphibia & Reptilia of North America."[11]

In addition to essays, Say sent Gilliams his manuscript for the third volume of *American Entomology*; Gilliams had offered to oversee its printing. Say also asked Bonaparte to give his advice to the publisher if it were needed. The plates were being corrected and colored at New Harmony, Say said, and before departing for Mexico, he had left instructions that as soon as fifty impressions of each were finished they should be sent to Philadelphia so the volume could appear as soon as possible. He had also left the completed manuscript for the first volume of *American Conchology*, which he hoped to see published on his return.

Publishing and all the controversy over scientific firsts were apparently far from Thomas Say's mind as he headed for Mexico in early January 1828 to search for insects and shells to augment his studies. En route, he wrote Gilliams about his reaction to New Orleans and its burgeoning economy, which, benefiting as it was from the agriculture of the southern and western United States, was radically altered from his brief stop there nearly ten years earlier on his way back from the Rockies:

> I am much surprised at the great increase & improvement of the City since my visit in 1819. The quantity of business now transacting here is prodigious. Bales of Cotton & Hogsheads of Sugar without end, tumbled out of one vessel into another, destined to various parts of the world. The river is high & affords the numerous & fine steam boats a ready passage in transporting to this great mart, the superabundance of the West. But the Cotton business is beginning to be overdone, & we hear of many planters, who are about to remove with their slaves further south on the Mississippi & commence the Sugar cultivation, which, although vast already in this quarter may yet be much extended to great profit under the present tarif.[12]

Say mentioned that he and Maclure had taken passage aboard the brig *La Grange,* bound for Vera Cruz and due to sail the following day. Before leaving they visited Maclure's favorite haunt, "Miss Carroll's" bookshop, where they encountered Fanny Trollope (mother of the future novelist Anthony Trollope), just arrived from England with Frances Wright. Mrs. Trollope later described Maclure in her book *Domestic Manners of the Americans* as "a venerable personage, of gentleman-like appearance, who, in the course of five minutes, propounded as many axioms, as 'Ignorance is the only devil;' 'Man makes his own existence;' and the like."[13]

The voyage aboard the *La Grange*, as was typical of Say's boat journeys, was an ordeal. The vessel had no ballast and tossed about like a cork in the violent storms that persisted for all thirteen days of the crossing. Say suffered such severe seasickness that he would attribute the bad state of his health in succeeding months to this journey. To Tappan he wrote that his stomach was "in a constant state of nausea, which produced a bilious complaint that prevented me from availing myself of the opportunity of making collections, with as much zeal & devotion as I should otherwise have done."[14]

At Vera Cruz Maclure hired a coach pulled by ten mules and driven by two mixed-blood Indians. By this conveyance they proceeded in a leisurely fashion to Mexico City, accompanied by an acquaintance from Philadelphia, Lardner Vanuxem, who had taken a job as manager of a silver mine and was traveling to his new situation. Vanuxem told them that Say's former fellow explorer William Keating was also in Mexico, managing a mine only two miles away from where he himself would be.

On reaching Mexico City, Vanuxem would write to Isaac Lea in Philadelphia of the journey with his "old friends," adding that "it was a great surprise to me I assure you & I was much pleased to travel in company with them."[15] Some months later he modified this statement:

> Say I found as pleasant a companion as ever. Not so our friend Maclure who is more dogmatic than I am; & of course must be a bore; I found him to be such. Entre nous I was pleased when our journey was at an end & I am & was sorry that such was the case. He has much altered & I am not surprised that almost all who accompanied & followed him to Harmony so soon deserted him; Say's pecuniary situation & M[aclure's] good feelings at times, which are truly great in degree, combined with his exertions for science, I suppose keeps Say to our president & a most invaluable being the former is to the latter.[16]

Another American Say would meet in Mexico City was Joel Roberts Poinsett, who had served since 1825 as the first minister to Mexico from the United States. This cosmopolitan South Carolina statesman and future United States secretary of war under Martin Van Buren was interested in agriculture and botany and brought back from Mexico the following year the plant that was subsequently named for him, the poinsettia. Say wrote Haines proposing Poinsett for Academy membership on Maclure's behalf.[17]

From the swaying carriage Say looked with fascination at the unfolding landscape. He wrote to Benjamin Tappan:

> We had left our own country at a season in which "nature sleeps," & when the forest is stripped of its verdure, & we were now in the midst of an eternal

spring, surrounded by a vegetation as interesting as strange to us; by animals that we then saw for the first time, & by men whose appearance & habits, whose dwellings, agriculture & mechanics differed widely from anything we had before seen. The very composition of the soil, the face of the country, is so totally different from those of our own United States, that we seemed, indeed, to have arrived in a new world.[18]

The plethora of volcanoes stretching from Vera Cruz to Mexico City astonished him: "Besides the majestic snowcapped Orizaba & Popocatapetl . . . we saw numerous extinct volcanoes, ancient & modern streams & fields of lava, cinders, ashes etc., constituting unequivocal evidences of mighty changes & operations, of which this country has been the theatre. No part of the globe presents such a scene;—three hundred miles, at least, of uninterrupted volcanic matter, I believe is without a parallel."[19]

Say found the large, well-built Mexican haciendas, or plantation houses, in marked contrast to the miserable huts of the poor with their walls of corn stalks and roofs of thatched palm, banana, or agave leaves. Agave, he observed, "which in our greenhouses is called the Great American Aloe," was used to concoct the stimulating drink of the country, the Pulque [Tequila], of which, you may recollect, Humboldt has said so much."[20] Say gathered seeds of one hundred different Mexican plants and sent samples of each to Colonel Robert Carr at Bartram's botanic garden in Philadelphia. The seeds Say collected included various fruits and vegetables: "avocata or Alligator Pear," nectarine, Mexican pumpkin, musk melon, "miraculous wheat," peppers, "Upland Rice (from China)," and many varieties of beans. A wild *Pelargonium* (geranium), "Grenadilla—a *Passiflora* with eatable fruit," a *Lobelia* from Lake Chalco, and a *Linum* from Chapultepec constituted some of the flowers, while trees were represented by a cedar from the Mexican mountains and vines by a *Bignonia* from Tacubya.[21] Lucy was most likely responsible for Say's botanical enthusiasm; she once told a friend it was a "passion" with her.[22] Say noted that good quality wheat was the most extensive crop grown in Mexico. He marveled at the primitive plough employed on even the largest plantations, commenting that it was "absolutely unimproved since the time of Virgil."[23]

During his travels Say obtained ancient flint and obsidian blades, sheathed with copper, which were similar to those he and Lesueur had excavated from Indian burial mounds at New Harmony. When Say returned to Indiana he wrote about this interesting coincidence: "We presume not to say, how far this fact may go towards corroborating the hieroglyphic records of the Azteques, relative to their migration and that of the Toultecs from the North, but it seems to strengthen the conjecture that the remote ancestry of the present Mexican Indians, erected those mounds and embankments so liberally scattered over this country, the origin of which is unknown to the tradition of our red men."[24] Say could speak with first-hand knowledge of these embankments, in addition to the ones at New Harmony, because of the burial mounds he and Titian Peale had excavated near St. Louis and the many others he had seen along the St. Peter's River.

The majority of Say's observations in Mexico concerned insects and shells, though he had not found the latter abundant. Vanuxem wrote Isaac Lea, at the Academy, that it was not a country for land or freshwater shells. But Say gathered a variety of new species, the descriptions of which would embellish his future writings. He was even more successful with insects. Many new species named in his paper "Descriptions of North American Dipterous Insects," published in the 1829 *Journal*, specified "inhabits Mexico." And a long essay he sent to the American Philosophical Society several years later on new North American insects included many of Mexican origin.

Say would include descriptions of Mexican shells in his second major work, *American Conchology*, and in the *Disseminator of Useful Knowledge*, the newspaper published by Maclure's school in New Harmony. This erudite biweekly, which served as a mouthpiece for Maclure's often longwinded ideas, featured articles on philosophy, natural science, and morality. Begun in January 1828, shortly after Say's departure for Mexico, the paper would eventually involve much of his time as its editor.

Say and Maclure arrived back in New Harmony in early May 1828. Maclure had been enchanted with Mexico. "I never have been in any place where I found more to agree with me in opinion," he wrote, before returning, in a letter to the *Disseminator*. "I shall leave their fine climate, their urbanity, civility and friendly toleration with regret, tho' both Say and myself are cooped up in a small room not ten feet square, I never spent my time more agreeably, nor more to my satisfaction."[24] The journey was equally successful for Say. It had given him access to shell and insect specimens from a new and unique climate, which broadened the scope of his work to cover Central as well as North America. European naturalists, sitting at their desks across the Atlantic, could not achieve the accuracy that Say could now employ on his descriptions of American fauna found in its native habitat.

Say's correspondence with these men and his scientific colleagues in the United States was of the utmost importance to him. It served as a lifeline to the outside world and the mainstream of world science. His disappointment was thus keen when, upon his return to New Harmony, he found no letters waiting for him. He complained to Gilliams: "I wrote you from New Orleans on our voyage to Mexico, & again from this place sometime after our return here & also to my brother, but have not yet received any reply." He had also not heard from Bonaparte, Lea, or Hays. "What the cause can be of all this I am at a loss to divine. Can you withdraw the mysterious veil? for if the fault be my own, I may be able to correct it; do write I pray you without any fear of giving me offence for my most sincere friendship has been too long yours to be in danger of extirpation." Say asked Gilliams if he ought to send shells "as a recompense" to those who had packed his things, thinking perhaps that lack of acknowledgment from him might have been part of the trouble.[26]

The same fear of having been forgotten is sounded again in a letter several months later to Bonaparte: "How could you depart from our shores without bestowing upon me a parting farewell or the legacy of a single line? I do not even know how long you intend to remain in Europe, or indeed whether or not you propose ever to return."[27] That all Say's friends neglected to write him at this time seems to have been mere coincidence, because they continued to correspond with him for the rest of his life. Say was then so far removed from their everyday lives and concerns that he was not immediately important to them—an inescapable consequence of physical distance. For their part, they never understood why he had left Philadelphia, nor why he continued to live in such a backwater as New Harmony.

Say's feelings of isolation were unquestionably intensifying. Since he had only recently returned from a foreign country where he had been out of touch for some months, his reestablishment in the relatively remote town of New Harmony, with his only colleague, Lesueur, then on a trip to New Orleans to secure his government pension from France, left him feeling more detached than ever from the centers of scientific activity. In December he confided his frustration to Bonaparte, then living in Europe: "In this remote region we have not even a loophole through which to peep at the scientific world, but we must be content with the evidence of our ears, which however, experience proves, are not always worthy of credit. And if we were not occasionally to revisit that world with a communication or a letter we should even be in the predicament of annihilation in respect to it."[28] Say's remarks were justified in that he had only learned by hearsay that one of his books had been published. The previous August the Academy *Minutes* had recorded that "the third volume of American Entomology by Thomas Say was received."

Having heard nothing of the Maclurian Lyceum, Say asked Bonaparte if it had been abandoned. The Academy and the New-York Lyceum seemed equally dormant. He had sent several papers on new insect species to Philadelphia the previous year, but since their receipt had not been acknowledged he assumed they were "sleeping." These papers would in fact be read at an Academy meeting in March 1829 and published in the *Journal* the same year.

The reason for the long delay was the state of chaos that existed in the publication committee. Say had been the prime mover of the *Journal* during his years in Philadelphia, and after his departure no one took his place. Committee members were appointed and promptly resigned in dizzying succession. The *Minutes* of 31 July 1827 note that the entire publication committee resigned en masse. Not until 1829 was the *Journal* again in capable hands with the appointments of Dr. Charles Pickering, Timothy Abbott Conrad, and Dr. Samuel George Morton as its editors.

Although Say feared he was being deliberately ignored at the Academy of Natural Sciences, the neglect of its members could be attributed to the disorganization and transition through which the institution had struggled in the two-and-a-half years since his departure. Members in Philadelphia could not worry about far-flung members when they had so many problems with each other. William Cooper wrote to Bonaparte that he was sorry to hear of the disagreements among Academy members because the "cause of science" would suffer by it. He added that he hoped they would "be content with shedding a few gallons of ink, instead of a drop of blood; and sharpen their pens rather than draw their swords."[29]

Pens had indeed been sharpened and had proved nearly as deadly as swords. After Richard Harlan's *Fauna Americana, being a Description of the Mammiferous Animals Inhabiting North America* was published in 1825, John Godman, in a scathing review, accused Harlan of plagiarizing information already published by the French naturalist Anselme Gaetan Desmarest in his *Mammalogie, ou description des espèces de Mammifères* (Paris, 1820). A furious Harlan issued a small pamphlet refuting these charges by asserting that, as he had stated in his book, he had intended to correct and add to Desmarest's classifications.

Harlan subsequently turned the knife on Godman by claiming that

Godman's book, *Anatomical Investigation, Comprising Descriptions of Various Fasciae of the Human Body* (1824), was merely a rehash of old ideas.[30] "Unfortunately for the parent his immature productions were not 'dead born' from the press," Harlan wrote acidly, "but will descend to posterity, like flies in amber, preserved by the medium that surrounds them. They are in reality far beneath the dignity of criticism, and never would have been dragged from neglect and oblivion, but for the arrogance and effrontery of their author."[31]

Harlan was essentially more scientific than Godman. In effect, both men were entirely sincere in their work, but their approach to science was different. Harlan's *Fauna* was devoted mainly to classification and nomenclature, for example, while Godman's three-volume *American Natural History* that followed it (1826–28) was written for the general reader.

Historiographers see the controversy between these two men as a clear illustration of the significant change that was then occurring in the study of natural science.[32] Godman was in the tradition of earlier naturalists such as Charles Willson Peale, to whom nature was a book open to all who would read it. Alexander Wilson exemplified this thesis in his *American Ornithology,* which gives pages of lively and delightful anecdotes about each bird he discusses but little in the way of specific scientific description. Harlan, on the other hand, is seen as representing the emerging method of exacting descriptions with relatively few or no "histories."

Say had a foot in each camp. Brought up under the tutelage of Peale and later Wilson, he was of course much influenced by them. The quotation on the title page of his *American Conchology* (1830), "Read Nature; Nature is a friend to truth," could surely be seen as homage to Peale whose logo for his museum was an open book with the word *Nature* written across it. And, when appropriate, Say was not above including anecdotes about where he found a particular shell or insect, and under what conditions. Yet Say's descriptions were so thoroughly detailed and scientific that he was designated by the conchologist W. G. Binney in 1858 as "our greatest Naturalist."[33]

At least one of the controversial personalities Thomas Say had known in Philadelphia was accomplishing his goals. "I have lately received Audubon's prospectus," Say wrote to Bonaparte. "It appears that he is now engaged in publishing his magnificent work on our Ornithology. This it would seem is on a grander scale than anything of the kind that has been ever attempted; I sincerely wish him success & that he may bring forth the

whole, altho' it is not likely that I shall ever see so expensive a production."
Audubon was in England at the time, having failed to interest an American
publisher in his book.

Concerning his own most recent attempt in this area, Say said he
supposed Bonaparte had heard he had undertaken an "American Conchology," for which eighteen or twenty plates had been engraved and several
hundred impressions colored. "I shall include the whole of N. America &
the W. India islands, so you see here is a pretty extensive field." He asked his
friend to send him European shells for comparison.[34]

Although expeditions and fieldwork were his favorite pursuits, from
now on Say would have to rely on others to do his collecting. The trip to
Mexico was his last journey far afield in search of natural history specimens;
from 1828 onward he led a more or less sedentary life at New Harmony,
separated by distance from his scientific colleagues. No more opportunities
for exploring presented themselves, and Say felt a binding obligation to
safeguard Maclure's investment in New Harmony because the older man
had helped him become a scientist and publish his works. Aware that the
Academy had been in disarray since his departure from Philadelphia in 1825,
Say may have been apprehensive about what might happen at New Harmony if he left. And, after all, it was where he had fallen in love with and
married Lucy, and where he had established a home. The coarse "live-and-
let-live" philosophy of a town that until only recently had been on the
frontier appealed to his austere Quaker sensibilities more than the traditional society life of Philadelphia, as did the freedom to pursue scientific
endeavors without the politics and gossip prevalent in a big city. In addition, his chronic abdominal illness may have debilitated him more than he
was willing to admit, even to himself.

At the end of 1828, eight months after returning from Mexico, Say
wrote to Peter S. Du Ponceau, president of the American Philosophical
Society, requesting that Edward M. Bell, a young philologist living at New
Harmony, be given a place on a proposed expedition. Known unofficially
as the Wilkes Expedition after its eventual commander—the expedition
would not actually depart for ten more years—this venture must have
engendered serious regret in Say that he was not in a position to solicit such
an assignment for himself. In spite of his uncertain health, Say would have
welcomed the opportunity to explore the vast and uncharted reaches of the
Pacific.

"By the President's [John Quincy Adams] message it appears that one
or more of our public vessels are 'to be sent to the Pacific ocean & south sea

to examine the coasts, islands, harbours & reefs in those seas & to ascertain their true situation and description,'" he addressed Du Ponceau. Say then proceeded to assess the great advance of American science since the century's beginning, and to anticipate the specialization and professionalism that were emerging in natural science:

> In the present state of knowledge, an expedition of this kind presupposes the employment of such scientific persons as are capable of producing the most beneficial results, and we are not to believe that, as in the day of Lewis & Clark and Pike, we are only to reap the barren narration of the existence of a rock here, a tree there, of a singular unknown animal etc. The enquirers of the present day are more specific: the naturalist must be told, in language that he cannot mistake, the nature of that rock, tree or animal, its affinities, uses etc. the philologist is not content with the mere tale of the existence of an extraordinary race of men on one of those islands; he must be so far informed of the nature of their language as to be able to make his comparisons.[35]

While composing the letter, Say must have thought about his own role on two expeditions—how he had taken meticulous notes describing animals, birds, insects, and shells, and compiled Indian vocabularies. But his days as a field naturalist were over, and he would now become a cabinet naturalist. The principal adventure left to him lay in writing and printing his works in New Harmony. His only means of contact with the world beyond this small outlying town, aside from his correspondence, was the printing press that had been shipped from New Orleans several years earlier by Maclure. Within a few months of Say's return from Mexico his life revolved around publishing. Besides being editor-in-chief of the *Disseminator*, a full-time job in itself, he wrote pamphlets and supervised numerous other productions of the New Harmony press. None would be more important to science than his own book on American shells.

CHAPTER 13
Out of the Crowd

Great industry is requisite in this remote region to compensate for the disadvantages under
which a naturalist must here labour . . .

Thomas Say to Charles Lucien Bonaparte
New Harmony, 5 July 1830

S AY BEGAN THE YEAR 1829 enthusiastically. He wrote to
Thaddeus Harris that he had numerous publishing ventures in mind,
foremost of which was *American Conchology*. To his delight Lucy was
proving a skillful artist: so far she had produced twenty beautiful drawings
to illustrate his shell descriptions. As Marie Fretageot's pupil in Philadelphia she had studied drawing and painting with Lesueur, and she
continued to receive lessons from him in New Harmony. The engraver
Cornelius Tiebout prepared plates from Lucy's drawings, and when they
were printed Lucy took over the tedious task of coloring them by hand.
Under her delicate brushwork each engraving became an exquisite miniature. There was ample working space because the printing press was set up
in New Harmony hall, but the hours were long and it was often well after
dusk when she finally blew out the candles. Even so, she and Thomas
worked together, and Lucy was as excited about the project as he was.

To write *American Conchology*, which would be the first American
book on indigenous shells, Say had to amass sufficient shell specimens from
many localities to enable him to accurately compare minute differences. He
thanked Harris for sending samples and told him that he had to "call loudly
& beg sturdily for shells of all my correspondents, shells from any part of
North America to the Pole & including those of the West Indies; & shells
from any other part of the globe for comparison."[1] Although the prospectus for *American Conchology* had appeared in the *New Harmony Gazette* of
October 1827, the first part—for it would appear in installments—would
not be published for three years, in December 1830. Sickness had much to
do with the delay. "I am now convalescent from my second bilious attack

Fig. 39. *Lucy and Thomas Say,* by Titian Ramsay Peale, 1831. Silhouettes. Historic New Harmony, Inc. These silhouettes must have
been cut by Peale when the Says visited Philadelphia in the fall
of 1831.

this season," Say wrote his old school friend Reuben Haines at the end of
1829, "& Lucy is recovering from a three months most severe illness, during
which period her life was twice despaired of by every one."[2] Six weeks later
he announced that Lucy was now able to walk with the assistance of two
people and that his own health was at last restored. But within a month Say
was again seriously ill. "It is my old enemy, the bilious, or rather perhaps
the Liver complaint that causes me so much loss of time, of which I have
not an hour to spare of my allotment," he said to Bonaparte in a letter Lucy
wrote for him.[3] It is possible Say had suffered a gall bladder attack.

Say felt that his life was reaching a crisis. Along with ill health, the
frustration of not receiving boxes of specimens sent to him from the East
Coast and from abroad undermined his spirit and seriously hampered his
work on both shells and insects. He asked his brother Ben, who was always
solicitious of his needs, to go to the customs house in New York and locate
a box of insects sent to him from Germany in 1825. Maclure's agent in
Philadelphia, Andrew Spence, was charged with handling Say's affairs, but
he was exasperatingly negligent. Many boxes of specimens that Say was
sure Spence had received in his name were not sent on to him. "This most
extraordinary & unaccountable detention is of great disadvantage to me,"

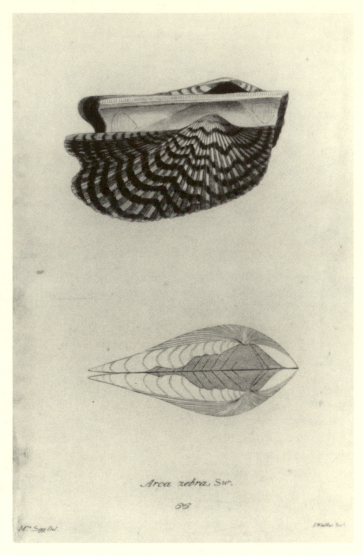

Fig. 40. *Arca zebra,* "inhabits the coast of the peninsula of Florida," by Lucy Say, plate 66 of *American Conchology.* Watercolor. Courtesy of the American Philosophical Society.

he wrote Haines. "The detention of boxes of insects, I need not say, is their destruction. That which you informed me of, as having been found by Mr. T. Peale to be destroyed, contained some insects which I long wished to possess, to exemplify some difficult points in Entomology, which, however, I have now lost all hopes of."[4]

Not receiving shell specimens was equally annoying. Had he gotten the shells Harris had sent him several years earlier—in 1828—Say could have added descriptions of important new species to a shell essay he had recently published. Say became so frustrated with the handling of his boxes that he actually asked that any sent to him in Philadelphia from overseas be immediately returned to the European sender with instructions to ship them to him in New Harmony via New Orleans. This would be faster than his agents could reroute them from Philadelphia.[5]

In addition to these obstacles, Say suffered increasingly from disadvantages inherent in living far from urban centers of culture: the dearth of current books necessary to keep him abreast of the ever-changing scientific scene; the absence of museums in which he could compare other collections with his own; and most important, the lack of stimulus from fellow naturalists. "It would give me pleasure to see the library & collection of the Academy, & the members also, but this perhaps may never be," he told Haines, "but wherever I may journey & whatever may be my lot, I cannot do otherwise than retain the most vivid remembrance of the gratification & instruction I have received in that school."[6]

Say feared he was lapsing into a state of apathy, "like the carelessness and indifference characteristic of the backwoodsman," as he expressed it in the following year to Bonaparte.

> That I have partaken of this presiding spirit of our forests in some degree cannot be denied, and when you ask me what I have achieved in Nat. Hist., I fear that my bouts of habitual ill health and the aforesaid opposing circumstances will prevent me from giving a very satisfactory account of myself. I have, however, managed to hammer out a paper on Diptera, another on Coleoptera, a third on Fresh water and Land shells, the Mss. for the first and second numbers of my Conchology (which will I hope be published sometime previous to the day of judgement) and I am now occupied with another essay, "Descriptions of New N[orth] Am[erican] insects and observations on some already described," which will be a work of some time, and will be published in the "Disseminator of Useful Knowledge," a Weekly paper of liberal character.[7]

But in January 1829, in addition to his *Conchology*, Say was hoping to publish a less expensive version of *American Entomology*. Mitchell had refused to continue with the project because he had lost money on it, and Maclure suggested that Say print it himself in New Harmony and make it cheaper and thus more accessible to the general public. In writing to Harris early that month about the idea, Say said that he did not mean to "detract from the accuracy of the plates" or from "their beauty," except in respect to their size. He thought he could proceed rapidly with this project if it were under his control and not "subject to the caprice of a bookseller, whose perpetual fear of pecuniary loss is a phantom that embitters his existence." Say added that a publisher (undoubtedly Mitchell) could not "conceive how an honest fame for fine work, unattended by money, can reward him, by drawing the attention of the public & thus extending his other business."[8]

The idea for a cheaper edition of Say's insect book may have been reinforced by Say's friend James DeKay at the New-York Lyceum of Natural History, a copy of whose address to the society on the state of natural science at that time (1826) possibly reached him: "The want of a good entomological manual is still felt by our young naturalists. . . . This is indeed partially supplied by the *American Entomology* of Mr. Say . . . but its expensive form puts it beyond the reach of most private individuals."[9] Rafinesque had said the same thing in 1817 about Say's first attempt at publishing *American Entomology*.

In the spring of 1827, Say had sent the plates and remaining impressions of the book to Mitchell in Philadelphia, completing what the publisher expected of him, but a year and a half later he still had not had word of their arrival, nor had he received the fifty copies which were to have been his only remuneration. Maclure observed in a letter to Mme. Fretageot that the promise of fifty copies was simply a lure, and that Mitchell had no intention of giving Say even a single copy. If Say had remained in Philadelphia, Maclure said, Mitchell would have made him his "pack horse," working without pay, and that Say's reputation as a scientist would have sold the book while Mitchell "pocketed" all the money.[10] Say never received his copies, but the third volume of *American Entomology* was published in August 1828 in Philadelphia.

Regardless of obstacles, Say's writing and publishing plans were prodigious, particularly for someone whose health was poor. In addition to *American Conchology* and the new *American Entomology*, he still intended publishing the book on reptiles he and Gilliams had discussed for years, another on species of North American insects, and yet another on the genera of insects. Say wrote Bonaparte that he hoped to make progress with all of these, but that they were as yet "in the prolific womb of futurity."[11] And as time-consuming as any of the endeavors Say enumerated was editing the *Disseminator*, the weekly newspaper printed by students from the School of Industry in New Harmony.

Not all Say's projects remained in the "womb of futurity," however; *American Conchology* would soon be born. Say planned to publish it in installments at three-month intervals and price it at $1.50 a copy. Book publishing in New Harmony involved special difficulties, however. Although the printer's type could be purchased in Cincinnati, the paper, ink, and watercolor paints all had to come from Philadelphia. At the end of 1829, Say had asked Haines to send him twelve reams of paper for the *Disseminator* of a better quality than what he had previously ordered because it would also be used for the *Conchology*. Delivery through the inefficient postal system was so uncertain that the best way to get something from place to place was by private conveyance; even this means depended on other people's timetables and illnesses, and involved countless delays. For some reason mail from Philadelphia to New Harmony was more undependable than the other way around. "We should suppose that letters sent from Philada. would have a much better chance, than those from this noted town so far 'within the bowels of the land,'" Say told Haines.[12]

Publishing works with colored plates required advance subscribers in order to defray the considerable expenses of production, however, and Say discovered that, from his location in New Harmony, finding enough to make the book feasible was a painstaking job. He regularly implored his friends and connections to find subscribers, but in America only Benjamin Tappan made a real effort on his behalf. The majority of those who signed up lived in Ohio and South Carolina; only three or four lived in Philadelphia. "We begin with but few more than 100 subscribers and these almost exclusively West of the mountains [Alleghenies] and in Europe," the *Disseminator* announced at the end of November 1830. The notice requested that specimens be sent to the author, including marine, freshwater, and land shells, from both north and south of the United States borders and from the northwest coast.

In mid-December, the first part of *American Conchology* appeared. The format was the same as that Say had used for *American Entomology*. Generic and specific characteristics of each shell were given first, followed by "synonyms" or other references from American or European publications. Then came a description and observations, which generally included where the particular specimen was found and by whom. The first number, containing shells with evocative names like Astarte, Pandora, and Delphinula, was confined to sea and freshwater shells from New Jersey, south to east Florida, and west to the falls of the Ohio and the Wabash. Besides Say, the shells had been collected by his brother Ben on the New Jersey shore, the botanist Stephen Elliott on Sullivan's Island off Charleston, and Lesueur from the Wabash.

Reuben Haines was Say's oldest friend, a fellow enthusiast in natural science since the early days at Westtown School. As Say became ever more frustrated with the difficulties of living in New Harmony, he turned increasingly to Haines for aid. This included not only assistance with his affairs in the East but moral support in defending his position at the Academy. "My dear friend!" he wrote in November 1829, "accept my thanks for your kind attention to my interests in Philadelphia, & the assurance of the high gratification which I cannot but express, for your good opinion of my character & reputation. It is extremely grateful, in my exile to learn that I am not forgotten by those whom I esteem: it is a consolation which I cherish & cleave to, & which I hope my future deportment will never obliterate."[13]

Say's impassioned feelings were called forth by a certain letter from Haines, who like many others could not understand why Say remained in New Harmony. "In common with all thy real friends, I have never ceased to deplore the infatuation that induced Lesueur & thyself to leave us, not withstanding all our protestations against it, & I am often puzzled to answer the question why you do not come back to Philadelphia."[14]

Say responded at once:

> Now this cause I thought was well understood by all my friends in that city: but as I find myself mistaken, I feel it my duty to explain to you what may indeed appear an infatuation, nearly allied, if you please, to partial inanity. This explanation may be given in the single word—poverty. My means of living were exhausted & I should have been under the necessity of relinquishing the pursuit of Natural History, had it not been for the pecuniary disinterestedness of my friend Gilliams, who always pressed me, with so much urgent kindness & hospitality to remain with him, that I felt it to be his wish that I should do so. But as my friend had a family to provide for, I considered it my duty to avail myself of the first opportunity to relieve him. Much against his wishes I accepted Mr. Maclure's invitation to visit Mexico & stop a few days at Mr. Owen's establishment in this place on our way, & to return to Philadelphia in the following spring. So confident was I that we should return at that time, that I left my insects unprotected against summer depredations; in conse-

quence of which, the greatest part of them was destroyed. Finding that Mr. M. concluded to remain here, & having no resort for a living in Philadelphia, I could not choose but remain also, & take a part in the singular & unique drama or farce enacted here. Mr. Maclure has treated me with uniform kindness & partiality, but should I survive him, I know not where my lot may be cast, this, however, is a matter which gives me no concern.[13]

What he would do if Maclure died concerned Say in every way. But he apparently could no longer conceive of being without his patron's support, and so chose to disregard the thought. For Say there was no other life than the pursuit of natural science. His statement of unconcern may have resulted also from an intuitive feeling that with his history of liver disorder he would not survive the sturdy old geologist, who lived frugally but not without attention to his health's requirements.

On his part, Maclure corroborated Say's account of his situation in Philadelphia but held a different view of his life in New Harmony, a view undoubtedly narrowed and simplified by distance and the plain fact that it suited him to have Say remain there in charge of his affairs. In a long letter to Haines, Maclure said he had heard that Ord and Isaac Hays were "very much enraged at Say and Lesueur for remaining at Harmony" and that he did not blame them for wanting to have the assistance of two such expert scientists, especially because their work had been gratis. Worried that Haines might share these "misapplied and unnecessary sentiments," Maclure wanted to set the record straight and did so in his invariably verbose manner:

Mr. Say was eating, lodging and fixed as a hermit in a corner of one of the academies' rooms, working for their journal and with all his industry could not keep it up so as to have a means of publishing his labours. Mr. Lesueur was designing and engraving both for himself and other contributors to their journal without any pecuniary benefit or advantage, and the subscribers to the journal could not keep up the expense of printing—so that its circulation was even less extensive than the Disseminator . . . Mr. Say has a house and a garden to any extent he pleases in which he finds amusement. At Harmony he is on a new field for all the objects he studies, and has a printing press at his command, for which even if his works should pay, it won't cost him half what it would at Philadelphia, and if the proceeds of his publications should not, he will not be burthened with any demands—he is perfectly free to follow his amusements in all the branches of science which pleases him without any let or hindrance . . . he is modest and unassuming; not well calculated for scrambling amongst the intrigue and forward ambition of your artificial superiority of ranks depending on the length of purse and the quantum of property. Mr. Lesueur is on the field favorable for his collections, either for himself or his European correspondents, the same advantage of printing press at his command; lives just as it suits him with a house and garden and wears his beard or any other dress he thinks proper.

New Harmony was one of the freest and most independent places in the country, Maclure concluded, where living was so cheap that no one was ever in want. "These advantages may appear trifling to those accustomed to the bustle, confusion and strife of large cities, but it is gratifying to those who have their independent occupations and amusements to be out of the crowd."[16]

Say would certainly not have described his scientific pursuits as "amusements," and being "out of the crowd" was becoming more and more of a disadvantage. "I wish we had some events here that might interest you, to compensate for the news you give me," he wrote Haines, "but ours is a monotonous region as respects the occurances of civilized life."[17] Nevertheless, when Haines offered him a post teaching at the school he had established in Germantown, Say declined, explaining that he considered himself under an "implied" obligation to Maclure to remain in New Harmony and manage his patron's publishing concerns.

Part of Say's responsibility to Maclure included editing the *Disseminator*, that "weekly newspaper of liberal character" whose chief function was to "disseminate" Maclure's ideas of social reform. From Mexico, to which he had soon returned, Maclure sent Say long treatises on reforming the world through education. "We recommend them to the careful reading and serious consideration of every Working Man, whose cause, the writer if not the very first, was one of the first of our countrymen to advocate," Say wrote in the *Disseminator*.[18] He dutifully printed Maclure's ponderous essays in the paper, and later, as directed by Maclure, collected and published them under the title *Opinions on Various Subjects, Dedicated to the Industrious Producers* (1831–38).

In addition to essays, the *Disseminator* contained excerpts of news gleaned from major centers in the country. The *Philadelphia United States Gazette, Baltimore American, Albany Daily Advertiser, New York Workingmen's Advocate*, and *Boston Sentinel* were but a few of the East Coast papers received in exchange. The news contained therein—much of it from Europe and as far away as Constantinople—was read by Say, evaluated, and reprinted in the *Disseminator* in the same way these news stories were treated by the newspapers of the large cities.

Say also included his own natural history essays, which he could offprint and send to his correspondents at home and abroad. He had of course sent articles to Philadelphia for various journals, but the exasperation of not receiving the extra copies due him as the author eventually made him reconsider this avenue of publication. The decision involved a definite sacrifice, however, because the circulation of the *Disseminator* was limited, even though its readership included some distinguished people. "They send the *Disseminator* to Jackson, the President," Mme. Fretageot wrote Maclure.[19] Andrew Jackson, whose election in 1828 had marked the rise in power of the common man in America, would certainly have approved the paper's liberal democratic tenor.

Say wrote articles for the scientific citizen in whom he hoped to awake an interest in entomology. In semipoetic language he personified insects and evoked a world previously unobserved:

> Few of our readers who have not made themselves conversant with the history of insects, will, perhaps, believe, that among them are to be found miners, masons, carpenters, and upholsterers, who were perfect in their different trades six thousand years ago! The common spider has made everybody familiar with his proficiency in the art of weaving; a similar insect, [that] has taken up his abode in the water, might have suggested the idea of the diving bell many centuries before it was discovered; and if we had our senses about us, when wandering in the fields of a fine evening in summer, the honour of inventing the air balloon would not have belonged to the French; we might have derived the principle of it from the little spider, who lifts himself in the air upon his tiny web of gossamer, an elevation which he could not otherwise have any chance of attaining.[20]

In the *Disseminator* Say discussed certain insects injurious to agriculture. An essay in the *New York Farmer* about the peach fly—named by Say *Aeperia exitiosa*—held that the insect responsible for destroying peach trees was an ichneumon (wasp). Say drew a moral from *Aesop's Fables* (a book being printed in New Harmony) to take exception to the *Farmer's* claim. "Now there is evidently some gross error here, as great as that made by the young mouse in the fable, who sought the acquaintance of the innocent looking cat, but was frightened away by an ugly cock. If the insect which those gentlemen speak of be in reality an Ichneumon, it is a benefactor, and the farmer who is acquainted with the manners of that numerous genus, will do all in his powers to encourage it." Say concluded that if, however, the insect in question was the *Aeperia exitiosa*, the farmer should condemn it as he would a "wolf found in his sheep fold."[21]

Say looked at everything with the eyes of a scientist, although he continued to relate his observations to literature—an eighteenth-century practice that would be abandoned as the study of natural history became increasingly scientific. He called his readers' attention to the fable "The Fox and the Grapes," in which the fox tries eagerly to reach some fruit. This would appear extremely unnatural, Say wrote, because the foxes he was familiar with did not eat grapes. "This fable comes from the East," he explained. "Shaw relates that the fox of Palestine is a great destroyer of grapes."[20]

Although the social discourses from Mexico, the *Disseminator*'s funding, and even its motto—"He who does his best, however little, is always to be distinguished from him who does nothing" (Samuel Johnson)—are attributable to William Maclure, the basic philosophy of the publication was Thomas Say's. As time went on Say became increasingly drawn to the cause of the working people through Robert Dale Owen's influence as well as Maclure's, and the *Disseminator* reflected this.

Robert Dale Owen had edited the *New Harmony Gazette*, his father's mouthpiece for socialist ideas, almost since his arrival in the town in 1826. But in the fall of 1828, with the outspoken young Englishwoman Frances Wright, whose own theories of social reform had filled its pages, Robert Dale moved the *Gazette* to New York City and rechristened it the *Free Enquirer*. Frequent excerpts from the paper appeared in the *Disseminator*, which by then had taken over the cause of reform at New Harmony even though the Owen experiment had failed.

Say wrote to Bonaparte in October 1830:

> No remnant now exists of our communities of common property, this town is now like all other towns, every one for himself & God for all. The fact is we never had common property . . . the true experiment has not been tried here. The houses, furniture and land . . . all belonged to Mr. O., who was not a member, and therefore the term "common property" was a mockery. But the experiment was so far conducted as to convince us that in order to succeed, it would be necessary that the individual should be educated from infancy for that form of society, just as we have been all educated for the form under which we live.[23]

From his extensive culling of newspapers Say could give Bonaparte, living in Rome, an overview of American society as he saw it:

> The greatest good of the greatest number is now advocated in this country with much zeal & talent. There are a great many working men's newspapers

which boldly put forth the rights of the producers. They call for a reform of the numerous abuses which have gradually crept into our institutions. They call for a general system of education, by which all the children of the Union may be educated in the best manner; the child of the plebian as well as that of the patrician. For the abolition of imprisonment for debt, for a simplification of the laws etc, etc. But all the world seems gradually reforming. Abuses must be finally destroyed by the omnipotence of the press. The poor silly, priest-ridden Bourbon of France [Charles X] could not fetter the press. What a glorious revolution [of 1830] was there, how sudden & how complete! The tide does not stop there. No tyrant can now much longer say "thus far shalt thou go & no farther".[24]

Perhaps to explain his involvement with political and social ideas, Say added, "I am editing a little paper here, for the want of a better editor, & although it is out of my line of work." Editing the paper may have been out of his field, but Say's increasingly liberal ideas were not out of character and were undoubtedly as much the result of heritage as that of association. The defiant Huguenots who fled the tyranny of Louis XV; the Quakers who departed England rather than submit to indignities from their intolerant countrymen; and Say's own father who seceded from the pacifist Quaker church during the American Revolution—all these forebears had bequeathed him a legacy of rebellion against injustice.

Say's accumulated anger and frustration at his impotence in frontier America poured forth on hearing from Bonaparte that the French naturalist Cuvier, in the new edition of his animal study *Le Règne animal distribué d'après son organisation*, had used many descriptions supplied by John Le Conte of American insects. In addition, Say found them to be erroneous. He was glad to hear that Bonaparte had undertaken a review of Cuvier's book, because "a man who has partially deserted [Natural] History, for the grovelling and vulgar ambition of ministering to a stupid, and besoted and bedevilled king [Charles X], deserves to have every error held up like a mirror in alto relievo to his eye." Disgusted with the mistakes attributable to Le Conte that he considered rampant in the book, Say exclaimed to Bonaparte:

> If this be a sample of the improvements in the new edition of Regne Animale we would have done much better with the first edition and to have believed the Grouse & Pheasant the same thing etc. etc. But what business have such poor miserables in intellect as we are, to judge of the handy work, the condescending dispensations of a minister of a king!! and so great, good and learned a king!! No! we must humbly receive what may be thus graciously vouchsafed to us and thank God for the favor. Whether or not Leconte has published on the subject I do not know.[25]

Could this anger be self-directed? At this point did Say feel that he had to "humbly receive" what Maclure gave him and be grateful? Say's years in the radical atmosphere of New Harmony had not been without their effect. They had decidedly influenced his ideas concerning education and religion, for example. In his letter to Haines in which he refused the teaching post in Germantown, Say stated his pragmatic beliefs on education, strongly influenced by those of Maclure. "In my opinion, a *complete* school establishment, ought to commence with the infant; train both mind & body; withhold all superstition & the whim whams of imagination; banish heathen greek & Latin, as well as every other monkish contrivance to prevent the application of the mental powers of the pupil to what is immediately around him, to what is immediately useful."[24] In another letter he made clear his antipathy to the church. "The prospectus of the 'Female School at Germantown' I conceive to be an excellent one; to which, with all my heterodoxy, I should feel no hesitation to subscribe; particularly as amongst the trustees I do not see the name of any hireling priest."[27]

Say's self-professed obligation to Maclure also served to turn away requests that he consider leaving New Harmony. He had recently declined another opportunity to return to Philadelphia, the previous summer—1830—a certain E. J. Pierce had asked him to come east to handle the natural history portion of a newspaper he intended publishing in support of the working classes. Say's answer was invariable; he was "fastened" in New Harmony.

Did he really feel so obligated to Maclure that in spite of everything—health, friends, and happiness—he was bound to the little western town? Or had Maclure been right in his assessment that Say was content to stay in New Harmony because he had a house and garden, a printing press, an excellent library of natural history books that Maclure continually purchased for him in Europe, and, more than anything else, the independence to do as he pleased? More than likely the truth lay somewhere in between. Say's awareness of his ongoing impecuniousness is evident in a postscript to Bonaparte. He confided that he and Lucy still had no children "and do not wish to have until we shall be well able to support them."[28] But even the prospect of having his own children was not incentive enough for Say to accept the proffer of employment in the East.

A final opportunity to change his circumstances occurred in the early fall of 1830 when Robert Dale Owen offered Say the editorship of the *New York Daily Sentinel*, a successful newspaper with a reasonably wide circulation. The remuneration from this job would surely have been enough to allow the Says to start a family. "I must hasten to express to you my most sincere acknowledgements for the kind & advantageous proposal you have made relative to the Sentinel," Say answered Robert Dale enthusiastically. "This paper is, beyond a doubt, by very great odds the best working man's paper in the Union, & I cannot but consider it the best of all our political papers, for various reasons; & therefore it must become, if indeed it is not at present, a leader not only in the great reform at which it so nobly & vigorously aims, but also in the reform of the press of this country, to which it may justly be said to be a pattern worthy of imitation."[29]

Several months earlier, Robert Dale Owen had attempted to enlist Haines's assistance in securing Maclure's financial backing for the *Sentinel*. "The good old man's money will *be lost to society*, if it remains as at present, as you know," Owen wrote Haines from New York. A week later he went into more detail: "It is so seldom that a rich man is really inclined to devote his riches to public & useful purposes, instead of leaving them—(I crave pardon if I offend your orthodoxy)—to bible societies & missionary follies; that I cannot think with patience of so large an amount of money going to swell the private coffers of a woman [Mme. Fretageot] who I am sure does not deserve it: and, at a moment, when the cause of the people here requires its aid so much, & where, even a small share of it [would] produce so much good."[30] Haines tactlessly sent this letter to Maclure, who certainly did not share Owen's antipathy to Mme. Fretageot. He rejected the idea out of hand.

Say declined the job of editing the *Sentinel*. "To conduct such a paper would be highly creditable to anyone, and ought to be an object of the commendable ambition of many good writers," he wrote Owen:

> Of the number of these, however, & perhaps I should say unfortunately, I have no right to consider myself one. I am but little versed in literature, still less in the arcana of modern politics, & not at all in the circumvention & chicanery of the politics of this country. I should therefore be a mere cipher in the establishment, or, if unassisted, injurious to the cause, by such incapacity. But even were talent & taste in my favour; I do not conceive it would be proper for me to determine, without previously consulting Mr. Wm. Maclure who is yet in Mexico, although there exists no express engagement on my part to him."[31]

As he had in the past, Say underrated his literary abilities in order to escape a commitment he did not want. By nature he was naive in the world of politics; in this he was candid. But his repeated claim of obligation to Maclure smacks of an oft-used but dubious excuse. He does not suggest conferring with Maclure concerning Owen's offer. For Say, his calling as a naturalist was all that really mattered, and he was willing to give up a great deal to pursue it.

Even Lucy's influence was not enough to sway him. About this time, when Maclure urged Say to join him again in Mexico, Mme. Fretageot assured Maclure that Say was satisfied with "his situation" and would not go east. "I do not relish his project to go next fall to you, for two reasons," she said, "one is that the Disseminator and his conchology would suffer in his absence and he is as careless about that as he can be. The second reason is that Lucy proposes to go to New York in his absence and then will contrive anything to get him there."[32] Lucy had few friends in New Harmony besides Lesueur, Maclure's younger brother, Alexander, and his two unmarried sisters, Anna and Margaret. Alexander had lived in the United States for some years before moving west, but the two women had emigrated directly from Scotland. They were all much older than Lucy. Mme. Fretageot's reference to Say as "careless" in regard to the *Disseminator* and his *Conchology* stemmed both from Say's wont of dropping everything to hunt shells and insects in the wild and from his habit of procrastination, of which he often accused himself. But what seemed like carelessness or procrastination was probably putting off one scientific pursuit in favor of another.

Perhaps Thomas Say's greatest frustration was his uphill battle to assure that only American naturalists name American species. In the spring of 1830, Bonaparte had written to tell him of Le Conte's latest indiscretion, which in Say's eyes amounted to a virtual betrayal of American science. With indignation he relayed the information to Harris:

> In your observations relative to Capt. Leconte I perfectly agree with you; but you are probably not aware of the full extent of his offending. Finding himself unable to describe the insects in his possession, even with the assistance of Dejean, he took with him to Paris his whole immense collection of American Coleoptera [beetles], the fruit of his researches for years, from N. to S. & presented them all at once to that truly eminent Entomologist [Dejean]. This I had in a letter from Prince Musignano [Bonaparte], who expressed his surprise, that they should not rather have been given to an Amer[ican] Entom[ologist], & I find the donation acknowledged by Ct. Dejean himself in his 3rd Vol. [of *Spécies des Coléoptères*] "une immense collection d'insectes des États Unis qu'il m'a donneé avec la plus rare génerosité." Accordingly in that Vol., as well as in his 4th he gives truly a great number of Amer[ican] new insects from that collection. This I leave without comment.[33]

But there was even more to Le Conte's scientific treason, and Say continued:

According to my correspondent, Capt. Leconte has made arrangements with a naturalist in Paris [M. J. A. Boisduval] for the publication of all the Lepidoptera [moths] of the U.S.—of these I believe, that by far the greater portion are as yet undescribed. . . . Here then is a field that urgently requires the attention of an Amer[ican] Entom[ologist], & from the study that I think you have devoted to that Order, it unquestionably awaits your labours. Do then, if agreeable to you, give us a paper descriptive of the unknown insects of this beautiful & neglected Order, & let them not be wrested from their own countrymen, thus unnaturally."[34]

Say was all the more incensed when he learned from Harris that Alexander Wilson's old friend John Abbot of Georgia had drawn the illustrations for the book Le Conte had published in Paris. Harris had explained that Le Conte "supported" Abbot in his old age.[35]

Say told Harris that it would give him great pleasure to send him moth specimens and to publish his essay in the *Disseminator*. As to Harris's offer to make drawings depicting the wing veins of moths for the less expensive edition of *American Entomology* about which they had corresponded, Say answered, "I would accept them most gratefully, did I know that my patron, who is now in Mexico, would warrant it by entering with sufficient extent into this business of Nat[ural] Hist[ory], for I have learned by experience that a capital, & not a small one is required to publish plates . . . especially coloured ones." In order to go on with the work, Say continued, he would either have to await Maclure's return or, as soon as his own health was "sufficiently reestablished," visit him in Mexico. There he would be able "to make clear & permanent arrangements in respect to issuing . . . a new & cheaper series of the work." Say added that "a work of this kind would be more useful because more generally attainable, & still more so if it should be also the record of your observations as well as my own."[36]

Harris's reply did not come for five months. He explained that he too had been ill, and although the study of lepidoptera had always been of interest to him, he could not write an essay on the subject for lack of a collection of European species complete enough to compare with his own. Harris confessed that as he had not heard from Say in so long, he had accepted a proposition from Le Conte the previous winter to exchange insects. "Among 193 species of Coleoptera sent to him," Harris wrote, "52 were nondescripts [undescribed], but had received names from Count Dejean, and 61 were new to Majr. Leconte; making in all above 100 which are probably undescribed." However, Harris assured Say that "these are but a small part of my supposed new species, and I shall send no more to Majr.

Leconte at present; nor would I have sent any of them if I could have been sure of your advice and assistance."[37]

Say responded at once:

> I greatly regret that circumstances prevented my reply to your former valued letter, otherwise the loss of so many species to *Amer[ican] Science*, might have been prevented; as my descriptions, in future, will antedate those of Ct. Dejean & of course be adopted by future naturalists. I expect also to elucidate them in my continuation of the Amer[ican] Ent[omology] . . . I am aware that your sentiments, as expressed in your former letter, agree perfectly with mine, as regards the describing of our productions by foreigners, & that you would have sent the insects to me, rather than to an European author, had you not, by my long silence, good reason to suppose that my labours had terminated. But I assure you that my zeal in this cause augments greatly with years, & I am resolved, if I can obtain the aid of my correspondents in various parts of the Union, to devote myself, yet even more exclusively to the describing of insects.[38]

Unfortunately, time would not permit Thomas Say to continue *American Entomology*, and most of the papers on insects he would write from now on would not be published until after his death.

At New Harmony Say gave his time liberally to pursuits other than science. Weather permitting, he spent many hours in the large garden behind George Rapp's old mansion, Community House No. 5, where he grew fruits and vegetables. Six young boys worked with him, including his favorite, a little Mexican boy, Zavalla, whom Maclure had sent to be educated at the School of Industry. The constant presence of Zavalla perhaps compensated Say somewhat for not having his own child.

Although edible plants were greatly needed in New Harmony, Say was always delighted to receive flower and tree seeds from his friends. Haines, horticulturist as well as farmer, sent him many packets. "Do you want any of our Backwoods seeds?" Say asked him in return. "If so please indicate them; but we have not fine Rhododendrons, Azaleas, Kalmia [mountain laurel] etc."[39] Maclure sent him seeds from Mexico of the lovely Chinese ornamental golden-rain tree, which he planted in front of No. 5, and from Colonel Carr at Bartram's Garden he ordered a quantity of fruit trees. To Bonaparte Say mentioned birdsightings: "The Wild Pigeons [passenger pigeons] were flying to the South overhead & on every side yesterday as far as the eye could reach in inconceivable numbers, the noise of their wings was like the commencement of a tempest."[40] Say noted that grouse were abundant around New Harmony—one shot in the winter had come close to the house and frightened the chickens—and the woods were filled with wild turkeys. In summer, hummingbirds, sometimes three or four at a time, visited the honeysuckle that "clustered" over his "piazza."[41]

In a small garden house behind No. 5 Say spent as much time as he could salvage from other activities examining, classifying, and describing insects and shells. Here he maintained his voluminous scientific correspondence and composed many papers as well as his *American Conchology*. Absorbed in the multifaceted science he adored, Say was probably happiest during these long hours alone—though slowly and irrevocably they took their toll on his delicate constitution. Indeed, Say's health seems to have deteriorated in direct proportion to his engrossment in science. Lucy did her utmost to encourage him to maintain regular habits but without success.

Say's duties also included overseeing the printing office of the School of Industry, run by William Kellogg, the chief hand-printer, and Kellogg's

Fig. 41. *Residence of Thomas Say at New Harmony* (Community House No. 5), by Charles Alexandre Lesueur. Watercolor. Courtesy of the Historical Society of Pennsylvania.

two young assistants, Lyman Lyon and James Bennett. Setting the *Conchology*, which had been promised to Say's subscribers in installments every three months, was their main concern. The second number would adhere closely to this timetable, but subsequent issues would continue to grow farther apart. Obtaining enough paper of the proper quality caused many delays.

It constantly worried Say that his situation in New Harmony crippled his work. On the back cover of the *Conchology's* second number, issued in April 1831, he printed an appeal to his readers:

> The insulated residence of the author, precluding a reference to any other cabinet than his own limited one, or to any extensive library, excites a fear that some errors in nomenclature may occur in this work, that under more advantageous circumstances might be avoided. In order therefore to render the "Conchology" as perfect in this respect as possible, and that the interests of science may not be endangered by his local disadvantages, the author invites judicious criticism, which shall be inserted on the cover of the number with due acknowledgment to the writer.

The fear that his chosen science might be "endangered" by his work certainly contributed to Say's growing depression.

Only his friend Joseph Barabino, the New Orleans apothecary and naturalist, responded to his plea for corrections. Say claimed that a certain shell had been found near New Orleans, but Barabino informed him that he had discovered it two hundred miles northwest of the city. In his ongoing attempt to fix the exact location where certain shells were found, Say once gave a friend an engraving of one he thought inhabited the Mississippi and asked him to show it to any Indians he encountered because they were known to be accurate observers. But not even the Indians had seen this shell in the "father of rivers."[42]

Other publications, for which proposals were sent out by the School Press, were not proceeding as smoothly as the *Conchology*. A reprint of *North American Sylva* by the French botanist François André Michaux had been announced in the fall of 1828, but as the necessary hundred subscribers had not been found, the work was postponed. Even the possibility of such an elegant work being produced by an obscure press on the American frontier, was an extraordinary notion. Originally published in Paris between 1810 and 1813, the book had later been translated into English. When Maclure learned that Michaux planned to sell to a London bookseller the copperplates and the few hundred copies that had been struck off, he bought the whole lot. "I thought it a stock book that ought to be in all our libraries," Maclure explained in the *Disseminator*'s prospectus, "as the only register of the greatest part of our forest trees—after the cutting down of our woods will leave only the most useful in preservation."[43] The prospectus noted that trees not included by Michaux would be added to make the work complete. Many years later this was carried out by Say's old friend Thomas Nuttall.

Lesueur's book on the fishes of North America, the first work announced by the press, never appeared. Say had told Benjamin Tappan in 1827 that two numbers of Lesueur's fish book, each with four colored plates, had been published and that a third was nearly ready. Twelve numbers were to constitute a book.[44] But for some reason it was not completed. A surprising statement from Mme. Fretageot to Maclure casts some light on why the project was abandoned: "Lesueur refuses to associate Say in his publication and this last refuses the translation of it if he is not put his name in partnership for the description, so much for author vanity."[45] Acknowledging credit was a sine qua non with Say, whether in describing new natural history species or in work as a translator. But to Lesueur, Say's rigidity may have seemed excessive, especially since the only book being published in addition to Maclure's *Opinions* was the *Conchology*. Even the *Disseminator* was discontinued in June 1831. Say explained in an editorial that the young printers were so completely occupied with a job "for our patron Mr. Maclure" (the *Opinions*) that proceeding with the paper was impossible.

In early March the printing office had been moved into No. 5 where Mme. Fretageot lived and conducted her school. She told Maclure she wanted the press there so she could keep an eye on it and "be in there often." Her constant presence was exceedingly annoying to Say, who began to withdraw from the project. "I am astonished that Say don't take more interest in it," she wrote archly to Maclure. Mme. Fretageot was one of the few who saw through Say's modesty, and she complained to Maclure that if she asked Say something about the printing office he would say he did not know. She noticed, however, that when Say headed Maclure's business he knew more than he pretended, and she said it was "false delicacy" for Say to withhold his advice because he was unwilling to "meddle" in others' business.[46]

Isolation, frustration, and ill health were combining at this stage to make Say increasingly testy, bitter, and critical. He would not have much longer to contend with Mme. Fretageot's interference, however, because she would soon depart for France and leave all Maclure's New Harmony affairs in his hands.

CHAPTER 14
A Toad Under a Harrow

Mr. Say writes he wishes I return as fast as possible that he may be able to return to his occupations that are much neglected on account of his new ones.

Marie Fretageot to William Maclure
Paris, 2 February 1832

I N J U N E 1 8 3 0 G E O R G E O R D wrote from Paris to Reuben Haines that he had heard Maclure was so pleased with Mexico he had no desire to return. "This is ominous, be assured. What, abandon that earthly Paradise and all his enlightened brethren, so soon! Do not you think that that brazen fraud—Madame—has been the cause of his forsaking his Utopia?"[1] Haines probably agreed with Ord, but Maclure did not think of Mme. Fretageot as a fraud, and he had moved to Mexico because of his health. To observers from a distance, however, Madame's control over New Harmony was scandalous, particularly in 1830 when the position of women was still such that it would be ninety years before they could vote. Maclure looked at women's rights differently from most of his contemporaries. He regarded Mme. Fretageot not only as an equal, but quite rightly as a clever businesswoman who could competently manage his affairs in New Harmony.

Maclure was fully aware that she was more capable in business matters than Say, although Madame herself suggested that he be given more responsibility: "I think Say very worthy of your esteem, and have thought many times that he deserves to be my partner in your affairs . . . [but] he does not like to be troubled with money, and dislikes business, as much as I like it."[2] She offered Say a salary on Maclure's behalf, but he refused it, claiming he did not like money and had everything he wanted. He had remarked, however, that if Maclure recovered his property in Spain he would ask him for a number of books.

The lack of a steady supply of scientific works and other naturalists to confer with continued to make Say's distance from the Academy a tremen-

Fig. 42. *Marie Duclos Fretageot and Charles Alexandre Lesueur,* by John Chappelsmith. Silhouettes. Courtesy of Historic New Harmony, Inc.

dous disadvantage. "I suppose I should hardly know one half of the members of the Academy now," he wrote Haines, "but I hope the spirit & interest of the meetings are kept up. How I envy them all the treasures of books that surround them. I should now if give Mr. Vaughan [the librarian] . . . more trouble than ever."[3] He mentioned that he hoped the Academy would soon find a larger building for its quarters than the one acquired in 1826, a few months after he had left Philadelphia for New Harmony. "These buildings may be had cheaper by & by, and they would be appropriated to objects of real utility if turned into museums & Societies of Nat[ural] Hist[ory], & the tilting spear of the theological polemic would then perhaps be beaten into the ploughshare & pruning hook of the cultivator of nature," he said, turning a biblical quotation back on itself to leave no doubt as to his attitude in this regard.[4]

By 1831 Say felt that he was again on a firm footing with the Academy, once spoken of by Bonaparte in reference to Say as "the only river of harmony in his philosophical, but still more scientific head."[5] Say commented to Haines that, ideally, he wanted all the naturalists of Philadelphia to make up a package of shells and insects to help with his work. He was eager to proceed with his studies after another serious illness. "I am just on my legs again from a short bilious attack, the first of any importance since my dangerous one of 1829; mercury is my specific, & my mouth is now sore with the effects of it."[6] Mme. Fretageot told Maclure that Say was tormented with these attacks and had more to do than the state of his health would permit. Say's illness may have been another reason for the demise of the *Disseminator* in June 1831. In its place the students from the School of Industry, under his supervision, printed a small bimonthly paper, the *Western Hive*, devoted principally to local activities.

Say was relieved to discontinue the *Disseminator*, for now, besides overseeing the School Press, he could devote himself to his writing and studies. As much as possible he kept in touch with Philadelphia—principally, as always, through Haines. Say's interest in most areas of natural history prompted him to ask Haines about a certain genus of fossil bones established by John Godman that had been under question. Say was amazed that anyone would doubt Godman, whom he considered an authority on the subject, and expressed his acute sensitivity to the honor of science in America: "If I recollect arright the genus Neotoma & another, made by Ord & myself, were denied also; yet these very genera have been adopted by the first authority in Europe. Is not this a sufficient admonition to others to make themselves somewhat acquainted with a subject, before they attempt to write upon it, lest they belittle American science still more in the eyes of foreigners?"[7]

Say's respect for the naturalists of France was enormous, in spite of his occasional outbursts against them. For years they had been world leaders in the field of natural science. When Haines told him of Ord's trip to Paris, Say responded with a mixture of envy and discouragement at his own prospects for such a journey, and particularly for the chance to see the type specimens from which so many scientific descriptions had been taken: "What an immense harvest Ord must be reaping in the French Museum! What an opportunity to solve an infinity of doubts & difficulties by simple inspection of the objects themselves, labeled by the French professors. Such an opportunity can never be mine, but I must continue to labour against wind & tide."[8] This is an interesting reference for Say to have used—it comes from Shakespeare's Henry VI, Part 3: "What fates impose, that men must needs abide; It boots not to resist both wind and tide." There is a certain fatalism in Say's attitude toward the conduct of his life.

Actual physical forces were indeed against him as well. He had to depend on ships sailing from Philadelphia to New Orleans to bring the mail up the Mississippi, Ohio, and Wabash rivers to New Harmony. Even if his requests were answered at once—which they were not—it took a long time. He had much trouble retrieving a number of papers on insects he had sent to Philadelphia several years earlier, especially a group of descriptions from his article on Diptera (flies) that had been unaccountably excluded when the essay was published in the *Journal* in 1829. "I cannot divine the reason why they were omitted or rather, I should say, rejected," he wrote Haines in July 1831.[9] By November, Say still had not received these descriptions, which considerably hampered his work. He again pleaded with Haines to look into the matter and to ask the members to give him reasons for the rejection so he could make corrections. "I do assure the Academy, that however unimportant those descriptions may appear, they cost me a great deal of labour & I am very unwilling to lose them."[10] Over a year later Say was still trying to discern what had happened to his lost insect descriptions, but he told Samuel George Morton at the Academy (with another reference to Shakespeare) that he was calling a truce "with so disagreeable a subject of 'Still harping on my daughter [his descriptions].'"[11] In fact, the pages from this essay were not rejected but lost. They had been omitted accidentally by the printer when the paper was originally published.

Say hoped someone in Philadelphia would either incorporate his article on Hymenoptera (wasps and bees), which Gilliams had in his possession, into another he was currently writing on the same subject and would send to Philadelphia, or else return the paper so he could accomplish the task himself. Say also wished to have a long paper on Coleoptera published in a scientific journal that would reach other naturalists. Some of the article's descriptions had been printed in the *Disseminator*, and a few others had been offprinted at the New Harmony press. He asked Haines to attend to these requests as he saw fit, but Haines, who for years had suffered from recurring depression and had become increasingly engulfed by it, neglected them. Say thought his repeated requests had probably exhausted the forbearance of his friends. "You will have good reason to think me a very troublesome correspondent," he wrote Haines. "I fear I wore out the patience of our excellent friend Gilliams, & I must therefore be more cautious in the future."[12] (Say's papers on new species of Hymenoptera and Coleoptera would not be published in his lifetime. Some years after his death Lucy would arrange with Harris to include them in the newly established *Boston Journal of Natural History*.)

To John Speakman Say had sent several copies of the first two numbers of *American Conchology* in the hope that Speakman would find subscribers for them. But since he had no reply Say assumed his friend was too occupied to attend to the matter. Speakman had left New Harmony in 1827 and moved some thirty miles up the Wabash. He had "turned shepherd," as Say had said at the time, by buying the community's flock of eight or nine hundred sheep.[13]

Although the third issue of the *Conchology* appeared in September 1831, it would be six months before the next number was published. Fate had intervened in the person of Marie Fretageot's brother Jean Duclos, who arrived in New Harmony from Paris at the beginning of August. Duclos's move to the small community on the Wabash had been inauspicious from the start: on his journey up the Mississippi he narrowly escaped death when a boiler burst on the steamboat in which he was traveling, killing three people and injuring him seriously in one leg.

Duclos brought his sister news that a friend of hers had died in France. Some time previously this friend had given her a copy of his will, in which he left her a yearly income of eight hundred francs. Anxious to discover if the document was still valid and to attend to other business concerning an inheritance from her father that she wished directed to her invalid husband—a casualty of the Napoleonic wars who had long been incarcerated in a Parisian veterans' hospital—Mme. Fretageot left New Harmony in early November 1831 on the first leg of her journey to France.

She had been ill for most of September and October and wrote Maclure en route that her health remained poor. She said that because of it she had been unable to attend to any business for the past two months and could not prevail on Say to act in her place as long as she was in charge. So, finding her health unimproved and Maclure's affairs neglected as a consequence, she had decided to leave and to make Say her substitute.

When she and Say reached Mount Vernon, Indiana, where she was to board the steamboat, they learned that a certain Count de Leon was at Rapp's settlement of Economie and was preparing to head west. (This count would prove a fraud who would severely disrupt the Harmonist community by undermining Rapp's strictures and leading away a third of his followers.) Since Madame had heard the count was interested in buying land and houses in New Harmony, she assured Say that should she meet him on her way she would return to New Harmony and negotiate the deal. She said of Say:

> I was looking at him in the mean time, and I was surprise to see him change colour and with quivering lips answer, with great agitation, that I should do better not to return. I caught his glance in the same instant. He could not help perceiving my astonishment and, being quite out of his gard, he was a while without speaking. Put yourself at your ease, Sir, said I. As I never expected your friendship, I am not unaware of your feelings, tho I did never think they had such extension; not a word any more on that subject. Fulfil your duty now toward Mr. Maclure, and I will remain satisfied.[14]

Maclure had informed Madame that two thousand dollars had been placed to her credit in Philadelphia the previous June. She was therefore astonished to receive a letter from the banker Stephen Girard the day before her departure saying the account was empty. She had asked Say repeatedly to write Haines about her financial status, but a letter had arrived from Haines in the same mail with the one from Girard without a word about it. "You see very well that it is impossible for me to continue your affairs," she had written Maclure in exasperation. "Your friends drive me away. . . . You will have by this an idea of my situation, in bed with a violent fever and delirious for about two weeks, and not a being around me who felt disposed to do the least thing to lighten the burden." She contrasted what she had done when Lucy was ill to the manner in which the Says treated her: "I was three days and nights by [her] bedside. Their ingratitude has overcome me. It is a fact that when they came in the morning about ten o'clock, they were not sufficiently master of faces for not showing they were disappointed at my being yet alive. It was sometime amusing. I was obliged to tell them that I wonndered at their not knowing that people good for nothing cannot die; they must be killed." Despite her acrimonious feelings toward the Says, Madame left her son Achilles in their care during her absence, though she told Maclure, "they are no friend of mine."[15]

On arriving in Philadelphia she heard the news that Reuben Haines had died suddenly on 18 October 1831, leaving five children and a pregnant wife. It was said that he expired in his sleep after attending an Academy meeting where he had appeared to be in perfect health. Madame wrote the somber truth to Maclure from New York, where she stayed with Lucy's mother before embarking for France:

Spence [Maclure's financial agent] told me that Ruben Hain came to his death by 4 ounces of laudanum that he took before he went to bed and was found in the morning too far gone for recovery. Spence says that a week before he was at his counting house and was relating to him that his father and grandfather had both killed themselves and thought it would be the same with him, that this idea was continually hanting his mind and that he kept himself as busy as he could to avoid such thoughts, but could not get rid of them.[16]

Rembrandt Peale painted a touching posthumous portrait of Haines (figure 43) and presented it to his widow. In the eyes there is a melancholy faraway look of despair that reflects, perhaps, Haines's mental state before his death. As a young man Haines had been aware of an unusual habitual despondency, and on his twenty-second birthday he wrote in his diary: "From some unaccountable propensity in my nature I do not possess that enjoyment of life which my youth, health, the attentions of a dearly beloved mother and my outward circumstances would warrant."[17] Nine years before Haines's death Madame Fretageot, in writing to Maclure of Haines's kindness to her, had added that, even if he did not have a "sound mind," he was a "good man."[18]

When Say heard the news he no doubt felt as though part of himself had died with his friend. Since their youth at Westtown where they had shared the rigors of an austere Quaker education, and through their years at the Academy where a mutual interest in natural history had cemented their friendship, the two had been very close. Say had spent countless hours with Haines searching for insects and other fauna in the fields surrounding Wyck. Distance had done nothing to diminish their relationship; indeed, it had only deepened through their correspondence when Say moved to New Harmony. For one is apt to reveal in letters feelings never expressed in conversation. Haines's death meant the end of Say's principal line of communication with the naturalists of Philadelphia, since Ben was now living in New Jersey and rarely attended Academy meetings. Haines had also handled financial matters for Say and Maclure, and his demise left those affairs temporarily unattended until the unsatisfactory appointment of Andrew Spence.

It had been Maclure's practice to deposit sums of money regularly, through Haines, into his account at Girard's bank. Say could then draw from this account to pay for supplies needed at the printing press, as well as to buy food, gardening equipment and seeds, clothing, and other staples necessary for his own life and the lives of those dependent on him. When Maclure learned that Mme. Fretageot planned to pass through Philadelphia

Fig. 43. *Reuben Haines III*, by Rembrandt Peale, ca. 1831. Oil portrait. Courtesy of the Wyck Association, Germantown, Philadelphia, Pennsylvania.

on her way to France, he had allocated two thousand dollars for the purchase of books in Paris for Say. He also allowed her to draw three thousand dollars in order to buy stock for a new store she proposed opening in New Harmony. The old one she had managed, now in the hands of her teen-aged son Achilles, was not doing well, and she planned to start it over again.

In January 1832, Say wrote Madame in Paris that, because it was not likely she would receive money for either her store or his books for some time, he would not trouble her with a list of all the works he wanted.

Instead, he asked her to look out for an agent who might take book orders in future. "What would I not give to enjoy the opportunities you now have to consult the magnificent museum & libraries!" he told her. "But I must attend to the trouble & perplexities that seem to thicken here & wait with what patience I may, in the delectable condition of a 'toad under a harrow,' until the coming of spring, which is the promised era of my deliverance."[19]

He had realized soon after Mme. Fretageot's departure that, surprisingly, her absence caused more difficulties than her presence, and he now eagerly awaited her return to relieve him of the onerous duties he had been obliged to assume. (Neither he nor Lucy seems to have been aware of the animosity Madame had felt toward them, and they wrote her many letters describing their activities and the concerns of New Harmony.) When Madame left for France, the Says' obligation to take over from her included moving into Community House No. 5 from the small Harmonist house behind it where they had been living. Say had taken on so many new responsibilities that he could hardly afford any time at the cottage. "I visit our house in the garden every day," he told her, "& the time will roll on heavily until we can return to occupy it once more in tranquility, without which every other advantage is to me of little importance; it seems to grow more desirable in my estimation the longer we remain absent from it."[20]

In addition to the Says, Achilles, and several boys from the school, the boarders at No. 5 included Duclos, his two young sons, Victor and Peter, who had come to New Harmony on the *Philanthropist*, and his French cook and her daughter. Relations between the Says and the elder Duclos, an irascible and difficult man, became increasingly strained. Duclos refused to eat at the same table with them and ignored any attempt at conversation, yet he appeared to have no intention of leaving. Lucy wrote testily to Mme. Fretageot: "You wish me to say how I get along in my new situation, I reply as well as I can but not as I wish—I have many *counteracting circumstances* to contend with and as Say can't, or pretends he can't, speak a word of french I have most of the differences to settle." Duclos had treated the French cook and her daughter badly on several occasions, prompting Lucy to speak "pretty freely" to him. This had "incurred his dislike," but, she concluded, "Thomas has approved of my conduct so I am satisfied."[21]

In addition to drawing illustrations for her husband's *Conchology* and coloring thousands of engraved impressions, Lucy cooked, washed, cleaned, and mended clothes. Every morning before rushing off to the printing office she fixed breakfast for at least five people—herself and Say,

Achilles, and the two Mexican boys—despite the presence of the two Frenchwomen. Say complained to Maclure that they had to pay them $1.50 a day for washing and scrubbing "whilst a backwoods woman would do the whole with more cleanliness & less trouble for a much less sum." He added that the sun had "caught" him and Lucy in bed but once since they had moved to No. 5.[22]

When Lucy had first arrived in New Harmony she had raised silkworms as a hobby, but she eventually turned to flower gardening in her free time. She dried and studied plants and would eventually become an accomplished amateur botanist. The previous year she had sent a collection of dried local plants to the botanist Charles Wilkins Short at Transylvania University in Lexington, Kentucky for his herbarium. In a letter to her husband, Short sent Lucy a list of all their botanical names. Say told Short that his wife's "incessant occupation" as artist had prevented her from pursuing botany as she wished, but they both hoped to "gather a few specimens" the following summer. But, he said, "unfortunately, a small prairie within three miles of us has been converted into a cornfield & nothing at all remains of it to attract the observation of the botanist."[23] To Mme. Fretageot, Lucy directed requests for flower seeds suitable to the New Harmony climate. She asked for "bulbous plants such as Tulips, the Tuberoses and a few double Hyacinths," adding, "you may think I wish you to purchase the whole Garden of Plants, you know my passion for all these things, but you must exercise your own judgement."[24]

In mid-January 1832, the contentious Duclos announced his plan to bring a lawsuit against Maclure for misrepresenting the education his sons were to have received at New Harmony. He threatened to publish a number of letters in his possession to substantiate his claim. Two weeks later Duclos applied to the local judge, accompanied by William Owen as his lawyer, to prosecute Maclure for compensation. The judge told him there were no grounds for such a suit, but that he could bring one against his sister. That night Duclos warned Say in strident tones that he would go to Mt. Vernon the next day to start proceedings against her. "A more disagreeable or a meaner man I think I never met with," Say told Maclure.[25]

Say informed Madame of the suit and of Duclos's intention to use some of her letters as evidence against her—letters presumably describing the education she was to have given his sons. The amount of the suit was $1,662, and if the money was not raised the furniture from No. 5 would be seized in lieu of it. Say had to give his personal bond to assure this. In order to save the furniture from a sheriff's sale, he told Madame, he had to prove it did not belong to her. Say urged her to return at once.

Throughout the summer and fall the case dragged on, with Say repeatedly delaying the trial in expectation of Madame's arrival. Duclos was decidedly not yet through with his sister. Achilles wrote to his mother in consternation: "Did Mr. Say ever mention to you that Mr. D. was going to publish your biography! and was writing most all day in his room? . . . There's no doubt but what he will make it as bad as possible."[26]

Aside from Duclos, Say had other problems to contend with in his unwanted role as manager of Maclure's New Harmony affairs. A new fence had to be erected around the orchard, and the one around the pasture, nearly swept away by the flooding Wabash, needed repair. The tenant farmers brought in precious little "rent corn," complaining that cattle broke through their fences and ate the crop. Say found it nearly impossible to get money from them. In January 1832 he told Mme. Fretageot that they preferred "running away to paying," and that while they remained many of them burnt and destroyed the property, "so that they cost more than they come to."[27] Say advised Maclure to sell the frame houses that were in such bad repair, since refurbishing them would far exceed their rent. Another problem was getting supplies for the printing press. Madame had forgotten to get printer's ink on her way through Louisville, so Say had ordered a keg sent by stage. It never came, and when notified that the stage had stopped running for the winter Say was forced to send Kellogg to Vincennes for it.

During all these diversions the printing of *American Conchology* continued. Say introduced the third issue with a genus new to science that he called *Alasmodonta*, a genus he had formed to include several species of aquatic bivalves that did not fit into the other bivalve genera. He explained that "Cuvier in the first edition of his Regne Animal unites all the genera of this family in Anodonta and Unio; and is still followed in this arrangement by some other naturalists, upon the principle that inosculating species destroy genera. They appear to forget that the same principle would reduce those two genera to a unit, and would in fact eliminate a great portion of those groups, in all departments of Natural science."[28] In this issue, as in many of his published observations, Say at times digressed into nonscientific particulars of special interest: he noted that *Venus mercenaria* was the shell used by American Indians as wampum, and that the "Wentletrap, or royal staircase shell," was the largest and most beautiful of its species. One of his English correspondents had written him in 1815 that the treasured wentletrap was worth more than forty pounds, which in those days came to the rather large sum of two hundred dollars.

By March 1832 the fourth part of the *Conchology* was published. Say was "dashing on with the printing office at a great rate, with plenty of ink & paper & force."[29] The freshwater shells he described represented both a large portion of the country and the efforts of many collectors whose names figured in the exploration of America and in the early history of natural science. The explorer Henry Schoolcraft located one species in Lake Superior; Augustus Jessup, initial geologist on the first Long Expedition, discovered another in "Canadaigua lake," New York; Joseph Barabino pulled a third from Bayou Teche near New Orleans; and Stephen Elliott, "the first botanist of the South," had sent Say a fossil shell from the Santee River in South Carolina. Say himself had found several examples during his encampment at Council Bluffs. One of these shells, *Helix profunda*, he had originally named and described in a *Journal* article of 1821, shortly after returning from the Rockies. A year later, the preeminent French naturalist Jean-Baptiste Lamarck had called the same shell *Helix richardi* in the last volume of his *Histoire naturelle des animaux sans vertebres*. Say wrote in *American Conchology* that his own name of *profunda* had priority and therefore must be adopted. This kind of insistence was mandatory in establishing the credibility of science in America.

The plates for the fourth issue would be the last engraved by Cornelius Tiebout. According to Achilles, Tiebout's serious illness was attributable to consumption and "hard drinking."[30] He died in early March 1832. Tiebout's death left Say no alternative but to employ his inexperienced apprentice, Lyman Lyon, as full-time engraver. Lucy had colored well over two thousand impressions since the beginning of winter, but she would be unable to keep up such a grueling pace, no longer having the assistance with the coloring of Madame's schoolchildren. Say mentioned to Maclure that David Dale Owen, yet another son of Robert Owen, might be able to print in the new medium of lithography upon his return to New Harmony, but this was not to be. Lyon's engraving steadily improved, but disease would again take its toll, for less than two years later this aspiring young artist would also be dead.

In regard to his *Conchology*, Say agreed with Maclure's suggestion of putting English as well as Latin scientific names to the shells, but he admitted he did not know them and had no books to help him. Say suggested to Maclure that many English works on conchology had been published recently which might be useful. Also, he had sent Madame a long list of books in French, with some in German and Latin, in the hope that arrangements could eventually be made for their purchase. That Say ordered so many difficult scientific works in French suggests that he could read the language (substantiating Lucy's claim that he only pretended not to know it when dealing with Duclos and his cook). Indeed, Say had written Harris some years earlier: "I do not see the necessity of thus using [Latin] in preference to the French, German & English languages, for I believe that almost every naturalist of any distinction can read a description in either. If any part is to be latinized I conceive it ought to be the history which is always the most difficult to read in a foreign language."[31]

One of the works he told Madame he needed most was, ironically, a monograph on bivalves of the Ohio River by his old bête noire Constantine Rafinesque, which had been published ten years before in a Belgian natural history journal. Say had also asked Short to send him a copy if one could be located at Transylvania University, where Rafinesque had taught botany, materia medica, and modern languages from 1819 to 1826. Since Rafinesque's descriptions of mussels had been published, Say had no choice but to quote them, not daring to publish any species as new without consulting this essay. Say told Short: "I never expect to find all his species, so often have I pursued his researches in vain, in relation to many animals that he has described, which may very possibly be in consequence of my own deficiency in acute perception of natural distinctions."[32]

Could Say have been referring to failing eyesight? Once, in cautioning John Melsheimer to take care of his eyes, Say had acknowledged that he too needed this advice. He told his friend, who was afflicted with opthalmia, that it was a disease more distressing to an entomologist than anyone, and although some eminent naturalists, including Lamarck, had continued their observations in blindness, "yet it falls to the lot of but few persons to extend the boundaries of science even when blest with all their organs of sense in full perfection."[33]

Say's magnifying lenses were essential to him in identifying minute differences in shells and insects. It thus came as a sharp blow when in February 1832 thieves broke into Say's study through a loose window and made off with his case of microscope glasses, his spectacles, and his dissecting instruments. He wrote Madame at once asking her to price a set of lenses such as French entomologists used. A month later, he told Maclure he was "endeavouring to get rid of some vile tenants" who had robbed him, and that he was determined while he remained to "purge the property" of such "wretches."[34]

Say mentioned to Maclure that he had heard from Ben that Spence had the "unblushing effrontery" to deny he owed Maclure any money, insisting his commissions and other expenses equaled Maclure's note of three thousand dollars. Ben had also told him that the printer Little, who now owned the copperplates and remaining stock of *American Entomology*, wanted nine hundred dollars for the unsold copies. This price made the book's purchase impossible. Say had written Haines a year earlier asking him to negotiate the matter with Little, not knowing that Haines was already dead.

At the end of August 1832, Say was at last able to write to Mme. Fretageot: "You are fearful that I have trouble with yr. business here; I think you will find on your return that there is not business enough of the estate, to employ the time of one person, so that there will be not any occasion for me to remain at No. 5; & I shall be able again to devote my time to Nat. Hist. exclusively; but you may always command my advice, if such as I can give may be useful, & it will, in all instances, be given conscientiously." He said he would send a box of American beetles for a friend of hers but that the friend need not send him European insects, as he already had too many to protect from destruction by parasites. He wanted to obtain European marine shells, however, with their names and localities attached.[35] In an earlier letter Say had told her he had plenty of European freshwater and land shells, and "if more are sent me, I propose to make lime of them for our bricklayers."[36] Say had sent twenty-five copies of the *Conchology* to his London bookseller and regretted not having thought to send her a few in Paris because Baron de Ferussac had intimated his book would be popular there. The baron had sent him a set of his own twenty-one-part work on shells.

The *Conchology*'s fifth number was published under a new imprint, called "M Press" for Maclure; it replaced "School Press," as the School of Industry no longer existed. To those subscribers who had promised to pay, Say sent a glossary of his work, hoping thereby to speed their payments. The previous year's experience had given him a modicum of business sense, forcing him to conclude that publishing the *Conchology* certainly did not pay. Even so, he planned to continue it as long as Maclure agreed.

In order to hasten the publication of the sixth issue, Say assisted Lucy with coloring plates—he told Madame he wished he could spend a few days in Paris in order to buy an assortment of paints and brushes and to improve himself in this art.[37] But of even more assistance to Lucy than Say's painting was Lesueur's agreement to make two of the drawings. A few months earlier Say had told Short the *Conchology* progressed more slowly than he wished because it was so difficult to obtain artists in New Harmony.[38] Lucy had more than she could handle drawing the shells and coloring thousands of engraved impressions, in addition to housework and clothesmaking, and Lesueur had been too absorbed in his own pursuits until then to become involved. Perhaps, too, he was still annoyed that Say had refused to translate his book on American fish. Lucy's duties at No. 5 had been reduced since her teaching ended with Madame's departure; in addition, other than Duclos and his two children, only Achilles, Tiebout's son Henry, and the two Mexican boys still remained, and the latter were soon to go home. It was just as well, because by November cholera was rapidly approaching New Harmony; several people had already died of it in Evansville, only twenty-eight miles away.

The previous August, Say had had reason to believe that his own health was improving. He told Ben that it was even possible he would outgrow his bilious attacks, and that he still planned to tour the East Coast, the West Indies, and Mexico in search of shells. He was pleased at Ben's plans for paying off the taxes on their father's estate without selling the Chestnut Street property but thought that in order to do so Ben "must really have discovered a silver mine." "It will certainly be a most unexpected degree of success to me," he assured his brother. He was confident Ben would settle "the whole estate business" in the best possible way but warned, "the veto, so much against the aristocracy in all parts of the Union, may perhaps diminish for a time the value of property & the Chestnut St. estate [if he had to sell it after all] may not bring as much as you anticipated, yet for one, I am perfectly willing to bear my portion of the pecuniary loss, for the sake of the ultimate moral good for our Republic."[39]

Two months later Say's spirits took another turn for the better when a cultured German naturalist arrived for a visit.

CHAPTER 15

Final Years

There is here a distinguished foreigner, a German, who is a very zealous
naturalist, & is travelling to make collections.

Thomas Say to Marie Fretageot
New Harmony, 21 November 1832

I
N 1832, MAXIMILIAN, prince of Wied-Neuwied, on his way to
explore the far West, stopped in New Harmony especially to see
Thomas Say, whose reputation as a distinguished American scientist
was known to him. Maximilian arrived on 19 October, accompanied by
Karl Bodmer, a young Swiss artist of exceptional talent he had hired to
visually record landscapes, natural specimens, and the Indians he hoped to
encounter on his travels through North America; and Maximilian's retainer
David Dreidoppel, an excellent hunter and taxidermist who had journeyed
with him to the jungles of Brazil from 1815 to 1817.

Maximilian, descended from an ancient family whose baroque castle
stood on the Rhine near Koblenz, was an avid naturalist. He had followed
in the footsteps of his mentor, the great scientist and explorer Alexander
von Humboldt, by collecting plant and animal specimens in South America. These he described and published in two volumes issued three years
after his return to Germany (in 1820). Maximilian's fascination with the
native peoples he encountered in Brazil prompted him to embark for North
America some twelve years later in search of fast-disappearing Indian tribes,
as well as the continent's unique flora and fauna.

After landing in Boston, Maximilian was so anxious to reach the
American wilderness that he bypassed the country's major cultural and
scientific institutions, overlooking Harvard University while in Boston and
visiting only Peale's museum in Philadelphia. There he had been welcomed
by Titian Peale, then proprietor, and had learned of Thomas Say, about
whom he may have already heard from German colleagues who corresponded with Say. Peale had shown Maximilian the collections he and Say

had made on their expedition together across territory the prince planned to explore.

Upon his arrival in New Harmony, Maximilian wasted no time in seeking out Say, later noting in his diary that he had "made the acquaintance of this interesting man, who had undertaken important journeys to the Rocky Mountains and into the westerly countrys with Major Long and is a celebrated writer on natural history."[1] Say showed Maximilian his extensive library and the press on which he was currently printing *American Conchology*. In the afternoon they visited Lesueur, whom the prince described as "an original, already old [he was 54] with very clearly defined features, and despite the long time he lived here had still not learned to speak English. He was delighted to speak French with us [himself and Bodmer] and immediately brightened up."[2]

Maximilian drew a detailed verbal picture of Lesueur's studio in a hall of the old Harmonist church. The entrance to his quarters was decorated by several backdrops he had painted for the New Harmony theater—one depicting the town, another Market Street in Philadelphia, showing Joseph

Fig. 44. *Lesueur, the Naturalist, at New Harmony,* by Karl Bodmer, 1833. Watercolor. Courtesy of the Joslyn Art Museum, Omaha, Nebraska.

Bonaparte's town house. Within the studio, natural history specimens, including a preserved whooping crane and a great blue heron, hung from pillars, while stuffed animals and rows of shells from the Wabash and Mississippi covered benches, tables, and chairs. Lesueur's painting and drawing equipment filled every other space. Maximilian and Bodmer spent the afternoon looking at the artist's sketches and watercolors of New Harmony. The following morning Say invited them to see his garden and insect and shell collections.

In spite of his enthusiasm, it was evident Maximilian was ill, and Say persuaded him to consult a doctor. Cholera by then was epidemic in New Orleans, Louisville, and Cincinnati, but Say and Maximilian theorized that New Harmony had probably escaped contagion so far because of its isolation: water in the Wabash was then too low to accommodate steamboats, so few carriers of the disease could reach the town. Although the prince's severe intestinal disturbance suggested cholera, it was not diagnosed as such. Nevertheless he was advised to stay in bed for a week. Say dropped by daily bringing books and engravings, including, to Maximilian's surprise, such magnificent volumes as the *Oiseaux Dorés* of the French ornithologist Louis-Jean-Pierre Vieillot and his artist Jean-Baptiste Audebert.

When he was well enough, Maximilian accompanied Say on walks along the Wabash and Fox rivers to observe birds and collect plant and animal specimens. Flocks of vivid Carolina parakeets brightened the dreary autumn woods, as did mallards, golden-eyes, wood ducks, bluebirds, and several varieties of woodpeckers. Maximilian noted swamp hickories, pecans, catalpas, pawpaws, and Kentucky coffee trees. Even poison ivy, poison oak, and dandelions were of interest to him, and he carefully cited each of these by its Latin name in his diary. How pleased Say must have been with the companionship of this fellow naturalist, whose enthusiasm for everything around him matched his own. Say identified forty-three species of mussels (Unio) from the Wabash for his attentive listener. Maximilian later noted in his journal that Say was the first to describe these shells in his 1816 article for William Nicholson's *Encyclopedia*, and that only later had they been described by Lamarck and Rafinesque. In "October or November 1831," the prince recorded, Rafinesque had published several new genera and approximately twenty-four new species of mussels, to which, when he told Say about it, Say had responded by "shrugging his shoulders."[3]

Rafinesque's habit of publishing at his own expense small tracts of only several copies, just so that he could claim priority in naming species, was frowned on by other scientists, who disregarded these hasty slipshod papers even though they were usually original and were penned by an acknowledged, albeit eccentric, genius. In 1831 the Academy's Isaac Lea wrote Dr. Edmund Ravenel in Charleston that he regarded Rafinesque as a poor authority and wished he had listened to his friends, who advised that he pay no attention to him. James DeKay reminded a friend over a decade later, "I gave you notice, you know, that I never would cite that clever but notorious rogue in Nat. Hist., Rafinesque."[4] The historian Henry Savage described him as "a tragic figure, too erratic, undisciplined, and unreliable in his scientific work to be fully accepted by the scientific community of his day."[5]

Say often entertained Maximilian in the evenings with stories of his encounters with Indians and his collecting forays on expeditions. After one such congenial occasion the prince recorded that with Thomas Say he could always have "a fruitful discussion about American natural history . . . over a cigar by an open fire."[6] Occasionally they visited Lesueur, who was always willing to bring out his numerous drawings of mammals, amphibians, and mollusks made years before when he journeyed around the world with Peron. He told Maximilian that he planned to return to France to publish his work—a statement indicative of his feelings of discouragement with New Harmony, and perhaps with Say, since, after all, the town had its own printing press and could reproduce colored plates. Then again, for his own reasons, Lesueur may never have broached the subject to Maclure, even though Maclure had once said Lesueur had the "same advantage" of the printing press "at his command" as Say.

On 5 November 1832, the presidential election pitting Andrew Jackson against Henry Clay brought hordes of hard-drinking farmers to town to vote. Noting the careless life led by these people, Maximilian commented that if one asks a farmer how many horses or cows he has he is apt to answer: "'As many as I can find.'"[7] Around New Harmony there was much local enthusiasm for Jackson, because he was a man with whom the local people could easily identify—a backwoodsman—who had risen from poverty to run for the nation's highest office.

Maclure's renters kept Say busy, for they arrived daily at his house to settle their accounts. Because the crop was better that season, they were more reliable about paying. The aristocratic Maximilian described them as "extremely crude" and was shocked to see them "walk past the lady of the house with their hats on, grab the nearest chair, immediately plunk themselves down by the open fire, spit frequently, and make themselves at home."[8]

By the end of November Maximilian's health had improved, but his retainer Dreidoppel was quite ill with the same affliction. The prince ascribed this to the locality's severe changes in weather, observing that illness, especially abdominal complaints, was common in New Harmony. Say tried to make Maximilian's enforced stay as pleasant as possible by loaning him books on travel and the American West, including an account of Baron de Lahontan's early eighteenth-century journey to North America, Lewis Cass's invaluable articles on Indians, William Dunbar's record of his expedition on the Red River in Arkansas, and many books and articles on Indian languages. By means of Linnaeus's book of classification, *Systema Naturae*, Maximilian was able to identify the quantities of natural history specimens he, Bodmer, and Dreidoppel collected or purchased from the local inhabitants, who were only too glad to hunt for this generous visitor. Maximilian noted paying two dollars for a "splendid" bobcat and twenty-five cents for a prairie hen. His stay in New Harmony, according to the historian William H. Goetzmann, "was the key educational experience for Maximilian as regards all aspects of frontier America."[9]

One afternoon in mid-December when Say and Maximilian were walking together, Say suddenly felt acute pains in his liver which forced him to turn back. This reawakening of his chronic problem—probably gall stones, a condition inoperable in Say's time—foretold the seriously deteriorating health he would experience during the next two years.

Maximilian's health was nearly reestablished, but since winter had set in, resuming his travels was out of the question. Since he was able to augment his collections without setting foot beyond New Harmony he was fully occupied. Some specimens were even brought to him on Christmas Eve as presents—just as small children receive in Germany, he observed. But Christmas Eve in New Harmony had other less attractive aspects, as Maximilian was to discover when gunfire exploded in the street beneath his window. He noted that "there is no trace of a celebration these days because there is no church; and only by drinking, hunting, singing, and dancing does the wild and sometimes coarse population of this area celebrate the most solemn festivals of Christendom."[10]

On Christmas night a boisterous dance was held in the tavern where Maximilian had rooms. He described it as "raging since nightfall, with the large drum and a pair of violins and pipes or flageolets creating an uninterrupted music pounding the ears."[11] As Say was then still living at No. 5 directly across the street, he must also have spent a sleepless night. On New Year's Eve a similar party was held, but Maximilian escaped his throbbing quarters to spend the evening with Say. Lucy had once lamented to Mme. Fretageot that though she and Thomas were invited to balls, they never attended any.[12]

In mid-March 1833, Maximilian left New Harmony after a stay of five months. Say gave him letters of introduction to his acquaintances along the Missouri River, one of whom was Lieutenant Martin Scott, the famous sharpshooter with whom he had journeyed up the Red River of the North to Fort Pembina on his second expedition with Major Long. Say spent the prince's last two evenings in discussions with him and reluctantly saw his enthusiastic and knowledgeable friend depart.

Life in New Harmony settled back into its monotonous routine. Say's hopes of relief from his troublesome managerial tasks had been renewed at the end of 1832, however, when he learned that his November letter to Mme. Fretageot describing his ongoing problems with Duclos had at last convinced her to return to America. She sailed from Le Havre on 30 December, on a crossing of forty-eight days. Because she had not seen Maclure for years and had much to discuss with him, she directed her travels to Mexico—a move she may have contemplated for some time. From the beginning of their relationship her letters had intimated a regard exceeding that of friendship. In mid-February she landed in Vera Cruz and wrote to Maclure: "You will be astonished at my coming but it was absolutely necessary that I should talk with you about my business at home. . . . It is the last letter I received from Mr. Say and Achilles that have determined my leaving."[13] She added that most of the books Say requested had been sent from Paris. After several days rest she took a carriage to Mexico City.

In New Harmony Say had been ill for most of February and was barely well enough to answer a summons to appear in court against Duclos on the 26th. Once again he stalled the proceedings in anticipation of Madame's return in the spring. But at the end of April his long-cherished hopes of relief were suddenly dashed on receiving word that Mme. Fretageot, stricken with cholera in Mexico, had died in a matter of days. Maclure wrote to a friend that by her death he had suffered a greater loss than he had ever known. Perhaps in his gruff way he had returned the affection she had so obviously felt for him. For Say, her death tightened inexorably the bonds that tied him to New Harmony.

During that spring of 1833 little was accomplished on the *American Conchology*. Lyman Lyon, the engraver, was seriously ill, and Say found himself again afflicted with the insidious apathy he had once described to

Bonaparte, more than likely exacerbated by his own declining health. As a result his only published paper that year was a small pamphlet entitled "A Catalogue of Exotic Shells from My Cabinet," an impressive list of hundreds of shells from all the oceans, the Adriatic and Mediterranean seas, and the Straits of Magellan, as well as from Europe, Africa, China, New-Holland (Australia), New Zealand, and South America. He also continued to exchange specimens with European naturalists, a practice he found consistently rewarding. A letter from the German entomologist Johann Ludwig Christian Gravenhorst of the University of Breslau told of boxes containing books and hundreds of insects that he had sent Say in care of Barabino in New Orleans.[14] Since Joseph Barabino, the wealthy and philanthropic apothecary who for years had received Say's shipments for him, died that spring, Say may have had difficulty obtaining these gifts.

In the summer of 1833, Lucy, increasingly anxious to see her family in New York after an absence of nearly eight years, at last persuaded Say to accompany her on a trip east. Say's need for sound medical advice, his earnest desire to see his friends at the Academy in Philadelphia once again, and the opportunity to examine certain type specimens and books made him acquiesce. Toward the end of July, the Says boarded a stagecoach for Louisville, then a steamboat to Pittsburgh, and finally a carriage to Philadelphia.

A letter from Samuel Carpenter, Maclure's new agent at Girard's bank, informed his client that Thomas Say had arrived in the city indisposed, but was recovering. Dr. Benjamin Coates at the Academy saw with dismay that "the ravages of sickness were but too visible." Say was thin and hollow-eyed, and had an unhealthy yellow pallor; a stooped drained aspect replaced his once erect and confident bearing. To Coates he confided the depression he had felt for so long at being isolated from his colleagues and from the mainstream of science. Coates, in later noting how low Say's spirits had been, observed that "his last days cannot be said to have passed away without regrets . . . he appeared to feel, though surrounded by friendship and munificence, that he had not the independence to which his extraordinary talents and industry entitled him."[15] Say's implied obligation to Maclure, to which he had adhered so tenaciously out of honor, duty, necessity, and certainly at times out of preference, had weighed ever more heavily on him as the years passed. Say now felt acutely a sense of personal tragedy that circumstances had not permitted him the scope he had envisioned for his work. Certainly he realized at heart that a significant part of that tragedy was his own doing.

In September the Says traveled to New York to see Lucy's family, as confirmed by a letter Maclure received from an old friend, who told him that Say had called twice but that he had been out both times. Say had himself written Maclure the previous June, telling him of his intended eastern journey, but he had forgotten to give Maclure a date for his departure until just before he left New Harmony in July. When Maclure received Say's letter he wrote at once to Carpenter arranging credit for Say to purchase books in Philadelphia, but by the time the letter arrived Say was on his way back to Indiana. He learned of Maclure's intended generosity only upon his return to New Harmony in an admonishing letter from Mexico: "Had you timed your matters well so to receive 10 or 12 memorandums with an [order] for 2,000 dollars, I haven't a doubt but you would have been able to purchase the greatest part of the books you wanted in Philadelphia, New York, Boston, Baltimore etc. without being swindled by the booksellers."[16]

Maclure asked Say to persuade Achilles to come to Mexico, if not to live at least to visit, because he wanted someone "active and young" on whom he could rely when his "dotage" came on. As for New Harmony, he advised Say to handle the town as if it were his own, adding, "rest assured I shall never complain only consider I am a great egoist and would be more pleased to hear something about my o[ctavoes] [his book of *Opinions*]— and the success of the working men than all you can write to me about Camelots or even printing proofs—the one is the means I have employed the other the object. Harmony is a distant consideration in which I have no great interest."[17]

This statement must have been something of a shock for Say. He had been aware of Maclure's disillusionment with his educational experiment in New Harmony, which had come to an end even before Mme. Fretageot's departure for France, but he had thought that Maclure cared about the press and the town generally. Undoubtedly Say was relieved in one sense by Maclure's attitude, since it left him free to follow his own pursuits, but he must have been apprehensive in another, because Maclure's interest in and subsidy of the press was essential to its continuing. At least Maclure was concerned about the publishing of his *Opinions*. He said that if Say were bored with his ideas, he must remember they had been formed over fifty years and were not to be dismissed lightly. "I do not expect you or anyone else to ride my hobby [horse]," Maclure assured Say, "or to find pleasure, gratification or satisfaction in studying his paces, frisks or gambols, nor that you can yet foresee his utility, but you may consider him harmless and nourish the poor beast now and then, tolerating him sometimes to jog alongside of your own."[18]

Maclure's letters to Say often upbraided him for not writing, and when Say did write, for not answering Maclure's questions. "Your letters are no answer to mine, filled with lists of books that I am no judge of and complaints against the vogues of booksellers." Nevertheless, he advised Say on his own project: "Be sure you have a copious index to every volume, it is a bill of fare which every reader has a right to expect from every author to inform him whether it will be worth the trouble of turning the pages."[19] Maclure was pleased to hear that Say had hired an engraver but would have cared even more had he taken on a bookbinder, without whom it would not be possible to produce inexpensive books. He instructed him to publish François André Michaux's *North American Sylva* as he pleased, but to remember that "cheapness is the end and sole object of our free press." Say had his hands full with *American Conchology*, and whether or not he had any plans for printing the *Sylva* is unknown, but it was not undertaken in his lifetime. Maclure told Say: "I always believed your pleasure and amusement in diffusing knowledge was similar to mine," but understanding Say's single-mindedness, he added with sympathetic insight that Say was "so much of a naturalist as to be indifferent to the other branches of knowledge & rather neglect the little hobbies that were nothing along side of yours, that is so natural that it would perhaps be unreasonable to expect otherwise."[20]

With the help of his new engraver, James Walker, Say brought out the sixth number of *American Conchology* in April 1834. Included were descriptions of shells sent to him by Titian Peale and Edmund Ravenel, the conchologist from South Carolina. Say's knowledge of classical literature and art are evident in his observations on scallop shells (genus *Pecten*): "Aristotle and Pliny indicated several species, and compared them to a comb or pecten from the similitude of their ornamental rib-formed radii. Distinguished artists have judged them worthy of representation on their canvas, and the voluptuous form of *Venus* is seen supported on the waves by the valve of a *pecten*."[21]

Could Say have seen a copy of Botticelli's *Birth of Venus* at the home of Joseph Bonaparte? Because there were at the time no art museums in America containing European works, the famous collection at Point Breeze is the most likely place he may have seen a print of the painting. Say's connection of Pliny's "encyclopedic" *Natural History* with the figure of Venus standing on ocean waves may have derived from the Peales. Rembrandt Peale wrote an 1820 article for the *National Gazette* on allegorical painting, including Pliny's discussions of art, and in 1822 his brother Raphaelle exhibited a painting entitled *Venus Rising from the Sea—A Deception* at the Pennsylvania Academy of Fine Arts. Their father had referred to Pliny as early as 1801 in his public lectures on natural history, which the precocious Say may have attended, although he would have been only fourteen.[22]

Say quoted Pliny in a description of the remarkable behavior of certain mollusks: "When the sea is calm, troops, or little fleets of Scallops, are often observed swimming on the surface. They raise one valve of their shell above the surface, which becomes a kind of sail, while the other remains under the water, and answers the purpose of an anchor, by steadying the animal and preventing its being overset. When an enemy approaches, they instantly shut their shells, plunge to the bottom, and the whole fleet disappears!" Say added: "We have not learned that this remarkable flotilla has been observed since the time of Pliny."[23]

For his discussion of oyster shells (genus *Ostrea*), Say again drew on his knowledge of antiquity to give his description historical significance: "The shells were used by the Athenians in the performance of their right of suffrage, during the earlier periods of their government, and the sentence of condemnation or acquittal of the arraigned, was marked upon a shell; whence the word *ostracism* had its origin." Never failing to replace myth with science, he mentioned that earlier writers had had the mistaken notion that crabs, on finding an oyster shell open, would cast in a pebble to prevent the shells from closing, then extract the animal and eat it. He quoted one writer as remarking on the amazing craft of these creatures, who had no voice or powers of reason. "We scarcely need to add," Say noted dryly, "that the craft existed only in the imagination of a person who may have seen a crab feeding on an oyster that had fortuitously closed on a pebble."[24]

In the *Conchology*'s sixth number, another artist—Lesueur—is represented along with Lucy for the first time. Later she was to say she persuaded Lesueur to draw two plates for the *Conchology* because he had been her first teacher "and always my friend," and she wanted him associated with her part of the work.[25] It was mid-April when this issue was published, and Say hastened on with the seventh. He also would have published *American Entomology* in smaller size, with only one species to a plate, had he been able to find "a good draughtsman of Insects," as he wrote to Harris.[26] There is no mention of Lesueur.

In the fall of 1833, to Say's relief, the troublesome Duclos departed for Mexico. He was intent on badgering Maclure about his sister's estate. Maclure wrote Say that Duclos had given him "an immense history of the destruction of my property, not one word of which I believe." He said that the vindictive Frenchman complained much about Say, but more about Lucy, whom he described as "having a bad tongue in her head." Maclure added that Duclos "fully confirmed the opinion I have often given you that he was mad."[27]

The following June, 1834, Prince Maximilian returned to New Harmony for several days on his journey back to Europe. He and Karl Bodmer regaled Say and Lesueur with tales of their fascinating though harrowing experiences of a year-long stay among Indian tribes of the upper Missouri River. Bodmer showed the two naturalists his magnificent watercolor portraits of Indian leaders, and vivid landscapes of the grand, wild country they had seen. While in St. Louis, Maximilian had decided, at General William Clark's suggestion, to accompany members of John Jacob Astor's American Fur Company up the Missouri, in lieu of following his original plan of crossing the great plains to the Rockies and the old Spanish town of Santa Fe.

Since last seeing Maximilian, Say had worked steadily on his *Conchology* and had compiled many descriptions of new American insects. During the summer following the prince's brief visit, Say wrote often to Harris and exchanged lists of new insects. Still exasperated over the loss of his manuscripts, which he had not located on his eastern visit the previous year, Say lamented: "You mention my unpublished Mss in Philadelphia, this reminds me that I have probably in the lists I sent you, sometimes quoted them as published & sometimes as unpublished; the delay of my Philad[elphia] friends of several years, has been of serious inconvenience to me. They inform me that the Mss are mislaid, & I have no copy of them."[28] He was doubly annoyed at himself for not having made copies.

Say told Harris he would be glad if the essay he had sent him—"Descriptions of New Species of North American Insects"—could appear in the *Boston Journal of Natural History*. He explained that he had offered the work to the American Philosophical Society in Philadelphia in answer to a request for an article to be included in its *Transactions*, but he had since received a letter saying that, by mistake, a paper he had written on Curculionidae (weevils) had been sent to the press instead. In any case, Say felt sure the essay would be published much sooner in the Boston periodical, as the *Transactions* came out "at very remote intervals," and in the meantime his paper could be "overtaken & its species anticipated by European works."[29] Say persistently worried that he would be preempted in his discoveries.

He also mentioned to Harris, in the same letter, Titian Peale's project of painting American butterflies, depicting the different states of each species. "If anyone will undertake to describe them," he suggested, "I will contribute by furnishing those of our environs. I endeavoured to persuade Mr. Peale to do this, but I doubt if he will."[30] (Peale had published a few plates and pages of his butterfly book in 1833 in Philadelphia and presented the Academy with a copy, which is still in the library.)[31]

Say's last letter to Harris, dated 26 August, expressed concern for not having asked his friend's permission to publish the names of new species Harris had sent him. Because he had printed them himself in New Harmony, Say suggested that if Harris objected he would obliterate them so they could not be read, and of course he would not send off "a single copy" until he received Harris's reply. He did not mention his failing health.

Less than a month later, Say's condition took a sudden turn for the worse and he was prostrated with a severe attack of his long-recurring malady—what he had always called "bilious fever." His temperature rose alarmingly, and as the hours passed his body shook increasingly with tremors and muscle spasms. Lucy and Lesueur watched in consternation at his bedside, unable to alleviate his violent tossing and turning. It was all too evident that his strength was relentlessly ebbing away.

During a slight remission, Maclure's brother and sister, Alexander and Anna, had the presence of mind to prevail upon Lucy to have Say sign three drafts for money on which they all depended. Maclure's sisters had planned a trip to Mexico with Achilles, and they needed funds for the trip. Only Say had the power to tap Maclure's resources, and his sudden incapacity had taken them all unawares. With Lucy and Lesueur holding him in a sitting position, Say summoned all the energy left in his wasted body and painstakingly described the letters of his name in oversized figures. His huge signature resembled that of a blind man. Three witnesses signed the drafts.[32]

Lucy, barely able to see his face through her tears, then sought her husband's advice concerning the disposition of his specimen collections and his library. Say managed to whisper that he thought her entirely competent to handle his affairs and that he left everything up to her. Lucy suggested the Academy, and Say nodded. Shortly afterward he lapsed into a coma. At seven o'clock on the night of 10 October 1834, Thomas Say died, "without any struggle or emotion, just like a person whose system had been gradually worn out by natural decay," observed Alexander Maclure.[33] Lucy wrote Harris that Say's bilious fever had "soon assumed a Typhoid form of an extremely nervous character which with the supervention of the Dysentery proved fatal."[34] According to Anna Maclure, "a general sickness in this quarter" had resulted in more deaths in the last four months in New Harmony than in the previous six years.[35]

Say's constitution had been weakened by years of neglecting his health as he pursued his life's work. What was probably acute liver failure, in combination with typhoid fever and dysentery, was more than his worn-out body could withstand. He was forty-seven, at the height of his powers as a naturalist, and as deeply involved as ever with his struggle for the world's recognition of American science.

CHAPTER 16
Aftermath

He was the pride of my heart . . . and the recollection of his virtues shall stimulate me to
the exercise of the limited talent which I possess to the advancement of that Science for
which he sacrificed riches and health.

Lucy Say to William Maclure
New York, 30 December 1834

L UCY WAS DEVASTATED by Thomas's death. Lesueur wrote
Maclure that she was "inconsolable" over her loss, and Alexander
Maclure told his brother that while Say's death was "severely" felt
by them all, "the bereavement to poor Lucy [was] truly afflicting."[1] Lucy's
world had been centered around Say for the last nine years; now, at thirty-
four, her life's focus was gone. She most wanted to see her mother, and as
nothing was left to keep her in New Harmony except memories, which
were too painful at present, she made immediate plans to return east. A
local workman hired to pack her things wrote and tacked up a sale notice
listing a small house, a "first rate" milk cow, oats and corn, a loom, and
"varis artickles two tegis to mention."[2]

At the end of November, having bid farewell to her closest friends in
the town—Lesueur, Achilles, and Alexander, Anna, and Margaret Maclure—Lucy left for Vincennes to catch a steamboat to Louisville. From
there she boarded another boat for the trip up the Ohio to Cincinnati. Only
a year and a half had passed since she and Say had made the same journey
together, and it must have seemed as though he were elsewhere on deck or
reading below in his cabin. Her loneliness undoubtedly deepened as she
watched the western country slip away with the boat's wake. In Cincinnati
she stayed three days with Dr. William Price and his wife—old and sympathetic friends who had voyaged with Lucy and Say aboard the *Philanthropist*—and their lively family of seven daughters.

From Cincinnati Lucy traveled to Philadelphia, where she was met
by the Academy of Natural Sciences representative, the tall, cadaverous-
looking physician Samuel George Morton. Robert Dale Owen had written

to Morton from New Harmony on Lucy's behalf concerning Say's death and his wife's intention to visit the city. Morton expressed the members' appreciation for the donations of specimens she had brought with her and for those she arranged to have shipped from New Orleans by Maclure's sisters on their way to Mexico. He presented her with a letter of sympathy, in which, as Lucy wrote Maclure, Say was spoken of as "the brightest ornament to American Science."[3]

On 16 December Lucy was present at an Academy meeting when Say's old friend and colleague Benjamin Coates read a biographical address in which he praised Say's untiring and multitudinous efforts on behalf of the institution and stated that "the value of such assiduous attention by such a man, may be easily imagined." Coates concluded his remarks with a fitting epitaph: "Thomas Say was the greatest American naturalist of his day, with a field of knowledge in vertebrates, insects, mollusks, crustacea and fossils not equalled by an American of his time."[4]

Say would be praised as well in other parts of the country. Lesueur wrote Maclure (in French) that his death was "an irreparable loss for the United States, and also for New Harmony, which he had made famous by his publication [*American Conchology*]."[5] Benjamin Silliman of Yale wrote in his *American Journal of Science and Arts*, "It is no exaggeration to assert, that [Say] has done more to make known the zoology of this country, than any other man."[6] And the *North American Review* in Boston described Say's impact in Europe: "Ask the savants of Germany; of France; of England, and they will, with one accord, thankfully acknowledge the discoveries due to his labours."[7]

When Lucy at last arrived in New York to the comforting embraces of her mother, brothers, and sisters, her ordeal became easier to bear, but she found that New Harmony was still a "proscribed place" in their estimation, and she gradually stopped talking about it. Lucy wrote to the Prices in Cincinnati, "Mother is careful that no one [of the boarders] in the house shall know that Frances and Sarah [her sisters] were ever at N[ew] Harmony, and they, of themselves do not like to mention it."[8]

Lucy had found the same attitude in Philadelphia, where Academy scientists attempted to separate Say from the "utopian" society of New Harmony. "His residence there, as well as that of several other learned men, should not be confounded with the eccentric experiment of which, by the agency of Mr. Robert Owen, the same place was made the theater," Coates declared in his memoir.[9] Lucy wrote Achilles in Mexico that "the opprobrium which formerly existed against N[ew] Harmony still only slumbers. When the place is mentioned I am questioned most minutely upon the state of society there, and not infrequently, have been obliged *to state the fact* that the society has *been extinct* for seven years and that it was upon a par with any other place in the west, excepting there had been more *intelligent people* there than in any other small town in its neighborhood." She added that she had never concealed any "particulars" of her life there, nor the interest that she would always take in the town, though she could "never think of living at it again." In concluding, she asked Achilles to write often and let her know his future plans because, she said, "I shall always take a deep interest in every thing that interests you."[10] Achilles may have substituted for the son Lucy never had.

After her return to New York, she made arrangements to place the *Conchology* and Maclure's *Opinions* in the hands of the Philadelphia bookseller Judah Dobson. She planned to return to Philadelphia a few weeks later, or, if the weather continued so bitterly cold, to wait until Say's boxes arrived, at which time Dobson agreed to send for her.

The biting temperature was not the only discomfort to provoke the young widow. In late December she learned that George Ord had presented an offensive memoir of Say before the American Philosophical Society. Say's friends were so furious at Ord's remarks, which they considered a cruel caricature of the Academy, a libel of Say, and, in the end, a mere eulogy of Ord himself, that the text of his talk was rejected for publication. Particularly repugnant to his audience was Ord's characterization of the Academy founders as "a club of humorists" who held weekly meetings "merely for the purpose of amusement" and whose specimen collections could only "excite merriment."[11]

Lucy wrote Harris in great indignation that Ord had spoken of Say as "having been very deficient in 'Elementary learning,' and especially 'indifferent to polite literature.'" He had also said, wrote an astonished Lucy, that "[Say's] printed papers, at least while he lived in Philadelphia, underwent the *revision* of some of his particular friends!!" "My private opinion," she confided, "is that he forgot his friend and contemporary, and made poor Say the vehicle through which to vent his ill nature upon Mr. Maclure and others, whom he thought instrumental in causing him to leave Phila.— the limits of a letter will not permit me to give you the minutiae of the circumstances which excited his jealousy of Mr. Say."[12]

Ord, believing himself unjustly maligned, related his own version of the event and its outcome to his friend Charles Waterton in England—a correspondent with whom he shared a sharply critical view and dislike of Audubon:

> In one of my letters of December last, I spoke of a Discourse which I had been requested to compose on the life and character of the late Mr. Thomas Say, the entomologist. This Discourse was read to the Philo. Society, and received with approbation; but there were three or four persons, also members of the Academy of Natural Sciences, present, who thought fit to take exception to it; and who, communicating to the other members of the Academy an erroneous idea of my sentiments and intention, were the cause of a cabal, which deprived me of the chair of Vice President, a situation which I had held for many years. At the head of this conspiracy was Audubon's dear friend, Rich. Harlan, M.D., a fellow whose moral character is so infamous in Phila., that he is excluded from the society of gentlemen.[13]

Ord's description of this incident gives some insight into the warring factions that had existed at the Academy for some time, seriously disrupting its business and perhaps accounting, at least in part, for Say's presumed exclusion. It is ironic that Richard Harlan was the leader of the "conspiracy" supporting Say, because Say had once strongly opposed him on behalf of John Godman. Say had earlier described Harlan as "very unpopular" in Philadelphia[14]—possibly, strangely enough, because of Ord's opinion of him.

There are several probable reasons for Ord's offensive memoir. The trouble may have begun in July 1825 when Say was helping Charles Bonaparte with the writing of his continuation of Wilson's *Ornithology*. Ord, who had completed Wilson's work after his death and was extremely defensive of it, objected to a part of Bonaparte's book. Say dashed off a note to Bonaparte from the "Hall of A.N.S.": "I had not an accurate recollection of the passages in p. 37 of y[ou]r Ornithology that offended Mr. Ord. Mr. Mitchill [the publisher] brought the sheet here today and as soon as I read it, I told Mr. Mitchill that I could not see anything in it that could give serious offence to any person." Say said that he immediately took it over to Zaccheus Collins (an old and respected Academy member) for his opinion. Collins returned the page and agreed with Say, and when Ord came in they both told him what they thought. Say concluded that he supposed the business "was for the present at rest, though Mr. Ord persists that he is right & he says he hopes to make this appear in a paper on the subject that he intends to write."[15]

The following fall, when Say left Philadelphia for New Harmony, Ord undoubtedly saw this move as desertion. He must have felt betrayed and disgusted that Say, a long-admired associate, would give up his position of eminence at the Academy of Natural Sciences to join what Ord later termed "schemers of newfangled modes of education," "propagators of illegitimate morality," and "factors of grubstreet literature."[16]

There is certainly some justification for Ord's outrage. The Academy was just beginning to establish an international reputation and Say was one of its brightest stars. After Say's departure, the *Journal*—so important to the Academy's prestige—collapsed and was not successfully resurrected for many years.

By joining the proscribed New Harmony community, Say, in Ord's opinion, undermined everything the Academy had been attempting to do for American science. With regard to professions in general, George H. Daniels has written, "A member becomes dangerous when he either violates the methodological canons of the profession or makes some attack on societal values that may cause the public to look askance at the profession as a whole. In order to deal with such a member the defenders of orthodoxy try to associate these two sins with each other."[17] This is exactly what the rigidly orthodox Ord attempted to do in his memoir by denigrating Say's approach to science. "Some persons," Ord had said, had maintained that "the insufficiency of our author's technical phraseology may lead to confusion or doubt."[18] Daniels further states that denying a scientist access to publishing in journals was an effective way of punishing him. Say's difficulty in getting his papers published in the *Journal* after his move to New Harmony is evidence of this method of castigation. No doubt Ord had a hand in it.

Although Lucy was thoroughly shaken by Ord's ill-chosen remarks, Say's death had overwhelmed her too completely to worry long about the memoir; it had been suppressed, so she allowed the incident to fade in her memory. But like the mythical Hydra, the hated "creation" had not been cut off and would reappear unexpectedly long afterward.

In 1859, twenty-five years later, the entomologist John Lawrence Le Conte, son of Say's old adversary, collected all Say's entomological writings—from the *Western Quarterly Reporter*, *Contributions to the Maclurian Lyceum*, the *Disseminator*, and other obscure journals—and published them in one volume. When Lucy opened a copy of this treasured, long-desired compilation, she was aghast to see Ord's memoir printed in full at the beginning of the book. The ironic juxtaposition of something she had looked forward to for years and Ord's scurrilous paper shocked her so thoroughly it took her a full year to control her anger, shape her response to Le Conte, and institute a plan to counteract the insidious memoir. "Our long acquaintance and pleasant social intercourse, when you resided in New York, was, I thought, a sufficient reason why you should have informed me of Mr. Ord's intention to avail himself of this most effectual means of exhuming this address, which, was so obnoxious to Mr. Say's personal friends," she reproved Le Conte.[19]

Nearly all were dead who would vindicate her husband's name from Ord's charges, Lucy asserted. Therefore, she had resolved to write out her own comments, and send them to a few naturalists who could have no knowledge of Thomas Say other than his published writings and the several memoirs in print. She enclosed a copy of these comments for Le Conte. After stating the case, and pointing out Ord's imputations that Say was indifferent to classical literature, that he had no "technical precision" in his papers, and that he had disdained "a sacrifice to the muses"—"Think of Say's emulating the Muses!" wrote Lucy heatedly to Harris—she went on to clarify her objections:

> Really, I am unable to understand Mr. Ord, in his assumption of Mr. Say's deficiency in elementary learning. True, his father, particularly his grandfather [Thomas Say, senior] had the peculiar objections of the "Society of Friends" to Colleges, and in the beginning of his N[atural] History career, he may have experienced some embarrassment from this want of a Collegiate education.
>
> But his assiduity in remedying this scholastic defect, speedily supplied him with all the resources necessary to his profession.
>
> His scientific text books, which he continually used, were written in the German, French and Latin languages, and it were indeed presumptuous to suppose him incapable of fully comprehending their contents.
>
> With regard to his choice of profession, I know his Father had no wish for his son to succeed to his own professional calling; but wished him to acquire a knowledge of Medicine for the literature and learning incidental to medical studies.
>
> And this, I think, he did to a respectable degree. But his distaste for business, "trade," "buying and selling," was probably exaggerated, from the fact of his prospective inheritance being such as to stifle the usual incentive to thrift, and to the emulation so essential to success in business.
>
> His endorsement for his brother, whose partner had embezzled money to an amount which ultimately involved his House [Say's apothecary business with Speakman] beyond the power of retrieving its former credit, was the chief cause of the loss of his ample patrimony, which, consisting mostly of real estate, was submitted to forced sale ruinous to the proprietor, though portions of the same, at the present valuation, would be an independence to his heirs.
>
> But this disaster was one of the means of fixing his attention upon the study

of Zoology, his favorite branch Entomology claiming his particular attention; and how far he indemnified himself and the scientific world for his "mis-employed youth" those can but judge, whose studies have induced like inves-tigations.

"Despite his want of 'classical phraseology,' concluded Lucy, "there will be more than one 'Erichson' to give him that true commendation, which his devotion to Natural History entitles him to. For we may reason-ably infer, from the encomium of this learned man, that the obscurity of diction ascribed to Mr. Say by some may find an interpretation in the obtuseness of those who cannot define his meaning."[20] Lucy may have had "a sharp tongue," as Duclos once claimed, but it was also witty and articulate.

Three months after Say's death, she had written Harris about re-publishing Say's miscellaneous papers, printed at New Harmony and else-where. She approached the Academy of Natural Sciences first because it was the most obvious choice. Morton had told her the members were sincerely interested, but on being advised that no funds were available to pursue her objective, she had looked to the scientific societies in Boston to take over the project. "For myself, I feel as if his writings belong to the World," she told Harris, "and that regardless of country, city or society they ought to be published in that style, and by them who will do the most justice to his memory."[21]

Harris was unable to persuade anyone in Boston to undertake the plan, so he turned at last to Maclure, explaining that because Say's papers had been printed in so many obscure journals and in such limited editions at New Harmony they were virtually unattainable for other entomologists. Most of the descriptions of North American insects contained in these papers had been presented to science for the first time.

> The *right of the names* applied by Mr. Say to these insects is exclusively his, his friends, therefore, must feel an interest in securing to him this right, which has already been infringed upon by Count Dejean, & other foreign naturalists, to a great extent; it is essential to his reputation that it should be recognized & made known to European entomologists. Unfortunately, the descriptions, upon which this right is founded, are accessible to but very few persons, even in this country; and to foreign Entomologists they are, for the most part, absolutely unknown.[22]

Harris offered his services to arrange Say's papers for publication and asked Maclure, as Say's friend and patron, to back the project financially.

"Allow me to hope, Sir," he concluded with dignity, "that the freedom with which I have addressed you will not be considered as presumption; and be assured that, in doing so, I am actuated by no selfish or sordid motives, but, on the contrary, by a true love of science & a regard for the fame of a most laborious naturalist. Your own friendship for Mr. Say, and your philanthropy and liberality, as they have encouraged this appeal to you, will, I am sure, be my best apology."[23]

Maclure did not finance the project. This decision was no doubt a surprise to Harris, who must have expected that Maclure, who had backed Thomas Say financially and morally for nearly twenty years, would publish Say's collected papers. With Say's death, however, Maclure may have felt the thin thread sever that had tied him to natural science in America. Perhaps he had no interest in supporting the spirit of Thomas Say, but only Say himself. His means had made possible the publication of Say's work in the first place; now he may have felt that issuing Say's collected writings should be left to the booksellers. Since the booksellers looked upon the project as unprofitable, it was not until W. G. Binney published *The Complete Writings of Thomas Say, on the Conchology of the United States* in 1858, and John Lawrence Le Conte brought out *The Complete Writings of Thomas Say on the Entomology of North America* in 1859, that Say's books and numerous papers on shells and insects were finally brought together.

Lucy spent the month of February 1835 in Philadelphia. One of her first tasks was to procure a marble slab to mark Say's grave in New Harmony. She told Maclure she thought it "perfectly in unison with the character of him whose memory it is intended to perpetuate—pure white marble, with simply his name, birthplace and period of decease, to which is added 'One of the founders of the Academy of Natural Sciences of Philadelphia.'" She also had lithographs made of the portrait that Joseph Wood had painted of Say in 1812. Lucy referred to this picture as "one of the best likenesses that I ever saw—his friends say that at that time he was rather stout and full faced."[24] All Say's friends recalled that when they saw him again after his many years in New Harmony, during his visit to Philadelphia in the late summer and early fall of 1833, they thought his looks had altered radically.

While Lucy was still in the city, Say's boxes arrived from New Orleans. Unfortunately, many specimens had been mutilated by bad handling and microscopic insect predators. The collection was eventually sent to Harris for preservation, but Harris found the specimens almost beyond salvage, with heads and wings missing and bodies disintegrated. It was later revealed that in order to get rid of the predators he had baked the collection in his oven, a process that virtually destroyed them. He returned only a fraction to the Academy.

Determined to complete the seventh issue of *American Conchology*— the majority of which Say had finished—Lucy took up the art of engraving upon her return to New York. Since it was the most expensive part of the work, she decided that by engraving the plates herself she could be surer of getting them published. In her feministic spirit, she wrote to the Prices: "I am looked upon as being very singular, particularly since I have commenced Engraving—a gentleman remarked 'Well! at what do you think the ladies will stop?' I replied, I hoped at nothing, short of breaking up the Monopoly so long held by the Gentlemen—that we were tired of cramping our genius over the needle and distaff."[25]

Lucy took engraving lessons from a Mr. Pilbrow, an English artist recommended to her by James Walker, the engraver at New Harmony. Before Say's death, five plates of the *Conchology*'s seventh number had already been engraved, printed, and colored, so Lucy asked the conchologist Timothy Abbott Conrad at the Academy to assist with Say's manuscript of descriptions and to help her finish the work. She told Maclure that Conrad had agreed to add three more plates, making eight in all, and that if he should be "patronized" in this undertaking she would contribute all in her power toward the "mechanical" part of the book. She assured Maclure that "as this is the only resource of which I can avail myself, satisfactorily for my own maintenance, I am very anxious as to the success of the undertaking."[26] She thought seriously of a career in engraving, but after three or four months of lessons her teacher changed his business and she was forced to give up the idea.

A year later she wrote Maclure that Conrad was at last editing Say's manuscript descriptions for the seventh number. As for the plates, "I have so far succeeded with those I began, as to have them *pass* with touching up by the engraver, and in the course of the Spring [1836], this No. which poor Say left unfinished will be published by Mr. Dobson who has interested himself in it."[27] Five plates had been engraved by Walker, but the remaining three (62, 65, and 67) must have been done by Lucy, since hers is the only name on the page. Instead of being in the lower left-hand corner, as on her other plates, "Mrs. Say, del[ineator]" appears at the lower right, the spot traditionally reserved for the engraver.

Lucy could have been an artist of note had circumstances been more favorable to her talent's development, for her early instruction had been of the finest. At Marie Fretageot's boarding school at Twelfth and Walnut Streets in Philadelphia, both Lesueur and Audubon had been her teachers. In describing to Benjamin Tappan her nine-week stay in Philadelphia during the summer of 1837, she mentioned that in addition to meeting Thomas Nuttall for the first time, "[I] saw also my old teacher in drawing Mr. Audubon whom I had not seen since 1824—and then his great work had not yet been put into the hands of the engraver."[28]

When Audubon had come to Philadelphia in the spring of 1824 in his unsuccessful attempt to find a publisher for his bird paintings, he was as usual in need of money and had looked for work teaching drawing to young ladies, as he had done elsewhere in the past. Through his friendship with his fellow Frenchman Lesueur, whom he had met at the Academy of Natural Sciences, Audubon most likely secured a temporary position at Mme. Fretageot's school, where Lesueur had been teaching for three years.

Lucy had also seen part of the printed version of Audubon's *Birds of America* (the publication was not concluded until 1838) at the Academy that summer; the members had subscribed for a complete copy of the elephant folios for five hundred dollars. She observed to Tappan: "Many and various opinions are expressed as to the merits of the work and the author—I am disappointed in the execution of the *plates*—considering the immense *aid* which he had at command and the price demanded for each volume."[29] In mentioning the diversity of opinions expressed about Audubon and his work, Lucy alluded to the controversy over his scientific accuracy in depicting birds. One plate showed mockingbirds under attack by a rattlesnake, for example, and some Academy members refused to believe that such a confrontation was possible. In fact, later observers proved Audubon correct: it is now known that the canebrake rattler, common in the south, does indeed climb trees to dine on birds and their eggs.[30] As to Lucy's remarks on the quality of the engraving, one can only surmise that her own attempts at the art had given her a thoroughly critical eye.

Of Lucy's two teachers, one achieved a fame that would become monumental with the years, while the other would remain unknown to all but a few. "But what can be done in regard to Lesueur?" Harris had written to her in 1835. "[He] seems forever lost to his friends & to the world, after a debut the most brilliant. Will he too pass away without leaving behind him any memorials of his eventful career, or any one to record this history of his life & labours?"[31]

After Say's death and Lucy's departure, no one remained in New Harmony about whom Lesueur really cared, except his ward, Virginia

Dupalais, who had married and settled there. He had planned for years to return to France, so in 1837 he at last boarded the steamboat for New Orleans and sailed to Le Havre. For a while he lived in Paris near the Jardin des Plantes, earning a marginal living by teaching drawing, until in 1845 he was chosen to direct a new natural history museum in his native Le Havre. Lesueur moved there with his brother to a small house near the sea, to begin at last a career with both the prestige to which he had so long been entitled and the scope to use his prodigious talents. But he died suddenly of heart failure the following year, on 12 December 1846, at the age of sixty-eight.

Lesueur's countless drawings and valuable specimen collections from his voyage to Australia with Peron, the journey to the West Indies with Maclure, and his wide-ranging travels in North America formed the basis of the new museum. This institution existed for nearly one hundred years until it was bombed during World War II. Lesueur's scientific collections were destroyed, but his portfolios of drawings and watercolors, which had been moved for safekeeping to an old abbey nearby and stored in trunks, miraculously survived the war and are housed at the rebuilt Museum of Natural History in Le Havre.[32] Several publications of Lesueur's drawings of North America have been recently issued by the museum.[33]

Lucy's later life as a single woman in mid-nineteenth-century New York City was not easy. Women were still a long way from achieving the emancipation that such a spirited individual as Lucy wanted. In a letter to Maclure in 1836, she mentioned that Benjamin Silliman was lecturing in New York that winter, "but as no one of my acquaintance whose protection I could avail myself of, attended, I remained at home, lamenting the dependence of females in large communities."[34] She missed the freedom she had enjoyed in New Harmony and regretted not appreciating it at the time. A few years later she told Alexander Maclure she had made everyone laugh at the dinner table when she told them she was tired of being pent up in New York and yearned for the West. "One said, have you not enough to enjoy here. No—was my reply; everything is too circumscribed, I long for the freedom I used to enjoy when I lived on the Banks of the Wabash."[35]

Maclure freed Lucy somewhat from financial worry by leaving her $5,000 in Pennsylvania 5 percent bonds in his will. He died at seventy-seven of pneumonia on 27 March 1840 at San Angel, Mexico, on his way back to New Harmony for a visit, a curious old man still full of ideas for reforming the world. Three years earlier, he had written Lucy of a bizarre, egocentric, although typically pragmatic bequest he planned for the institution of which he had been president for twenty years: "I mean to have my body dissected after my death and the bones sent to the Academy of Natural Sciences to be scraped and made into [a] skeleton as a memento mori and to serve for the study of geology and craniology—as I conceive there are some boxes in my cranium not common."[36] In spite of his eccentricities, Maclure had been a great benefactor of the Academy, and after Say's death he gave his entire library in New Harmony to the society. The Academy librarian, Charles Pickering, journeyed to the small frontier town to select and ship this remarkable collection of over two thousand books. Most of these volumes can still be found in the Academy's library, with bookplates designating them as gifts of William Maclure.

In New Harmony, Maclure's endowment of the Workingmen's Institute in essence established the first public library in America. His will provided for the inauguration of a system of free libraries for the workingmen of America: a sum of five hundred dollars was to be donated to any group that possessed a collection of at least one hundred volumes. Because no such organizations existed at the time, the bequest went through years of vicissitudes. Eventually eighty thousand dollars was distributed to 144 libraries in Indiana and 16 in Illinois, though most of these were abandoned or absorbed by the end of the century.[37] Nevertheless, Maclure can be credited with initiating this invaluable form of education in the United States. It has been written that what was original about Maclure's ideas was "their combination in one mind and the creation of a complex that was his alone. His contribution to civilization was in the application of these principles to new enterprises in new places and under new conditions."[38]

Lucy returned several times to New Harmony but never lived there again. After her mother died she made her home for many years with a sister on Staten Island. After the death of Say's unmarried brother Ben in May 1836, Lucy no longer had much communication with her husband's family. She informed Maclure that Ben, whom she considered "an uncommonly fine man," had died of "hydrothorax or water on the chest."[39] Say's sister, Rebecca Corbin, had predeceased him by four years, so his stepmother (who shortly succumbed to typhus), her three children, and Rebecca's three young daughters were all that remained. Lucy had hardly known any of them.

In her eighties, Lucy wrote to a young friend, Arthur Gray, who had interested himself in Thomas Say: "I have walked alone for nearly half a

Fig. 45. Lucy Say in old age, ca. 1880. Photograph. Courtesy of The
Academy of Natural Sciences of Philadelphia.

century." During those years she had maintained her interest in botany and
conchology, although, as she assured Gray in regard to the latter, "I make
no pretence of any critical knowledge—for at the death of my husband, I
had only learned the a.b.c. of the science—and had no opportunity after-
wards of improving myself—had my lot been art in Phila. I should have had
resource in the collections of the Academy of N[atural] Sci[ences] but I
have ever retained the interest developed in my married life, and when opportunity occurred, have contributed such materials as I possessed whether
in book or specimens. The Academy made me a life member for my good
intentions."[40] Lucy's contributions to science—principally her exquisite

drawings of shells—and her donations of Say's books and papers earned her the distinction of becoming, in 1841, the first woman elected to Academy membership.

Although her eyesight had diminished with age, Lucy's memory of her time with Say was as vivid as ever. "My married life," she wrote Gray, "was replete with happiness far beyond that which is ordinarily attained—we lived for each other."[41] Lucy died of pneumonia on 15 November 1886 in Lexington, Massachusetts, and was buried in New York City. She was almost eighty-six years old.

Since she had shared Say's most difficult years, Lucy had known all too well the disadvantages under which he had labored, "but it were of little consequence now," she had said to Gray. "The verdict has long since been passed upon his merits as a Natural Historian and I think he will be appreciated as one, who gave to his own Country the earliest impetus to the study or investigation of the immensities of its products."[42]

Epilogue:
Thomas Say's Legacy

Naming and classifying are as essential as the use of nouns in language—therein lies the basic importance of Thomas Say's taxonomic contributions to natural science.

Daniel Otte, Chairman, Department of Entomology, Academy of Natural Sciences
of Philadelphia
January 1991

AFTER SAY'S DEATH, Benjamin Coates wrote, "It is not that there is no more gold in the mine; but in raising his own ore, Mr. Say has opened the shafts and galleries, pointed out the veins, and indicated, by his example, the best manner of working them."[1] Say was significant in the development of this "gold mine" of American science for four accomplishments: the credit and respect he brought to American scientists; his lasting contributions to American entomology and conchology; his founding and initial support of the Academy of Natural Sciences of Philadelphia, as well as his participation in the American Philosophical Society, both of which played such an important part in making Philadelphia the "Athens of America" for so long; and his role as one of the earliest scientific participants in western exploration, in which he contributed in a more immediate but less lasting way to American history and self-knowledge.

An American context of pragmatism shaped the character of Thomas Say's scientific endeavors. By applying his knowledge of insects to medicine and agriculture, he contributed significantly to both of these vitally important fields in the American economy. Scientific theories in natural history as to relationships between and origins of species, or what is termed *pure science*, would develop after Say's death, most significantly, of course, with the publication of Darwin's *Origin of Species* in 1859.

Numerous species of plant and animal life were being discovered almost daily in the United States. The collecting of facts by nineteenth-century naturalists enabled these species to be named, described, and classified, and there was a great rush among scientists to be first with the names and descriptions. *Species-splitting*, or creating new species names because of minute differences, was common among Say's contemporaries. Rafinesque, as the most notorious practitioner, seems to have provided an archetype of American naturalists, at least for Europeans, who believed Americans rushed into print to seize priorities without regard to the necessary specific descriptions. This impression persisted for a long time. In an 1885 address before the American Association for the Advancement of Science it was said that "we are in fact a fast people," and because of "the demon of haste," American scientists continually spoiled their own performances."[2]

In hotly denouncing this practice of "overwhelming the science," Thomas Say was a harbinger of the future. Scientists of a later day would be called *lumpers* because they combined so many different species—a practice of which Say would have approved. In the year of Say's death, the botanist John Torrey wrote to his brilliant young colleague Asa Gray with dismay at the "great number of nominal species with which our Flora are crowded." He added, "I do intend to cut them down without mercy and have already decimated two or three regiments."[3]

Say also deplored the practice of changing the name of a species in order to promote oneself, as some scientists were wont to do. He wrote to Thaddeus Harris in 1830 that "great abuses" had "crept" into natural history because of this practice. "Innumerable instances of such fraudulent attempts, or ignorant blunders are familiar to every Naturalist, burdening Nat. Hist. with names & rendering it obscure, repulsive, & laborious, for the gratification of individual vanity."[4]

In the course of his life Say bridged several significant developments in American natural science. The early naturalists had a broad interest in all areas of study. Say's enthusiasms initially embraced not only insects and shells but also amphibians, mammals, birds, and fossils. Increasingly, however, he confined himself to the study of insects and shells. His refusal to take on botanical duties—other than collecting plants—for the second Long Expedition demonstrates his attitude toward specialization. As the years progressed and more and more knowledge was accumulated, all branches of science became increasingly specialized.

It can also be said of Say that he bridged the gap between the so-called field naturalists and cabinet naturalists. Since he had been on several important expeditions to the West, as well as to Florida and Mexico, he was much in the tradition of the field naturalists. His later years in New Harmony, however, when he studied the smallest components of insects and shells with advanced optical equipment provided by Maclure, qualified him for the designation of cabinet naturalist. The years after Say's death saw the rise of the latter as natural science became ever more exacting.

Early science in America had been more concerned with the diffusion of knowledge than its advancement. Natural history publications were important to spread new information as well as to establish scientific authority. For so long American books had been pirated renditions of European works. In his publication of his two seminal works—*American Entomology* and *American Conchology*—with their magnificent hand-colored plates, Say showed himself to be a man of his times. He clearly wished to establish the authority of American expertise. But he must be credited, too, with organizing and advancing these sciences in the first place.

Perhaps one of Say's most innovative contributions to the advancement of science was in pointing out—in an 1818 article for Silliman's *American Journal of Science and Arts*—the uses of the fossil record in geology as a guide for dating rock strata. Even in Europe this connection was not fully understood. In an 1819 article for the same journal, Say observed that geology "must be in part founded on a knowledge of the different genera and species of reliquiae, which the various accessible strata of the earth present." He conceded that little was known about North American fossils, but that comparisons must be made with those of Europe—so ably described by Lamarck and other naturalists—before progress in this field could be made. He wrote that America was "rich in fossils" and that the task of studying them required a knowledge of all their different states, from the "unchanged specimen" to that of the present.[5] Although a hint of evolutionary belief exists in these observations, Say was so involved with classification that, even at this stage of his career, he had no time for theories.

Nevertheless, Say's writings are occasionally suggestive of concern with the impact of the environment on species. He once wrote to John Melsheimer: "Your remark respecting the diminution of numbers of *hirsuta*, has often struck me with regard to other animals. Many birds which Wilson described as rare in his time, are common now, & others which he informed us were common, are now seldom seen. May not the northern migration of the *Citonia nitida* be owing to some amelioration in our climate?"[6]

During Say's lifetime a fundamental change took place in taxonomy,

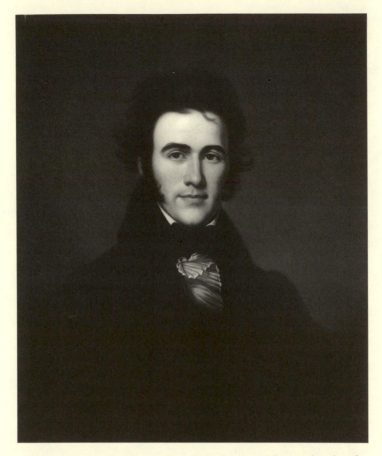

Fig. 46. *Thomas Say,* by Rembrandt Peale, 1841. Oil portrait painted posthumously by order of the members of The Academy of Natural Sciences of Philadelphia, after the portrait of Say by Charles Willson Peale. Courtesy of the Academy of Natural Sciences of Philadelphia.

of which he was an early proponent: the establishment of the natural system of classification in place of the Linnaean artificial system. Certainly this approach was more suited to use by professional, and hence presumably more advanced workers, because large numbers of specimens needed to be compared in order to judge affinities. No longer could a specimen be classified by looking only at its obvious physical characteristics. Say was, however, typical of his time in that he disregarded what George H. Daniels has called "the vestigal, the abortive, and the useless" in determining relationships between species—exactly those characteristics most significant to scientists of a later era.[7]

The quality and scope of education available to young scientists would change dramatically during and after Say's life. Say's early years at the Academy of Natural Sciences in a sense constituted his university experience, while the Long expeditions may be said to have served as his graduate education. What we take for granted today concerning the necessity of acquiring academic degrees was not applicable then.[8] Early on, learned societies such as the Academy rather than colleges and universities—where courses in natural science were, for the most part, yet to be established—were the repositories of scientific study. Before 1800 natural history had been taught more as philosophy than as science. But with the century's progress, the vast quantity of knowledge amassed by scholars split natural science into many different disciplines. After the Civil War the country's great universities would take education over from the learned societies, and government agencies would fund scientific research to a degree far beyond the abilities of institutions like the Academy. Being self-taught was virtually the only means available to Thomas Say of educating himself in natural science.

Had he lived, and had he remained in New Harmony, Say would undoubtedly have been left behind as the years wore on, for natural science of necessity became more and more concentrated in urban centers, and different fields of natural science more interdependent. Without the books, collections, or colleagues essential for learning, comparisons, and discussions—factors essential for the advancement of science—Say's isolation would have rendered him obsolete. Of this fact he was acutely aware, and the Hamlet-like dilemma of knowing what he should do, and not doing it, was part of the tragedy of his life's story.

In Europe Say was recognized in his lifetime as an eminent American naturalist. In 1818 he was elected a foreign correspondent of the Société de Philomatique of Paris, among whose members were the leaders of world science: Lamarck, Laplace, Cuvier, and Desmarest. In 1830, the Linnaean Society of London placed him in the distinguished company of Aimé Bonpland and Alexander von Humboldt by electing him one of only fifty foreign members—the only American on the list.

Say's papers on many different zoological subjects appeared in the first issues of the foremost American scientific periodicals of his day. Aside from his many essays on insects, crustaceans, amphibians, and mammals in the

Academy of Natural Sciences *Journal*, his work was represented in volume 1 of the *Transactions of the American Philosophical Society* (new series) in 1818, with an article on tiger beetles; the first volume of Benjamin Silliman's *American Journal of Science and Arts* (1818), with the first American paper on fossil shells; in the first number of John Godman's *Western Quarterly Reporter* (1823), with an essay on wasps and bees; in the first issue of *Contributions of the Maclurian Lyceum* (1827), with remarks on reptiles; and posthumously, in volume 1 of the *Boston Journal of Natural History* (1835), with a paper on beetles.

Whether he was explaining away the literal truth of the Bible by proving that the mouth of a whale is not large enough to admit a man, or demonstrating that "walking" sticks were in fact insects, or showing that sea serpents were composed of harmless fish swimming in rows, Say applied, in Coates's words, "his strong intellect and accurate powers of observation" to combat the remnants of medieval superstition that lingered in nineteenth-century culture.

By founding the Academy of Natural Sciences with his peers in the auspicious year of 1812—the War of 1812 marked the true beginning of American self-reliance—Say helped establish an institution in which American scientists, impelled by their growing sense of national pride, could base scientific disciplines and describe and classify their country's flora and fauna—an aspect of science today called systematics. Still it would be after 1900 before Americans were considered on a par with European scientists, and twenty to thirty years later than that before they would take the lead.[9] The Academy's insect collection today contains 3.5 million specimens from around the world and is ranked first in historical importance in the United States, as is the malacology collection with 10.3 million specimens.[10]

Say has been immortalized by his fellow scientists in the names of birds, reptiles, mammals, insects, and shells. Say's phoebe (*Sayornis saya*) was named in his honor by Charles Lucien Bonaparte, and the genus *Sayornis* was established later by W. G. Gray at the British Museum; Say's squirrel (*Sciurus sayi*) by John James Audubon and his zoological collaborator John Bachman; Say's blister beetle (*Pomphopoea sayi*) by John Lawrence Le Conte, Say's lettered olive (*Oliva sayi*), a shell, by Edmund Ravenel; and most recently, a daddy-longlegs (*Eumesosoma sayi*) by James C. Cokendolpher in 1980. Thomas Nuttall named a flower from the forests of the Rocky Mountains *Aster sayianus*, although this name was subsequently changed by others.

Say's most important scientific contributions were in the field of entomology, a science of as much value to medicine as to agriculture. Today, the study he made into a science in America encompasses well over 900,000 named species of insects, representing three-quarters of the animal kingdom. For having named approximately 1,500 new North American insects, Thomas Say has been called the father of American descriptive entomology. According to a modern historian, "[Say's] descriptions have furnished the basis for a large amount of the taxonomic work in practically all orders of the insect fauna. Without his careful treatment of the species the further elucidation of the life history, habits and controls of the native species would have been greatly hampered if not almost impossible. We often forget how essential it is that we have a definite name and description for the animals we discuss."[11]

The mosquito is a case in point. In the 1980s, approximately twelve hundred to fifteen hundred papers were published every year on mosquitos and mosquito-borne diseases alone.[12] In 1824, after his return from the second Long Expedition, Say described in the appendix of the expedition's report his female specimen of the mosquito, *Anopheles quadrimaculatus*, as "pale brownish" and having wings with "four fuscous spots." Seventy-four years later, during the hot summer of 1898 in Italy, Dr. Giovanni Battista Grassi sought to prove the link between malaria and mosquitos by risking his life in the malaria-infested swamps of Campania, a region of Italy. He realized that where malaria existed mosquitos were always present, but when mosquitos were present malaria did not necessarily accompany them. Reasoning that the disease was carried by only certain species, by the process of elimination he found that of the forty kinds of mosquitoes in Italy, only a handful were responsible for the spread of malaria. In America, it was discovered that Say's *Anopheles quadrimaculatus* carried malaria. Without Say's primary observation, description, and classification it is probable many more years would have passed before the crucial connection could have been made.[13]

It has been said that "unlike researchers in either the physical or, to some extent, medical sciences, those working in the biological and zoological sciences (including entomology) need to make a constant reference to the older literature. Early descriptions of insects are essential to further research, along with the need to trace and examine collections of type-material. It is imperative for taxonomy, because of its inextricable link with zoological nomenclature, to carry its past into its present."[14] In 1819 Say emphasized the importance both of type specimens and of museums as repositories for natural objects. "It is, I conceive, an incumbent duty on the describer of a natural object, to deposit his specimen . . . in some cabinet or museum, to which he should refer, in order that subsequent writers may be satisfied with the accuracy of his observations, by examining for themselves."[15]

Thomas Say's entomological descriptions were considered excellent in his day. The German entomologist Wilhelm Ferdinand Erichson wrote (in Latin) in his *Genera et Species Staphylinorum* (1840) that "in brevity I see that no one excels the American Say who published descriptions so concise that they hardly go beyond the extent of a diagnosis, nevertheless, so clear that you will hardly ever find doubtful a form exhibited by him."[16]

Say was the first to identify the American dog tick. Although he was unaware of it, this tick is the principal vector of Rocky Mountain fever in the central and eastern United States. He also named the cattle tick, which was responsible for untold depredation among cattle herds until tick erad-ication programs were introduced.

In agriculture, Say's groundwork in identifying for science notorious crop predators has been of long-term economic importance. Asa Fitch, an entomologist with the New York Agricultural Society, in 1858 called Say "the greatest zoologist America has produced" because of his original insect descriptions.[17] Say was the first to describe the chinch bug, an insect damaging to corn, wheat, and sorghum in the Midwest; the Colorado potato beetle, a major pest of potato and tomato plants; the grape leafhop-per, a significant factor in the yearly loss of grape yield; the green stinkbug, which feeds on mature seeds of soybeans, causing poor quality at harvest; the peach tree borer, responsible for the decline in vigor and eventual death of peach, almond, and apricot trees; the walkingstick, at times a serious defoliator of eastern deciduous trees; and the Hessian fly, known to cause millions of dollars in wheat crop losses. The development of resistant wheat varieties has lessened but not eliminated this destruction.[18]

Say's work in classifying shells and mollusks was second only to his work in entomology. His paper for the American edition of William Nich-olson's *British Encyclopedia* (1816) was the first essay written on conchology (malacology) by an American, and it founded the science in this country. And his *American Conchology*, issued in what was then the virtual wilderness of Indiana, was the first such publication in America. Thus Say is also called the father of American conchology.

Of the more than twenty-five mollusks with medical significance first described by Say, several stand out. One is the North American freshwater mollusk *Pomatiopsis lapidaria*, a potential transmitter of the disease schistosomiasis, which afflicts nearly 200 million people worldwide and is second to malaria as the earth's most prevalent disease. A related mollusk, found throughout China, Japan, and Southeast Asia, is host to a particular species of schistosome worm which, following expulsion from its snail host into a body of water, enters a human body to reproduce and there causes severe anemia by ingesting blood cells. Schistosomiasis, although seldom fatal in itself, can create lesions damaging to the heart and liver and can lead to cancer. The American species of mollusk, found from Michigan to Louisiana, has the genetic makeup necessary to carry Asian schistosomiasis, but because of weather conditions, and because the disease has not yet been introduced, it has remained free of infection. *Schistosoma mansoni*, another disease-carrying species found in South America, is carried by the pulmonate snail *Biomphalaria glabrata*, first described by Say.

Of concern to veterinary medicine is a disease of cattle carried by another snail, *Helisoma bicarinatus*, that Say first brought to the attention of science in his pioneering article of 1816. Many of Say's names have been moved from their original genus as new discoveries have been made, but many others, such as *Physa gyrina*, the mollusk responsible for transmitting trichobilharzia to poultry, remain where he placed them.[19]

Some marine mollusks described by Say also have an economic impact. Two east North American pyramidellid snails are parasites that live on the outside of oysters and other mollusks. Recent research has shown that these small snails injure their hosts by blood sucking. Since all marine mollusks are potential food for crabs and fish, they are essential in the food chain. Say also named a large number of freshwater mussels whose pearly shell interiors have been used commercially for years to make buttons, although for the most part they have now been replaced by plastics.[20]

When we speak of western animals such as the coyote, plains gray wolf, and swift fox, and birds such as the band-tailed pigeon, orange-crowned warbler, and lazuli bunting, we allude without knowing it to Thomas Say, who was the first to describe for science every detail of the bodies of these creatures, so that for all time there would be no doubt as to their scientific identification.

His contributions to Indian ethnology during both Long expeditions—including studies of Indian customs, beliefs, health, and diet, and vocabularies of Indian languages—were significant at the time because of the scarcity of such information. No-one with a scientific background had been to the West and conducted this type of investigation. But Say's name is not associated with the development of ethnology in America, because he did not interpret his material. Although Say, at least in his known letters, did not concern himself with slavery—and it was then becoming a major issue—in his correspondence he often denounced the harsh treatment of Indians. But he would leave the study of their culture, which had been initiated by Benjamin Smith Barton, for Peter S. Du Ponceau, Albert Gallatin, and Henry Rowe Schoolcraft. Du Ponceau, whose researches provided a strong impetus to Indian studies in both Europe and America, used the vocabularies of the northern plains tribal groups that Say collected on the first Long Expedition as a resource.[21]

Because of his government employment as a scientist on two expeditions, and because he devoted his life to natural science without other means of support, Thomas Say can be considered one of the first true American professionals in a field that until his time had been thought of as only an amateur pursuit. In order to adopt science as a profession, however,

Fig. 47. *Swift Fox, Vulpes velox, Say,* by John James Audubon, from *The Viviparous Quadrupeds of North America* (1845–46).

it was necessary for Say to depend entirely on patronage, a situation he allowed almost to the point of intellectual and social prostitution. Even though his choice was more acceptable in his day than it would be in ours, like much else in nineteenth-century life the attitude toward patronage was changing; it is not surprising that Emerson idealized self-reliance.

Say also had a tendency simply to turn away from responsibilities he found distasteful, without any apparent effort to delegate them to an assistant or replacement. Because of his antipathy to business he was totally unsuited to run Maclure's affairs in New Harmony, and in accepting the task he was untrue to himself as well as to Maclure. His remaining in New Harmony—never apparently a deliberate decision—was severely damaging not only to himself but to the Academy of Natural Sciences as well, especially to the *Journal*. In his latter days, because of illness and deleterious frustration at what he assumed was his exclusion from the scientific community, Say became critical and testy. He may have brought Ord's censure on himself by his tactless way of simply publishing his reproofs of others without making any effort to communicate his objections more privately. Until his departure for New Harmony, Say's professional life had been increasingly successful, but by removing himself from the mainstream of science he brought about his own intellectual and physical destruction.

Thomas Say was thus not without some shortcomings in personality and judgment, but there is no denying his contributions to science, even though time may nearly have eradicated his name. In his introduction to Say's collected writings on conchology, W. G. Binney wrote in 1858 that his classification of species was known to most American conchologists "rather by tradition than from a careful study of his excellent descriptions." Although Binney was referring to the obscurity of the publications in which Say's work could then be found, his statement is now truer than ever. Born in the eighteenth century, Thomas Say is indeed known to modern natural scientists mainly through tradition. But though his specific contributions may have been long forgotten in the constant shifting of biological nomenclature, and in the enormous scientific advances of the more than 150 years since his death, in the words of Benjamin Silliman, Say "will ever be remembered as one who did honor to his country and enlarged the boundaries of human knowledge."[22]

Say's challenge to Americans to study their own multifarious fauna may indeed have been his most valuable contribution. That he named and described thousands of North American insects and mollusks, and many mammals, reptiles, and birds suggests the lasting impact of his life's work.

And that he did not send these creatures to Europe to be classified testifies to the scientific importance of his career. In the year of the American Constitutional Convention, Thomas Say began a life that would be devoted to establishing natural science in the United States as an institution deserving of international honor and respect.

Notes

The following abbreviations are used in these notes.

ANSP   Academy of Natural Sciences of Philadelphia, Philadelphia, Pennsylvania

APS   American Philosophical Society, Philadelphia, Pennsylvania

MNHN   Musée National d'Histoire Naturelle, Paris

HSP   Historical Society of Pennsylvania, Philadelphia, Pennsylvania

MCZ   Museum of Comparative Zoology, Harvard University, Cambridge, Massachusetts

MHNH   Musée d'Histoire Naturelle du Havre, Le Havre, France

QCHC   Quaker Collection, Haverford College, Haverford, Pennsylvania

WMI   Workingmen's Institute Library, New Harmony, Indiana

INTRODUCTION

1. Harry B. Weiss and Grace M. Ziegler, *Thomas Say, Early American Naturalist* (Springfield, Ill.: Charles E. Thomas, 1931).

2. Richard Holmes, *Coleridge: Early Visions* (New York: Viking, 1989), preface, xviii. Coleridge's famous *Biographia Litteraria* was initially reviewed (negatively) in the same issue (Dec. 1817) of the *American Monthly Magazine and Critical Review* as Thomas Say's first book, *American Entomology*.

3. Thomas Say, *The Complete Writings of Thomas Say on the Entomology of North America*, ed. John L. Le Conte, M.D., 2 vols. (New York: Bailliere Brothers, 1859).

4. Thomas Jefferson, *Notes on the State of Virginia* (1785; reprint, New York: W. W. Norton & Company).

5. Alexander Wilson, *American Ornithology* (Philadelphia, 1811), 3: preface, viii.

6. Frederick Pursh, a German, published descriptions of plants collected by Lewis and Clark in his *Americae Septentrionalis* (London, 1814).

7. Robert V. Bruce, *The Launching of Modern American Science, 1846–1876* (New York: Alfred Knopf, 1987), 7.

8. Henry David Thoreau, *The Heart of Thoreau's Journals*, ed. Odell Shepard (Boston and New York, 1927), entry for 23 March 1853, p. 165.

9. James E. DeKay, *An Address Delivered before the New-York Lyceum, February, 1826* (New York, 1826).

10. Bruce, *Modern American Science*, 5.

Chapter 1: A Heritage of Science

1. The month of Thomas Say's birth is a matter of debate. The Say Bible record as published in the *Pennsylvania Magazine of History and Biography* 29 (1905): 222, states: "Thomas Say, son of Benjamin & Ann Say was born on the 27th of 6 mo called June 1787, about ¼ of an hour after 4 o'clock in the morning being the 4th day of the week." Say's white marble monument in New Harmony, Indiana, is marked July 27, 1787, however.

2. E. Digby Baltzell, *Puritan Boston and Quaker Philadelphia* (New York: Free Press, 1979), 169.

3. Frederick B. Tolles, *Meeting House and Counting House: The Quaker Merchants of Philadelphia 1682–1763* (Chapel Hill: University of North Carolina Press, 1948).

4. "Collection of Various Pieces Concerning Pennsylvania," *Pennsylvania Magazine of History and Biography* 6 (1882): 323–28.

5. Caspar Morris, "Contributions to the Medical History of Pennsylvania," *Memoirs of the Historical Society of Pennsylvania* (May 1876): 344–45.

6. Ibid.

7. Penn Manuscripts, Indian Affairs, vol. 3, 1757–72, p. 89, HSP. The historian Daniel J. Boorstin states that this nongovernmental association, although true to its Quaker principles, did more harm than good by meddling in government affairs and confusing the issue with pacifism when stronger measures were needed to protect embattled settlers on the Pennsylvania frontier from Indian massacre. Boorstin, *The Americans: The Colonial Experience* (New York: Random House, 1958), 57.

8. Eric P. Newman, *The Early Paper Money of America* (Racine, Wis.: Whitman, 1967).

9. Document of manumission, Thomas Say Papers, QCHC.

10. Baltzell, *Quaker Philadelphia*, 153.

11. Wilson, Alexander, *The Poems and Literary Prose of Alexander Wilson*, ed. Alexander B. Grosart, 2 vols. (Paisley, Scotland: Alexander Gardner, 1876), 359.

12. William Darlington, M.D., *Memorials of John Bartram and Humphry Marshall* (Philadelphia, 1849; reprint, New York: Hafner, 1967), 477.

13. J. H. Powell, *Bring Out Your Dead: The Great Plague of Yellow Fever in Philadelphia in 1793* (Philadelphia: University of Pennsylvania Press, 1949), 30.

14. Benjamin Say to Benjamin Rush, 21 Sept. 1793, HSP.

15. Robert Elman, *First in the Field* (New York: Mason/Charter, 1977), 31–32.

16. George W. Norris, M.D., *The Early History of Medicine in Philadelphia* (Philadelphia: 1886), 100.

17. Brooke Hindle, *The Pursuit of Science in Revolutionary America 1735–1789* (Chapel Hill: University of North Carolina Press, 1956), 189. From APS minutes 30 July 1773, p. 148.

18. Ann Sharpless, *Historical Essays,* Westtown Literary Union, 17.

19. Reuben Haines to Caspar Wistar Haines, 19 May 1799, Wyck Papers, APS.

20. Reuben Haines to Hannah Haines with added note from Catherine Hartshorne, 25 June 1799, Wyck Papers, APS.

21. Notebook of Reuben Haines, Wyck Papers, APS.

22. Dr. Benjamin Coates, *A Biographical Sketch of the Late Thomas Say, Esquire, read before the Academy of Natural Sciences, December 16, 1834* (Philadelphia: W. P. Gibbons, 1835), 6.

23. Westtown School Archives, Westtown, Pa.

24. Thomas Say Papers, fragment, n.d., Manuscript Collection, ANSP.

25. John Bartram to Peter Collinson, 3 Dec. 1762, in Darlington, *Memorials,* 243.

26. Newspaper clipping, 7 May 1870, Kennedy Collection, box 15, HSP.

27. Lucy Say to John L. Le Conte, M.D., Newburgh, N.Y., 25 June 1860, Lucy Say Papers, APS.

28. Will extracts, file 105, book 5, 56, HSP.

29. Lucy Say to selected naturalists, June 1860, enclosed with a letter to John L. Le Conte, M.D., Newburgh, N.Y., 25 June 1860, APS.

30. Edward Potts Cheyney, *History of the University of Pennsylvania, 1740–1940* (Philadelphia: University of Pennsylvania Press, 1940), 237.

31. *A Brief Sketch of the Military Operations on the Delaware During the Late War* (Philadelphia, 1820), 22.

32. First City Troop, *By-Laws, Muster-Rolls and Papers Selected from the Archives of the First Troop Philadelphia City Cavalry from 17 Nov. 1774 to 7 Sept. 1815* (Philadelphia, 1815).

33. First City Troop, *History of the First Troop City Cavalry, 17 Nov. 1774 to its Centennial Anniversary 17 Nov. 1874* (Princeton, N.J., 1875).

34. *A Brief Sketch,* 25.

Chapter 2: Birth of the Academy

1. George H. Daniels, *American Science in the Age of Jackson* (New York: Columbia University Press, 1968), 8.

2. Peale was a great showman who conducted his museum as a lucrative business for many years. When he died in 1827 at the age of eighty-six, his sons attempted to carry on the quasi-scientific exhibition. But by 1843 the museum was bankrupt and the building was sold at a sheriff's sale. Six years later P. T. Barnum and Moses Kimball bought the collections at auction. Barnum's holdings were destroyed by fire in 1851, but most of Kimball's eventually ended up at the Museum of Comparative Zoology at Harvard.

3. *Poulson's American Daily Advertiser,* 6 May 1812.

4. *Minutes of the ANSP,* Saturday, 25 Jan. 1812, ANSP.

5. *Minutes of the ANSP*, 17 March 1812, ANSP.

6. Peter J. Bowler, *Evolution: The History of an Idea* (Berkeley: University of California Press, 1984), 77.

7. Daniels, *American Science*, 53.

8. Gerard Troost to Samuel George Morton, 10 January 1847, Library Company Manuscript Collection, HSP.

9. Transcription by Edward Nolan of the original minutes of the ANSP, 1912, ANSP.

10. Ibid.

11. Samuel George Morton, *Memoir of William Maclure*, read before the ANSP, 1 July 1841, ANSP (Philadelphia: Merrihew and Thompson, 1841).

12. *Minutes of the ANSP*, 21 Dec. 1813.

13. George W. Norris, M.D., *The Early History of Medicine in Philadelphia* (Philadelphia, 1886), 130. The quote is from Dr. Thomas Bond's introductory lecture to a "Course of Clinical Observations Delivered at Pennsylvania Hospital, 3 December 1766," 130.

14. Ibid. 131.

15. George H. Daniels, *Science in American Society* (New York: Alfred Knopf, 1971), 137.

16. Daniel J. Boorstin, *The Americans: The Colonial Experience* (New York: Random House, 1966), 261.

17. Antonello Gerbi, *The Dispute of the New World: The History of a Polemic, 1750–1900*, trans. Jeremy Moyle (Italy, 1955; rev. and enl. ed. Pittsburgh: University of Pittsburgh Press, 1973), 254.

18. Thomas Nuttall, *The North American Sylva: or, A Description of the Forest Trees of the United States, Canada and Nova Scotia not Described in the Work of F. Andrew Michaux* (Philadelphia, 1857), 1: 141–42.

19. Benjamin Coates, M.D., *A Biographical Sketch of the Late Thomas Say, Esquire, read before the Academy of Natural Sciences, December 16, 1834* (Philadelphia: W. P. Gibbons, 1835), 10–11.

20. Ibid.

21. *Philadelphia Ledger*, 16 March 1891, Kennedy Collection, HSP.

22. Thomas Say to Jacob Gilliams, Pittsburgh, 17 April 1819, Thomas Say Papers, APS.

23. Charles Alexandre Lesueur and François Péron, *Voyages de découvertes aux terres australes* (Paris, 1807), 1: preface.

24. Gilbert Chinard, "The American Sketchbooks of Charles Alexandre Lesueur," *Proceedings of the American Philosophical Society* 93, no. 2 (1949): 114–18.

CHAPTER 3: THE *JOURNAL*'S OUTREACH

1. *Journal of the ANSP* 1, pt. 1 (May 1817): page A.

2. Thomas Jefferson to Charles Thomson, 20 Sept. 1787, quoted in Silvio A. Bedini, "Jefferson: Man of Science," *Frontiers: Annual of the Academy of Natural*

Sciences of Philadelphia 3 (1981–82): 15. See also Silvio A. Bedini, *Thomas Jefferson: Statesman of Science* (New York: Macmillan, 1990), 180.

3. R. Tucker Abbott, preface to a reprint of Thomas Say, "Conchology," William Nicholson's *American Edition of the British Encyclopedia, or Dictionary of Arts and Sciences, Comprising an Accurate and Popular View of the Present Improved State of Human Knowledge*, 3d ed. (1819; facsimile, Melbourne, Fl.: American Malacologists, Inc., 1981).

4. Thomas Say, "Conchology," in Nicholson's *British Encyclopedia*," C-5.

5. James E. DeKay, "An Address delivered before the New-York Lyceum, February 1826" (New York, 1826).

6. George H. Daniels, *American Science in the Age of Jackson* (New York: Columbia University Press, 1968), 38.

7. Say, "Conchology," in Nicholson's *British Encyclopedia*, A-4.

8. Ibid.

9. Thomas Say, "On a South American species of Oestrus which inhabits the human body." *Journal of the ANSP* 2, pt. 2 (1822):353–54.

10. See Wilhelm Ferdinand Erichson, *Genera et species staphylinorum insectorum coleopterorem familiae* (Berolini, Germany 1840), vii.

11. C. S. Rafinesque to Reuben Haines, New York, 25 April 1817, QCHC.

12. Thomas Say, *American Entomology* (Philadelphia, 1824), 1: preface.

13. Thomas Say, "An Account of the Insect known by the name of Hessian Fly and of a Parasitic Insect that feeds on it," *Journal of the ANSP* 1, pt. 3 (1817):46.

14. Say to Thaddeus Harris, Philadelphia, 10 November 1823, Harris Papers, Houghton Library, Harvard University.

15. Ibid.

16. Say, "South American species of Oestrus."

17. Lists of persons and institutions to whom the *Journal* was sent are found in Reuben Haines's stud book of hogs and cows for 1817, Wyck Papers, APS. Haines, a Quaker farmer, was corresponding secretary of the Academy.

18. Correspondence of Reuben Haines, QCHC.

19. Haines's stud book.

20. Thomas Jefferson to Haines, Monticello, 10 May 1818, QCHC.

21. George Ord to Haines, Paris, 23 March 1829, Wyck Papers, APS.

22. Say to Baron J. D'Audebert de Férussac, letter draft (1822?), Thomas Say Papers, APS.

23. Say to Harris, Philadelphia, 10 November 1823, Harris Papers, Houghton Library, Harvard University.

24. *Journal of the ANSP* 1, pt. 2 (1818):385–86.

25. Say to Baron de Ferussac, Philadelphia, 5 June 1824, Thomas Say Papers, APS.

26. Asa Gray, "Notice of the Botanical Writings of the Late C. S. Rafinesque," *American Journal of Science* 60 (April 1841): 241. Quoted in Daniels, *American Science*, 61.

27. Ibid.

28. Thomas Say, *American Entomology* 1: opp. pl. 17.

29. Ord to Haines, Paris, 3 June 1830, QCHC.

30. Gerard Troost to Say, Cape Sable, 1 September 1818, QCHC.

31. Charles Bonaparte to Say, Point Breeze, 15 October 1824, Thomas Say Papers, APS.

32. Ibid.

33. Charles Lucien Bonaparte was the son of Lucien Bonaparte, Joseph's brother. In 1822, Charles married his cousin Zenaide, Joseph's daughter. They had twelve children.

34. "Joseph Bonaparte as recorded in the Private Journal of Nicholas Biddle," with introduction and notes by Edward Biddle. *Pennsylvania Magazine of History and Biography* 55 (1931).

35. Reuben Haines to Ann Haines, Germantown, 3 July 1825, Wyck Papers, APS.

36. Ord to Reuben Haines, Paris, 26 August 1820, Reuben Haines Papers, ANSP.

37. *Journal of the ANSP* 2, pt. 1 (December 1821):192.

38. Thomas Say, "On a Quadruped, belonging to the order, Rodentia." *Journal of the ANSP* 2, pt. 2 (1822):331.

39. Thomas Say, "Descriptions of Three New Species of Coluber inhabiting the United States," *Journal of the ANSP* 4, pt. 2 (1825):241.

40. Thomas Say to Benjamin Say, Philadelphia, October 1822, Charles Roberts Autograph Collection, Haverford College Library.

41. C. A. Lesueur, "Description of a Squalus, of a very large size, which was taken on the coast of New-Jersey." *Journal of the ANSP* 2, pt. 2 (1822):343.

CHAPTER 4: SPANISH FLORIDA

1. Portions of this chapter are based on a manuscript in the Titian Peale Papers at the American Museum of Natural History, New York, "A Visit to Florida in the early part of the Century," by L. Peale—presumably Titian's grandson, Louis.

2. Thomas Say to John L. Melsheimer, Philadelphia, 30 July 1816, Thomas Say Papers, ANSP.

3. Say to Melsheimer, Washington, D.C., 12 December 1817, Thomas Say Papers, ANSP.

4. Say to Jacob Gilliams, St. Marys, Georgia, 30 January 1818, Manuscript Collection, vol. 7, HSP.

5. William Bartram, *Travels through North & South Carolina, Georgia, East & West Florida* (Philadelphia, 1791).

6. L. Peale manuscript, "A Visit to Florida."

7. William Bartram, *The Travels of William Bartram*, ed. Francis Harper (New Haven, Ct.: Yale University Press, 1958), 41.

8. Say to Gilliams, St. Marys, Georgia, 30 January 1818, Manuscripts Department, vol. 7, HSP.

9. Ibid.

10. Ibid.

11. Ibid.

12. Constantine Samuel Rafinesque, review of *American Entomology* in *American Monthly Magazine and Critical Review* 2, no. 2 (December 1817): 143.

13. Thomas Say, "On the Fresh Water and Land Tortoises of the United States," *Journal of the ANSP* 4, pt. 2 (1825):207.

14. Bartram, *Travels*, 52.

15. Thomas Say, "Observations on some of the animals described in the Account of the Crustacea of the United States," *Journal of the ANSP* 1, pt. 2 (November 1818):443.

16. Bartram, *Travels*, 61.

17. Say to Melsheimer, Philadelphia, 10 June 1818, Thomas Say Papers, ANSP.

18. Say to George Ord, Savannah, 11 April 1818. Dreer Collection of American Scientists, HSP.

19. Ibid.

20. Benjamin Coates, M.D., *A Biographical Sketch of the Late Thomas Say, Esquire, read before the Academy of Natural Sciences of Philadelphia, December 16, 1834* (Philadelphia: W. P. Gibbons, 1835), 12.

21. Say to Ord, 11 April 1818, Dreer Collection, HSP.

22. Say to Melsheimer, Philadelphia, 10 June 1818, Thomas Say Papers, ANSP.

23. Say to Melsheimer, Philadelphia, 6 November 1817, Thomas Say Papers, ANSP.

24. Daniel J. Boorstin, *The Americans: The National Experience* (New York: Random House, 1965), 222.

CHAPTER 5: DESTINATION: COUNCIL BLUFFS

1. William H. Goetzmann, *Exploration and Empire: The Role of the Explorer and Scientist in the Exploration and Development of the American West 1800–1900* (New York: Alfred Knopf, 1967), 183.

2. Dr. Benjamin Coates, *A Biographical Sketch of the Late Thomas Say, Esquire, read before The Academy of Natural Sciences of Philadelphia, December 16, 1834* (Philadelphia: W. P. Gibbons, 1835).

3. Major Stephen Harriman Long to Secretary of War John C. Calhoun, Pittsburgh, 24 December 1818, Records of the Office of the Secretary of War, Record Group 107, National Archives Microfilm publication M221, roll 82, "Letters Received by the Secretary of War, Registered Series, 1801–1870." National Archives, Washington, D.C. (Torrey became a distinguished botanist.)

4. Roger L. Nichols and Patrick L. Halley, *Stephen Long and American Frontier Exploration* (Newark: University of Delaware Press, 1980), 72.

5. Jeanette E. Graustein, *Thomas Nuttall, Naturalist: Explorations in America, 1808–1841* (Cambridge, Mass.: Harvard University Press, 1967), 130. Italics added.

6. Calhoun to Dr. Thomas Cooper, Washington, 3 September 1818, in W. Edwin Hemphill, ed., *The Papers of John C. Calhoun* (Columbia: University of South Carolina Press, 1967), 3: 95.

7. Nuttall's other sponsors were José Correa da Serra, the Portugese minister to the United States and an avid naturalist; Zaccheus Collins, wealthy farmer and

member of the APS and the ANSP; and John Vaughan, treasurer and librarian of the APS.

8. Brooke Hindle, "Charles Willson Peale's Science and Technology" in Edgar P. Richardson, Brooke Hindle, and Lillian B. Miller, *Charles Willson Peale and His World* (New York: Harry N. Abrams, 1983), 166.

9. William Baldwin to William Darlington, 21 March 1819, reproduced in William Baldwin, *Reliquiae Baldwinianae, selections from the correspondence of the late William Baldwin*, compiled by William Darlington (Philadelphia, 1843; reprint New York: Hafner, 1969).

10. Coates, *Biographical Sketch*.

11. Calhoun to Long, Department of War, 1 September 1819, RG107, NA M221, roll 82, National Archives. Calhoun was secretary of war in President James Monroe's cabinet, 1816–1824.

12. George H. Daniels, *American Science in the Age of Jackson* (New York: Columbia University Press, 1968), 21.

13. William H. Goetzmann, *Army Exploration in the American West 1803–1863* (New Haven, Ct.: Yale University Press, 1959), 39.

14. *Aurora General Advertiser* (Philadelphia), 12 October 1818.

15. Calhoun to General Andrew Jackson, Department of War, 28 December 1818, RG107, NA M221, roll 82, National Archives.

16. Calhoun to Robert Walsh, 11 March 1819. From the *Minutes of the ANSP*, 23 March 1819.

17. Long to Calhoun, Pittsburgh, 24 December 1818, RG 107, NA M221, roll 82, National Archives.

18. Robert Cushman Murphy, "Sketchbooks of Titian Ramsay Peale," *Proceedings of the American Philosophical Society* 101, no. 6 (1957).

19. Nichols and Halley, *Stephen Long*, 75–76.

20. Long to Calhoun, Pittsburgh, 24 December 1818, R G 107, NA M221, roll 82, National Archives.

21. Thomas Say to John Melsheimer, Philadelphia, 13 March 1819, ANSP, reproduced in Harry B. Weiss and Grace M. Ziegler, *Thomas Say: Early American Naturalist* (Springfield, Ill.: Charles E. Thomas, 1931), 61–64.

22. "Nuttall's Travels into the Arkansa Territory," *Port Folio* (October 1823): 337.

23. Baldwin, *Reliquiae Baldwinae*, 313.

24. Say to Jacob Gilliams, Pittsburgh, 17 April 1819, Thomas Say Papers, APS.

25. Titian R. Peale, Journal from the Long Expedition, Library of Congress. Lillian B. Miller, ed., *The Collected Papers of Charles Willson Peale and His Family*, microfiche (Millwood, N.Y., 1980).

26. Say to Melsheimer, Philadelphia, March 13, 1819, Thomas Say Papers, ANSP.

27. William Elford Leach to Say, London, 1 January 1819, Conaroe Collection, HSP.

28. Say to Gilliams, Pittsburgh, 17 April 1819, Thomas Say Papers, APS.

29. Baldwin, *Reliquiae Baldwinae*, 312.

30. Say to Gilliams, Pittsburgh, 17 April 1819, Thomas Say Papers, APS.

31. Edwin James, ed., *Account of an Expedition From Pittsburgh to the Rocky Mountains* vol. 15 of *Early Western Travels 1748–1846*, ed. Reuben Gold Thwaites (Cleveland: Arthur H. Clark, 1905), 178n.

32. "Le Serpent de mer d'Amérique, extrait d'une lettre de T. Say Esq., de Philadelphie, au D. Leach," *Bulletin des Sciences par la Société Philomatique de Paris* (1818).

33. C. S. Rafinesque, "Museum of Natural Sciences," *American Monthly Magazine and Critical Review*, October 1817, article 5, 433.

34. Thomas Nuttall, *A Journal of Travels into the Arkansa Territory During the Year 1819* (Philadelphia, 1821), vol. 13 of *Early Western Travels*, ed. Reuben Gold Thwaites (Cleveland: Arthur H. Clark Co., 1906), 65.

35. Edwin James, ed., *Account of an Expedition from Pittsburgh to the Rocky Mountains* (London, 1823), 1: 23 (see Bibliography for full title).

36. Dr. Daniel Henry Drake (1785–1852) was president of the Medical College of Ohio, chartered in 1818.

37. Maria R. Audubon, *Audubon and His Journals* (New York, 1897), 1: 37.

38. Nuttall, *Journal of Travels*, 81.

39. Titian Peale, Journal, The Collected Papers of Charles Willson Peale and His Family, Library of Congress.

40. Titian R. Peale, "Ancient Mounds in St. Louis, Missouri, in 1819," *Smithsonian Institution Annual Report of 1861* (Washington, D.C., 1862), 388. The Cahokia Mounds, located four miles northeast of East St. Louis, Illinois, were excavated, beginning in 1920, by W. K. Moorhead of the University of Illinois. He dated them A.D. 1200–1500. Highly developed pottery, copper, pipes, mica ornaments, and projectile points were found on the site (Paul Wilhelm, *Travels in North America 1822–1824*, ed. Savoie Lottinville [Norman: University of Oklahoma Press, 1973]).

41. Peter Farb, *Man's Rise to Civilization as Shown by the Indians of North America from Primeval Times to the Coming of the Industrial State* (New York: E. P. Dutton, 1968), 223–24; Stephen Williams, *Fantastic Archaeology: The Wild Side of North American Prehistory* (Philadelphia: University of Pennsylvania Press, 1991).

42. Baldwin, *Reliquiae Baldwinae*, 317.

43. Say to Gilliams, U.S. Steam Boat Western Engineer, Franklin, Missouri Territory, 15 July 1819, Thomas Say Papers, ANSP. I have been unable to locate this reference in Pindar and believe Say may have meant Bunyan.

44. Baldwin to Long, Franklin, Missouri Territory, 18 July 1819, enclosure to a letter from Major Stephen H. Long to Secretary of War John C. Calhoun, 19 July 1819, RG 107, NA M221, roll 86, National Archives.

45. Thomas Say, *American Entomology or Descriptions of the Insects of North America*, 3 vols. (Philadelphia: Samuel Augustus Mitchell, 1824–28), unpaged, v. 1, observations accompanying plate 16.

46. Ibid. vol. 1, text opposite plate 16.

47. James, *Account*, 133.

48. George E. Hyde, *The Pawnee Indians*, 2d ed. (Norman: University of Oklahoma Press, 1974), 166.

49. Farb, *Man's Rise*, 115.

50. James, *Account*, 134.

51. Nichols and Halley, *Stephen Long*, 75.

CHAPTER 6 WINTER ENCAMPMENT

1. Edwin James, ed., *Account of an Expedition from Pittsburgh to the Rocky Mountains* (London, 1823), 1:140.

2. George E. Hyde, *The Pawnee Indians*, 2d ed. (Norman: University of Oklahoma Press, 1974).

3. James, *Account*, 1:146. The Pawnee picked up from the Spaniards the custom of riding fine mules instead of horses on ceremonial occasions. For years they had been raiding Spanish settlements in the Southwest and were inclined to borrow Spanish customs. Hyde, *Pawnee Indians*, 187n71.

4. Hyde, *Pawnee Indians*, 167.

5. Ibid., 166–67.

6. James, *Account*, 1:293.

7. Hyde, *Pawnee Indians*, 167.

8. Thomas Say to Benjamin Say, Engineer Cantonment, 10 October 1819, Gratz Collection, HSP.

9. James, *Account*, 1:151–52.

10. Observation in the catalog for an exhibition at the APS *Titian Ramsay Peale, 1799–1885, An Exhibition of His Sketches, Watercolors and Oils* by Stephen Catlett, manuscripts librarian, APS.

11. James, *Account*, 1:153–55.

12. Ibid., 2:355. The zoological information was supplied the author by Dr. Karl F. Koopman at the American Museum of Natural History, New York.

13. Robert Walsh to J. C. Calhoun, Philadelphia, 30 March 1819, APS.

14. "Concerning Inquiries to be made by Major Long of the Indians"—notes in various hands included with Walsh's letter to Calhoun, March 30, 1819, APS.

15. James, *Account*, 1:181.

16. Thomas Say to Jacob Gilliams, Engineer Cantonment, 10 October 1819, reprinted in Harry B. Weiss and Grace M. Zeigler, *Thomas Say: Early American Naturalist* (Springfield, Ill.: Charles E. Thomas, 1931), 73–74.

17. James, *Account*, 1:191.

18. Ibid., 196–97.

19. Ibid., 212.

20. Ibid.

21. Ibid., 250.

22. Ibid., 2: 3.

23. Ibid., 43.

24. Ibid., 65–66.

25. Ibid., 52.

26. Ibid., 59–60.

27. Ibid., 1:164.

28. Hyde, *Pawnee Indians*, 132.

29. Richard Edward Oglesby, *Manuel Lisa and the Opening of the Missouri Fur Trade* (Norman: University of Oklahoma Press, 1963), 195.

30. William H. Goetzmann, *Exploration and Empire: The Explorer and the Scientist in the Winning of the American West* (New York: Alfred Knopf, 1966), 28–29. Manuel Lisa would die in August 1820 of an undiagnosed disease.

31. James, *Account* 2:68. Information from Gary L. Krapu and Jan Eldridge, "Crane River," *Natural History* (January 1984) states that the area near and along the Platte River in Nebraska is today recognized as the principal stopover for sandhill cranes migrating to their Arctic breeding grounds from the south. Water drained from the Platte for irrigation has shrunk the river's main channel alarmingly since the nineteenth century (see Chapter 7, note 8), but the consequent crowding of cranes into smaller areas has not diminished their food supply. They have adapted to a different diet since Say saw them in 1820, and now feed on waste corn left by mechanical cornpickers the previous fall.

32. James, *Account*, 2:75.

33. Ibid., 2:79–80.

34. Ibid.

35. Prince Maximilian of Wied, on visiting the upper Missouri in 1833, recorded that the Arikaras had formerly practiced this custom. Hyde, *Pawnee Indians*, 161.

36. James, *Account*, 2:90.

CHAPTER 7: TO THE SHINING MOUNTAINS

1. Roger L. Nichols and Patrick L. Halley, *Stephen Long and American Frontier Exploration* (Newark: University of Delaware Press, 1980), 110–11.

2. Edwin James to John James, New York, 4 March 1820, letterbook, Western Americana, Beinecke Rare Book and Manuscript Library, Yale University Library.

3. Thomas Say to John F. Melsheimer, Philadelphia, 29 August 1821, Thomas Say Papers, ANSP.

4. James, Edwin, ed., *Account of an Expedition from Pittsburgh to the Rocky Mountains*, 3 vols. (London, 1823), 2:126.

5. Ibid., 2:137. Gary L. Krapu and Jan Eldridge in "Crane River," *Natural History*, January 1984, 71, state that in the Platte river "quicksand was commonplace and at times created treacherous conditions for wagon trains and horsemen crossing the channel."

6. James, *Account*, 2:335.

7. Alexander Wilson and Prince Charles Lucien Bonaparte, *American Ornithology: or, the Natural History of the Birds of the United States* (London: Chatto and Windus, 1876), 3:223.

8. Today, as a result of massive irrigation projects, the flow of water in the Platte has been drastically reduced. John C. Fremont noted in 1843 that the river's width just below the confluence of its two forks was 1,785 yards. Now the width of the channel at this point measures less than 100 yards. Krapu and Eldridge, "Crane River," 70.

9. James, *Account*, 2:161.

10. Ibid., 2:173.

11. Ibid., 187.

12. Wilson and Bonaparte, *American Ornithology* 3:177.

13. Patricia Trenton and Peter H. Hassrick, *The Rocky Mountains: A Vision for Artists in the Nineteenth Century* (Norman: University of Oklahoma Press, 1983), 28.

14. George H. Daniels, *American Science in the Age of Jackson* (New York: Columbia University Press, 1968), 26.

15. George Ord's article on the grizzly bear was included in William Guthrie's *New Geographical, Historical, and Commercial Grammar*, 2d ed. (Philadelphia, 1815).

16. James, *Account*, 2:243.

17. Ibid., 255.

18. Ibid., 3:42.

19. Ibid., 43–44.

20. Ibid., 44.

21. Ibid., 51.

22. Ibid., 60–61.

23. Ibid., 96.

24. Ibid., 98.

25. Richard G. Beidleman, "The 1820 Long Expedition," *American Zoologist* 26, no. 2 (1986): 309.

26. Walter Prescott Webb, *The Great Plains* (Boston: Ginn and Co., 1931), 147.

27. James, *Account*, 3: 102–3.

28. Ibid., 2:45.

29. Webb, *Great Plains*, 153.

30. Say to Melsheimer, Philadelphia, 29 August 1821, Thomas Say Papers, ANSP.

31. Richard H. Dillon. "Stephen Long's Great American Desert," *Proceedings of the American Philosophical Society* 3, no. 2 (April 1967):93–108.

32. Martyn J. Bowden, "The Great American Desert in the American Mind: The Historiography of a Geographical Nation," in *Geography of the Mind: Essays in Historical Geology in Honor of James Kirtland Wright*, ed. David Lowenthal and Martyn J. Bowden (New York: Oxford University Press, 1976), 138.

33. Michael H. Glantz, "Running on Empty: Irrigation is Depleting a Vast Reservoir Under the Great American Plains," *The Sciences* (November/December 1990).

34. Dillon, "Great American Desert," 104–5.

35. Edwin James to John James, Cape Girardeau, 6 October [1820], letterbook, Western Americana, Beinecke Rare Book and Manuscript Library, Yale University Library.

36. Ibid.

37. Say to Jacob Sturm, Philadelphia, 2 May 1821, Thomas Say Papers, MCZ Archives.

38. Edwin James to John James, Smithland, Kentucky, 1 March 1821, letterbook, Western Americana, Beinecke Rare Book and Manuscript Library, Yale University Library.

39. Thomas Say to Benjamin Say, Philadelphia, October 1822, Charles Roberts Autograph Collection, Haverford College Library.

40. Edwin James to John James, Philadelphia, 22 November 1821, letterbook, Western Americana, Beinecke Rare Book and Manuscript Library, Yale University Library.

41. Thomas Say to Melsheimer, Philadelphia, 9 May 1822, Thomas Say Papers, ANSP.

42. Nichols and Halley, *Stephen Long*, 179.

43. Rubens Peale to Titian R. Peale, Philadelphia, 6 July 1821, Peale Papers, APS.

44. Say to Melsheimer, Philadelphia, 29 August 1821, Thomas Say Papers, ANSP.

45. *Account*, preface.

46. Robert Elman, *First in the Field: America's Pioneering Naturalists* (New York: Mason/Charter, 1977).

47. Letter draft by Thomas Say, addressee unknown, Thomas Say Papers, ANSP.

48. Bernard Jaffe, *Men of Science in America* (New York: Simon and Schuster, 1944), 153.

49. Major Stephen H. Long to Secretary of War John C. Calhoun, 3 January 1823, in *The Papers of John C. Calhoun*, ed. W. Edwin Hemphill, vol. 8, *1822–1823* (Columbia: University of South Carolina Press, 1973). *Port Folio* 15 (1823): 175.

50. Quoted in Maxine Benson, ed., *From Pittsburgh to the Rocky Mountains, Major Stephen Long's Expedition* (Golden, Col., 1988), xiii.

51. John C. Ewers, *Indian Life on the Upper Missouri* (Norman: University of Oklahoma Press, 1968), 190.

52. Ewers, *Indian Life*, 191.

53. Charles Willson Peale to Rubens Peale, 23 March 1823; quote courtesy of the Peale Family Papers, National Portrait Gallery, Smithsonian Institution, Washington, D.C.

54. Say to Sturm, Philadelphia, 2 May 1821, MCZ Archives.

55. Say to Daniel H. Barnes, Philadelphia, 17 July 1821, MCZ Archives.

56. Edward Potts Cheyney, *History of the University of Pennsylvania 1740–1940* (Philadelphia: University of Pennsylvania Press, 1940), 237.

57. William H. Goetzmann, *Army Exploration of the American West, 1803–1863* (New Haven, Conn.: Yale University Press, 1959), 17.

CHAPTER 8: EXPEDITION TO ST. PETER'S RIVER

1. Lucile M. Kane, June D. Holmquist, and Carolyn Gilman, eds., *The Northern Expeditions of Stephen H. Long* (St. Paul: Minnesota Historical Society Press, 1978), 24–26.

2. William H. Keating, ed., *Narrative of an Expedition to the Source of St. Peter's River, Lake Winnepeek, Lake of the Woods, etc. Performed in the Year 1823, by Order of the Hon. J. C. Calhoun, Secretary of War, Under the Command of Stephen H.*

Long. U.S.T.E. Compiled from the Notes of Major Long, Messrs. Say, Keating &
Colhoun (London, 1825), 1:76.

3. Stratford Canning to "Any officer of His Majesty or other person having authority in the Posts or Settlements situated within His Majesty's North Western American Territories," Washington, D.C. 1 May 1823, reprinted in Kane, Holmquist, and Gilman, *Northern Expeditions*, 363–64.

4. Stratford Canning to George Canning, Washington, D.C., 5 May 1823, reprinted in Kane, Holmquist, and Gilman, *Northern Expeditions*, 364–65.

5. Kane, Holmquist, and Gilman, *Northern Expeditions*, 16–17.

6. Keating, *Narrative*, 1:76.

7. Ibid., 86.

8. Ibid., 146.

9. Ibid., 166.

10. Ibid. n 230.

11. Ibid., 219.

12. Ibid., 277.

13. Thomas Say, "Notes on Herpetology," *American Journal of Science and Arts* 1 (1819):256–65.

14. J. C. Beltrami, *A Pilgrimage in Europe and America, Leading to the Discovery of the Sources of the Mississippi and Bloody River* (London, 1828; reprint Chicago: University of Chicago Press, 1962), 2:370.

15. Keating, *Narrative*, 1:456. Say probably refers to Thomas Bewick (1753–1828), an English wood engraver whose *General History of Quadrupeds* (1790) and *History of British Birds* (1797–1804) were popular in Say's time.

16. Keating, *Narrative*, 1:457.

17. Ibid., 2:14.

18. Ibid., 19–20.

19. William H. Goetzmann, *Exploration and Empire: The Role of the Explorer and Scientist in the Exploration and Development of the American West, 1800–1900* (New York: Alfred Knopf, 1967), 88–89.

20. Edwin James, ed., *A Narrative of the captivity and adventures of John Tanner, United States Interpreter at Sault de Ste. Marie, during thirty years residence among the Indians in the Interior of North America* (New York: G. and C. H. Carvill, 1830). James, a surgeon in the United States Army, was stationed at a number of military posts. While at Fort Crawford he began a study of the Chippewa language, and later at Mackinac became friendly with the Chippewa Indians. He translated the New Testament into Chippewa and made hundreds of converts to Christianity through his missionary work. James was also a dedicated abolitionist. John Torrey and Asa Gray named the genus of the Saxifrage family, *Jamesia*, in his honor, as well as the type species *J. americana*. Susan Delano McKelvey, *Botanical Exploration of the Trans-Mississippi West 1790–1850* (Jamaica Plain, Mass.: Arnold Arboretum, Harvard University, 1955), 247.

21. Keating, *Narrative*, 2:173.

22. *North American Review* 21 (July 1825): 128ff.

23. *The Monthly Review, or Literary Journal* 108 (September to November 1825).

CHAPTER 9: *AMERICAN ENTOMOLOGY*

1. William Maclure to Marie Duclos Fretageot, 18 January 1824, Correspondence of William Maclure and Marie Duclos Fretageot, WMI.

2. Thomas Say to John F. Melsheimer, Philadelphia, 30 November 1823, Thomas Say Papers, ANSP.

3. Thomas Say to John F. Melsheimer, Philadelphia, 9 May 1822, Thomas Say Papers, ANSP.

4. Thomas Say, *American Entomology*, 3 vols. (Philadelphia: Samuel Augustus Mitchell, 1824–1828), preface.

5. *North American Review* (July 1825).

6. *Minute Book* of the ANSP, 14 December 1824.

7. Say to Prof. C. A. W. Wiedemann, letter draft "in reply to his of 16 May 1824," MCZ Archives.

8. Say to Baron de Ferussac (letter draft) May 1825, Thomas Say Papers, APS.

9. Say to Nicholas M. Hentz, Philadelphia, 2 August 1825, MCZ Archives. Hentz (1797–1856) died long before his own book was published in 1875. Illustrated with twenty-one plates after his drawings, it was the "first noteworthy work on American spiders" (Arnold Mallis, *American Entomologists* [New Brunswick, N.J.: Rutgers University Press, 1971], 408).

10. Mallis, *American Entomologists*, 406.

11. *North American Review* (July 1825).

12. Say, *American Entomology*, vol. 2, text to accompany plate 26.

13. Ibid., vol. 1, text to accompany plate 17.

14. Ibid., vol. 2, text to accompany plate 34.

15. Ibid., text to accompany plate 22.

16. Reuben Haines to Jane B. Haines, Reading, Pa., 25 August 1825, Wyck Papers, APS.

17. "Notes and Queries," *Pennsylvania Magazine of History and Biography* 5 (1881).

18. Ibid.

19. John J. Audubon to Reuben Haines, Bayou Sarah, 5 May 1825, QCHC.

20. Ibid.

21. Audubon to Haines, Bayou Sarah, 25 December 1825, Wyck Papers, APS.

22. Charles Lucien Bonaparte to William Cooper, 9 February 1826, MNHN, quoted in Alice Ford, *John James Audubon* (Norman: University of Oklahoma Press, 1964).

23. Say, *American Entomology*, vol. 3, text to accompany plates 37 and 38.

24. Ibid.

25. Ibid., text to accompany plate 42.

26. Ibid., text to accompany plate 54.

27. Vivian Rogers Price, *John Abbot in Georgia: The Vision of a Naturalist Artist (1751–ca. 1840)*, catalogue of an exhibition, 25 September–31 December 1983, Madison-Morgan Cultural Center, Madison, Ga.

28. Mallis, *American Entomologists*, 23.

29. Reuben Haines to Jane B. Haines, Reading, Pa., 25 August 1825, Wyck Papers, APS.

CHAPTER 10: "THE BOATLOAD OF KNOWLEDGE"

1. Arthur E. Bestor, Jr., ed., *Education and Reform at New Harmony: Correspondence of William Maclure and Mme. Frétageot, 1820–1833* (Indianapolis: Indiana Historical Society, 1948; reprint New York: Augustus M. Kelley, 1973), 304–5.

2. John F. C. Harrison, "Robert Owen's Quest for the New Moral World in America," in *Robert Owen's American Legacy: Proceedings of the Robert Owen Bicentennial Conference, New Harmony, Indiana, October 15 and 16, 1971*, ed. Donald E. Pitzer (Indianapolis: Indiana Historical Society, 1972), 35.

3. John Speakman to Thomas Say, [Pittsburgh?], [1823?], Thomas Say Papers, WMI.

4. Harrison, "Robert Owen's Quest," 37–39.

5. Robert Dale Owen, *Threading My Way: An Autobiography* (New York, 1874; reprint New York: Augustus M. Kelley, 1967), 241.

6. Henry Savage, Jr., *Discovering America: 1700–1875* (New York: Harper and Row, 1979), 179.

7. J. Percy Moore, "William Maclure—Scientist and Humanitarian," *Proceedings of the American Philosophical Society* 91, no. 3 (1947): 234–49.

8. *Minutes of the ANSP*, 18 April and 6 June 1812.

9. William Maclure to Benjamin Silliman, *American Journal of Science* 9 (June 1825): 157.

10. Bestor, *Education and Reform*, 305.

11. Ibid., 312.

12. Donald MacDonald, *The Diaries of Donald MacDonald, 1824–1826*. Indiana Historical Society Publications, vol. 14, no. 2 (Indianapolis: Indiana Historical Society, 1942), 209.

13. Marie Fretageot to William Maclure, 11 February 1825, in Bestor, *Education and Reform*, 315.

14. Say to Thaddeus Harris, Philadelphia, 21 November 1825, Harris Papers, Houghton Library, Harvard University, and Say to Nicholas Hentz, Philadelphia, 12 October 1825, MCZ Archives.

15. Robert Owen to Maclure, 27 March 1825, in Bestor, *Education and Reform*, 317.

16. Maclure to Mme. Fretageot, 15 July 1825, in ibid., 322.

17. Ibid., 323.

18. Reuben Haines to Ann Haines, Germantown, 6 July 1825, Wyck Papers, APS. Owen's wife and two daughters remained in Scotland, but all his sons and one daughter, Jane, joined him at New Harmony. Several years later Owen returned to Scotland for the rest of his life.

19. MacDonald, *Diaries*, 302.

20. Say to Hentz, Philadelphia, 12 October 1825, MCZ Archives.

21. Charlotte M. Porter, *The Eagle's Nest: Natural History and American Ideas, 1812–1842* (University: University of Alabama Press, 1986), 110.

22. *Aurora General Advertiser* (Philadelphia), 19 November 1825.

23. Say to Harris, Philadelphia, 21 November 1825, Harris Papers, Houghton Library, Harvard University.

24. MacDonald, *Diaries*, 334.

25. Josephine M. Elliott, ed., *To Holland and to New Harmony: Robert Dale Owen's Travel Journal, 1825–1826* (Indianapolis: Indiana Historical Society, 1969), 243.

26. Ibid., 243, 247.

27. Ibid., 253–54.

CHAPTER 11: UTOPIA CONFRONTED

1. George B. Lockwood, *The New Harmony Movement* (New York: D. Appleton, 1905), 22.

2. Lord Byron, *Canto XV, Don Juan*, in *The Works of Lord Byron* (London, 1833), 17:167.

3. Donald E. Pitzer and Josephine M. Elliott, "New Harmony's First Utopians," reprinted from *Indiana Magazine of History* 75, no. 3 (September 1979): 255.

4. Donald MacDonald, *The Diaries of Donald MacDonald 1824–1826* (Indianapolis: Indiana Historical Society, 1942), 231.

5. William Owen, *Diary*, 129–30 (24 March 1825), quoted in Arthur Bestor, *Backwoods Utopias: The Sectarian Origins and the Owenite Phase of Communitarian Socialism in America: 1663–1829*, 2d ed. (Philadelphia: University of Pennsylvania Press, 1970), 116.

6. Marie Fretageot to Hannah Haines, 13 March 1826, Wyck Papers, APS.

7. William E. Wilson, *The Angel and the Serpent: The Story of New Harmony* (Bloomington: Indiana University Press, 1964).

8. Bestor, *Backwoods Utopias*, 174.

9. Ibid., 181.

10. Karl Bernhard, Duke of Saxe-Weimar, *Travels Through North America during the Years 1825 and 1826* (Philadelphia, 1828) quoted in Lockwood, *New Harmony Movement*, 126. The Wistar parties were private gatherings instituted in the late eighteenth century by Dr. Caspar Wistar to bring together the intellectuals of the city. After Wistar's death in 1818 the parties were held at various members' houses. Today the Wistar parties are continued by a group within the American Philosophical Society in Philadelphia.

11. Thomas Say to Charles Lucien Bonaparte, Columbus, Ohio, 13 July 1826, Charles Lucien Bonaparte Correspondence from American Scientists, MNHN, microfilm at APS.

12. Ibid.

13. Ibid.

14. William Pelham to his son, New Harmony, 8 February 1826, quoted in Harlow Lindley, ed., *Indiana As Seen by Early Travelers* (Indianapolis: Indiana Historical Collections, 1916).

15. Arthur E. Bestor, Jr., ed. *Education and Reform at New Harmony, Correspondence of William Maclure and Marie Duclos Fretageot 1820–1833* (Indianapolis: Indiana Historical Society, 1948; reprint New York: Augustus M. Kelley, 1973), 338n.

16. Karl Bernhard, Duke of Saxe-Weimar, *Travels Through North America*, quoted in Lockwood, *New Harmony Movement*, 130.

17. Fretageot to Maclure, New Harmony, 7 July 1826, Maclure-Fretageot Correspondence, WMI.

18. Maclure to Fretageot, Cincinnati, [18–]21 August 1826, quoted in Bestor, *Education and Reform*, 354–56.

19. Maclure to Fretageot, Springfield, Ohio, 11 August 1826, quoted in Bestor, *Education and Reform*, 348–49.

20. Wilson, *Angel and Serpent*, 132.

21. Maclure to Fretageot, Cincinnati, 20 June 1826, quoted in Bestor, *Education and Reform*, 339.

22. Maclure to Fretageot, Springfield, 11 August 1826, quoted in Bestor, *Education and Reform*, 349.

23. Maclure to Fretageot, Cincinnati, 29 August 1826, quoted in Bestor, *Education and Reform*, 362.

24. Maclure to Fretageot, Cincinnati, 30 August 1826, quoted in Bestor, *Education and Reform*, 366.

25. Gerard Troost to Benjamin Tappan, New Harmony, 10 May 1827, Tappan Papers, Manuscripts Division, Library of Congress.

26. Tappan to Reuben Haines, Steubenville, Ohio, 14 April 1827, Robert B. Haines Papers, QCHC.

27. Troost to Tappan, 10 May 1827, Tappan Papers, Library of Congress.

28. Paul Brown, *Twelve Months in New-Harmony* (Cincinnati, 1827; reprint Philadelphia: Porcupine Press, 1972), 82.

29. Fretageot to Maclure, New Harmony, 2 March 1827, quoted in Bestor, *Education and Reform*, 390.

30. Say to Jacob Gilliams, New Harmony, 9 June 1827, Thomas Say Papers, APS.

31. Ibid.

32. Say to Tappan, New Harmony, 30 August 1827, Tappan Papers, Library of Congress.

33. Say to Isaac Hays, New Harmony, 20 October 1827, Silliman Papers, Yale University.

34. Ibid.

35. Troost to Tappan, New Harmony, 10 May 1827, Tappan Papers.

36. Joseph Neef to Tappan, Cincinnati, 20 April 1828, Tappan Papers.

37. Robert Dale Owen, *Threading My Way: An Autobiography* (New York, 1874; reprint New York: Augustus M. Kelley, 1967), 284.

38. Say to Tappan, New Harmony, 30 August 1827, Tappan Papers.

CHAPTER 12: TRAVELS AND TRIALS

1. Thomas Say to Charles Lucien Bonaparte, New Orleans, 6 January 1828, Charles Lucien Bonaparte Correspondence from American Scientists, MNHN, microfilm at APS.

2. William Cooper to Bonaparte, New York, 4 April 1826, Charles Lucien Bonaparte Correspondence from American Scientists, MNHN, microfilm at APS.

3. Say to Bonaparte, 6 January 1828, Charles Lucien Bonaparte Correspondence from American Scientists, MNHN, microfilm at APS.

4. James Ellsworth DeKay to Bonaparte, New York, 5 March 1825, MNHN, microfilm at APS.

5. Say to Bonaparte, 6 January 1828, Charles Lucien Bonaparte Correspondence from American Scientists, MNHN, microfilm at APS.

6. George H. Daniels, *American Science in the Age of Jackson* (New York: Columbia University Press, 1968), 32.

7. Say to Bonaparte, 6 January 1828, Charles Lucien Bonaparte Correspondence from American Scientists, MNHN, microfilm at APS.

8. *Contributions of the Maclurian Lyceum to the Arts and Sciences* 1, no. 1 (Philadelphia) (January 1827).

9. Thomas Say, "Capt. Leconte's paper on 'New Coleopterus Insects of North America,' published in the first volume of the Annals of the Lyceum of Natural History of New York," *Contributions of the Maclurian Lyceum to the Arts and Sciences* 1, no. 2 (July 1827): 37–38.

10. Say to Bonaparte, 6 January 1828, Charles Lucien Bonaparte Correspondence from American Scientists, MNHN, microfilm at APS.

11. Say to Benjamin Tappan, New Harmony, 19 November 1827, Tappan Papers, Manuscripts Division, Library of Congress.

12. Say to Jacob Gilliams, New Orleans, 3 January 1828, Thomas Say Papers, APS.

13. Fanny Trollope, *Domestic Manners of the Americans* (1832; reprint Oxford: Oxford University Press, 1984), 8.

14. Say to Tappan, New Harmony, 20 July 1828, Tappan Papers, Library of Congress.

15. Lardner Vanuxem to Isaac Lea, Mexico, 16 February 1828, Isaac Lea Papers, ANSP.

16. Vanuxem to Lea, near Temascaltepec, Mexico, 10 September 1828, Isaac Lea Papers, ANSP.

17. In 1840, Poinsett (1779–1851) helped found the National Institute for the Promotion of Science and the Useful Arts, a forerunner of the Smithsonian Institution.

18. Say to Tappan, 20 July 1828, Tappan Papers, Library of Congress.

19. Ibid.

20. Ibid.

21. List of seeds sent to Colonel Carr, n.d., Say Papers, ANSP. Robert Carr and his wife, Say's cousin Ann Bartram Carr, had owned and managed the famous botanic garden as a nursery since 1814, when Ann had inherited it from her father, John, son of the botanist.

22. Thomas and Lucy Say to Marie Fretageot, New Harmony, 1832, series 1, New Harmony Correspondence, WMI.

23. Say to Tappan, 20 July 1828, Tappan Papers, Library of Congress.

24. *The Disseminator of Useful Knowledge* 1, no. 52 (25 June 1831).

25. *Disseminator*, 10 September 1828.

26. Say to Gilliams, New Harmony, 25 September 1828, Thomas Say Papers, ANSP.

27. Say to Bonaparte, New Harmony, December 1828, Charles Lucien Bonaparte Correspondence from American Scientists, MNHN, microfilm at APS.

28. Ibid.

29. Cooper to Bonaparte, 5 April 1826, Charles Lucien Bonaparte Correspondence from American Scientists, MNHN, microfilm at APS.

30. Patsy Ann Gerstner, "The Academy of Natural Sciences of Philadelphia, 1812–1850," in *The Pursuit of Knowledge in the Early American Republic: American Scientific and Learned Societies from Colonial Times to the Civil War*, ed. Alexandra Oleson and Sanborn C. Brown (Baltimore: Johns Hopkins University Press, 1976), 184–85.

31. Richard Harlan, *Refutation of Certain Misrepresentations issued against the author of "Fauna Americana," in the Philadelphia Franklin Journal No. 1, 1826 and in The North American Review No. 50* (Philadelphia, 1826), 25.

32. Charlotte M. Porter, "The Demise of the Wilsonian Naturalists," chap. 5 in "The Excursive Naturalists; or the Development of American Taxonomy at the Philadelphia Academy of Natural Sciences, 1812–1842" (Ph.D. diss., Harvard University, 1976), 173ff.

33. W. G. Binney, "Preface," in Thomas Say, *The Complete Writings of Thomas Say on the Conchology of the United States*, ed. W. G. Binney (New York: H. Bailliere, 1858).

34. Say to Bonaparte, December 1828, Charles Lucien Bonaparte Correspondence from American Scientists, MNHN, microfilm at APS.

35. Say to Pierre S. Duponceau [Peter S. Du Ponceau], New Harmony, 28 December 1828, Thomas Say Papers, ANSP.

CHAPTER 13: OUT OF THE CROWD

1. Thomas Say to Thaddeus W. Harris, New Harmony, 4 January 1829, Harris Papers, Houghton Library, Harvard University.

2. Say to Reuben Haines, New Harmony, 20 November 1829, Robert B. Haines Papers, QCHC.

3. Say to Charles Lucien Bonaparte, New Harmony, 19 October 1830, Charles Lucien Bonaparte Correspondence from American Scientists, MNHN, microfilm at APS.

4. Say to Haines, New Harmony, 12 February 1830, QCHC.

5. Ibid.

6. Say to Haines, New Harmony, 6 June 1829, QCHC.

7. Say to Bonaparte, New Harmony, 19 October 1830, Charles Lucien Bonaparte Correspondence from American Scientists, MNHN, microfilm at APS.

8. Say to Harris, New Harmony, 4 January 1829, Harris Papers, Houghton Library.

9. James E. DeKay, *An Address Delivered before the New-York Lyceum, February, 1826* (New York, 1826).

10. William Maclure to Marie Fretageot, New Orleans, 8 February 1827, Maclure-Fretageot Correspondence, WMI. I am indebted to Josephine Elliott for this letter.

11. Say to Bonaparte, New Harmony, 19 October 1830, Charles Lucien Bonaparte Correspondence from American Scientists, MNHN, microfilm at APS.

12. Say to Haines, New Harmony, 2 September 1830, QCHC.

13. Say to Haines, New Harmony, 20 November 1829, QCHC.

14. Ibid.

15. Ibid.

16. Maclure to Haines, Mexico, 25 June 1831, Wyck Papers, APS.

17. Say to Haines, New Harmony, 18 August 1830, QCHC.

18. *The Disseminator of Useful Knowledge*, 9 November 1830, ANSP.

19. Fretageot to Maclure, New Harmony, 6 January 1830, Maclure-Fretageot Correspondence, WMI.

20. *Disseminator*, 3 August 1830, ANSP.

21. *Disseminator*, 5 March 1831, ANSP.

22. *Disseminator*, 9 April 1831, ANSP.

23. Say to Bonaparte, New Harmony, 19 October 1830, Charles Lucien Bonaparte Correspondence from American Scientists, MNHN, microfilm at APS.

24. Ibid.

25. Ibid.

26. Say to Haines, New Harmony, 6 January 1831, Wyck Papers, APS.

27. Say to Haines, New Harmony, 12 July 1831, Wyck Papers, APS.

28. Say to Bonaparte, New Harmony, 19 October 1830, Charles Lucien Bonaparte Correspondence, MNHN, microfilm at APS.

29. Say to Robert Dale Owen, New Harmony, 12 October 1830, series 1, New Harmony Correspondence, WMI.

30. Owen to Haines, New York, 10 August 1830, series 1, New Harmony Correspondence, WMI.

31. Say to Owen, New Harmony, 12 October 1830, series 1, New Harmony Correspondence, WMI.

32. Fretageot to Maclure, New Harmony, 24 January 1831, Maclure-Fretageot Correspondence, WMI.

33. Say to Harris, New Harmony, 20 May 1830, Harris Papers, Houghton Library, Harvard University.

34. Ibid.

35. M. J. A. Boisduval and John Leconte, *Histoire générale et iconographie des lépidoptères et des chenilles de l'Amérique septentrionales*, illus. John Abbot (Paris, 1829).

36. Say to Harris, New Harmony, 20 May 1830, Harris Papers, Houghton Library, Harvard University.

37. Harris to Say, Milton, Mass., 15 October 1830, Thomas Say Papers, MCZ.

38. Say to Harris, New Harmony, 28 November 1830, Say Papers, MCZ.

39. Say to Haines, New Harmony, June 1829, QCHC.

40. Say to Bonaparte, December 1828, Charles Lucien Bonaparte Correspondence from American Scientists, MNHN, microfilm at APS.

41. Say to Bonaparte, 19 October 1830, Charles Lucien Bonaparte Correspondence from American Scientists, microfilm at APS.

42. Thomas Say, F.M.L.S. [Foreign Member Linnean Society], *American Conchology, or Descriptions of the Shells of North American Illustrated From Coloured Figures From Original Drawings Executed from Nature*, part 1 (New Harmony, Ind., March 1830).

43. *Disseminator*, 19 November 1828, ANSP.

44. Say to Benjamin Tappan, New Harmony, 30 August 1827, Tappan Papers, Library of Congress.

45. Fretageot to Maclure, New Harmony, 28 July 1831, Maclure-Fretageot Correspondence, WMI.

46. Fretageot to Maclure, New Harmony, 1 April 1831, Maclure-Fretageot Correspondence, WMI.

CHAPTER 14: A TOAD UNDER A HARROW

1. George Ord to Reuben Haines, Paris, 3 June 1830, QCHC.

2. Marie Fretageot to William Maclure, New Harmony, 13 December 1830, Maclure-Fretageot Correspondence, WMI.

3. Thomas Say to Haines, New Harmony, 6 January 1831, Wyck Papers, APS.

4. Ibid.

5. Charles Bonaparte to Isaac Hays, M.D., New York, 25 January 1825, Isaac Hays Papers, ANSP.

6. Say to Haines, New Harmony, 6 January 1831, Wyck Papers, APS.

7. Say to Haines, New Harmony, 12 July 1831, Wyck Papers, APS.

8. Ibid.

9. Ibid.

10. Say to Haines, New Harmony, 2 November 1831, QCHC.

11. Say to Samuel George Morton, 5 March 1833, Morton Papers, APS, reprinted in Nathan Reingold, ed., *Science in Nineteenth-Century America: A Documentary History* (New York: Octagon Books, 1979), 40.

12. Say to Haines, New Harmony, 31 July 1831, Conarroe Papers, vol. 7, HSP.

13. Say to Jacob Gilliams, New Harmony, 3 January 1828, Thomas Say Papers, APS.

14. Fretageot to Maclure, "bettwin Louisville and Cincinnaty," 8–26 November 1831, Maclure-Fretageot Correspondence, WMI. I am indebted to Josephine Elliott for this letter.

15. Ibid.

16. Ibid.

17. Reuben Haines diary, n.d., Wyck Papers, APS.

18. Fretageot to Maclure, Philadelphia, 5 September 1822, Maclure-Fretageot Correspondence, WMI. I am indebted to Josephine Elliott for this letter.

19. Say to Fretageot, New Harmony, 14 January 1832, WIL.

20. Thomas and Lucy Say and Achilles Fretageot to Marie Fretageot, New Harmony, 5 January 1832, series 1, New Harmony Correspondence, WMI.

21. Ibid.

22. Say to Maclure, New Harmony, 29 March 1832, Boston Public Library.

23. Say to Charles Wilkins Short, New Harmony, 1 March 1831, and 14 January 1832, Short Papers, Manuscript Department, Filson Club, Louisville, Kentucky.

24. Thomas and Lucy Say and Achilles Fretageot to Marie Fretageot, New Harmony, 5 January 1832, series 1, New Harmony Correspondence, WMI.

25. Say to Maclure, New Harmony, 2 February 1832, series 1, New Harmony Correspondence, WMI.

26. Say and Achilles Fretageot to Marie Fretageot, New Harmony, 6 November 1832, series 1, New Harmony Correspondence, WMI.

27. Thomas and Lucy Say and Achilles Fretageot to Marie Fretageot, New Harmony, 5 January 1832, series 1, New Harmony Correspondence, WMI.

28. Thomas Say, *American Conchology, or Descriptions of the Shells of North America Illustrated from Coloured Figures from Original Drawings Executed from Nature* (New Harmony, Ind., September 1830 [1831]), part 3, unpaged.

29. Say to Fretageot, New Harmony, 20 February 1832, series 1, New Harmony Correspondence, WMI.

30. Achilles Fretageot to Marie Fretageot (included in Say's letter to Fretageot), Ibid.

31. Say to Thaddeus Harris, Philadelphia, 8 January 1825, Harris Papers, Houghton Library, Harvard.

32. Say to Short, New Harmony, 11 January 1832, Short Papers, Filson Club, Louisville.

33. Say to John Melsheimer, Philadelphia, 1 December 1824, Thomas Say Papers, ANSP.

34. Say to Fretageot, New Harmony, 20 February 1832, series 1, New Harmony Correspondence, WMI. Say to Maclure, New Harmony, 29 March 1832, Boston Public Library.

35. Say to Fretageot, New Harmony, 23 August 1832, series 1, New Harmony Correspondence, WMI.

36. Say to Fretageot, New Harmony, 20 February 1832, series 1, New Harmony Correspondence, WMI.

37. Say to Short, New Harmony, 14 January 1832, Short Papers, Filson Club.

38. Thomas Say to Benjamin Say, New Harmony, 23 August 1832, Thomas Say Papers, APS. Say is no doubt referring to the democratization of the United States under the presidency of Andrew Jackson.

CHAPTER 15: FINAL YEARS

1. Maximilian, Prince of Wied, *Diary of Travels in North America, 1832–1834,* pre-publication manuscript trans. William J. Orr (Omaha, Neb.: Center for Western Studies, Joslyn Art Museum, 1986), 20 October 1832.

2. Ibid., 21 October 1832.

3. Ibid., 19 November 1832, note.

4. James E. DeKay to D. H. Storer, M.D., Oyster Bay, 17 September 1843, quoted in William Martin and Mabbel Sarah Coon Smallwood, *Natural History and the American Mind* (New York: Columbia University Press, 1941), 119, 164.

5. Henry Savage, Jr., *Discovering America: 1700–1875* (New York: Harper and Row, 1979), 182.

6. Maximilian, *Diary*, 30 November 1832.

7. Ibid., 26 November 1832.

8. Ibid., 5 December 1832.

9. William H. Goetzmann, introduction to Karl Bodmer, *Karl Bodmer's America* (Omaha: Joslyn Art Museum and University of Nebraska Press, 1984), 8.

10. Maximilian, *Diary*, 24 December 1832.

11. Ibid., 25 December 1832.

12. Thomas and Lucy Say to Marie Fretageot, New Harmony, 5 January 1832, series 1, New Harmony Correspondence, WMI.

13. Fretageot to William Maclure, Vera Cruz, Mexico, 17 February 1833, Maclure-Fretageot Correspondence, WMI.

14. J. L. C. Gravenhorst to Say, Breslau, 19 March 1833, MCZ Archives.

15. Benjamin H. Coates, M.D., *A Biographical Sketch of the Late Thomas Say, Esquire read before The Academy of Natural Sciences of Philadelphia, December 16, 1834* (Philadelphia: W. P. Gibbons, 1835), 15.

16. Maclure to Say, Mexico, 16 November 1833, series 1, New Harmony Correspondence, WMI.

17. Maclure to Say, Mexico, 12 October 1833, series 1, New Harmony Correspondence, WMI.

18. Maclure to Say, Mexico, 31 October 1833, series 1, New Harmony Correspondence, WMI.

19. Maclure to Say, Mexico, 16 November 1833, series 1, New Harmony Correspondence, WMI.

20. Maclure to Say, Mexico, 7 November 1833, series 1, New Harmony Correspondence, WMI.

21. Thomas Say, *American Conchology, or Descriptions of the Shells of North America Illustrated from Coloured Figures From Original Drawings, Executed from Nature* (New Harmony, April 1834) part 6, unpaged.

22. Dorinda Evans, "Raphaelle Peale's Venus Rising From the Sea: Further Support for a Change in Interpretation," *American Art Journal* (Summer 1982): 63–69.

23. Say, *Conchology*, part 6, text accompanying plate 56.

24. Ibid., text accompanying plate 58.

25. Lucy Say to Arthur Gray, Danversport, Mass., 13 February 1883, Lucy Say Papers, APS.

26. Say to Thaddeus W. Harris, New Harmony, [10] April 1834, Harris Papers, Houghton Library, Harvard University.

27. Maclure to Say, Mexico, 12 February 1834, series 1, New Harmony Correspondence, WMI.

28. Say to Harris, New Harmony, 7 August 1834, Harris Papers, Houghton Library, Harvard University.

29. Say to Harris, New Harmony, 13 August 1834, Harris Papers, Houghton Library, Harvard University.

30. Ibid.

31. Titian Ramsay Peale, *Lepidoptera americana: or, original figures of the moths and butterflies of North America; in their various stages of existence, and the plants on which they feed* (Philadelphia: Printed by William P. Gibbons, 1833).

32. Say to Harris, 26 August 1834, Harris Papers, Houghton Library, Harvard University.

33. Draft in WMI.

34. Alexander and Anna Maclure to William Maclure, New Harmony, 14 October 1834, series 1, New Harmony Correspondence, WMI.

35. Lucy Say to Thaddeus Harris, New Harmony, 15 October 1834, Harris Papers, Houghton Library, Harvard University.

36. Alexander and Anna Maclure to William Maclure, New Harmony, 14 October 1834, series 1, New Harmony Correspondence, WMI.

CHAPTER 16: AFTERMATH

1. Charles Alexandre Lesueur to William Maclure, New Harmony, 1 December 1834, dossier 1743, no. 834, MNHN, copy of this letter was kindly shown the author by Josephine Elliott of New Harmony. Alexander Maclure to William Maclure, New Harmony, 14 October 1834, series 1, New Harmony Correspondence, WMI.

2. "Notice" in manuscript collection 433D, WMI.

3. Lucy Say to Maclure, New York, 30 December 1834, series 1, New Harmony Correspondence, WMI.

4. Benjamin H. Coates, M.D., *A Biographical Sketch of the Late Thomas Say, Esquire, read before The Academy of Natural Sciences of Philadelphia, December 16, 1834* (Philadelphia: W. P. Gibbons, 1835), 20.

5. Lesueur to Maclure, New Harmony, 1 December 1834, New Harmony, series 1, New Harmony Correspondence, WMI.

6. Benjamin Silliman, in *American Journal of Science and Arts* 27 (January 1835): 394.

7. *North American Review* (1835).

8. Lucy Say to Dr. William Price, New York, 29 January 1835, Lucy Say Papers, ANSP.

9. Coates, *Biographical Sketch*.

10. Lucy Say to Achilles Fretageot, New York, 7 January 1835, series 1, New Harmony Correspondence, WMI.

11. George Ord, "A Memoir of Thomas Say, Foreign Member of L.S. and Z.S. London, Read before the American Philosophical Society, on the 19th of December 1834," in Thomas Say, *The Complete Writings of Thomas Say on the*

Entomology of North America, ed. John L. Le Conte (New York, 1859; reprint New York, Arno Press, 1978), 1: x.

12. Lucy Say to Thaddeus W. Harris, New York, 24 January 1835, MCZ Archives.

13. George Ord to Charles Waterton, 17 April 1835, Ord Papers, APS.

14. Thomas Say to Baron de Ferussac, May 1825, letter draft, Say Papers, APS.

15. Thomas Say to Charles Bonaparte, Hall of A.N.S., Thursday evening, n.d. [probably July 1825 because of the reference in the same letter to Maclure, who had recently arrived back in Philadelphia after many years abroad], Charles Lucien Bonaparte Correspondence from American scientists, MNHN, microfilm at APS.

16. Ord to Reuben Haines, Paris, 20 April 1830, QCHC.

17. George H. Daniels, *American Science in the Age of Jackson* (New York: Columbia University Press, 1968), 57.

18. Ord, "Memoir," 8.

19. Lucy Say to John L. Le Conte, M.D., Newburgh, N.Y., 25 June 1860, Lucy Say Papers, APS.

20. Lucy Say to selected naturalists, June, 1860, enclosed with a letter to John L. Le Conte, M.D., Newburgh, N.Y. 25 June 1860, Lucy Say Papers, APS. Wilhelm Ferdinand Erichson (1809–1849) was a German entomologist. His encomium of Say is in *Genera et species staphylinorum insectorum coleopterorem familiae* (Berolini, Germany 1840), vii.

21. Lucy Say to Harris, New York, 6 January 1835, Harris Papers, Houghton Library, Harvard University.

22. Harris to Maclure, Cambridge, 8 December 1836, series 1, New Harmony Correspondence, WMI.

23. Ibid.

24. Lucy Say to Maclure, New York, 6 May 1835, series 1, New Harmony Correspondence, WMI.

25. Lucy Say to Price, New York, 29 January 1835, Lucy Say Papers, ANSP.

26. Lucy Say to Maclure, New York, 15 March 1835, series 1, New Harmony Correspondence, WMI.

27. Lucy Say to Maclure, New York, 2 February 1836, series 1, New Harmony Correspondence, WMI.

28. Lucy Say to Benjamin Tappan, New York, 1 October 1837, Tappan Papers, Library of Congress.

29. Ibid.

30. Robert Elman, *First in the Field: America's Pioneering Naturalists* (New York: Mason/Charter, 1977), 82.

31. Harris to Lucy Say, pencil draft dated 1835, Harris Papers, Houghton Library, Harvard University.

32. Robert W. G. Vail, "The American Sketchbooks of Charles Alexandre Lesueur 1816–1837," *Proceedings of the American Antiquarian Society* (April 1938).

33. Jacqueline Bonnemains, "Charles-Alexandre Lesueur en Amérique du Nord (1816–1837)," *Annales du Musée du Havre*, dossier 41, no. 29 (March 1984); no. 30 (March 1984).

34. Lucy Say to Maclure, New York, 2 February 1836, series 1, New Harmony Correspondence, WMI.

35. Lucy Say to Alexander Maclure, 28 March 1844, series 1, New Harmony Correspondence, WMI.

36. Maclure to Lucy Say, Mexico, 26 September 1837, Charles Roberts Autograph Collection, Haverford College.

37. George B. Lockwood, *The New Harmony Movement* (New York: D. Appleton, 1905), 323–27.

38. J. Percy Moore, "William Maclure—Scientist and Humanitarian," *Proceedings of the American Philosophical Society* 91, no. 3 (1947).

39. Lucy Say to Maclure, New York, 3 September 1836, series 1, New Harmony Correspondence, WMI.

40. Lucy Say to Arthur H. Gray, Staten Island, 13 February 1883, Lucy Say Papers, APS.

41. Lucy Say to Gray, Staten Island, 24 April 1883, Lucy Say Papers, APS.

42. Lucy Say to Gray, Staten Island, 8 March 1883, Lucy Say Papers, APS.

Epilogue

1. Benjamin Coates, M.D., *A Biographical Sketch of the Late Thomas Say, Esquire, read before The Academy of Natural Sciences of Philadelphia, December 16, 1834* (Philadelphia: W. P. Gibbons, 1835), 19.

2. Robert V. Bruce, *The Launching of Modern American Science: 1846–1876* (New York: Alfred Knopf, 1987), 70.

3. Nathan Reingold, ed., *Science in Nineteenth-Century America: A Documentary History* (New York: Octagon Books, 1979), 46.

4. Thomas Say to Thaddeus Harris, New Harmony, 20 May 1830, Harris Papers, Houghton Library, Harvard University.

5. Thomas Say, "Observations on some species of zoophytes, shells, etc., principally fossil," *American Journal of Science and Arts* 1, no. 4 (1818): 381–87.

6. Say to John Melsheimer, 30 November 1823, Say Papers, ANSP.

7. George H. Daniels, *American Science in the Age of Jackson* (New York: Columbia University Press, 1968), 116.

8. Alexandra Oleson and Sanborn C. Brown, eds., *The Pursuit of Knowledge in the Early Republic: American Scientific and Learned Societies from Colonial Times to the Civil War* (Baltimore: Johns Hopkins University Press, 1976), 37.

9. Pamela Gilbert and Chris J. Hamilton, *Entomology: A Guide to Information Sources* (Great Britain: Mansell Publishing, 1984).

10. Information supplied the author by Margaret Fischer, administrative director, Division of Systematics and Evolutionary Biology, Academy of Natural Sciences of Philadelphia.

11. Herbert Osborn, *A Brief History of Entomology* (Columbus, Oh.: Spahr & Glenn, 1952), 142.

12. Gilbert and Hamilton, *Entomology*.

13. *Frontiers*, promotional booklet written by academy scientists (Philadelphia: Academy of Natural Sciences of Philadelphia, 1936).

14. Gilbert and Hamilton, *Entomology*.

15. Thomas Say, "Notes on Herpetology," *American Journal of Science and Arts* 1 (1819): 256–65.

16. Quoted in Bernard Jaffe, *Men of Science in America* (New York: Simon and Schuster, 1944), 150.

17. Asa Fitch, M.D., *Fourth Report on the Noxious and other Insects of the State of New York* (Albany: C. Van Benthuysen, printer, 1858).

18. Entomological information supplied the author by Dr. Charles E. Mason, Department of Entomology and Applied Ecology, College of Agricultural Sciences, University of Delaware.

19. Malacological information supplied the author by Dr. George Davis, chairman, Department of Malacology, The Academy of Natural Sciences of Philadelphia. Dr. Davis is a world-renowned authority on the mollusks that carry schistosomiasis.

20. Additional malacological information supplied the author by Dr. Robert Robertson, curator, Department of Malacology, Academy of Natural Sciences of Philadelphia.

21. John C. Greene, *American Science in the Age of Jefferson* (Ames: Iowa State University Press, 1984), 396.

22. *American Journal of Science and Arts* 27 (1835): 394–95.

Bibliography

Academy of Natural Sciences of Philadelphia. *Journal of the Academy of Natural Sciences of Philadelphia* 1–8 (1817–42).

———. *Minutes of The Academy of Natural Sciences of Philadelphia* 25 January 1812–Dec. 1834.

Audubon, John James. *Journal of John James Audubon Made during His Trip to New Orleans in 1820–1821.* Edited by Howard Corning. Cambridge, Mass.: Harvard University Press, 1929.

———. *Ornithological Biography: or, an account of the habits of the birds of the United States of America, accompanied by descriptions of the objects represented in the work entitled The Birds of America.* Philadelphia, 1831–39.

Audubon, Maria R. *Audubon and His Journals.* New York, 1897.

Aurora General Advertiser, Philadelphia, October 1818.

Baatz, Simon. "Patronage, Science, and Ideology in an American City: Patrician Philadelphia, 1800–1860." Ph.D. diss., University of Pennsylvania, 1986.

Baldwin, William. *Reliquiae Baldwinianae, selections from the correspondence of the late William Baldwin.* Compiled by William Darlington. Philadelphia, 1843. Reprint, New York: Hafner, 1969.

Baltzell, E. Digby. *Puritan Boston and Quaker Philadelphia.* New York: Free Press, 1979.

Banta, R. E. "The American Conchology: A Venture in Backwoods Book Printing." *The Colophon* n.s. 3 (Winter 1938): 24–40.

Bartram, William. *The Travels of William Bartram.* Naturalist's edition, edited by Francis Harper. New Haven, Conn.: Yale University Press, 1958.

Bedini, Silvio A. "Jefferson: Man of Science," *Frontiers: Annual of the Academy of Natural Sciences of Philadelphia* 3 (1981–82): 10–23.

———. *Thomas Jefferson: Statesman of Science.* New York: Macmillan, 1990.

Beidleman, Richard G. "The 1820 Long Expedition." *American Zoologist* 26, no. 2 (1986): 307–13.

Benson, Maxine, ed. *From Pittsburgh to the Rocky Mountains: Major Stephen Long's Expedition—1819–1820.* Golden, Col.: Fulcrum, 1988.

Berkeley, Edmund, and Dorothy Smith Berkeley. *The Life and Travels of John Bartram From Lake Ontario to the River St. John.* Tallahassee: Florida State University Press, 1982.

Bestor, Arthur. *Backwoods Utopias: The Sectarian Origins and the Owenite Phase of Communitarian Socialism in America: 1663–1829.* 2d ed. Philadelphia: University of Pennsylvania Press, 1970.

———. *Education and Reform at New Harmony: Correspondence of William Maclure and Mme. Fretageot, 1820–1833.* Indiana Historical Society, 1948; reprint New York: Augustus M. Kelley, 1973.

Biddle, Edward. "Joseph Bonaparte as Recorded in the Private Journal of Nicholas Biddle." *Pennsylvania Magazine of History & Biography* 55 (1931).

Bieder, Robert Eugene. *The American Indian and the Development of Anthropological Thought in the United States, 1780–1851*. Master's thesis, University of Minnesota, 1972.

Bodmer, Karl. *Karl Bodmer's America*. Introduction by William H. Goetzmann. Annotations by David C. Hunt and Marsha V. Gallagher. Biography by William J. Orr. Omaha: Joslyn Art Museum and University of Nebraska Press, 1984.

Boisduval, J. A. and John Leconte. *Histoire générale et iconographie des lépidoptères et des chenilles de l'Amérique septentrionales*. Illustrated by John Abbot. Paris, 1829.

Bonnemains, Jacqueline. "Charles-Alexandre Lesueur en Amérique du Nord (1816–1837)." *Annales du Musée du Havre*, dossier 41, no. 29 (March 1984); no. 30 (March 1984).

Boorstin, Daniel J. *The Americans: The Colonial Experience*. New York: Random House, 1958.

———. *The Americans: The National Experience*. New York: Random House, 1965.

Borror, Donald J. and Richard E. White. *A Field Guide to the Insects of America North of Mexico*. Boston: Houghton Mifflin, 1970.

Bowler, Peter J. *Evolution: The History of an Idea*. Berkeley: University of California Press, 1984.

Bridenbaugh, Carl and Jessica Bridenbaugh. *Rebels and Gentlemen in the Age of Franklin*. New York: Reynal and Hitchcock, 1942.

A Brief Sketch of the Military Operations during the Late War together with a copy of the muster-rolls of the several Volunteer-Corps which composed the Advance Light Brigade as they stood at the close of the campaign of one thousand eight hundred and fourteen. Philadelphia, 1820.

Brown, Chandos. *Benjamin Silliman: A Life in the Young Republic*. Princeton, N.J.: Princeton University Press, 1989.

Brown, Paul. *Twelve Months in New-Harmony*. Cincinnati, 1827. Reprint Philadelphia: Porcupine Press, 1972.

Bruce, Robert V. *The Launching of Modern American Science, 1846–1876*. New York: Alfred Knopf, 1987.

Carmony, Donald F. and Josephine M. Elliott. "New Harmony, Indiana: Robert Owen's Seedbed for Utopia." Reprint from *Indiana Magazine of History* 76 (September 1980): 161–261.

Cheston, Emily Read. *John Bartram, 1699–1777: His Garden and His House*. Philadelphia: John Bartram Association, 1938.

Chinard, Gilbert. "The American Sketchbooks of Charles Alexandre Lesueur." *Proceedings of the American Philosophical Society* 93, no. 2 (1949): 114–18.

Claussen, W. Edmunds. *Wyck: The Story of an Historic House, 1690–1970*. Germantown, Pa., published by Mary T. Haines, 1970.

Coates, Benjamin, M.D. *A Biographical Sketch of the Late Thomas Say, Esquire, read before the Academy of Natural Sciences, December 16, 1834*. Philadelphia: W. P. Gibbons, 1835.

Contributions of the Maclurian Lyceum to the Arts and Sciences 1, nos. 1–3 (January 1827–January 1829).

"Contributions to the History of North American Natural History." A symposium at The Academy of Natural Sciences of Philadelphia, 21–23 October 1981. *Archives of Natural History* 3 (Oct. 1983). Published by the Society for the Bibliography of Natural History, British Museum (Natural History), London.

Cutright, Paul Russell. *Lewis and Clark, Pioneering Naturalists*. Urbana: University of Illinois Press, 1969.

Dall, William H. "Some American Conchologists." *Proceedings of the Biological Society of Washington* 4 (1886–88).

Daniels, George H. *American Science in the Age of Jackson*. New York: Columbia University Press, 1968.

———, ed. *Nineteenth Century American Science, A Reappraisal*. Evanston, Ill.: Northwestern University Press, 1972.

Darlington, William, M.D. *Memorials of John Bartram and Humphry Marshall*. Philadelphia, 1849. Reprint New York: Hafner, 1967.

Debo, Angie. *A History of the Indians of the United States*. Norman: University of Oklahoma Press, 1970.

De Voto, Bernard. *Across the Wide Missouri*. Cambridge, Mass.: Houghton Mifflin, 1947.

Dillon, Richard H. *Meriwether Lewis: A Biography*. New York: Coward-McCann, 1965.

———. "Stephen Long's Great American Desert." *Proceedings of the American Philosophical Society* 3, no. 2 (April 1967).

Disseminator of Useful Knowledge; containing hints to the youth of the United States from the 'school of industry'. Vols. 1–2 (16 June 1828–3 December 1829). Vol. 1 (June 1830–June 1831) (new format). New Harmony, Indiana.

Doskey, John S., ed. *The European Journals of William Maclure*. Notes and introduction by John S. Doskey. Philadelphia: American Philosophical Society, 1988.

Dumbauld, Edward. *Thomas Jefferson: American Tourist*. Norman: University of Oklahoma Press, 1946.

Dupree, A. Hunter. *Asa Gray: 1810–1888*. Cambridge, Mass.: Harvard University Press, 1959.

Earnest, Ernest. *John and William Bartram: Botanists and Explorers, 1699–1777, 1739–1823*. Philadelphia: University of Pennsylvania Press, 1940.

Eckhardt, Celia Morris. *Fanny Wright: Rebel in America*. Cambridge, Mass.: Harvard University Press, 1984.

Elliott, Josephine M., ed. *To Holland and to New Harmony: Robert Dale Owen's Travel Journal 1825–1826*. Indianapolis: Indiana Historical Society, 1969.

Elman, Robert. *First in the Field: America's Pioneering Naturalists*. New York: Mason/Charter, 1977.

Essig, E. O. *A History of Entomology*. New York, 1931.

Ewan, Joseph. "A Short History of the Botany of the United States." In *XI International Botanical Congress*, ed. Joseph Ewan. New York and London: Oxford University Press, 1969.

Ewers, John C. *Indian Life on the Upper Missouri*. Norman: University of Oklahoma Press, 1968.

Ewers, John C., Marsha V. Gallagher, David C. Hunt, and Joseph C. Porter. *Views of a Vanishing Frontier*. Exhibition catalogue. Center for Western Studies, Joslyn Art Museum, Omaha, Nebraska, 1984.

Fagin, N. Bryllion. *William Bartram: Interpreter of the American Landscape*. Baltimore: Johns Hopkins University Press, 1933.

Farb, Peter. *Man's Rise to Civilization as Shown by the Indians of North America from Primeval Times to the Coming of the Industrial State*. New York: E. P. Dutton, 1968.

First City Troop. *Book of the First Troop Philadelphia City Cavalry, 1774–1914*. Philadelphia, 1915.

———. *By-laws, Muster-Rolls and Papers Selected from the Archives of the First Troop Philadelphia City Cavalry from 17 Nov. 1774 to 7 Sept. 1815*. Philadelphia, 1815.

———. *History of the First Troop City Cavalry, 17 Nov. 1774 to its Centennial Anniversary, 17 Nov. 1874*. Princeton, N.J., 1875.

Fitch, John. *The Autobiography of John Fitch*. Edited by Frank D. Prager. Philadelphia: American Philosophical Society, 1976.

Ford, Alice. *John James Audubon*. Norman: University of Oklahoma Press, 1964.

Gerbi, Antonello. *The Dispute of the New World: The History of a Polemic, 1750–1900*. Milano-Napoli: 1955. Rev. and enl. ed. translated by Jeremy Moyle. Pittsburgh: University of Pittsburgh Press, 1973.

Gerstner, Patsy Ann. "The Academy of Natural Sciences of Philadelphia, 1812–1850." In *The Pursuit of Knowledge in the Early American Republic: American Scientific and Learned Societies from Colonial Times to the Civil War*, edited by Alexandra Oleson and Sanborn C. Brown. Baltimore: Johns Hopkins University Press, 1976.

———. "The Philadelphia School of Paleontology: 1820–1845." Ph.D. diss, Cleveland, OH: Case Institute of Technology, 1967.

Gilbert, Pamela and Chris J. Hamilton. *Entomology: A Guide to Information Sources*. Great Britain: Mansell Publishing, 1984.

Godman, John D. *American Natural History*. 3 vols. Philadelphia, 1826.

———. *Rambles of a Naturalist*. Philadelphia, 1833.

Goetzmann, William H. *Army Exploration in the American West, 1803–1863*. New Haven, Conn.: Yale University Press, 1959.

———. *Exploration and Empire: The Explorer and the Scientist in the Winning of the American West*. New York: Alfred Knopf, 1966.

Gordon, Maurice Bear, M.D. *Aesculapius Comes to the Colonies*. Ventnor, N.J., 1949.

Graustein, Jeanette E. *Thomas Nuttall, Naturalist: Explorations in America 1808–1841*. Cambridge, Mass.: Harvard University Press, 1967.

Greene, John C. *American Science in the Age of Jefferson*. Ames: Iowa State University Press, 1984.

Hamy, E.-T. *The Travels of the Naturalist Charles A. Lesueur in North America 1815–1837*. Translated by Milton Habor. Kent, Oh.: Kent State University Press, 1968.

Harshberger, John W. *The Botanists of Philadelphia and Their Work*. Philadelphia, 1899.

Hemphill, W. Edwin, ed. *The Papers of John C. Calhoun, 1818–1819*. Vol. 3. Columbia: University of South Carolina Press, 1967.

Hindle, Brooke. *The Pursuit of Science in Revolutionary America, 1735–1789*. Chapel Hill: University of North Carolina Press, 1956.

Hole, Helen G. *Westtown Through the Years 1799–1942*. Philadelphia: Westtown Alumni Association, 1942.

Horine, Emmet Field. *Daniel Drake, 1785–1852: Pioneer Physician of the Midwest*. Philadelphia: University of Pennsylvania Press, 1961.

Howe, S. R., T. Sharpe and H. S. Torrens. *Ichthyosaurs: A History of Fossil "Sea-Dragons."* National Museum of Wales, Cardiff, 1981.

Hunter, Clark, ed. *The Life and Letters of Alexander Wilson*. Philadelphia: American Philosophical Society, 1983.

Hyde, George E. *The Pawnee Indians*. 2d ed. Norman: University of Oklahoma Press, 1974.

Jaffe, Bernard. *Men of Science in America*. New York: Simon and Schuster, 1944.

James, Edwin, ed. *Account of an Expedition From Pittsburgh to the Rocky Mountains, Performed In the Years 1819, 1820, by Order of the Hon. J. C. Calhoun, Secretary of War, under the Command of Maj. S. H. Long of the U.S. Top. Engineers. Compiled from the notes of Major Long, Mr. T. Say, and Other Gentlemen of the Party*, 3 vols. London, 1823.

Johnson, Oakley C. *Robert Owen in the United States*. American Institute for Marxist Studies (AIMS). New York: Humanities Press, 1970.

Johnson, Paul. *The Birth of the Modern: World Society 1815–1830*. New York: Harper Collins Publishers, 1991.

Karl Bernhard, Duke of Saxe-Weimar-Eisenach. *Travels through North America, during the Years 1825 and 1826*. 2 vols. Philadelphia, 1828.

Kastner, Joseph. *A Species of Eternity*. New York: E. P. Dutton, 1978.

Keating, William H., ed. *Narrative of an Expedition to the Source of St. Peter's River, Lake Winnepeek, Lake of the Woods, etc. Performed in the Year 1823, by Order of the Hon. J. C. Calhoun, Secretary of War, Under the Command of Stephen H. Long, U.S.T.E. Compiled from the Notes of Major Long, Messrs. Say, Keating & Colhoun*. 2 vols. London, 1825.

Kohlstedt, Sally Gregory and Margaret W. Rossiter, eds. *Historical Writing on American Science: Perspectives and Prospects*. Baltimore: Johns Hopkins University Press, 1985.

Lewis, Meriwether and William Clark. *The Journals of the Expedition Under the Command of Capts. Lewis and Clark . . . performed during the years 1804–05–06*. Edited by Nicholas Biddle. 2 vols. New York: Limited Editions Club, 1962.

Lindley, Harlow, ed. *Indiana as seen by Early Travelers*. Indianapolis: Indiana Historical Commission, 1916.

Lockwood, George B. *The New Harmony Movement*. New York: D. Appleton, 1905.

Long, Stephen H. *The Northern Expeditions of Stephen H. Long: The Journals of 1817 and 1823 and Related Documents*. Edited by Lucile M. Kane, June D. Holmquist, and Carolyn Gilman. Minneapolis: Minnesota Historical Society Press, 1978.

Lovejoy, Arthur. *The Great Chain of Being*. Cambridge, Mass.: Harvard University Press, 1936.

McCracken, George E. *Welcome Claimants, Proved, Disproved and Doubtful, with an Account of Some of their Descendents*. Baltimore: Genealogical Publishing Co., 1970.

McDermott, John F. "Samuel Seymour: Pioneer Artist of the Plains and the Rockies." *Smithsonian Institution Annual Report, 1950*. Washington, DC, 1951.

MacDonald, Donald. *The Diaries of Donald MacDonald. 1824–1826*. Vol. 14, no. 2. Indianapolis: Indiana Historical Society, 1942.

McKelvey, Susan Delano. *Botanical Exploration of the Trans-Mississippi West 1790–1850*. Jamaica Plain, Mass.: Arnold Arboretum of Harvard University, 1955.

Maclure, William. *Education and Reform at New Harmony: Correspondence of William Maclure and Marie Duclos Frétageot 1820–1833*. Indianapolis: Indiana Historical Society, 1948. Reprint, Clifton, N.J.: Augustus M. Kelley, 1973.

MacPhail, Ian. "Natural History in Utopia: The Works of Thomas Say and François-André Michaux. Printed at New Harmony, Indiana." Lisle, Ill.: Morton Arboretum.

Mallis, Arnold. *American Entomologists*. New Brunswick, N.J.: Rutgers University Press, 1971.

Matthiessen, Peter. *Wildlife in America*. New York: Penguin Books, 1959.

Maximilian, Prince of Wied. "Stay of Four and a Half Months at New Harmony." Chapter 5 in *Diary of Travels in North America, 1832–1834*. Pre-publication manuscript, translated by William J. Orr. Omaha, Neb.: Enron Art Foundation, Center for Western Studies, Joslyn Art Museum, 1986.

———. *Travels in the Interior of North America 1832–1834*. Vol. 23 of *Early Western Travels 1748–1846*, edited by Reuben Gold Thwaites. Cleveland: Arthur H. Clark Co., 1906.

Moore, J. Percy. "William Maclure—Scientist and Humanitarian." *Proceedings of the American Philosophical Society* 91. no. 3 (1947).

Morris, Caspar, M.D. "Contributions to the Medical History of Pennsylvania." *Memoirs of the Historical Society of Pennsylvania* (May 1826).

Morris, Percy A. *A Field Guide to Shells of the Atlantic and Gulf Coasts and the West Indies*. Boston: Houghton Mifflin, 1947.

Morris, Stephanie. "John Davidson Godman (1794–1830): Physician and Naturalist." *Transactions and Studies of the College of Physicians of Philadelphia* 41, no. 4 (April 1974).

Moulton, Gary E., ed. *The Journals of the Lewis and Clark Expedition*. 5 vols. to date. Lincoln: University of Nebraska Press, 1983–.

Murphy, Robert Cushman. "Sketchbooks of Titian Ramsay Peale." *Proceedings of the American Philosophical Society* 101, no. 6 (1957).

Nash, Roderick. *Wilderness and the American Mind*. New Haven, Conn.: Yale University Press, 1967.

Newman, Eric P. *The Early Paper Money of America*. Racine, Wis.: Whitman, 1967.

Nichols, Roger L. and Patrick L. Halley. *Stephen Long and American Frontier Exploration*. Newark: University of Delaware Press, 1980.

Nolan, Edward J. "A Short History of the Academy of Natural Sciences of Philadelphia." Philadelphia: Academy of Natural Sciences, 1909. Collection 463, ANS.

Norris, George W., M.D. *The Early History of Medicine in Philadelphia*. Philadelphia: Collins Printing House, 1886.

Novales, Alberto Gil. *William Maclure in Spain*. Madrid: Iniciativas De Cultura, 1981.

Nute, Grace Lee. *Rainy River Country: A Brief History of the Region Bordering Minnesota and Ontario*. St. Paul: Minnesota Historical Society, 1950.

Nuttall, Thomas. *A Journal of Travels into the Arkansa Territory During the Year 1819*. Vol. 13 of *Early Western Travels: 1748–1846*, edited by Reuben Gold Thwaites. Cleveland: Arthur H. Clark Company, 1906.

———. *The North American Sylva; or, a Description of the Forest Trees of the United States, Canada and Nova Scotia not Described in the Work of F. Andrew Michaux*. 2 vols. Philadelphia, 1857.

Oglesby, Richard Edward. *Manuel Lisa and the Opening of the Missouri Fur Trade*. Norman: University of Oklahoma Press, 1963.

Oleson, Alexandra and Sanborn C. Brown, eds. *The Pursuit of Knowledge in the Early Republic: American Scientific and Learned Societies from Colonial Times to the Civil War*. Baltimore: Johns Hopkins University Press, 1976.

Ord, George. "A Memoir of Charles Alexandre Lesueur read before the American Philosophical Society, April 1849." *American Journal of Science and Arts* 2d ser. 8 (September 1849).

Osborn, Herbert. *A Brief History of Entomology*. Columbia: University of South Carolina Press, 1952.

Owen, Robert Dale. *Threading My Way: An Autobiography*. New York, 1874. Reprint New York: Augustus M. Kelley, 1967.

Peale, L. "A Visit to Florida in the early part of the Century." Titian Peale Papers. American Museum of Natural History, New York.

Peale, Titian R. Journal from the first Long Expedition. Library of Congress. Also in *The Collected Papers of Charles Willson Peale and His Family*, edited by Lillian B. Miller. Millwood, N.Y., 1980. Microfiche.

Pears, Thomas Clinton, Jr., ed. *New Harmony: An Adventure in Happiness: The Papers of Thomas and Sarah Pears*. Indianapolis: Indiana Historical Society, 1933. Reprint New York: Augustus M. Kelley, 1973.

Peattie, Donald Culross. *Green Laurels: The Lives and Achievements of the Great Naturalists*. New York: Simon and Schuster, 1936.

Peterson, Roger Tory. *A Field Guide to the Birds East of the Rockies*. Boston: Houghton Mifflin, 1980.

Phillips, Maurice E. *The Academy of Natural Sciences of Philadelphia in Historic Pennsylvania: From the Founding until The Early Nineteenth Century*. Edited by Luther P. Eisenhart. Philadelphia: American Philosophical Society, 1952.

Pindar. *The Odes of Pindar*. Translated by Richmond Lattimore. 2d ed. Chicago: University of Chicago Press, 1976.

Pitzer, Donald E., ed. *Robert Owen's American Legacy: Proceedings of the Robert Owen*

Bicentennial Conference, New Harmony, Indiana, October 15 and 16, 1971. Indianapolis: Indiana Historical Society, 1972.

Pitzer, Donald E. and Josephine M. Elliott. *New Harmony's First Utopians.* Reprint from *Indiana Magazine of History* 75, no. 3 (September 1979).

Poesch, Jessie. *Titian Ramsay Peale, 1799–1885, and His Journals of the Wilkes Expedition.* Philadelphia: American Philosophical Society, 1961.

Pond, Samuel W. *The Dakota or Sioux in Minnesota as They Were in 1834.* St. Paul: Minnesota Historical Society Press, 1986.

Pope, Alexander. *The Poems of Alexander Pope.* Edited by John Butt. New Haven, Conn.: Yale University Press, 1963.

Porter, Charlotte M. "The Concussion of Revolution: Publications and Reform at the Early Academy of Natural Sciences, Philadelphia 1812–1842." *Journal of the History of Biology* 12 (1959).

———. *The Eagle's Nest: Natural History and American Ideas, 1812–1842.* University: University of Alabama Press, 1986.

———. "The Excursive Naturalists; or the Development of American Taxonomy at The Philadelphia Academy of Natural Sciences, 1812–1842." Ph.D. dissertation, Harvard University, 1976.

———. "Following Bartram's 'Track': Titian Ramsay Peale's Florida Journey." Tampa: Florida Historical Society, 1983.

———. "Subsilentio: Discouraged Works of Early Nineteenth Century American Natural History." *Journal of the Society for the Bibliography of Natural History* 9, no. 2 (1979).

Poulson's *American Daily Advertiser.* Library Company of Philadelphia.

Powell, J. H. *Bring Out Your Dead: The Great Plague of Yellow Fever in Philadelphia in 1793.* Philadelphia: University of Pennsylvania Press, 1949.

Rafinesque, Constantine. *A Life of Travels.* Philadelphia, printed for the author by F. Turner, 1836.

Reingold, Nathan, ed. *Science in Nineteenth-Century America: A Documentary History.* New York: Octagon Books, 1979.

Richardson, Edgar P., Brooke Hindle, and Lillian B. Miller. *Charles Willson Peale and His World.* New York: Harry N. Abrams, 1983.

Rogers, Fairman. *History of the First City Troop 1774–1784.* Philadelphia, 1875.

Rogers-Price, Vivian. *John Abbot in Georgia: The Vision of a Naturalist Artist (1751–ca. 1840).* Catalogue of an exhibition, 25 September–31 December 1983, Madison-Morgan Cultural Center, Madison, Ga.

Savage, Henry, Jr. *Discovering America, 1700–1875.* New York: Harper and Row, 1979.

Say, Thomas. "An Account of the Insect known by the name of Hessian Fly and of a Parasitic Insect that feeds on it." *Journal of the Academy of Natural Sciences of Philadelphia,* vol. 1, pt. 1 (1817): 45–48.

———. *American Conchology, or Descriptions of the Shells of North America Illustrated From Coloured Figures From Original Drawings Executed from Nature.* Parts 1–6. New Harmony, Ind.; 1830–34. Part 7. Philadelphia, 1836.

———. *American Entomology, A Glossary of Terms.* Philadelphia, 1825.

———. *American Entomology, or Descriptions of the Insects of North America.* 3 vols. Philadelphia: Samuel Augustus Mitchell, 1824–28.

———. *Catalogue of Exotic Shells in My Cabinet.* New Harmony, Ind., 1833.

———. *The Complete Writings of Thomas Say on the Conchology of the United States*. Edited by W. G. Binney. New York: H. Bailliere, 1858.

———. *The Complete Writings of Thomas Say on the Entomology of North America*. Edited by John L. LeConte, M.D. 2 vols. New York: Bailliere Brothers, 1859. Reprint. New York: Arno Press, 1978.

———. "Conchology." In William Nicholson, *American Edition of the British Encyclopedia, or Dictionary of Arts and Sciences, Comprising an Accurate and Popular View of the Present State of Human Knowledge*. 3d ed. 1819. Facsimile. Melbourne, Fl.: American Malacologists Inc., 1981.

———. "Descriptions of Three New Species of Coluber inhabiting the United States." *Journal of the Academy of Natural Sciences of Philadelphia* 4, pt. 2 (1825):237–41.

———. "Observations on some of the animals described in the Account of the Crustacea of the United States." *Journal of the Academy of Natural Sciences of Philadelphia* 1, pt. 2 (1818):442–44.

———. "On a Quadruped belonging to the order, Rodentia." *Journal of the Academy of Natural Sciences of Philadelphia*. 2, pt. 2 (1822), 330–43.

———. "On the Fresh Water and Land Tortoises of the United States." *Journal of the Academy of Natural Sciences of Philadelphia*, 4, pt. 2 (1825), 203–19.

Say, Thomas (grandfather). *A Short Compilation of the Extraordinary Life and Writings of Thomas Say, In Which is Faithfully Copied, from the Original Manuscript, the Uncommon Vision, Which He Had When a Young Man, by His Son* [Dr. Benjamin Say]. Philadelphia: Budd and Bartram, 1796.

Scharf, J. Thomas and Thompson Westcott. *History of Philadelphia*. 3 vols. Philadelphia, 1884.

Sellers, Charles Coleman. *The Artist of the Revolution: The Early Life of Charles Willson Peale*. Hebron, Conn: Feather and Good, 1939.

———. *Charles Willson Peale, Volume II. Later Life (1790–1827)*. Philadelphia: American Philosophical Society, 1947.

———. *Mr. Peale's Museum: Charles Willson Peale and the First Popular Museum of Natural Science and Art*. New York: W. W. Norton, 1980.

Sheppard, Walter Lee, Jr., comp. *Passengers and Ships Prior to 1684—Penn's Colony*. Genealogical and Historical Materials Relating to the Settlement of Pennsylvania. Baltimore: Genealogical Publishing Co., 1970.

Simpson, George Gaylord. "The Beginnings of Vertebrate Paleontology in North America." *Transactions of the American Philosophical Society* 86 (April 1945).

Smallwood, William Martin. *Natural History and the American Mind*. New York: Columbia University Press, 1941.

Stapleton, the Reverend A. *Memorials of the Huguenots in America with Special Reference to their Emigration to Pennsylvania*. Carlisle, Pa., 1901.

Summers, Gerald. "A Bibliography of the Scientific Writings of Thomas Say (1787–1834)." *Archives of Natural History* 11, no. 1 (1982): 69–81. Published by the Society for the Bibliography of Natural History, British Museum (Natural History), London.

Tocqueville, Alexis de. *Democracy in America*. 1835. 2 vols. Translation with Introduction by Daniel J. Boorstin. New York: Vintage Books, 1990.

Tolles, Frederick B. *Meeting House and Counting House: The Quaker Merchants of*

Colonial Philadelphia 1682–1763. Chapel Hill: University of North Carolina Press, 1948.

———. *Quakers and the Atlantic Culture*. Chapel Hill: University of North Carolina Press, 1960.

Trenton, Patricia and Peter H. Hassrick. *The Rocky Mountains: A Vision for Artists in the Nineteenth Century*. Norman: University of Oklahoma Press, 1983.

Vail, Robert W. G. "The American Sketchbooks of Charles Alexandre Lesueur 1816–1837." *Proceedings of the American Antiquarian Society* (April 1938).

Webb, Walter Prescott. *The Great Plains*. Boston: Ginn and Co., 1931.

Weiss, Harry B. and Grace M. Ziegler. *Thomas Say: Early American Naturalist*. Springfield, Ill.: Charles E. Thomas, 1931.

Wilson, Alexander. *The Poems and Literary Prose of Alexander Wilson*. Edited by Alexander B. Grosart. 2 vols. Paisley, Scotland: Alexander Gardner, 1876.

Wilson, Alexander and Prince Charles Lucian Bonaparte. *American Ornithology: or, the Natural History of the Birds of the United States*. 3 vols. London: Chatto and Windus, 1876.

Wilson, Robert H. *Philadelphia Quakers 1681–1981: A Tercentenary Family Album*. Philadelphia: Philadelphia Yearly Meeting of the Religious Society of Friends, 1981.

Wilson, William E. *The Angel and the Serpent: The Story of New Harmony*. Bloomington: Indiana University Press, 1964.

Youmans, William J. *Pioneers of Science in America*. New York: 1896.

MANUSCRIPT COLLECTIONS
Permission to quote materials from these collections is gratefully acknowledged.

Library of The Academy of Natural Sciences of Philadelphia.
American Philosophical Society Library.
Rare Books and Manuscripts Collection, Boston Public Library. Materials quoted by courtesy of the Trustees of the Boston Public Library.
British Museum (Natural History) Library.
Library of the College of Physicians of Philadelphia.
Manuscript Department, The Filson Club, Louisville, Kentucky.
Historical Society of Pennsylvania, including the collection of the Library Company.
Houghton Library, Harvard University.
InterNorth Art Foundation, Center for Western Studies, Joslyn Art Museum, Omaha, Nebraska.
Linnaean Society of London.
Museum of Comparative Zoology Library, Harvard University.
Quaker Collection, Haverford College Library.
U.S. Library of Congress.
U.S. National Archives.
Workingmen's Institute Library, New Harmony, Indiana.
Wyck Papers, American Philosophical Society.

Index

Abbot, John, 127, 161, 225

Academy of Natural Sciences of Philadelphia, 5; and Audubon, 157–59, 260–61, 267; establishment of the *Journal,* 44–45, 51; founding of, 19, 30–33, 278; international correspondents and members, 39–40, 42, 43, 50; library, 34, 38–39, 56–57, 256; and Long Expedition, 78; Maclure's contributions to, 34, 56–57, 199, 269; Maclurian Lyceum schism, 198–99, 200; *Minutes,* 30, 31–32, 33, 35, 39, 54, 174, 187, 206; praise for Say in, 154; Lucy Say elected first woman member, 270–71; Say as curator of, 39, 129, 151; Say as founder of, 19, 30, 31, 265, 273, 278; Say as member of, 3, 23, 27, 33, 40–41, 60–61, 71, 151, 277; and Say's death, 258, 259, 260, 261, 264; Say's departure for New Harmony and, 174, 187, 197, 206, 208, 216, 230–32, 233, 261–62, 283; Say's lectures at, 35–36, 39, 58, 174; species names controversy, 197–200; specimen collection, 39–40, 129, 266, 278; sponsorship of expeditions, 66. *See also Journal of the Academy of Natural Sciences of Philadelphia*

Academy of Natural Sciences (Kennedy), 39

Account of an Expedition from Pittsburgh to the Rocky Mountains, 55, 122, 124–26, 127, 128

Adams, John Quincy, 172, 208–9

Advance Light Brigade, 26, 27

Aesop's Fables, 219, 220

Agriculture, 49, 88, 155–56, 219, 273, 278–79, 280

Alasmodonta (shell genus), 46, 240

Albany, N.Y., 149

Allegheny Mountains, 170

Allison (freedman), 137, 139, 149

Amelia Island, 59, 62, 63, 66

American Association for the Advancement of Science, 274

American Conchology (Say), 19, 280; cost of, 215; critical acclaim for, 161, 259, 275; first publication of, 201, 210, 215–16; illustrations in, 208, 241, 254, 275; later publications of, 228, 229, 234, 240–41, 243, 253, 254, 260, 266; Lucy Say's illustrations for, 196, 210, 238, 241, 243–44, 266; Say's work on, 208, 210, 213, 214, 224, 227, 228, 241–42, 246, 250–51, 255; shell descriptions in, 204, 207, 215–16, 240–41, 253, 254

American dog tick, 280

American Entomology (Say), 5, 19, 215; cost of, 5, 48, 63, 213–14, 243; critical acclaim for, 154, 161, 275; first publication of, 48, 57, 59, 60, 151, 152, 153–55; illustrations in, 48–49, 59, 153–54, 155, 161, 193, 214, 225; insect descriptions in, 155–56, 159–61, 174, 197; later publications of, 127, 155–56, 159–61, 193–94, 206, 213–14, 225, 226, 254; Rafinesque's review of, 63, 214; Say's work on, 46, 48, 84, 87, 125, 130, 151, 154, 193, 201, 214

American Fur Company, 255

American Indians, 38, 113, 228, 240; agriculture, 88–89; American hostilities with, 13, 59, 61, 63–64, 65, 66, 78, 286n.7; first Long Expedition and, 71, 82, 85–86, 87–89, 91–93, 102–7, 111, 115, 116–19, 120; Florida expedition encounters with, 61, 63–64, 65; and human sacrifice, 105–6; Maximilian and, 245, 248, 255; medicinal practices, 37, 99–100, 140; portraits of, 129; Say's ethnological studies of, 65–66, 85, 94, 96, 97–102, 111–12, 118, 119, 120, 136, 137–38, 140, 143–44, 150, 151, 203, 281–82; Say's respect for, 13, 67, 143, 282; second Long Expedition and, 136, 137–38, 141, 143–45; women, 98, 99, 100–101, 117–18, 138; in zoological studies, 78

American Journal of Science and Arts, 73, 259, 275, 278

This book has been set in Linotron Galliard. Galliard was designed for Mergenthaler in 1978 by Matthew Carter. Galliard retains many of the features of a sixteenth-century typeface cut by Robert Granjon but has some modifications that give it a more contemporary look.

Printed on acid-free paper.